Georg Brandes' *Main Currents*
A Companion

Georg Brandes' *Main Currents*
A Companion

Edited by
Jens Bjerring-Hansen
Lasse Horne Kjældgaard

Georg Brandes' Main Currents. A Companion
© The authors and U Press 2023
Cover design and layout by Rikke Vagner
Front cover: Harald Slott-Møller: *Georg Brandes at the University in Copenhagen*, 1889, oil on canvas, 105 x 93.3 cm. Detroit Institute of Arts, USA
© Detroit Institute of Arts / Bridgeman Images
Printed by Totem.com.pl
Printed in Poland
ISBN 978-87-93890-60-2

U Press
Bibliotheca Academiae Soranae
Akademigrunden 2
4180 Sorø – Denmark
www.upress.dk

This publication is generously supported by
The Carlsberg Foundation
Dr. Phil. Leif Nedergaards Fond
Konsul George Jorck og Hustru Emma Jorck's Fond
Svend Grundtvigs og Axel Olriks Legat

CONTENTS

7 Introduction
   Jens Bjerring-Hansen and Lasse Horne Kjældgaard

13 Brandes before *Main Currents*: The Making of a Critic
   Torben Jelsbak

31 The Textual History of *Main Currents*
   Per Dahl

65 Brandes after *Main Currents*:
   Political Journalism, Oppressed Peoples
   William Banks

97 *Emigrant Literature* (1872)
   Torben Jelsbak

133 *The Romantic School in Germany* (1873)
   Anna Sandberg

177 *The Reaction in France* (1874)
   Anders Engberg-Pedersen

205 *Naturalism in England* (1875)
   Robert William Rix

241 *The Romantic School in France* (1882)
   Carsten Meiner

271 *Young Germany* (1890)
   Adam Paulsen

306 Bibliography

325 Contributors

INTRODUCTION

Jens Bjerring-Hansen and Lasse Horne Kjældgaard

2021 marked the sesquicentennial of the opening lecture of Georg Brandes' *Main Currents in Nineteenth Century Literature* and thus the beginning of an audacious feat, which would take almost 20 years for the author to complete. Brandes' grand narrative of the evolution of European literature in the nineteenth century was delivered in person to a large audience at the University of Copenhagen, and soon after published in six volumes between 1872 and 1890.

The publication was a momentous event in contemporary culture not only in Denmark, but also on a global scale, by virtue both of translations (into German, English, Russian, Chinese, and more) and of Brandes' increasing prominence as a public intellectual. *Main Currents* became a kind of business card, or a letter of introduction, allowing Brandes to enter numerous national public spheres. By 1900, he was unquestionably one of Europe's leading intellectuals, as a scholar, a cultural critic, and a political activist. "It is one of those books creating a swallowing gulf between yesterday and today," Henrik Ibsen wrote to Georg Brandes from Dresden, in 1872, upon reading the first tome of *Main Currents*.

Due to its many agendas and layers, the impact of the work has been multifaceted. In literary studies, Brandes is considered a pioneer in the field of comparative literature studies (Régis Boyer: "Georg Brandes, le père de la littérature comparée," *Revue de littérature comparée*, 2013:2, pp. 135–144). His interdisciplinary views are also remarkable, including not least his belief in the relevance of scientific methods and views to the cultural sciences (positivism and Darwinism). As a literary scholar, Brandes' ambition was to deploy the tools of his discipline in the service of big causes, such as the promotion of freedom, peace, and modernity. In Danish circles, he constantly challenged national narrow-mindedness and worked to establish a dialogue between nations and cultures. In a wider context, he helped to put not only Denmark but the entire Scandinavian region on the global literary map. All of this was made possible by the publication of *Main Currents*.

Georg Morris Cohen Brandes (1842–1927) grew up in a secular, bourgeois Jewish family in Copenhagen. In April 1870, having successfully completed his university studies, which were grounded in the idealistic philosophical and aesthetical dogmas of the era and crowned by a doctorate degree in philosophy, Brandes traveled through Europe on a Grand Tour, making stops in Paris, London, and Switzerland before a longer sojourn in Italy. He left Denmark as the young hope of the literary and academic scene. In July 1871, he returned with an idea for a series of lectures and books on modern European literary history, to be called *Main Currents*. The work should have secured him a position as a Professor of Aesthetics at the University of Copenhagen. Instead, his attacks on the pillars of society – Christianity, patriotism, and patriarchy – put him in a precarious situation, denying him both tenure and access to the press in the conservative cultural climate of the day.

Independent of institutions, Brandes then pursued a career as a critic, journalist, author, and public lecturer; from 1877 to 1883 he based himself in Berlin, gradually expanding his readership beyond radical liberal circles and beyond Scandinavia. Finally, in 1890, he concluded his literary history with the publication of *Young Germany*, at which point he was more of a European intellectual than a Danish academic.

"The surest way for a beginning Danish writer to make a name is still, as it was 24 years ago, to write something or other against me," Brandes declared self-consciously in 1895 ("The Circumstances of a Danish Author," *Politiken*, March 2, 1895). In a Danish context, these words are still applicable today, as Brandes continues to evoke powerful emotions and statements in public debate, where he is one of the few surviving voices of the nineteenth century. He has managed to sow division ever since he first stepped up to the lectern in Auditorium 7 in the main building of Copenhagen University, on November 3, 1871, at 6pm, inaugurating his lecture series. In itself, this is a noteworthy achievement. Yet the local uproar over the lectures has tended to overshadow the literary work itself, and its immense and complicated international afterlife.

Although *Main Currents* was initially conceived as an intervention in the local Danish cultural situation, it told a much larger, European story: that of the great national literatures – French, German, and English – and their distinguishing traits, as well as their interrelations and their receptiveness to impulses from abroad.

Main Currents reads as a piece of comparative literary history, but also as literature in its own right, with its explicitly dramatic composition and sparkling prose. Perceiving imaginative literature as a product of the spirit of the times, it thus portrays European cultural history of the nineteenth century. With a rationalist-emancipatory point of departure ("Belief in the Right of Free Research and in the Final Victory of Free Thought"), the work depicts – via explorations of French, German, and English literature – how in the early nineteenth century Romanticism dismantled the eighteenth-century ideas of reason and freedom and ended in a political reaction, which was again overcome by a revolutionary spirit around 1848.

Furthermore, Brandes' *Main Currents* managed to combine scholarship with committed cultural criticism. It addresses the (literary) history of Europe's main countries, but also the provincial nature of contemporary Danish intellectual life. For the Danish audience, it was intended as instructional reading: "I believe that we can draw a lesson for ourselves from this great drama. We are now, as usual, forty years behind Europe," wrote Brandes, making use of the national "we," which clearly emerges as the addressee. Denmark appeared to him exceptional in a European context, but in a negative sense: "Nowhere in Europe are there so many exalted ideals and, in few places, a flatter spiritual life," he asserted polemically ("The 1872 Introduction to Main Currents of Nineteenth-Century Literature," transl. by Lynn R. Wilkinson, *PMLA* 132:3, 2017, p. 704).

With this attitude he further defined a role for himself in the national drama: as the one who would spur especially authors to action, and persuade them to write in a manner closer to reality and more engaged with the times. He urged them to "provoke debate," an expression that immediately became a cliché – and still is to this day. In doing so, Brandes inaugurated a new era in Denmark, "the Modern Breakthrough," as he would later label it. On the European literary scene, on the other hand, the work was a crucial element in establishing the "Nordic wave," which left its mark on the decades around 1900, orchestrated and promoted by Brandes himself.

One of the authors of the Modern Breakthrough, the Nobel laureate Henrik Pontoppidan, writes in his novel *Lucky Per* (1898–1904) of the "European cultural wave" that Brandes (in the novel portrayed in the character of Dr. Nathan) had unleashed over the country. This wave had engendered "a series of revolutionary poets, scientists and politicians" at the same time that "in the purely practical domain" it had "brought forth a surge of youthful and bold energy that sought outlets" (*Lucky Per*, 4th edition, 1918, Vol. 1, p. 333). This outburst of energy is seen by the novel's protagonist, the engineering student Per Sidenius, as just one of the innumerable consequences of Brandes' movement. He underlines the vastness of the Modern Breakthrough, which was much more than a literary phenomenon. Conceptually, it was an umbrella category encompassing an array of modernization processes, as well as a more sustained and closer engagement with the outside world, especially within the domains of culture, commerce, and science.

Brandes has reached a broader and more international audience than any other Danish humanist before or since. His works have been translated into 17 languages, *Main Currents* alone appearing during his lifetime in Danish, German, English, Russian, Polish, Yiddish, and Japanese, while individual volumes of the series were also published in Finnish and French. After his death Spanish and Chinese versions were also released.

In 1924, the author boasted: "I have my Readers in Europe, Asia and America." Brandes had sensed a new and difficult task for himself, which was expressed in the foreword to the Japanese edition of *Main Currents* (1915): "*Main Currents* begins with the old fable of 'The Raven and the Stork.' The work would open up the perspective of the various European nations to the advantages of one another, serve the raven's dishes on the stork's table and vice versa. Now the fable applies more broadly. It would please the author of *Main Currents* if he had served European intellectual nourishment in such a manner that it might now be appropriated by the Japanese palette" ("Foreword to the Japanese Edition of *Main Currents*," *Politiken*, July 23, 1915). Whereas the initial goal of the work was to compare and tie together European cultures, Brandes now understood that it was a matter of fostering an intercontinental dialog. This broadening of horizons was a reflection of a developing situation in which cultures, crises, and wars were becoming globalized. The First World War (1914–1918) was a pressing example of this, and Brandes' critical engagement with the conflict turned him into a global player whose commentaries on its unfolding developments were constantly in demand in all the world's newspapers.

Brandes' fame, however, was very much tied to his particular era. As a public speaker, he toured constantly; in 1912 alone he lectured in 42 European cities. Through his journalism and his criticism published in newspapers, Brandes understood how to make himself relevant to the new, fast-moving media environment. But just as importantly, he succeeded – as a speaker, journalist, and author – in reaching the younger generations on the cusp of the century of globalization and world war. When Brandes died, the German author and Nobel laureate Thomas Mann wrote that around 1900, *Main Currents* had been "the bible of the young intellectuals of Europe" (Thomas Mann, "A Master of Productive Criticism," *Politiken*, February 20, 1927). And Brandes was a genuine European, indeed "the Good European," as he was deemed by the German philosopher Friedrich Nietzsche, whom Brandes had "discovered", according to Nietzsche, and popularized around 1890 (Letter from Nietzsche to Brandes, Nice, December 2, 1887, in Paul Krüger (Ed.): *Correspondence of Georg Brandes*, 1966, Vol. 3, p. 441).

Brandes' magnum opus was a pioneering work in two respects: as a major contribution to the formulation of a modern European identity, and as an innovative effort in the development of the internationalization of literary studies. Both ventures are relevant to the globalized present, in which both disciplinary traditions and geopolitical constellations are under stress.

And current events have, on the whole, substantiated Brandes' theorizing and practice of his dual roles: as an academic and as an "intellectual" – to employ a term Brandes himself introduced into Danish – and as a Dane and a world citizen. An activist ethos underpins and unites all of these facets of his existence. Considered both as an academic accomplishment and as a critical intervention in contemporary culture, *Main Currents* had and continues to have an impact that is far-reaching and profound.

This is the reason why we have compiled this anthology of essays on the biographical background, overall structure, and individual volumes of *Main Currents in Nineteenth Century Literature*. Hopefully, it may serve as a resource for newcomers as well as experienced readers looking for an overview of – and new paths in – Brandes' work.

The chapters of this companion were originally produced for the research project Digital Currents, hosted by The Society for Danish Language and Literature and financed by the Carlsberg Foundation.

BRANDES BEFORE *MAIN CURRENTS*: THE MAKING OF A CRITIC

Torben Jelsbak

Introduction

In telling the story of Georg Brandes' education as a critic up to the appearance of *Emigrant Literature*, the first act of the six *Main Currents*, it is tempting to employ a narrative model from the principal genre of nineteenth-century literature, the bourgeois *Bildungsroman*. The path of the main character toward becoming himself is here normally portrayed as a process in three phases: first a departure from "home" in the form of a journey out into the world, then a series of formative experiences, and ultimately a return home to find a place in society. According to the Romantic-Idealist conception of *Bildung* underpinning the genre, becoming oneself means reconciling with one's background, ancestry, and milieu. The *Bildungsroman* thus understands the (self-)construction of the individual as a compromise between one's own internal drives and the external demands of society.

Brandes' life up to *Emigrant Literature* contains a series of foundational elements: growing up in the bourgeois Jewish milieu of Copenhagen, successful university studies, and a well-grounded academic education within the prevailing philosophical and literary value system of the era, crowned by a doctorate in aesthetics in 1871. This was followed by a European Grand Tour in 1870 and 1871, which took Brandes to Paris, London, and Switzerland, before a longer stay in Italy. But the journey did not result in a successful reconciliation with society for Brandes – in fact the opposite. When Brandes left Denmark in April 1870 he was the great young hope of the literary and academic Parnassus, yet when he returned in July of 1871 he had undergone a series of experiences that brought him into opposition with the dominant National Liberal culture of his home country. The lectures on émigré literature, which should have served as a proving ground for his appointment to the soon-to-be vacant chair of Professor of Aesthetics, instead ended up as a polemical attack on the National Liberal ideology and its fundamental pillars: Christianity, love of the fatherland, and marriage as a social institution. This resulted in a confrontation that – for better or worse – sealed his fate and defined the rest of his career.

Pathways of Life

In reconstructing the series of factors, events, and influences that led Brandes to the positions he took in *Emigrant Literature*, it is striking the degree to which the desire to rebel and to oppose – as well as a certain sense of martyrdom – was evidently written into his intellectual character from the very beginning. As the eldest son of a clothing wholesaler, Georg Morris Cohen grew up in a secular, bourgeois Jewish home in Copenhagen. During his school years he shone with his extraordinary gifts and insatiable appetite for book learning, yet at the same time his upbringing also seemed to have left the young Brandes with a degree of wariness regarding his Jewish origins – the result of an experience of foreignness and of not being acknowledged as a full member of the society into which he was born (compare Gibbons 1980:55–60; Knudsen 1985:12–16).

Recent scholarship has emphasized this particular element of Brandes' cultural background. On the one side, as a modern, secular Jew, he purposely kept his distance from Judaism in its most orthodox variants, but on the other he exhibited a lively interest, throughout a large measure of his authorship, in the role of the Jew in history and in the specifically Jewish contribution to the development of Western culture, in that he saw Jews as especially well disposed to critical, oppositional, and cosmopolitan thinking (Hjortshøj 2021).

Brandes' upbringing and family history contain all the ingredients of a modern *Bildungsroman* about the possible pathways available to a young man from a nineteenth-century bourgeois family, in social terms encompassing the business world, politics, and artistic-literary inclinations.

Following his father's wish, Brandes began his university studies as a law student, but quickly abandoned the law to pursue his less practical and potentially unprofitable passion for aesthetics and literature. His father's business folded in 1861, after which Brandes was compelled more often than not to support himself through various forms of teaching, while at the same time his studies and travels were financially supported by his younger brother Ernst (1844–1892).

In accordance with family tradition, Ernst had trained in business and had already acquired a significant fortune as a stockbroker by the time – still at a young age – he left the business world in order to work as a journalist and publicist. According to Georg, this was because as a Jew Ernst was denied a career within the official institutions of the banking industry (Brandes 1908:378). In 1889 he took over editorial and financial responsibility for the newspaper *Kjøbenhavns Børs-Tidende*, a business trade publication, which he attempted to transform into an organ for liberal social debate and critique, despite rising opposition from the paper's traditional readership. The project ended in tragedy when, burdened by financial problems and a defamation suit against the paper, he chose to take his own life in 1892.

The youngest brother, Edvard Brandes (1847–1931), chose a third career path. After a doctorate in Oriental and Semitic linguistics, he first worked as an author and theater critic, but gradually developed a long and influential career as a newspaper publisher and politician. From 1880 to 1897 he served as member of the Folketing for the liberal Venstre party, which served as the driving force for the transition to full parliamentarianism in Denmark. In 1884 he helped found the newspaper *Politiken*, which became the central organ for the culturally liberal and cosmopolitan wing of Venstre. After this faction broke from Venstre in 1905, forming the new Radikale Venstre party, Edvard Brandes became one of the chief architects of a modern political program that in numerous essential areas set its mark on the social development of Denmark in the twentieth century. At the peak of his political career, he twice served as finance minister, in the Radical governments of 1909–1910 and 1913–1920 respectively (Hvidt 2005).

This brief sketch of the family reveals how closely Georg Brandes' life was bound up with modern social development, and the radical social and political changes Danish society was undergoing at the turn of the twentieth century. At the same time the tragic fate of his brother Ernst is a reminder of the widespread anti-Semitism and xenophobia in Danish society at the time, which was also a factor in the story of Georg Brandes as critic and intellectual.

Academic Studies

Brandes' intellectual and academic years of apprenticeship, which are summarized in detail by Henning Fenger (Fenger 1955), played out between different disciplines and institutions – between the university and the press, between aesthetics and philosophy, and between Danish and European literature. As a student of aesthetics and literature he devoted himself to a comprehensive reading program, encompassing Goethe, Shakespeare, the Greek tragedians, Homer, and Plato, as well as the Romantic poetry of the Danish Golden Age, from Jens Baggesen and Schack Staffeldt through Adam Oehlenschläger to Chr. Winther, Fr. Paludan-Møller, Henrik Hertz, and J.L. Heiberg. During the same years he experienced an intellectual and religious crisis under the influence of the philosopher Søren Kierkegaard. Paul V. Rubow has argued that it was his relation to Kierkegaard, more than anything else, that shaped Brandes' personality (Rubow 1932:101–165). According to Rubow, it was the passionate idealism of Kierkegaard's religious existential thought, together with its uncompromising demand for individual self-realization and personal renewal in opposition to lethargic social norms and majority opinion, that appealed to and stimulated Brandes. But a series of other philosophical sources of influence also made an impact on him as his intellectual journey gradually unfolded.

As a student of literature Brandes quickly established a reputation as one of the most intelligent academics of his generation. In the fall of 1863 he was awarded the university's gold medal for a treatise on the concept of fate in Greek tragedy, and in the winter of 1864 he was well prepared for his MA defense. The topic of his exam, which was not chosen by Brandes himself but in accordance with the custom of the time was selected by the faculty, was, in full:

> To determine the reciprocal relationship between the pathetic and the symbolic in general, in order thereby to illuminate the contrast between Shakespeare's tragedies and Dante's divine commedia, along with the possible errors that might result from a one-sided over-emphasis on one of these two elements. (Dahl 1998: 9)

In order to pass the exam, Brandes also had to produce three smaller written exercises on the following – likewise related – themes: "To what extent can poetry be called idealized history?," "Demonstrate in which manner the philosophical orientation of Spinoza and of Fichte may lead to a misconstruing of the concept of beauty," and "Demonstrate the relationship of the comic to its limits and its various contradictions" (Dahl 1998:9).

These themes together provide a potent image of the university and the discipline from which Brandes emerged, and whose norms and criteria he was to honor in his first academic work. They are comfortably situated within the frame of the Idealist and speculative Hegelian aesthetics that functioned at the time as the dominant framework for all academic work on literature and in art in Northern Europe. According to this approach, the physical and sensual world and its phenomena are materializations of eternally valid abstract ideas and principles. The methodology of speculative aesthetics thus concentrated on relating works of art to abstract concepts such as the beautiful and the noble, the tragic and the comic, and so on, and thereafter evaluating the concrete works on how well they agree with the concepts. In 1866 Brandes embarked on an effort to complete his education within this tradition in the form of a planned dissertation on the theme of "the theory of the comic," but for the first time in his career he found himself in conflict with speculative aesthetics and the Hegelian system of thought, which up to then had shaped his academic training.

In the meantime, Brandes had also begun supporting himself as the theater reviewer for the Copenhagen newspaper *Dagbladet* and the weekly *Illustreret Tidende*. These journalistic venues meant that Brandes' prior, more theoretical or academic orientation was challenged by new, more worldly and socially engaged interests and questions. This experience is also evident in a stylistic change in his manner of writing; abstract Hegelian conceptual prose yields to a more emphatic and polemical approach. It was in his role as polemicist and social commentator that Brandes made his literary debut in 1866 with the pamphlet *Dualism in Our Recent Philosophy*.

The pamphlet was a contribution to the great debate of the time, that on the relation between faith and knowledge, which emerged in the wake of the historical and philological critique of the Bible and of Christianity forwarded by Left Hegelians such as Ludwig Feuerbach (*Das Wesen des Christentums*, 1841) and David F. Strauss (*Das Leben Jesu kritisch bearbeitet*, 1842–1843). New life was breathed into the debate in the 1860s with the appearance of the French philosopher Ernest Renan's *La Vie de Jésus* (1863, Da. *Jesu Levnet*, 1864), which on the basis of a study of historical sources denied the Christian dogma of the divine nature of Jesus. At the same time the Christian worldview was challenged on a second front in the form of more sophisticated natural science and natural history: in his *Principles of Geology* (1830–1833), the English geologist Charles Lyell had presented a positivistic and naturalistic explanation of the lifeforms of the Earth, which contradicted the Christian idea that all extant species had initially appeared in their finished forms through a divine act of creation a few thousand years prior. Lyell's geology was the most important inspiration for Charles Darwin's doctrines of the origin of species and of slow historical evolution through natural selection, as presented in *On the Origin of Species by Means of Natural Selection* (1859, Da. *Arternes oprindelse*, 1872).

The formal occasion for Brandes' intervention in this discussion involved his earlier teacher at the university, the philosophy professor Rasmus Nielsen. In his *Grundidéernes Logik* (1864–1866), Nielsen had attempted to reconcile the rising gulf between religion and science by arguing that faith and knowledge constitute two essentially distinct domains of human cognition, each of which should respect the limits of the other. In his pamphlet, Brandes objected to the dualism and the indolent spinelessness of this point of view, instead arguing that the dogmas and myths of Christianity must be subjected to the challenges and corrections of modern geology and biology. In other words, Brandes accepted neither Nielsen's "philosophy of reconciliation" (Brandes 1866:8) nor his declared truce between the worldly and the spiritual regimes. Instead he argued stridently and confidently for an open confrontation between the two.

Encounter with Hippolyte Taine

In the winter of 1866–1867, at the same time as the publication of *Dualism in Our Recent Philosophy*, Brandes took his first extended study trip to Paris, which would prove to be of decisive significance for his intellectual development. Especially important was his encounter with the French philosopher, historian, and literary critic Hippolyte Taine (1828–1893). Before the journey, Brandes had already acquainted himself with Taine's chief work, the grand *Histoire de la littérature anglaise* (3 vols, 1863–1864/1866), which contained a program for a new, positivist-inspired form of literary history that sought to explain literary works and developments using concepts and principles adopted from the modern natural sciences of geology and biology. But the influence of Taine on Brandes increased quite considerably during his stay in Paris, during which he attended the Frenchman's lectures on aesthetics at the École des Beaux Arts – so much so that Taine ended up as the theme of Brandes' doctoral dissertation, *French Aesthetics in Our Age* (1870).

There is a measure of agreement among Brandes scholars that his acquaintance with Taine should be viewed as a landmark event in his education as a critic. Bertil Nolin has thus designated the encounter with Taine as initiating a paradigm shift in Brandes' work (Nolin 1980). This shift may be summarized as a movement away from (German) idealism and metaphysics toward (French) positivism, psychology, and cultural history. In contrast to the speculative aesthetics in which Brandes had been trained, Taine represented a more secular, historical view of literature that attempted to explain literary phenomena on the basis of the life of the author, the composition of the public, and the historical context. For Taine it was not sufficient to discern that a tragedy was a tragedy and lived up to the eternal laws of such. He was more interested in getting to know the person who stood behind the work, and the culture or the civilization that shaped it. The central idea was to view literary works as psychological testimonies of human thoughts and feelings.

Taine thus emphasized human existence in literary history, yet at the same time argued that the creative abilities of human beings were determined by a series of external cultural, climactic, social, and historical factors. In the famous programmatic declaration from the introduction to *Histoire de la littérature anglaise,* he summarizes these factors as the three foundational forces [forces primordiales] of history: "la race, le milieu, le moment" (Taine 1866:XXIII), which can be translated as "the people, the environment, the age."

Taine's philosophy of history further rested upon the theory, first developed in his treatise on the ancient Roman politician and historian Titus Livius (*Essai sur Tite-Live,* 1854/1856), that all the domains of a given culture – its religion, art, philosophy, industry, family life, and so on – can be traced back to a collective cause in the form of a predominant characteristic (faculté maîtresse) among the given people. As a natural scientist of the soul, the literary historian is tasked with mapping the human faculties, abilities, and feelings that form the basis of literary history and revealing how these are determined by the previously mentioned foundational forces. All things, including human feelings and passions, must be treated and explained historically: "there is a cause for ambition, for courage, for truth, just as there is for digestion, for muscular movement, for animal heat; vice and virtue are products just as much as vitriol and sugar" (Taine 1866:XV). It was this kind of characteristic formulation from the introduction to Taine's English literary history that Brandes took to heart and employed in his dissertation (Brandes 1870a:182).

In his dissertation, Brandes loyally subscribes to the pillars of Taine's historical methodology, yet along the way he also registers a series of objections to the deterministic and reductive character of the Frenchman's explanatory model. Brandes was especially skeptical of Taine's endeavor to reduce poets and poetic works to a predominant characteristic and to a summation of the spirit of the age and the race. In this critique of Taine's determinism, Brandes found significant support in the more psychological-biographical method of the French critic Charles-Augustin Sainte-Beuve (1804–1869). Sainte-Beuve's profiles of the French Romantics in his book *Critiques et portraits littéraires* (1832–1839) were thus also a direct model for Brandes, when after his dissertation he published a series of his own author portraits, *Kritiker og Portraiter* (1870).

The essence of Brandes' critique of Taine is more or less that the latter's theoretical architecture does not provide sufficient space for the individual and for creative genius, and thus none at all for the kind of hero worship that became a steadily more prominent driving force in Brandes' own critical methodology. Yet this disagreement also points toward an important difference between the two regarding their conceptions of history itself. Whereas Taine is occupied with long, nearly unchangeable lines in the formation of national identity – or what the twentieth-century French Annales school of historical science would come to call the "longue durée" of historical time (Braudel 1997:151–152), Brandes' more impatient and combative attitude was better oriented toward dramatic rupture and renewal in history. If the key words for Taine were *nation* and *civilization*, for Brandes they are *rupture* and *revolution*.

It is thus only conditionally true, as stated in the opening of this section, to sum up the Tainean turn in Brandes' theoretical development as a transition from (German) idealism and Hegelianism toward (French) positivism. In his conception of history Brandes remained deeply indebted to Hegel's dialectical method and philosophy of history, as developed in the German philosopher's lectures on the subject (*Vorlesungen über die Geschichte der Philosophie*, 1819–1832, published 1833–1836). Hegel here portrays world history as a continuous narrative of the progressive penetration of human reason and freedom into the world through the steady movements of ideas (theses), which encounter their opposites (antitheses) and thereafter are sublated in a higher synthesis. It is this dialectic and this conception of history that forms the ground for the literary-historical drama of *Main Currents*, which is staged as a struggle between the principles of revolution and of reaction.

The Essays on H.C. Andersen and M.A. Goldschmidt: Towards a Literary Psychology of Race

From his theater reviews and literary portraits from the period following his stay in Paris, we can see how Brandes attempts to bring Taine's concepts into play. Two of the most express examples are the treatments of H.C. Andersen and M.A. Goldschmidt, both central yet quite distinctive figures from the Late Romantic Danish Golden Age. These two essays can be simultaneously read as reflecting on Brandes' own ambivalent relation to his double identity as a Danish Jew at a time when the public opinion in Denmark was moving steadily in a more nationalist and conservative direction.

In the case of H.C. Andersen, Brandes attempts to explain the secret of his popular tales with reference to the author's affection and empathy for "childlike imagination and childlike feeling" (Brandes 1870b:323), while identifying his "foundational idyllic tone" as particularly Danish (Brandes 1870b:345). Brandes here was on the trail of the poetic "naiveté" and the presence "of childishness in the national character" that later, in the introduction to *Emigrant Literature*, he polemically identified as a peculiarity of Danish culture (Brandes 1872a:17).

The counterpoint to Andersen is the Danish-Jewish author M.A. Goldschmidt, who in the manner of Taine is portrayed as a "stylist" and an "eclectic" – a predominant characteristic that is explained with reference to his Jewish origins. On the strength of his Jewish characteristics, Goldschmidt had been able to assimilate to Danishness and to contribute to the creation of a modern Danish prose style, but at the same time, Brandes argues, he maintained an unfortunate inclination toward mysticism and to playing the coquette with his Jewish background.

This leads Brandes to make a few general observations regarding the question of "the task of the Jew in modern culture" (Brandes 1870b:399).

He notes the strong Jewish presence in contemporary European music and literature, citing – as a counterpoint to Goldschmidt – the German Jewish composer Giacomo Meyerbeer (1791–1854) as an example of an artist who "manifests his Jewish origins in something cosmopolitan, something eclectic, which leads him to reconcile Romance and Germanic peculiarities" (Brandes 1870b:400).

These citations introduce a recurrent theme in Brandes' authorship, namely the connection between Jewish identity and modern cosmopolitanism, as well as the conception of the modern European Jew as a historical type particularly disposed to play the role of mediator between national cultures. For Brandes, the modern European Jew was possessed of the immense advantage of not being weighed down or burdened by a "home" and thus by a defined national inheritance and tradition. On the one hand this amounted to a tragic experience, but on the other it simultaneously rendered him especially well disposed to intellectual mobility, cultural renewal, and secular freethinking. As Brandes formulated it, the modern Jew was a "son of Spinoza … polemically inclined from birth against every form of European narrow-mindedness, oppositional, free born and born for scientific observation and poetic re-presentation" (Brandes 1870b:401).

As Henry J. Gibbons has proposed, there is also an element of the self-portrait in Brandes' characterization of the modern Jew as cultural reformer (Gibbons 1980:60–61). We encounter the same figure in the introduction to *Emigrant Literature*, in which Brandes makes a point of emphasizing that the most progressive poets of Young Germany, Heinrich Heine, Ludwig Börne, and Berthold Auerbach (Brandes 1872a:14), were all of Jewish descent. It may be argued that it was the influence of Taine that made Brandes newly aware of his own cultural identity as a Jew.

French Encounters

In April of 1871 Brandes embarked on a Grand Tour through France, England, Switzerland, and Italy, which came to last 16 months and can be identified as the second decisive event in his formation as a critic. If Brandes' intellectual education had up to this point been shaped essentially by the books he had read and written about, then his education and the development of his ideas during this journey were more spontaneous and desultory, based as they were on personal encounters and conversations and on observations of art, people, places, and landscapes. As Henning Fenger has asserted, Brandes was "an ingenious traveler," who by virtue of his social skills and talent for conversation quickly established personal contacts and networks in the places he visited (Fenger 1957:169). Through his expansive, almost daily correspondence with the family in Copenhagen, which functioned as kind of combined intellectual diary and archive of impressions and travel memories, we can follow his doings and also locate the first sketches of what, after his return home, would become *Emigrant Literature*.

His first destination was Paris, where the newly minted doctor was received like a son by the Taine family. Through Taine he was able to make contact with Ernest Renan, author of the scandalous biography of the historical Jesus, *La Vie de Jésus*, who, much to Brandes' surprise, revealed himself to be a man with strongly elitist and anti-democratic views. Brandes was further introduced to the circle around Philarète Chasles (1798–1873), a literary historian, librarian, and Professor of English at the Collège de France. Although largely forgotten today, Chasles was among the early pioneers of the discipline of comparative literature, especially by virtue of his surveys of German and English literary history. In addition, the 72-year-old man of letters was known as a walking encyclopedia of the private lives and scandals of the great French authors of Romanticism, whom he had known personally.

Though Brandes would affectionately refer to Chasles as "the old fuddy duddy" in his correspondence with his family, he did learn from him. In a letter written on the night of June 15, 1870, Brandes enthusiastically relates a visit to Chasles the evening before, in which the affable professor had held court with his colorful anecdotes and gossip on nineteenth-century literary life in France. "I sit like a sponge and take it all in. I listen with 24 ears," Brandes notes: "at last I glimpse behind the scenes of the whole of literary life here" (Brandes 1978, I:238–239).

It was also after one of Chasles' soirées that Brandes, in a letter home on June 20 of the same year, commits to paper the first sketch of a literary-historical presentation of "the great currents in new French literature" (Brandes 1978, I:249), which in broad strokes contains the central idea and plan of the three "French" volumes of *Main Currents* (vols 1, 3, and 5), as well as some of the main elements of Brandes' polemical attack on contemporary Danish literature featured in the introductory lecture. The sketch portrays the evolution of nineteenth-century French literary history from Romanticism toward Naturalism as a dialectical interplay between the spirit of Voltaire and the spirit of Rousseau, that is, between the regimes of reason and of nature and passion. Brandes identifies three phases or groups within this process. First is Romanticism – the French *Sturm-und-Drang* – represented by figures such as Alexandre Dumas père, early Victor Hugo, and George Sand, who place nature and passion at the center of literary production, thereby constituting a continuation of the spirit of Rousseau. Brandes positions the July Revolution of 1830 as the historical ground zero of this period. Thereafter follows the sudden shift toward the so-called "L'école de bon sens," the stolid and temperate school of French theater represented by Neoclassical dramatists such as Eugène Scribe and Émile Augier, with moralism and idealism as common traits. But around 1850 a new rupture begins a third period, the positivistic and naturalistic "*realism* with a *physiological basis*," represented by Taine, Renan, Dumas fils, the brothers Goncourt, and Flaubert.

After this literary-historical survey of nineteenth-century movements and groups in French literature, Brandes provides a few comparative perspectives on contemporary Danish literature. Oehlenschläger's position in early Romanticism is likened to that of early Victor Hugo in France, and a "moral" turn is dated to Søren Kierkegaard's *Either/Or* (1843). But the analogy can be stretched no further, and thus Brandes reaches the conclusion that would come to function as the polemical fulcrum of the introductory lecture of 3 November 1871: "You see that we have still not reached the third period" (Brandes 1978, I:252). Danish literature had stalled in moralistic reaction, and was therefore outside the main current of European literature.

With respect to this programmatic declaration in his introductory lecture, it cannot but be observed that Brandes himself was at least a generation or two behind in his literary points of orientation. His knowledge of modern French Naturalism was at this time severely limited. Furthermore, in looking forward to his program for literary debate on social problems launched in *Emigrant Literature* it is clear that the matrix of this program was not contemporary French Naturalism, but rather French and English Romanticism from the years around 1830, with the poet and freedom fighter Lord Byron as an important transition figure. In 1871 Brandes called for a literature that submitted modern problems concerning marriage, religion, and private property to debate. An early formulation of this call to arms was present in a letter from June 1870 – but here, noticeably, as part of a historical characterization of French Romanticism:

> Convergence in the Revolution of 1830 (…) attack on society, on property (Proudhon), on marriage (A. Dumas' Anthony, Forward to Victor Hugo's Angelo. Fourier, St. Simon. George Sand's initial burst of creativity. The god of Romanticism is *passion*. (Brandes 1978, I:250)

Brandes is confusing things when he mistakenly places the socialist and anarchist Joseph-Pierre Proudhon (1809–1865) as a partisan of the 1830 Revolution. Proudhon's seminal work on the question of private property, *Qu'est-ce que la propriéte?* [*What is Property?*], did not appear before 1840, forming a part of the intellectual context of the June Days uprising of 1848. But regardless of this and other temporal disparities along the way, the note bears witness to Brandes' attempt to link literary and political developments together. It also shows that he saw Romanticism not as a purely literary phenomenon, but as a broader intellectual, historical, and political current that also encompassed revolutionary utopian and socialist social thinkers such as Henri de Saint-Simon (1760–1825) and Charles Fourier (1772–1837).

The Encounter with John Stuart Mill – "a kind of turning point in my inner intellectual history"

In the course of Brandes' European journey, the encounter that would undeniably prove to be the most decisive for his development was with the British philosopher, economist, and liberal politician John Stuart Mill (1806–1873). The year before Brandes had produced a Danish translation of Mill's *The Subjection of Women*, in which the British philosopher argued for the emancipation of women and the equality of the sexes. In the beginning of July 1870, Mill passed through Paris, taking the opportunity to seek out his Danish translator at his quarters on the Rue Mazarine. This visit, which he described animatedly in his letters home, marked the beginning of an intense philosophical exchange that acquainted Brandes with a new manner of conceiving of literature and society. In a letter of July 16, Brandes proclaims that his conversations with Mill amounted to "a kind of turning point in my inner intellectual history" (Brandes 1978, I:275).

As a thinker, Mill belonged to the Empiricist tradition in English philosophy and social science, which proceeded from the idea that all knowledge and perception must be built on observation. On this foundation Mill developed a social and moral philosophy, so-called "utilitarianism," which began with the proposition that every human act must be evaluated according to its sum efficacy for society – and not according to the degree to which it cohered with any predetermined principles, whether determined by religion or by a conception of natural rights. Mill's utilitarianism was critical to Brandes' thinking in that it established an ethics founded not in religious but in worldly principles. Just as important for Brandes was the practical dimension of Mill's philosophy, which blended together conceptions of freedom with the social and political reform movements and the technological and economic developments of the age. "His ideas resemble railroads. Simple, without ornament, useful, grand. He bothers not with roads, but with railroads," notes Brandes in a letter of July 10, 1870 (Brandes 1978, I:269).

Brandes' enthusiasm for the philosophy of Mill was also motivated by a fascination with modern English society as the most progressive concerning democratic reforms and the relations between the sexes. At the same time his visit to England also strengthened the comparative observation he had already made in Paris, not just of the difference in manners and customs between the European countries, but also of how immensely ignorant they were of each others' cultures and intellectual lives. Just as in Paris he had been surprised by Taine's ignorance of Germany, so in England he could discern Mill's equally striking lack of knowledge of Hegel's philosophy. This experience made it clear to Brandes that there was a need for a cosmopolitan mediator between European literatures.

Italian Intermezzo: Brandes' Conversations with Alfredo Saredo and Georges Noufflard

When the Franco-Prussian War broke out in July 1870, Brandes left Paris, traveling southward by train over the Alps to Geneva and then on through Italy, visiting Turin, Milan, Florence, and Rome. This part of the journey resulted in the descriptions of Rousseau's land of birth around Lake Geneva and the ecstatic depictions of Italian landscapes, art, and architecture that would later be integrated in *Emigrant Literature* (chaps. I and XVI). Brandes' enthusiasm for Italy was first and foremost awakened by his encounter with the Renaissance and Antique architectural and artistic treasures of Florence, Rome, Naples, and Pompeii. Yet his fascination was also possessed of a more topical and political dimension, tied to the modern Italian movement for democracy and independence, and to the recent annulment of the Papal State in central Italy – an event that stirred up Brandes' revolutionary instincts.

Brandes' thoughts on these themes during his stay in Italy were stimulated by his acquaintance with two quite distinctive intellects and personalities: the law professor and later politician Giuseppe Saredo (1832–1902) from Rome, ten years his senior, and the 24-year-old French art student Georges Noufflard (1846–1897), who like Brandes found himself in Italy as part of an extended Grand Tour (see Knudsen 1985: 185–189).

Saredo was a fiery patriot, an advocate of young, independent Italy and thus an equally engaged liberal – a fighter for democracy, free trade, and modern industry as well as a follower of J.S. Mill's philosophical and political thought, which he saw as the very foundation of a modern liberal society. When in November of 1870 Brandes was afflicted with typhus, which nearly killed him and consequentially subjected him to four months of bedrest, it was Saredo who for a time served as his daily conversation partner. Again, this occurrence in Brandes' intellectual biography almost has the character of an episode in a modern *Bildungsroman*: much the same as the humanist Settembrini, in Thomas Mann's *The Magic Mountain* (1924), entertains the convalescent Hans Castorp with his liberal ideas, it was Saredo who in the winter of 1870–1871 held Brandes' feet to the fire with his hour-long discourses on the connection between humanism and the technical and material progress of the modern world.

Georges Noufflard was Saredo's diametrical opposite: a refined and distinguished aesthete, the son of a wealthy clothing factory owner in Roubaix, who was in Rome for research on a never-realized book on the city's monuments and artworks. Brandes and Noufflard met in the Scandinavian Club in Rome at the beginning of April 1871, just as Brandes had finished his convalescence. Subsequently, the two spent an intense few months as companions, visiting the art museums and churches in Rome, Sorrento, and Naples, which exerted a decisive influence on Brandes' conception of art. More specifically, it was with Noufflard as his guide that Brandes became attuned to the sensual and impassioned depiction of the human body in Italian Renaissance and Baroque art. The encounter with Italian baroque painting and sculpture was to produce a disruption of Brandes' aesthetic taste within the field of the pictorial arts.

To sum up, the Italian part of the *Bildungsreise* was to leave a pivotal imprint on Brandes' way of thinking and regarding the world, in terms of both aesthetics and politics. In a strange kind of synergy within one another, the conversations with Saredo and Noufflard added to the positivist Tainean aesthetics and cultural analysis present in his dissertation a more polemical and critical dimension. It may thus be argued that it was the Italian journey that caused the rebirth of Brandes as "Activist Critic" (Hertel and Kristensen 1980). It would no longer do for Brandes merely to describe and analyze how literary works and human moral doctrines came into being as results of cultural, climactic, and historical conditions. It was now also necessary to reveal the reformative and revolutionary potential of literature, which could be used to criticize and to change the prevailing moral doctrines of contemporary society.

At Home Again: The Confrontation of 1871

Brandes' Grand Tour was brought to an end in July 1871; he returned home to find a place in a society that, after his Italian experiences and encounters, seemed all the more barren and hostile to art and to humanity. His encounters with the philosophy of J.S. Mill, Saredo, and the liberal movements of Modern Italy had made Brandes a political radical, while his friendship with Noufflard had stimulated a more existentially and aesthetically motivated opposition to the Protestant art and culture of his fatherland.

These insights together explain why for Brandes his Grand Tour did not lead "homeward" toward a reconciliation, but instead initiated a fateful confrontation with the National Liberal culture of his homeland. As we shall see in the following chapters of this book, this confrontation would also have far reaching consequences for the future course of Brandes' life as a literary critic and public intellectual.

THE TEXTUAL HISTORY OF *MAIN CURRENTS*
Per Dahl

Design

Georg Brandes' *Main Currents in Nineteenth Century Literature* was published in six volumes between 1872 and 1890, and later in revised and translated editions.

Brandes' aim was to examine European literature as a unity and to elucidate a series of common traits in German, French, and English literature in the period between 1789 and 1848. In so doing he was one of the first European literary historians to establish a *comparative* point of view, with the intention – among others – of casting light on Danish literature, which according to Brandes was 40 years behind other parts of Europe in its development. "The comparative study of literature has the double advantage of bringing the foreign closer to us, so that we can understand it, and of distancing us from our own, so that we can see it in context," Brandes announced in his introductory lecture in November 1871, which also established his preeminent principles: "the belief in the right to free inquiry and in the eventual victory of free thought" (Brandes 1872a:8, 7).

Over the years Brandes delivered most of the lectures that form the basis of the six published volumes in his capacity as a lecturer at Copenhagen University. Prominent civil servants and politicians denied him the professorship in aesthetics that had been vacated in 1872, so that for the rest of his life he earned his living as an independent writer. Through political maneuvering, in 1902 he did eventually receive the title of professor, with a corresponding salary "to support free scientific research"; although funded by the university budget, this did not involve a formal post at Copenhagen University (see Pelle Oliver Larsen 2016:141, 386–391).

Brandes presented his narrative in the form of a drama in six acts, with liberalism as its structuring characteristic. In the foreword to the sixth edition of 1923, Brandes introduces the work by noting that:

> *Main Currents* relates an episode of the history of the European soul, in that the work presents the course of development in the literatures of the major countries throughout the first half of the nineteenth century. The design of the work is political, not literary. (Brandes 1923:3)

To begin with, he portrays the revolutionary movements of the eighteenth century, culminating in the French Revolution of 1789. After the Revolution, which constitutes the first action, follows the reaction, just as a thesis is followed by an antithesis. With the defeat of Napoleon and the Congress of Vienna of 1814–1815, the Church and the state came together in Catholic Europe; orthodoxy and authority became the new pillars of society. Ultimately there followed the overcoming of the reaction, that is, a renewal of action. This was heralded by the Greek War of Liberation against Ottoman rule (1821–1829), and specifically the heroic death of Byron in 1824, which in Brandes' account constitutes the decisive reversal. After this the liberal movement gained momentum in the French July Revolution of 1830, before its breakthrough in France and Germany in 1848.

This simple and clear construction is illustrated by the following model, which at the same time demonstrates how culture and politics in Denmark were mired in the traces of the reaction right up until 1870. Brandes saw it as his task to bring this reaction to a close, and thus to align Danish intellectual life with the liberal European "main current." The model was inspired by the dialectical philosophy developed by F.W.J. Schelling (1775–1854) and G.W.F. Hegel (1770–1831) at the beginning of the nineteenth century, which came to play a powerful role in the post-Hegelian tradition in which Brandes was schooled at university. Each concept leads to its own opposite – its negation – but in such a way that the negated concept is sublimated, entering into a greater relation – a

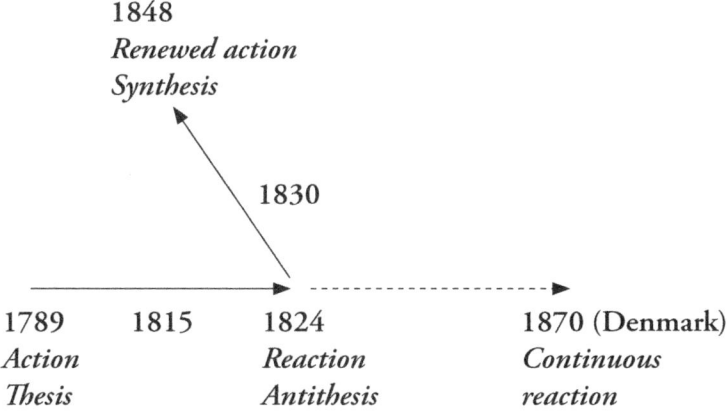

Fig. Brandes' Hegelian plot

synthesis – which forms a new unity of opposites. Brandes explains this in his introductory lecture as follows:

> Reaction as such is far from the same thing as regression. Far from it! A true, appropriate, correcting reaction is progress. But such a reaction is powerful and short-lived, and does not stagnate. After a time combatting the excesses of a previous period, after bringing to light what it suppressed, the new period takes up the content of the previous one, reconciles itself with it, and continues its movement.

Hereafter Brandes clarifies the challenge he is issuing, summarizing his reasoning with an image:

> This is not what has happened here. When a stick has been bent in one direction, one straightens it out by bending it in the other direction—but one does not keep doing this. (Brandes 1872a:12)

The rhetorical presentation of the lectures was brilliant and impactful. Brandes was a splendid, rhetorically conscious lecturer. The very form of his presentation appealed to the passion its content would encourage. His arguments culminated in images that encapsulated and completed the manner of thinking, supplied the feelings with associations and provided his powers of representation or imagination with perspective. When the argumentation itself was forgotten, its central points remained present in the consciousness of the spectators as images. In the introductory lecture Brandes refers to Aesop's fable of "The Fox and the Stork," which illustrates his point about the comparative perspective, and concludes by invoking the motif of the current of a river:

> The major part of the work will entail opening up a multiplicity of channels through which can flow the streams and currents that have their origin in the revolution and the age of progress, thereby putting a stop to reaction in all those areas in which its task has historically come to an end. (Brandes 1872a:28)

The goal of the lectures was to bring Danish intellectual life and politics into agreement with developments in Europe. Brandes adopted the contention of the French philosopher and literary historian Hippolyte Taine (1828–1893) that a country's literature reflects "the entire history of its views and feelings" (Brandes 1872a:9); as far as Denmark was concerned, this was a fragmented history, with sizable lacunae and without a great deal of independence, and therefore in a broad sense a history subordinated to influences and impacts from abroad. This takes into account the fact that not all European currents reached Denmark – indeed sometimes only those of the reaction, as was the case, according to Brandes, with the restorationist containment of Enlightenment ideals and revolutionary ideas. Now this backlog had to be overcome, and literature should relate to the conditions of the present instead of viewing life through the lens of the past. To be oneself is to be modern, and a literature is alive when it "provokes debate" (Brandes 1872a:15).

This polemical sting in the form of the juxtaposition of the literatures of Europe's major countries with stagnated Danish culture was the launching point for *Main Currents*, particularly its first two volumes. In the revised editions of all six volumes, which were released between 1891 and 1898, some of the polemical remarks and comparisons were removed, such that the work came across more as a European literary history written for European readers. In the English translation, for example, the introductory lecture was nearly entirely edited out. This meant that the work lost a measure of the polemical bite that had resulted in such intense attention in Denmark and Scandinavia; in a wider European context, it was evaluated according to a more general, literary-historical approach.

In the meantime, as the final two volumes were completed in 1882 and 1890, the movement that Brandes would come to call the "Modern Breakthrough" (initially in his 1883 book *The Men of the Modern Breakthrough*) became a living reality, even if he himself sought to revise his views.

The following describes in part the fundamental characteristics of the development – or perhaps change – that takes place between the first volume and the last, and in part how these characteristics were at the center of the textual revisions to which Brandes subjected his narrative over the course of time, not the least with respect to the first two volumes.

Brandes is cited here at length, because less well-known and less accessible texts are often discussed, and because it is important to view the critical individual passages in their original form and context.

Background: The Individual and the Formation of Consciousness

A functional relationship between the great and the small runs throughout the work of Georg Brandes, in his earlier and later aesthetics alike. The great is that which delivers an abundance of details and places them in perspective. The small or the singular, if it cannot be explained, appears as *chance*, and it is this that becomes the immense challenge of post-Hegelian aesthetics.

In his literary criticism at the end of the 1860s, in order to break with the harmonizing idealism of Biedermeier culture, Brandes, inspired by Taine, had pushed his framework for explanation and his perspective – "the great" – as far outward as was possible, while at the same time seeking out "the small" – the actual, earthy details. As suggested in the 1869 essay on *Henry IV, Part One*, "'The Infinitely Small' and the 'Infinitely Great' in Poetry" (published in the journal *Illustreret Tidende* and included a year later in the book *Criticism and Portraits*), the scope for the characterization of a literary figure should be as wide as possible.

In reality this demanded a difficult balance, which can be illustrated with a longer citation from Brandes' dissertation on Taine that concerns whether an individual should be viewed as a whole or should be divided up into analyzable parts:

> As far as the individual is concerned, it is often doubtful whether the natural groups of his intellectual production would lead us to group them with the individual himself as the center. Because of the imperfections of the individual, he only strives to be an intellectual organism, but in reality and at many points, intellectually as well as bodily, he is no more than an aggregate. Even the unity of consciousness is more or less like the freedom of the will only an ideal, not a reality. If *as I believe it to be correct* the task of scientific analysis is to dissolve artificial groups and form natural ones, then sometimes the correct scientific approach will be to treat a part of the work of the individual as literary history, another as military history, and a third as criminal history or the history of customs. Just as the gradient of a falling stone and the law of gravity belong more closely together than the gradient, color, and sound we unite in our minds when we think of the stone, so it will also be most effective to understand the different aspects of the diffused personality on the basis of the different intellectual currents of the age, rather than as emanating from the midpoint of the personality. (Brandes 1870b:33–34, my italics)

The individual can therefore be understood as either an aggregate or an organism. His productivity or his works can be interpreted as a manifestation or product of intellectual currents which lend themselves to analysis (as for example in *Emigrant Literature*), or with the midpoint of the personality as the source. In his dissertation Brandes asserts (as in the italicized text above) that although the goal has yet to be reached, the scientific method of analysis and the aggregate perspective constitute the proper path forward.

In *Explanation and Defense*, published just a few months after *Emigrant Literature*, Brandes wrote that he:

> only portrays works in so far as that they express the feelings and thoughts of the age in a lively manner, that is to say with constant reference to their cultural historical worth. My approach is thus not to provide summaries; I have continuously emphasized the critical points of view, I have comparatively drawn new parallels, and I have demonstrated the linkage between no small number of literary phenomena that previously were viewed as unrelated (…) I have long followed this method that I have developed and explained in my dissertation, I have employed it in a host of shorter critical pieces (…) I read the history of an age in its types (…) According to the method I follow, a work has value to the same degree that it is typical. (Brandes 1872b:7–9)

After his dissertation and a Grand Tour that lasted from April 1870 until the summer of 1871, Brandes attempted to develop the question of the formation of consciousness even further. *Main Currents* was initially envisioned according to this scientific orientation. Immediately after the appearance of the first volume and his defense of it in the spring of 1872, Brandes returned to his preoccupation in a series of lectures on recent French drama. Throughout the entire summer of 1872 he was occupied with a work on the association of ideas. Associationist psychology was an effort to break with the doctrine of innate ideas, and the unity of the "I" or the personality. Brandes' inspiration was provided by Stuart Mill and Taine, but perhaps also by his slightly earlier studies of J.F. Herbart.

In a letter to his friend Julius Salomonsen (1847–1924), dated "Sunrise, July 20, 1872," the project (or vision) is presented in this manner:

> And this idea is so lovely, oh so lovely!
> The Association
Conceived and Represented as
Foundational Principle
of Human Cognition
by
G. Brandes
>
> I've come no farther than this, but soon, soon it shall be four to five hundred pages and many shall read it with admiration (…) Dear friend, if I should kick the bucket before I finish this, you must tell everyone that I wanted to carry out a depiction of the above in Danish and thereby ground our philosophy here in Norden [Scandinavia] on a new basis, a true basis, which permits the demonstration of *altogether determinative, incontrovertible laws*, quite like in mechanics and chemistry. You can also let it be known that all the other philosophy here in Denmark amounts to figments of the imagination and so much chatter, idealistic dreams, and thus allow me to acquire the reputation of one who defined philosophy as a *science of the laws of the intellect*, and who ventured to assert that as such it is of the same rank as the natural sciences, which are sciences of the laws of nature. All philosophy is psychology. All psychology is based on observation. All psychology is the doctrine of associations, associations and sense impressions, of images, of ideas and of names. The associations are the mortar that holds together the bricks in the grand edifice of the intellect. (Georg and Edv. Brandes 1939:279–280)

That very same summer, however, Brandes had to abandon the project. In his memoirs he laconically noted that "my abilities were not up to the task of elaborating the fundamental thoughts occurring to me, and after a few months I let the work go" (Brandes 1907:92).

Traces of the problematic and its concepts, however, are found in the chapter on "Romantic Reflection and Psychology" in *The Romantic School in Germany* (Brandes 1873:207–213), in which the following passage at long last establishes a distance from the self-dissolving determinants of the aggregate point of view:

> But if the human being is now by the necessity of nature multifaceted and split and divided up by nature, then it is one through freedom. Freedom, will and resolve make a human whole. If the human being as a product of nature is only a multiplicity held together more or less securely by associations, then the human being as intellect is an individuality, and in the will collects all the elements of the intellect and thus functions like the edge of a sword. (Brandes 1873:213)

As so often in Brandes, the reasoning is summarized in an image. The sword elegantly cuts through the Gordian knots that had troubled his dissertation. In comparing this citation with the context and its resonance in the second edition of the book (Brandes 1891:257–269), it is evident that "idea-associations" as a concept had been supplanted by "idea-connections" and "thought-chains," such that the concealed reference to the contradiction ridden dilemma raised by the dissertation fades away. At the same time the "freedom" that made the human being whole (note the inserted "however" below) is supported by a doctrine of the *personality*:

> [the human being is] however as the healthy, vigorous personality, one. Purpose, will, resolve make the human being whole. If the human being as product of nature is only a multiplicity held together more or less securely by chains of thoughts, then

the human being as intellect is a unity, and in the will collects all the elements of the intellect and thus functions like the edge of a sword. (Brandes 1891:268)

A vitalistic and Nietzschean solution is therefore provided for the psychology of the self. This change in argumentation and conceptual formation, which has its roots in Brandes' dissertation, can be seen as a recurring feature in the revision of the first volume especially, but the emphasis on personality can be detected in all six volumes.

Composition

When Brandes returned from his travels in Europe in the summer of 1871 he had first thought of delivering a series of public lectures on "Recent French Drama," a subject with which he was familiar from his role as a theater critic for *Illustreret Tidende*, which he had held since 1867. (The lectures were published in 1978 by Henning Fenger as *Georg Brandes and Recent French Drama. Theater Reviews and Dramaturgical Lectures, 1865–1872*). The lectures on drama were delayed, however, until the spring of 1872, because his mentor of many years, the philosopher Hans Brøchner (1820–1875), found them too narrow and unimpressive. Instead, as noted in Brandes' memoirs, at the beginning of October, Brøchner proposed a broader theme for a series of lectures that would have a greater impact. Brandes also mentions in his memoirs that his chief concern at the time was a (polemical) diagnosis of "the cultural standpoint of Denmark at present and a critique of the literature of its past, which would function as my starting point" (Brandes 1907:62–63).

Shortly thereafter, Brandes came back to Brøchner with a proposal for six long series of lectures, collectively titled "Fundamental Currents" [Grundstrømninger]. After consultation with Brøchner, this was changed to "Main Currents" [Hovedstrømninger], which is the designation Brandes employs in a letter to Emil Petersen dated October 20, 1871 (Georg Brandes and Emil Petersen 1980:142).

The first of the lectures was delivered at 6pm on November 3, 1871, while the last was given on December 16. Shortly after, on December 27,

Brandes summarized his central theme for all six volumes in a letter to Taine, adding "mais je n'ose pas encore le faire imprimer; les orthodoxies sont trop en rage contre moi" [but I dare not allow this to be published, for the orthodox types are too angry with me] (Brandes 1952:7).

One last perspective on the relationship between Brøchner and Brandes is provided by the philosopher Carl Henrik Koch. His (prudent) conclusion is that the program of ideas – freethinking, freedom of intellect, free humanity – does indeed refer back to the conclusion of the eighteenth century, but that it is first and foremost the voice of Brøchner (rather than Hegel) that stands behinds these words. It was Brandes himself, however, who *radicalized* Brøchner's conception of freedom (Carl Henrik Koch 2000:128–150).

As noted, the six volumes of *Main Currents* were intended as a drama in six acts, determined by the literary groups characterized in each: first the emigrants exiled by the revolution; next the German Romantics and their reaction against the revolution; and in the third volume the corresponding course of reaction in France. The reversal in the drama arrives with English Naturalism in the fourth volume, where "Naturalism" signifies a love of nature rather than Émile Zola's later iteration of the impartial depiction of reality. Byron's death in 1824 during the Greek War of Liberation against the Ottoman Empire (1821–1829) for Brandes marks the decisive, positive turning point in European liberalism. The fifth volume concerns the liberal movement as manifested among other places in the July Revolution of 1830, with Balzac as its leading author, while the sixth and concluding volume treats the corresponding movement in Germany up until 1848, with Ludvig Börne and Heinrich Heine as the main figures.

This composition was first and foremost inspired by the liberal German historian and politician G.G. Gervinus (1805–1871) and his work *Geschichte des. 19. Jahrhunderts seit den Wiener Verträgen* (8 vols, 1855–1866), which Brandes had borrowed from the Royal Library in August 1871, and Hermann Hettners' *Literaturgeschichte des achtzehnten Jahrhunderts in drei Theilen* (8 vols, 1856–1872), also borrowed at the same time (see bibliography in Henning Fenger 1955:445, 447). These

41

were especially significant for the critical concept of the work as a drama (the term "emigrant literature" and the prominent placement of Madame de Staël are owed to Gervinus), and for the description of the genre-bending currents, born out of ideas and fixed into types that are representative of an epoch. The relatively plentiful portraits of individual women that Brandes supplies, especially in the first two volumes, are also primarily due to Gervinus: beyond Madame de Staël, he includes George Sand, Dorothea Veit, Caroline Schlegel, Madame de Krüdener, Rahel von Varnhagen, Bettina von Arnim, and Charlotte Stieglitz (see Gunnar Ahlström 1937).

Brandes' portrayal of political liberalism contains an inner tension between two main currents that he had lucidly described in the opening pages of *The Reaction in France* (1874). One emanated from Rousseau. This is the unifying principle of enthusiasm, by which the social feeling of solidarity counteracts the authority principle; socialism begins here, through Robespierre and the Jacobins. The other originated with Voltaire. It is a subversive principle, by which indignation and freethinking crush the authority principle; liberalism emerges here as individualism, through Condorcet and the Girondins. On the one side brotherhood, and on the other freedom. Yet both traditions demand equality. In this context it is worth recalling that the designation "liberal" first gained a foothold after 1800, just as "individualism" only acquired a positive valence after around 1860.

In order to put these ideas clearly into perspective, the Rousseauian thread can be traced forward to the image of the centralized state with subordinate civil servants, which Brandes himself imagined during his stay in Berlin between 1877 and 1883, albeit also – in an early, foreboding image of socialism – tempered by fear of the tyranny of the majority. In a more positive variant Brandes also considers a solidaristic social utopia, the idea of a better society with happiness for the many.

The Voltairean thread concerns the human being as an autonomous individual, described among other places in European Romanticism, with which the young Brandes was familiar. Here the individual begins where the state ends, and an elitist cultivation of intelligence and sophistication can thrive. The implications for society can be vague, but it generally involves a truer and more just society, in which the autonomy and value of the individual is respected.

In his *Den ensamme. En motivstudie i det moderna genombrottets litteratur* (1961), the Swedish literary scholar Thure Stenström has described the two traditions in the literature of the Modern Breakthrough as governed by a "naturalistic feeling of community" and "Romantic individualism" respectively. The two traditions can be traced as clear threads all the way through *Main Currents*.

In the first years of the 1870s, Brandes read up on socialist theory, especially the Saint-Simonians and Ferdinand Lassalle, about whom he wrote a book, first published in German in 1877 and then in Danish in 1881. In the introductory lecture to *Main Currents* he had emphasized how Danish society had developed such that "it bears the features of tyranny under the mask of freedom" (Brandes 1872a:15). Brandes had experienced and described the reaction as an amoral duality. A few years later, through Lassalle (as well as an image borrowed from Sainte-Beuve), Brandes came to understand the bourgeois reaction as an element of class struggle:

> it can be seen that the bourgeoisie tried to pull the ladder up with it as soon as it had reached the top. Its first action after having itself secured its status through the pen was to take the pen out of the hand of the proletariat (compare Lassalle: *Arbeiterprogramm*). (Brandes 1874:46; in the second edition the parentheses around the Lassalle citation are eliminated: Brandes 1892:41)

Yet later in the book Brandes declares his preference regarding the Rousseauian and Voltairean traditions:

> The central idea is that it is not the family, as is usually asserted, but the individual that constitutes the fundamental pillar of

society, and that the individual is sovereign. The sovereignty of the individual [means] freedom of the press, speech, travel, exchange, inquiry and freedom of feeling. From this point of view the only possible defense of a law that constrains freedom is that such a law, through the provisional impingement upon freedom, is the only means of acquiring a more perfect arrangement with complete freedom, for freedom is the ideal of individualism. (Brandes 1874:151–172)

Method

Types

In each of the six volumes of *Main Currents*, Brandes devotes an introductory chapter to describing the historical and political background of the works he will analyze, which is generally followed up by a corresponding summary in the conclusion. His assertion that "first and foremost and everywhere I trace the literature back to life" (Brandes 1873:4) functions as a recurring declaration of fighting words. Yet rather than delineating a relationship of dependency, it is more accurate to say that Brandes – as well oriented and well informed as he was – outlines the background and the context only for those works of literature that concern him. The connection between background and foreground is established with the help of *types*, in which the societal tensions of an epoch come to expression symptomatically. In *Emigrant Literature* it is especially Goethe's Werther and Chateaubriand's René that function as clear examples of a passionate individual who in the effort to emancipate himself collides with societal limitations: "the principal source of Werther's sorrows is the discordance between the infinity of the heart and the strictures of society" (Brandes 1872a:55). In the rhetoric of his presentation, these examples were accompanied by reassurances that the author "portrays for the reader, purely historically and scientifically, a state of the soul that historically has revealed and documented itself in the literature" (Brandes 1872a:89–90). "The literary historian who moves from one variation of a type of the age to another proceeds as does the natural scientist, who pursues the same transformation of fundamental forms" (Brandes 1872a:91).

In the course of the six volumes, Brandes found it increasingly difficult to maintain the typological matrix, and in the formulations in the revised editions it is often apparent that the abstract ideas and movements that originally functioned as the frame were rewritten as concrete influences and thoughts. This is why many of the thematic chapter headings in the first editions were replaced with authors' names in the second editions. This coheres with a positivistic biographical trait that is more comprehensively explained below.

At the same time it also became clearer to him that while the typological concept ensured a strong conception of the presentation and invited comparative characterization of the variants of types, this occurred at the expense of coherent readings of the individual literary works. This contributed to the weakening of *Main Currents* as a literary-historical handbook in comparison to more recent national literary histories (for a survey of Danish literary history writing, see Flemming Conrad 2006).

Comparatism and Positivism
Brandes' work was a forerunner to the kind of comparative literary studies that only began to develop in earnest in the years following. The concern of *Main Currents* was not so much comparative literary study in the modern sense of the word – that is, the study of impacts and influences between literatures – but a general or universal description of the major European literatures in (polemical) comparison with that of Denmark.

Methodologically speaking, the immediate inspirations for the six volumes were the theoretical books of Hippolyte Taine and his English literary history *Histoire de la littérature anglaise* (4 vols, 1864, Danish transl. 1874–1877). Brandes specifically employed Taine's analogies between aesthetics and classifying natural science in *Emigrant Literature*. The overarching and determinant factors that Brandes sought to identify were "race," "milieu," and "moment," while the material and the authors were arranged in "schools" around "the dominant quality" of a single figure.

In order to honor the triumphant practice of the natural sciences, scientific literary study began with a narrowing of perspective and interest to controllable and manageable individual processes, in which the principle of causality could be employed – and employed with success.

In Germany during the period in which Brandes worked, a positivistic literary studies and a praxis of literary history in a narrower sense developed, associated with figures such as Wilhelm Scherer (1841–1886) and his successor in Berlin, Erich Schmidt (1853–1913). At the same time this approach was marked as a distinctly national practice of literary history, appropriate to the German Reich that was established in 1871 under Bismarck's reliable leadership. Here the critical, source-based study of impacts and influences was developed and refined. In place of the open expanses of "race," "milieu," and "moment," the influential Wilhelm Scherer, whom Brandes got to know during his years in Berlin, inserted the "closed" categories of "das Ererbte," "das Erlernte," and "das Erlebte." In France, Taine's pupil Ferdinand Brunetière (1849–1906) isolated the cultural historical "moment," and within that the more narrowly literary, more specifically determined "genre."

Now literary studies began to seek the impacts and influences of individual concrete events, of personal incidents, or of a writer's reading. In a polemic against idealism, scholars sought out the laws of imagination in order to uncover empirically how the poetic imagination functions; these conditions lent themselves to isolation and description, while the more comprehensive – and decisive – societal logic, which is found between the individual events and tensions and renders them as manifest forms or as symptoms, was much more difficult to handle. Here the category of "experience" served a key function as the smallest possible unity whose impact could be definitively traced. Literary observation was interested in experience not for what it *resulted from*, but for what it *resulted in*. Biography or the biographical frame now became the manner of integrating the details investigated. At the same time it is an approach that regularly appeals to empathy, understanding, and identification. This development in the direction of positivism was catalyzed by the emergence of national philologies and the establishment of corresponding university curricula (see Klaus Weimar 1989 and König and Lämmert 1993; for its Anglo-American development, see Gerald Graff 1987; the French development is covered in Carl Fehrman 1999).

Yet *Main Currents* landed in Germany before all of this happened. The work fulfilled a characterizing and perspectivizing function in a period in which the establishment of national literary studies had yet to acquire a solid foundation as an independent discipline. As the new discipline was relatively rapidly developed at the university lectern, Brandes' work was correspondingly progressively dismissed and marginalized, since it did not fulfill the ever-growing demands of the national philological school.

Max Koch established *Zeitschrift für vergleichende Literaturgeschichte* in 1887, but around 1890 the center for wider comparative literary studies shifted from Germany to France. In 1896 Joseph Texte (1865–1900) took up the first chair in "littérature comparé" at the University of Lyon; later figures in the French comparative tradition include Fernand Baldensperger and Paul van Tieghem. In Denmark Valdemar Vedel (1865–1942) became first a lecturer and later, in 1911, a temporary professor in general and comparative literature; in 1918 the professorship was made permanent.

Over the course of time Brandes produced a number of lesser studies within the more narrowly defined comparative tradition, for example "Goethe and Denmark" in 1880 (republished in Brandes 1883b) and "Henrik Ibsen and his School in Germany" in 1890 (republished in Brandes 1906), but overall the rapid development of the discipline and the transfer of its scholarly center from Germany to France served to diminish the literary-historical significance of Brandes' opus magnum.

Brandes consequently used his status as critic and artist as a bulwark against the intrusive demands of the professionalized discipline. In the foreword to *Mennesker og Værker* (1883) he suggests that literary criticism could be viewed as an applied science: "it is this to a certain point; but it is no less an art; for no methodical investigation can provide us with the key to a coherent human intellect" (Brandes 1883b:V). At the conclusion of the sixth volume of *Main Currents*, Brandes defends himself against the condemnations of his Danish critics:

> Here is the answer, that viewed impersonally the literature of a half century is only a chaos of hundreds of thousands of works in a great number of languages, and that the genuine Procrustes who has grouped, contrasted, stylized, emphasized and de-emphasized, expanded and contracted, placed in full light, half light or in shadows, is none other than the power normally referred to as art. (Brandes 1890:573)

A Conflict over Publication Rights

Main Currents, from volume to volume as well as from the first editions to the later revised versions, is characterized by a clear and continual movement away from the broad, Taine-inspired foundation toward a narrower focus on the biographical. This was the result of the more or less conscious disciplinary and methodological development Brandes underwent during the more than 15 years the six volumes were under construction. But when because of his own lack of forethought he found himself in a conflict over the publication rights to the German editions, he wrote an account, blessed by the wisdom of hindsight, of the changes to the foundation of the work he had undertaken prior to the new German editions. This was thus a partisan brief in a court case, yet at the same time it is noteworthy as a testament of his methodological self-understanding. It was formatted as a letter to his (new) publisher, Hermann Credner (1842–1924) of the house Veit & Co., but a Danish version was published in *Politiken* on July 4, 1887.

The first four volumes of *Main Currents* were quickly translated into German by Adolf Strodtmann (1829–1879), and issued by Duncker of Berlin between 1872 and 1876. After the firm's bankruptcy in 1886 it was acquired by the book publisher Hermann Barsdorf. Brandes was not content with the arrangement and in 1880 had entered into an agreement with Veit & Co. for a new edition, now titled *Die Literatur des neunzehnten Jahrhunderts in ihren Hauptströmungen dargestellt*. Although the remainders were transferred to Veit & Co., the house did not, because of carelessness on its part as well as on Brandes', secure the rights to Strodtmann's translations. The Danish government did not sign the 1886 Bern Convention, which concerned publication rights in countries outside the native lands of authors, until 1903, so Barsdorf issued a whole series of new printings without Brandes' agreement and without paying royalties to him. To avoid additional legal troubles Brandes was compelled to revise the collected volumes of *Main Currents*; Veit & Co.'s edition was thus only completed in 1901 (the complex legal issues are explained in the chapter on "The Barsdorf Nightmare" in Jørgen Knudsen 1994:414–421; see also Jens Bjerring-Hansen 2008:150–167).

According to the agreement with Veit & Co., the new and revised editions of the first four volumes were to be made available in 1882. The first and the fifth were completed in 1882 and 1883 respectively. But when the second volume appeared in 1887, Hermann Barsdorf, who had acquired Duncker and thus the rights to the old translations, filed suit on the grounds that the new volume relied too heavily on Strodtmann. It was in this context that Brandes published his account. The case passed through several courts, concluding in 1889 when the *Reichsgericht* ruled in Barsdorf's favor. He was therefore permitted to continue to sell the published and the revised translations for which he himself made provision. They were priced much more cheaply than Veit & Co.'s revised editions, which consequently sold poorly.

When Brandes published his *Gesammelte Schriften* with Langen in 1902, he returned to the Barsdorf conflict in his foreword:

> The majority of the books published in Germany with my name on the title page are books I have never seen, much less examined or published (…) A thrifty publisher, whose reputation does not at all correspond to his vigor, has acquired my entire authorship in German against my will and in spite of nearly twenty years

of protest on my part; he has treated my books as he desired, equipped them with ballyhooed and arbitrarily chosen titles, supplied them with additions and supplements, or cut the majority of them to pieces and thus sold them on the retail market. I must here once again state what I have so often expressed, that I do not have the most minimal relationship to the innumerable books Hr. Barsdorf of Leipzig has published under my name, and would never acknowledge them as my own. (In Danish in Brandes 1906:285–289; cited portion 287)

The Key Biographical Concept of "Experience"
The following series of citations provides examples of how Brandes found his way to the category of "experience" as a central explanatory factor that secured causality in a positivistic sense while, at the same time narrowing the scope of his analysis by integration into a biographical frame. The point of departure is the account Brandes provided in the summer of 1887 during the conflict with Barsdorf, in which he explained how his aesthetics, and therefore his construction of *Main Currents*, changed over time. It was published as "A Letter from Dr. G. Brandes" in *Politiken* on July 4, 1887:

> The central understanding of aesthetics has changed since 1873.
> At that time my conception of history was still abstract. I evaluated literature before anything else as an intellectual orientation. My understanding of *freedom* and *progress* was still doctrinaire. My own combative position endangered my impartiality. Thus my judgement of the Romantics was determined especially by their religious and political attitudes. There was much less to say regarding their talent.
> This is now completely changed. By virtue of innumerable interpolations, excisions, changes, in many cases of small size yet consequential, an entirely different poetics and historical understanding have come into being (…)

When I began to work on *Main Currents* in 1871, I was in my intellectual orientation still metaphysically minded. I overlooked the personalities; they were only the organs of the Ideas. As the title indicates, I was interested only in the *currents* of the world of ideas. The individualities were carried along by the currents, pulled apart by them; they were the spokespersons of the ideas. The personalities remained uninteresting to the author.

Thus not a single biographical sketch is found in the first part of the oldest edition of *Main Currents*.

In the old edition of the second part there is progress, in that the biographies are included, but as a rule they are short and incomplete and – as is wholly characteristic – they are in general tacked on at the end as supplements less important than the portrayal of the works.

First the works are reviewed, such that when the whole intellectual life of the person is characterized, there follows, as noted, a short description of the life of the personality, in which all that is portrayed has its roots. The works do not unfold themselves from these roots. They are breathed into life by the ideas. The human being, this "slack" that is left over when the ideas are treated, this nonetheless indispensable slack, was in the end included as a necessary evil. Compare for example the treatment of Kleist.

There is therefore not a single actual portrait found in the book. I was not capable of doing as much.

It was only much later that I learned that precisely on this point I was possessed of a strength. And when I no longer subscribed to the Hegelian contempt for the individual, no longer believed that the abstract world spirit brought forth the works, I began to immerse myself in the historical personalities and show *how their production followed from their lives* (…)

Therefore: the task of the work, which initially was to agitate, became purely scientific in the second edition, what was national and

Danish became universal. The understanding of poetry and art was at that time conditioned by the tendentiousness; it is now otherwise. Ultimately the relation between the ideas and the personalities has been reversed, and to this change corresponds the wholly distinct composition of the work. (Essential sections of this letter were worked into the article "The Heibergian Aesthetic" published in the journal *Ny Jord*, 1889, III:1–23; this was thereafter published in *Essays. Danish Personalities*, 1889:136–185, as well as, with changes to the language, in the *Samlede Skrifter*, I, 1899:494–512; cited portion 496)

Brandes' article was a plea in a dispute about copyright, so it was useful for him to trace the lines precisely and to prove how thoroughgoing the changes had been. Yet it is evident that the biographical approach appeared in various preliminary forms and variants in the previously published editions, and at the same time that his eye for currents had hardly vanished completely in the final volume, or in the revised editions already undertaken. But it is important to recall that the majority of the translations of *Main Currents* into foreign languages relied on the revised editions, while in the case of Germany it was presumably the translations from the original editions that circulated most widely.

In a continuation of Brandes' account, the following examples demonstrate how, step by step, he established the structure by which the noun "experience" [Da. oplevelse, Ger. Erlebnis] entered the language, it having appeared for the first time in Danish in his 1877 monograph on Kierkegaard.

1. (…) to what degree the subjects are selected from purely formal points of view. One of our preeminent contemporary poets once in conversation made me aware that "The Virgin of Orleans" is not "experienced" [oplevet], not conceived from strong, personal impressions but construed. (Brandes 1873:41)
2. As obscure, as allegorical as this novel [*Heinrich von Ofterdingen*] is, it touches on something of value, such that as much as any other living work of poetry it is experienced [oplevet]. (Brandes 1873:259)

3. This trait was grounded in something that had been experienced [noget oplevet]. (Brandes 1874:204)
4. These works are not like those of the best poets products of (…) profoundly vital, personally experienced [oplevede] events. (Brandes 1875:181, on the novels of Walter Scott)
5. That which is mere poetry in this narrative (…) is *unexperienced* [uoplevet] and therefore uninteresting. That which is only copied from reality (…) is as merely *experienced* [oplevet], not poetry, and likewise uninteresting. (Brandes 1876:312)
6. But the degree to which Kierkegaard's life was now stirred up is amply testified by the immensity of the forthcoming production. For there is of course no feeling, no passion and no suffering in anything that has not lived within the heart of the author. The river cannot rise higher than its source. (…) There are creative spirits who require much great fortune or experiences [Oplevelser] in order to produce a minor work. These are the kinds of poets who produce a drop of rose oil from hundreds of pounds of rose leaves. And on the other hand there are talents whose nature is so fruitful, whose inner climate is so tropical, that out of the wholly peculiar conditions of daily life they experience [oplever] with the highest energies they are able to draw out a whole series of significant works. They resemble the treeless islands of the South Seas, on which passengers from a passing ship leave a few fruit seeds and which many years later are covered with mighty forests. Kierkegaard belonged to the latter type. He was unreceptive to the great mass of life impressions, because early on only a handful of them so entranced him that he could never escape them or create space for new ones. He had the poet's need to diffuse himself, to send out a host of different figures from the enclosure of his personality. Yet at the same time he did not possess the poetic powers to provide, through a complete transformation of his life impressions, an independent life for them outside of the various figures, figures that appeared in an abundance of forms that were

either irrelevant to him or only emerged from situations alien or heterogeneous to his personality. Instead of transforming his life impressions he only recast them; instead of transforming himself he disguised or masked himself. He never concentrated himself as intensely as his mere thoughts, he never diffused himself as intensely as does the true poet. (Brandes 1877:76–78)

7. He (Balzac) had still not experienced [oplevet] anything that could provide for his creations value or worth, yet his powers of imagination were lively and eternally fruitful and he had read enough to provide his creations with a passable form in the usual sense of entertaining material. (Brandes 1882:227)

8. This portrayal undoubtedly owes a part of its incomparable mastery to the faithful re-presentation of personal experiences [Oplevelser]. (Brandes 1882:300, on Stendhal)

Citation 6, from the book on Kierkegaard, reveals the path toward the principle in what was then a groundbreaking work. It was Brandes' first book dedicated to a single author, the aim of which was to provide an account of Kierkegaard's production by showing the works to be reflections on the decisive events or "experiences" of his life and development: his relation to his father, to The Corsair, and to Regine Olsen. Brandes sought – and found – the decisive genetic connection between life and work in the experiences that conditioned the poetry. Moreover, the understanding of causality with which Brandes operated was in no way simplified. His differentiated elucidation of the relationship between desire and powers, between thinkers and poets, is quite noteworthy.

Example: The Portrait of Byron
The change in Brandes' methodological and ideological approach can be clarified by looking at his understanding of the key figure of Byron.

As early as the introductory lecture of *Main Currents*, Byron was introduced as the man who brings about the reversal in the great drama: "the Greek War of Independence breaks out, and a breath of fresh air travels throughout

Europe; Byron falls a hero for the Greek cause, and his heroic deed makes an enormous impression on all the writers of the Continent" (Brandes 1872:13).

In April and May of 1872, some months after the publication of the introductory lecture of *Main Currents*, Brandes gave six lectures on recent French drama. At the conclusion of the first of these lectures, he reiterates and expands on the central position of Byron as an expression and a summation of the liberal movement:

> But in Byron himself the spirit of rebellion was incarnated. In his birth, his bodily development, his war against the pharisaic public opinion of England, his Rousseau-influenced love of nature, his hatred of civilization, which to him did not seem to have birthed any other fruits than pestilence and cancer, war and immorality, he stood outside of society (…) American republicanism, German freethinking, French rebelliousness, Anglo-Saxon radicalism seemed to be united in this one intellect. His death was a boon to the universal cause of freedom. The Holy Alliance seemed to have cowed the spirit of revolution for all time. Every bond that connected the Restoration to the Revolution was severed. Then this poet tied together the threads that had required a million soldiers to cut apart. When the rebellion had been suppressed in all countries, when the press had been gagged, when science had humbled and subjected itself, this son of the imagination, this poet as free as the air, entered himself into the lists and so awakened the spirit of the previous century. (Cited from Fenger 1978:102–103)

This vision is reiterated and modified in *The Reaction in France* (1874), in which Brandes in part compares literary types and in part summarily goes back and forth between them and the historic personages of Napoleon and Byron:

> Napoleon had displaced Werther, René and Faust; Byron's promethean and desperate heroism displaced Napoleon. He accorded wonderfully with the demand of the age (…) It was the spirit of

rebellion that radiated from him and through his mouth united the young generation to a society of world citizenship (…) Byron let loose all passions. It was not for him to attack at a single point, but to revolutionize the minds, to awaken indignation at tyranny. (Brandes 1874:348–349)

The point at which this citation ends is followed by a few lines in accordance with what Brandes had said in the spring 1872 lecture series, but in the published version it is now marked with a citation from Gervinus' *Geschichte des 19. Jahrhunderts seit den Wiener Verträgen*. Brandes relies on the view of the post-Hegelian Gervinus, according to which the great individuals of history can only be understood in their context, and the leader is only the leader of the masses, because he is an expression of a tendency of development in society.

In 1875's *Naturalism in England* Brandes escaped the post-Hegelian view and the practice of comparative characterization in favor of an interpretation grounded in biography. The material on Byron consumes the last six chapters of the book, in all more than 170 pages. In the previous volumes of *Main Currents*, Brandes had employed themes or problematics as chapter titles, but in this portrait of Byron the name of the author appears within the chapter titles. This was the longest piece Brandes had written on a single person up to this point, and in contrast to his previous work the first to be constructed purely biographically. Byron's development is portrayed with emphasis on his parents and upbringing, especially regarding decisive events and their significance in interplay with his character traits. These meaningful traits are not reflected against society, but in relation to the development of his personality. Brandes summarizes the troubles from which the poet emerged by noting that they "acquired their significance by early on driving Byron, who as a young aristocrat could easily have occupied himself with the sensibilities of his class and kin, exclusively toward the resources of the single, isolated personality" (Brandes 1875:378).

The event which "acquired decisive meaning in his life" (Brandes 1875:469) was falling in love with the young Teresa Guiccioli. The portrait is constructed such that Byron's life story proceeds from the desire for freedom: from society toward solitude and from culture toward nature. Byron sought escape from society toward "localities outside of civilization, where individuality could develop itself freely and without regard to any conventional strictures" (Brandes 1875:389). "He, who descended in a straight line from Rousseau, felt himself powerfully drawn to all the people living in a 'natural state'" (Brandes 1875:390). Feudal Albania became that "nature" in which the individuality and true humanity of the free world citizen could reveal itself: "He now grasped freedom in the wide and full and universally human sense of the word. He now sensed that free thought is the point of departure for all life of the spirit" (Brandes 1875:429).

The section "Byron. The Self-Absorption of the I" thus concludes:

> Thus the poet conducts his worship service and gathers his soul in devotions. He renounces all "houses of idols," Gothic churches as well as Greek temples, and like the Ancient Persians built their altars on the highest mountains overlooking the earth, he bows his head in the great church of nature, which consists of the earth and the air. (Brandes 1875:433)

Byron does not just reject culture here; even nature returns to its original meaning as paradise, with the human being as primordial as Adam. Brandes refers here to the "ur-history of the race." Logically enough, the revolutionary spirit culminates atop the Alps:

> On the lonely heights above the snow line, where human weakness and pliability no longer thrive, where his soul first breathes freely, and the Alpine landscape by the necessity of nature forms the frame round his hero who in his stern wildness is akin to it. (Brandes 1875:446–447)

Characteristic of Brandes' biographical interpretation is that it is precisely at this point that he, by virtue of his own experiences, inserts himself into Byron's situation:

> I recall that one evening I stood on Rigi Kulm and observed the lovely lakes at the foot of the mountain, and the small clouds that far down passed over them … It was visions of nature such as this that provided the material for the apparitions that overcame Manfred. Passage after passage of Byron's journal is incorporated into his poem. (Brandes 1875:436–437)

(Here Brandes is citing his article "A Few Notes on Travel. (From a Diary)" published in *Illustreret Tidende*, May 2, 1869:262; the article was based on a letter to his parents dated August 14, 1868, published in Brandes 1978:196–198.)

It is notable that "experience" now has two functions. First, it is an element in that which is understood, in that experience becomes the measure to which the literary work can be causally traced back; here the frame of understanding is defined as biography. Second, experience functions as understanding in and of itself – as the hermeneutic element or the similarity that conditions the relation between the object and the interpreting or understanding subject (here Brandes' corresponding experiences atop Rigi Kulm).

The chapter on Byron is paradoxical in that Brandes, who is wholly in revolt against Romanticism, chooses a Romantic as his principal subject. A foundational aspect of his approach, however – as was already evident in the introductory lecture – is that it is the reactionary social system that forces the seeker of freedom to choose solitude; in later iterations solitude acquires absolute value, while family and society are portrayed as destructive of the personality.

In *The Romantic School in France* (1882), this problematic receives a peculiar treatment in a contrasting of George Sand and Naturalism (the Balzac school, and Zola):

> Whenever Emile Zola registered his objections against the idealistic novel, he never forgot to point out the dangers that this continual aspiration beyond the bounds which restrain the individual, this

repeated desire for greater intellectual and emotional freedom, pose to the family and to society (…) He could have added that he and his successors in the Balzac school have never at all had need of a higher morality than the ordinary, and that they have never opened up a vision of society different from that which exists. They have subjected themselves to a violent constriction, in that they have committed themselves to the depiction of the external realities observable to them and refused to draw any conclusions therefrom. (Brandes 1882:198–199)

If literature and human beings are only products of circumstances, then the world cannot be changed; thus Positivism and Naturalism become that which in his dissertation Brandes had called "quietistic," meaning without feeling, or disengaged (Brandes 1870b:173). Only when human beings are free is critique as appeal made possible. Thus the world can be changed. If literature ought to criticize society, it cannot do so by simply being an expression of it. "The only literature that is alive today is one that provokes debate" – this provocative declaration in the introduction to *Emigrant Literature* (Brandes 1872a:15) represents a profound and continuous preoccupation of all six volumes of *Main Currents*.

Editions and Translations
Between 1872 and Brandes' death in 1927, *Main Currents* was published in five Danish editions, the last in 1923–1924. Thus some 14,250 copies were circulated, although *Emigrant Literature* was issued in 15,250 copies, since this first volume was published as a revised edition early on, in 1877. Apart from the fourth printing in 1906, Brandes revised each of the new editions.

The German edition was released in the same year as the Danish, in 1872, thanks to Adolf Strodtmann's translation for Duncker of Berlin. The next three volumes appeared in 1873, 1874, and 1876; after Strodtmann's death in 1879, the final two volumes of *Die Hauptströmungen der Literatur des neunzehnten Jahrhunderts*, translated by W. Rudow and A. v. D. Linden, appeared in 1886 and 1896.

When Brandes began to revise the individual volumes and, as previously noted, signed a new contract with Veit & Co. of Leipzig in 1880 for *Die Literatur des neunzehnten Jahrhunderts in ihren Hauptströmungen dargestellt*, this resulted in a court case that Brandes lost. The 1887 account of the revisions cited previously was a brief in this case.

At long last, in 1924, a "Vom Verfasser neu bearbeitete endgültige Ausgabe," translated by Ernst Richard Eckert, was published by Erich Reiss in Berlin in three closely printed volumes. The third volume includes a detailed index.

The German Duncker editions provided the foundation for the Polish translations of the five first editions (1881–1885), and likewise for the Russian versions of the four first editions (1891–1893). A translation from the Danish, edited by M.V. Lucickaja, was published in Kiev in 1902–1903. The fourth volume was translated from German by E. Zauer and published with a foreword by E.A. Solevev in Saint Petersburg in 1898; the other volumes, from German translations, were also published by different translators between 1895 and 1900.

Brandes' *Collected Writings* were published in Russian in twelve volumes in 1902–1903; volumes three to eleven contain *Main Currents*. The whole collection appeared in a revised and expanded edition between 1906 and 1914; of the twenty volumes, five through twelve contain *Main Currents*.

A Spanish edition in two volumes, which contained all six of the original books, appeared in Buenos Aires in 1946.

It was the appearance of Brandes' *William Shakespeare* (3 vols, 1895–1896) in English translation in 1896 that opened the English and American markets to his books, and thereafter those of India and Japan. *Main Currents in European Literature*, translated by Diana White and Mary Morison, appeared in London in six volumes between 1901 and 1905; illustrations were added in a 1906 edition, which was reissued in 1923 and 1924; and in 1975 the edition was reprinted in New York. The introduction to the work in the English editions is reduced to three and a half pages. The third volume, *The Reaction in France*, was separately reissued in 1960, the fourth, *Naturalism in England*, in 1957 and 1960, and the fifth in 1966.

A Japanese edition of *Main Currents* appeared in Tokyo in 1915, translated by Junsuku Suita. It was reissued in 1929 and then revised by S. Fukushima in 1953–1954. Brandes' foreword to the Japanese edition appears in Danish in *Napoleon and Garibaldi* (1917:257–261).

A Chinese edition of the first four volumes was published in Shanghai in 1936, translated from the English editions by Han Shiheng, who also made use of the Japanese edition. A Chinese edition of all six volumes appeared between 1980 and 1986, and was reissued in 1997 and 2018.

A Yiddish translation in eleven volumes was published in Warsaw between 1918 and 1921.

Beyond the complete editions of *Main Currents*, individual volumes have been translated to other languages. *Emigrant Literature* was made available in Finnish in 1887. *The Romantic School in France* was translated into Czech in 1894 and French in 1902.

Literature on Georg Brandes and *Main Currents*

Julius Moritzen (1863–1946) published a short introduction to Brandes, *Georg Brandes in Life and Letters*, in 1921. In 1924 there followed the small-format *A Guide to Georg Brandes's "Main Currents in 19th Century Literature"* in the series *Little Blue Book*, No. 531.

Paul V. Rubow (1896–1972) published *Georg Brandes' Briller* in 1932, which treated the elements of and changes in Brandes' aesthetic views. Rubow's discussion of the individual volumes of *Main Currents* can be searched in the index. His long article "Georg Brandes' Forhold til Taine og Sainte-Beuve" of 1916, published in *Litterære Studier* in 1928 (with a new edition in 1949), remains foundational.

Holger Ahlenius (1905–1956) published a work on reception history in 1932, *Georg Brandes i svensk litteratur till och med 1890. Hans ställning och inflytande*.

Gunnar Ahlström (1906–1982) published *Georg Brandes' Hovedstrømninger. En ideologisk undersökning* in 1938. This book was the first larger-scale analysis of the work, with emphasis on the themes of freedom, nature, humanity, and literature. Ahlström later wrote a broad introduction, *Det moderna genombrottet i Nordens litteratur*, published in 1947, with a second edition in 1974.

Henning Fenger (1921–1985) published the foundational work *Georg Brandes' læreår. Læsning, ideer, smag, kritik 1857-1872* in 1955, followed in 1957 by a biographical volume on the same period, *Den unge Brandes*. The two volumes were published together in 1963 under the title *Georg Brandes et la France. La formation de son esprit et ses goûts littéraires (1842–1872)*.

Thure Stenström (1927–) published *Den ensamme. En motivstudie i det moderna genombrottets litteratur* in 1961, which contains a long chapter on Kierkegaard and Brandes that includes an analysis of the Byron chapter in the fourth volume of *Main Currents*.

Sven Møller Kristensen (1909–1991) in 1964 published the useful article "Georg Brandes Research. A Survey" in *Scandinavica* (Vol. 3, 1964:121–132), and in 1980 the book *Georg Brandes. Kritikeren, liberalisten, humanisten*, which is an eminently clear outline of Brandes' central ideas.

René Wellek (1903–1995), in his voluminous *A History of Modern Criticism*, treats Brandes in the fourth volume, *The Later Nineteenth Century* (1965), in chapter 16: "The Lonely Dane: Georg Brandes," 357–369.

Bertil Nolin (1926–1996) wrote the foundational book on Brandes' relation to European literature, *Den gode europén. Studier i Georg Brandes' idéutveckling 1871-1893 med speciell hänsyn till hans förhållande till tysk, engelsk, slavisk och fransk litteratur* (1965). A bibliographic supplement contains many detailed explanations of difficult-to-access material. The relatively short introduction in Twayne's World Author Series, *Georg Brandes*, 1976, contains a fine chapter on *Main Currents*.

Klaus Bohnen (1941–2019) published *Der Essay als kritischer Spiegel. Georg Brandes und die deutsche Literatur* in 1980, which contains an introductory essay and a bibliography.

Jørgen Knudsen (1926–2017) published a reliable and relatively comprehensive Brandes biography in eight volumes between 1985 and 2004. It appeared in 2008 in an abridged single volume, *GB. En Brandes-biografi*.

Finally, four longer anthologies of articles on Brandes are available, which include sections on *Main Currents*:

Hans Hertel and Sven Møller Kristensen (Eds) (1973): *Den politiske Georg Brandes*.

Hans Hertel and Sven Møller Kristensen (Eds) (1980): *The Activist Critic. A Symposium on the Political Ideas, Literary Methods and International Reception of Georg Brandes* (*Orbis litterarum*, Supplement No. 5). See in this volume Per Dahl and John Mott, "Georg Brandes – a Bio-Bibliographical Survey," 303–360, which contains an overview of Brandes' books and the available translations in different languages.

Olav Harsløf (Ed.) (2004): *Georg Brandes og Europa. Forelæsninger fra 1. internationale Georg Brandes Konference, Firenze, 7-9 november 2002*.

Annie Bourguignon, Konrad Harrer, and Jørgen Stender Clausen (Eds) (2010): *Grands courants d'échanges intellectuels: Georg Brandes et la France, l'Allemagne, l'Angleterre. Actes de la deuxième conférence internationale Georg Brandes, Nancy, 13–15 novembre 2008*.

BRANDES AFTER *MAIN CURRENTS*: POLITICAL JOURNALISM, OPPRESSED PEOPLES

William Banks

Introduction

The completion of the immense enterprise that has been the *Digital Currents* project will surely go a long way toward generating new and deserved interest in the figure of Georg Brandes, he who for a half century was placed at the very center of the world republic of letters and yet, for a number of reasons, no longer occupies such a position within world literary-historical memory. The project has performed a critical service to the human sciences in making *Main Currents*, the single work upon which Brandes' formidable reputation was built, widely accessible to a new generation of readers. Given the extent of the impact of *Main Currents*, both at home in the North, in Europe and eventually across the world, Brandes could, after he delivered the manuscript for the sixth and final volume in 1890, have opted for an early retirement. Indeed, he could have done so relatively certain that his place in world literary history had been firmly secured. In the disciplinary (and international) domain, the work had contributed a great deal toward establishing comparative literature as an independent and autonomous branch of literary studies. Perhaps even more importantly, within the local Danish (and Scandinavian) context, *Main Currents* had fulfilled its equally significant aim of provoking literary (and, more broadly, cultural) change in relatively backward Scandinavia. The critic's call, in the famous inaugural lecture of November 3, 1871, for a new literature that "provokes debate" was very soon answered by the young writers of Scandinavia, so much so that only a dozen years later, Brandes could declare unconditional victory, issuing a celebratory volume of portraits of the leading lights of the movement he had deemed the Modern Breakthrough (*Det Moderne Gjennembruds Mænd*, 1883). Not only had Brandes and his many allies emancipated Scandinavia from its "long Romantic hangover," they had transformed Norden from a literary afterthought to a vital center of the world literary republic, effectively crashing the party so long the exclusive affair of France, Germany, and England, a rare moment in the sun for such a peripheral part of the globe that would not be relinquished until the First World War.

Given how restless and searching the spirit of Brandes was, the critic could hardly rest on the considerable laurels he had already acquired before reaching the age of fifty. His productivity after *Main Currents* accordingly shows no sign of abatement, right up until his death in 1927. The nature of this production, however, most certainly does change, and indeed had already begun to do so during the nearly two decades during which he labored on his master work. This essay provides a brief, although by no means comprehensive, overview of Brandes' work after *Main Currents*. All emphasis is placed on what is wholly new in mature Brandes, specifically his sustained activity as a political journalist, his tireless advocacy on behalf of all those to whom he referred as *undertrykte folkeslag*, "those oppressed peoples," beginning with his fellow Danes in Sønderjylland but eventually encompassing the manifold of national minority populations of Eurasia as well as, gradually, the colonized peoples of Europe's overseas empires.

Two Brandesian Radicalisms: Literary and Aristocratic

It is customary to divide Brandes' long career into two distinct phases, namely the early period of his specifically *literary* radicalism, which loosely corresponds to his work on *Main Currents* (1870–1880s), and the later period of his *aristocratic* radicalism, stretching roughly from the late 1880s until his death. This division is very useful in acquiring an understanding of the long-term evolution of the critic's thinking, although two important observations are in order. In the first place, contemporary readers of Brandes must be wary of overestimating the extent of the rupture that took place in the 1880s; his thinking and praxis did indeed change dramatically at this time, yet there is far more continuity between the "literary" and "aristocratic" iterations of his radicalism than might appear at first sight. In the second place, it must be kept in mind that while the general intellectual orientation of each of his two phases was characterized by a considerable degree of instability, the young Brandes was by and large a significantly more *coherent* figure than the mature critic – that is to say, the cracks and fissures in his literary radicalism were less severe than those in his aristocratic variant.

Young Brandes – the Brandes of literary radicalism – was in particular blessed with a relatively happy harmony between political and purely artistic concerns within his overall aesthetics. As he so forthrightly asserted in the November lecture, he had pressed young Nordic authors to reject their preoccupation with an imagined and idealized past in favor of immersion in the present and in reality. More importantly, at the same time he enjoined them to seek to transform that stagnant and reactionary reality into something modern, progressive, and freethinking, just as the poets and thinkers of Europe's major countries, beginning with Byron, had done fully 40 years prior. Literary radicalism, critically, thus understands politics and political engagement to be a constituent element of modern literature, not exactly on an equal footing with purely formal considerations, but very much a sine qua non. As Julie Allen has recently emphasized, Brandes would later note, in the foreword to the second German edition of *Main Currents* (1897) and thus after his views had changed fundamentally, that "the original orientation of the work is political, not literary" (cited in Allen 2012:63). A quarter century later, as stressed by Brandes' biographer Jørgen Knudsen, the critic would reaffirm this view of *Main Currents* in the preface to the sixth Danish edition (Knudsen 2004:424).

Brandesian literary radicalism as manifested in *Main Currents* was also, critically, deeply indebted to the dialectical Hegelian (and post-Hegelian) tradition in which the young critic had been educated. As carefully outlined by Anders Engberg-Pedersen in his article for this project (see especially the section "From Voltaire to Rousseau"), the dramatic structure of the work was staged as a dialectical interplay of a series of oppositions: Voltaire's kingdom of reason and Rousseau's kingdom of feeling; the principle of freedom and brotherhood as manifested in 1789 and the authority principle that followed in its wake; the spirit of freethinking of the eighteenth century and the stifling descent into reaction of the early nineteenth. In Brandes' peculiar appropriation of Hegel, poetic works (and the personalities that composed them) were viewed principally as (mere) expressions of the underlying intellectual and affective *currents* of the age. Brandes effectively attempts to look through the work and the personality for their more significant ideological underpinnings – the Idea at the expense of individual genius.

By the end of the 1880s, the literary radical theoretical foundation of *Main Currents*, never entirely secure in the first place, began to unravel, especially with respect to its Hegelian component. As Per Dahl has illuminated (see the section "A Conflict over Publication Rights"), Brandes provided us with a clear point of departure for his evolving thought in an open letter of 1887, in which he confesses that in the early stages of the project he was "still metaphysically minded," that is, Hegelian, and that he had "overlooked the personalities; they were only the organs of the Ideas" (Brandes 1887). During the long period of work on *Main Currents*, he thus gradually became increasingly preoccupied with the personalities of the poets and thinkers themselves, at the expense of the Ideas they expressed; in a different sense this further corresponds to a movement away from the sociology of Taine to the psychology of Sainte-Beuve. The consequences of this shift in understanding were immense, for now the significance of the individual talent was seen to be located within the constitution of the personality itself, rather than somewhere outside of it. As Dahl has demonstrated (see the section "Example: The Portrait of Byron"), there were already strong hints of this in the portrait of Byron, which so thoroughly dominates *Naturalism in England* (1875). By the late 1880s, Brandes' internal conflict had clearly been resolved, as from this point onward in his literary work, he becomes increasingly preoccupied with the great personalities of world history at the expense of Hegelian Absolute Spirit; as Adam Paulsen notes (the section "The Great Personality" in his contribution to this volume), mature Brandes practiced "an experiential and biographical aesthetics, according to which art was conceived as 'the expression of mental perturbations' with 'the aim of calling forth mental perturbations.'"

This general reordering of Brandes' views marks the point of transition from the early literary radicalism of his first phase to the specifically aristocratic radicalism of his mature period. Critical to this process of self-reinvention was his fateful encounter in the late 1880s with a then still obscure Friedrich Nietzsche; indeed, the name of Brandes' second phase is taken from the title of his seminal portrait of the philosopher from Basel, "Aristocratic Radicalism" (*Tilskueren*, August 1889), which was based on a series of lectures delivered earlier that year in Copenhagen. These lectures would soon come to rival the address of November 1871 with respect to their impact on Nordic (as well as German) literature. From Nietzsche Brandes acquired a new appreciation of what he would come to call *det store Menneske* [the great man]:

> This person willingly takes upon himself the sufferings of speaking the truth. His foundational insight is that a happy life is impossible; the highest a human being can reach is a heroic life, one in which he struggles against the greatest dangers for something that in one or another matter will benefit everyone. Only those authentic humans among us can rise up to the truly human, those who seem destined to be a leap in nature, thinkers and mentors, artists and creators, and those who make an impact more through their being than through their works: the nobility, those whose goodness is grand, those in whom the genius of the good manifests itself. (Brandes 1889:574)

Still the provocateur, Brandes proceeds to claim that such great personalities constitute no less than "the purpose of history," and that the role of us ordinary souls is thus limited to "the task of working, both inside ourselves and without, for the bringing forth of the thinker and the artist, the lover of the truth and of beauty, the pure and good personality" (Brandes 1889:574, 575). As Paulsen has noted (see the sections "The Great Personality" and "Aristocratic Radicalism"), the critic's new approach was already fully on display in the expansive portraits of Goethe and Heine in the sixth and final volume of *Main Currents*. For the remainder of his career as literary critic, Brandes would largely devote himself to a long series of monographs on the "great individuals of world history," among them Shakespeare (1895–1896), Ibsen (1898), Goethe (1915), Voltaire (1916–1917), Napoleon (1917), Julius Caesar (1918), and Michelangelo (1921).

Brandes contra Høffding

Like the November 1871 lecture, "Aristocratic Radicalism" was designed to provoke, and once more Brandes would not need to wait long for the inevitable fallout. Just a few months later, the Danish philosophy professor Harald Høffding, a representative of the intellectual establishment that had found no use for Brandes, responded with a vigorous critique, "Democratic Radicalism. An Objection," which appeared in the November/December number of *Tilskueren*. The ensuing debate, which reached ever greater magnitudes of intensity, would continue into the following spring, with each combatant weighing in twice more.

The feud between Brandes and Høffding is of significance here for the light it sheds on the former's transition toward his mature position of specifically aristocratic radicalism. The break with Hegel was a long time coming, but when it arrived it was in every way decisive. Another equally important question is whether Brandes' apparent affirmation of a new (intellectual and artistic, rather than hereditary) form of aristocracy also amounts to a rejection of the other component of literary radicalism, namely its insistence that if art is to be modern – and after Brandes, in the Germanic world all *should* be modern – it must be politically engaged. In other words, did the critic's movement from literary to aristocratic radicalism amount to a *retreat* from politics? In brief, the answer is most certainly no, yet much in his production during his mature period would seem to suggest otherwise.

In surveying the literary monography of Brandes' aristocratic phase, it certainly appears that the old harmony between progressive political engagement and purely artistic concerns has largely been abandoned. Indeed, the list of "world historical personalities" he chose to profile is conspicuous in that only Voltaire and Ibsen may be counted among those who consciously aligned themselves with the Enlightenment values so cherished by young Brandes; Ibsen, rather notoriously, was famously uncomfortable with such a designation. Two of Brandes "culture heroes," moreover, were arguably on the other side of history, Caesar and Napoleon having effectively ended their respective traditions of republican rule.

Even more dramatically, Brandes' reckless sallies against Høffding reveal a disturbing tendency toward contempt for "the mob," and even for the idea of democracy itself. Over and over again, he evinces a form of contempt for the masses so familiar to us from Nietzsche – a contempt also present, it must be remembered, in the thinking of another of Brandes' interlocutors, the consummate liberal J.S. Mill. Freethinking and progress, it seems, have far more to fear from the deprivations of the organized mob than from the actions of the "great men" appointed by history to lead humanity toward a brighter future:

> When the passions of the masses come into motion, the rational majority, even more the rational individual, will be overruled, shoved to the side, or crushed. The masses are not $1 + 1 + 1$ (up to the number they come to), but $1 + 1 + 1 \,(\ldots) + X$, that is the beastliness that is developed within the individual when he becomes the masses. (…) When Prof. Høffding, in a contradiction more apparent than real, thereby asserts the necessity of releasing steadily more of the masses to a free, humane life, this necessity is a testimony of precisely the meager human worth of the masses as masses, and of the danger the masses pose as opponents of the great men. This danger naturally also determines the usefulness of the masses as power in the hands of the great man, as a means of accomplishing his plans, which namely include the plans for the advancement of the masses. (Brandes 1890:19–20)

In parrying these attacks, Høffding comes off as by far the more sober – and humane – figure, effectively outflanking his opponent. Employing the nascent logic of social democracy to the domain of culture, Høffding asserts that the measure of the cultural development of a people is to be found in the mean, rather than at the top, and that single individuals of greatness, which he readily concedes are a necessity for a well-functioning human society, are to be evaluated according to the good they produce for society, as a means rather than an end in themselves. Perhaps most effectively, he offers up the eminently reasonable observation that the more ordinary people are educated and cultivated, the more likely they are to be capable of appreciating the great individual.

"Thoughts at the Turn of the Century"

Much in the seemingly illiberal and anti-democratic stance adopted by Brandes in his polemics against Høffding would appear to suggest that he had largely turned his back on politics, and yet, as has been noted, this is precisely not the case; indeed, beginning around the middle of the 1890s, he would dramatically *intensify* his involvement in affairs of state. However counterintuitive this might appear, there is in fact ample room for political activity within the mature, aristocratic iteration of Brandesian radicalism, although the nature of his political engagement, as indicated, changed in quality as well as in quantity. Whereas Brandes the literary radical had largely embedded his politics *within* his literary criticism and history – a fitting descriptor for the methodology of *Main Currents* is what the Danes would later come to call *ideologikritik* – the mature critic effectively sections off his politics from the relatively (but hardly entirely) apolitical literary monography. That he was conscious of the bifurcated nature of his mature production is clear in his 1905 essay "Zionism," written around the time that his first period of sustained activities as political journalist was coming to an end; here Brandes laments that such labors "have consumed three months of my working life this year" (Brandes 1910:407).

Brandes was motivated to make this fateful leap, from relatively abstract ideological critique to direct intervention in the form of political journalism, by a dramatically revised – and much more pessimistic – understanding of political developments in Europe's core countries. As clearly evident in the November 1871 lecture, the young Brandes held up France, Germany, and England as exemplars of progress and freethinking, as models worthy of study and emulation by backward Denmark. In the 1870s, the essential task for young Danes was working toward the closure of the "40-year gap" separating Denmark from Europe. By the 1890s, however, a series of disturbing developments in these countries had compelled Brandes to rethink his youthful valorization of them. He would outline his new views in a seminal 1899 address to the Danish Student Union, the association of freethinking young Danes that had long served as a forum for his evolving thinking. "Thoughts at the Turn of the Century," published in the January 1900 edition of *Tilskueren*, begins with an acknowledgement that as a young man he had overlooked two troubling developments within the core countries of Europe. In the first place he had failed to appreciate the significance of the outbreak of the Paris Commune in March of 1871, which is now understood as "the event that has most determined European politics" ever since, in that "fear of its repetition led the bourgeoisie of all the main countries" to forsake the very "freethinking" that had been the source of all their progress; the "social question" raised by events in Paris would come to "occupy all of the minds of the political class at the turn of the century," and "the social revolution" was seen as imminent (Brandes 1902a:143). Second, Brandes had failed to appreciate the intensity of French revanchist rage at the loss of Alsace and Lorraine, and because "both Germany and France had entered into powerful systems of alliances, the outbreak of a world war remained continuously plausible" (Brandes 1902a:143). That neither of these grim possibilities had realized themselves by the end of the century was hardly, the critic warned, cause for celebration:

> Although the world war and the social revolution have not come to pass, it is evident that they have only been postponed. But the decisive political event we have experienced at the end of the 19th century is this: the great powers divide the world among themselves. They try to do this as peacefully as possible, in that they attempt to avoid a world war. Yet still they act with an injurious recklessness,

because for the sake of economic advantage they sacrifice not only those peoples whom they conquer by fire and sword, but further all the small nations within their immediate orbit, which are either absorbed for the sake of national unity or exchanged as bounty or delivered up to brutality, all in order that the peace be preserved. (Brandes 1902a:144–145)

If the young Brandes had largely conceived of Europe as divided into free-thinking and reactionary blocs, the latter in desperate need of following the lead of the former, the mature Brandes perceived the world very differently, as a wholly unequal contest between predator nation and prey – between the major powers and everyone else.

The advent of Neocolonialism, in papering over social tensions at home and transferring great power rivalries to far-flung reaches of the globe, had indeed served to forestall catastrophe, yet this perilously flimsy peace had of course been purchased at the expense of the newly colonized, as well as the small nations of the European periphery:

In the new century there will be a new distinction between the states of Europe. The old division into great powers and powers of the second rank will be dissolved by that between the European (and perhaps Asiatic) world powers (Japan) and the merely local states of Europe, which will have lost all their political influence and any hope of expansion or growth. The smaller they are, the more miserable their political prospects seem. (Brandes 1902a:145)

It is evident from this that at the turn of the century Brandes does seem to privilege the unhappy fate of Europe's lesser countries; the far greater suffering of the newly subjugated peoples of Africa and Asia – those whom the major powers "conquer by fire and sword" – is noted here only as prelude to the larger point about the European periphery. This preoccupation can to a large extent be explained with reference to his gradually evolving conception of oppressed peoples. As has been noted, Brandes began his rights advocacy in the mid-1890s in the *national* sphere, as a response to the ascendancy of Ernst Matthias von Köller (1841–1928), who after his appointment as *Oberpräsident* of Schleswig-Holstein began to introduce increasingly harsh Germanization measures against the 300,000 ethnic Danes under the rule of the German Reich. Yet the seemingly national "we" employed in "Thoughts at the Turn of the Century" is actually something much larger, for by the expansive logic of solidarism, Brandes would in the coming quarter century continuously extend his advocacy work outward, first largely (but not entirely) toward similar subject populations of Eurasia and later toward the colonized abroad.

"Thoughts at the Turn of the Century" functions as a kind of annunciation of Brandes' coming foray into international rights advocacy, which would be launched the following summer with the appearance in *Politiken* of his critique of Kaiser Wilhelm's infamous "Hunnenrede," delivered on the occasion of the embarkation of German forces for the punitive campaign against the Boxer Rebels of China. That Brandes' long stint as an international tribune of oppressed peoples begins with a defense of a non-European people is of immense significance in that it demonstrates the essential universality of his conception of the rights of peoples, yet his initial burst of activity, as has been noted, is otherwise concerned almost exclusively with the subject populations of Eurasia, most prominently the partitioned Poles and the embattled Armenian community of the Ottoman Empire. It was really not until 1922, when Brandes delivered his monumental Christiania address on "Imperialism," that he fully articulated a critique of the domination of the weak by the strong that was truly planetary in its scope.

Finally, the 1899 address is also of interest because it so clearly demonstrates how the mature critic's essentially aristocratic orientation can relatively comfortably coexist with continued political engagement, specifically in defense of the weaker against the stronger. The first two thirds of the speech, as described, amount to a vigorous defense of the rights of the weaker peoples of the globe; if anything "Thoughts at the Turn of Century" demonstrates that Brandes in no manner or form attempts to apply the Nietzschean critique of "slave morality" to the contest of nations. If in the domain of national culture ordinary people are called upon to follow the lead of the great individuals in their midst, the same does not at all apply to relations between "major" and "minor" countries; indeed, the "lesser" peoples of the globe are continuously enjoined to resist the predations of the "greater" powers. The essential incongruity of the mature Brandes' intellectual orientation is fully on display here, for the final third of the speech consists of a long inventory of the individual "great men" he has come to know during his travels across the continent – hovering over them all, of course, Nietzsche himself. For the mature Brandes, up to the end, "human greatness remains the goal (…) the measure of all things" (Brandes 1902a:156).

Continuity in the Evolution of the Critic: National Sentiment

It should now be evident that Brandes' general theoretical orientation changed significantly over time, and we have every reason to uphold the consensus in the division of his long career into early literary and mature aristocratic phases. Yet two essential aspects of his intellectual and spiritual core largely survived this transition, features of his thinking and praxis that serve to explain – in part, but not entirely – the seeming contradiction at the very center of his mature position. The first is a profound (but by no means unconditional) love of country; the second, which is evidenced by the names ascribed to his two distinct phases, is his radicalism. Each of these facets deserves special attention.

The famous appellation bestowed on Brandes by Nietzsche, that of "the good European and cultural mediator," was by all means deserved, and yet we must be wary of making too much of it – of thinking of him as a kind of rootless cosmopolitan. Despite his Jewish ancestry, Brandes was in almost every important sense a thoroughly Danish figure, a self-understanding with which he was wholly comfortable, and he was a fervent patriot at that. As comprehensive and as damning as the critique of Danish culture presented in the November 1871 lecture is, Brandes in no way endorses the rather obvious solution taken up by so many similarly placed ambitious young intellectuals, namely self-imposed exile in one of the European cultural metropoles. His one extended period of exile, the Berlin sojourn of 1877–1883, was the result of financial necessity, and at no point during this period did he ever seek to cut off contact with home. Denmark was to be transformed, not abandoned.

His fellow Danes, of course, consistently accused him of disloyalty to his homeland. In a 1905 commentary by the American critic Albert Shaw, he reports that Brandes is viewed by his countrymen as "a traitor, a cosmopolite, an enemy of the nation" (Shaw 1905:107). The Dane's foray into international rights advocacy after the turn of the century – his ever-wider-ranging engagement with the manifold of oppressed peoples across the globe – only served to strengthen accusations that had plagued him from the very beginning, as he was seen by Denmark as neglecting issues much closer to home. The same, sadly enough, is also true of his relationship to the other half of his identity; European Jewry, especially proponents of Zionism (which Brandes largely opposed) regularly accused him of neglect. Nowhere is this tension more apparent than in his work on behalf of the Poles, that single people whom he loved most dearly and on behalf of whom he expended the most energy. For fear of damaging the cause of Polish independence he had made his own, Brandes remained almost totally silent on the matter of Polish anti-Semitism; indeed, his regular appearances in partitioned Poland were occasionally boycotted by local Jewish communities. It would not be until the outbreak of the war, when undeniable reports of Polish-led pogroms began to appear in the press, that he would finally speak out against his beloved Poles.

In spite of the efforts of his many enemies to paint him as a traitor, Brandes was, as has been suggested, deeply committed to the cause of his people. As Sune Berthelsen and Ditte Marie Egebjerg have carefully demonstrated, he was no rudderless cosmopolite; instead, his understanding of national identity is more properly qualified by what they call "national cosmopolitanism," a form of love of country that does not exclude an openness and a generosity toward the larger world, a kind of precursor to what Kwame Anthony Appiah has termed "rooted cosmopolitanism" (Berthelsen and Egebjerg 2004:99). As a radical thinker Brandes was of course categorically opposed to the kind of belligerent nationalism characteristic of the major powers (and, it should be remembered, all too many small nations as well) – what Thomas Nordby has aptly defined as "a nation's aggressive self-assertion at the expense of other peoples and races" (Nordby 1973:142). Rejecting such *nationalisme*, Brandes instead endorsed a love of country determined by what he calls *nationalfølelse*. This "national sentiment" is primary, yet wholly compatible with cosmopolitan generosity; indeed, the two sensibilities mutually reinforce one another:

> A sense of world citizenship built upon a foundation of national sentiment is not only quite possible, it is indeed unnatural without such a basis. Just as conceiving of oneself as a Scandinavian does not in any manner preclude conceiving oneself first and foremost as a Dane, so it is unnatural to conceive of oneself as a Northerner without first identifying oneself according to one's particular Nordic nationality — the same holds true with conceiving oneself as a European or a citizen of the world. First we are Danes! That is a matter of course. (Brandes 1902b:199)

Brandes delivered these remarks in another address before the Danish Student Union, "On National Sentiment," in 1894, 30 years after the nation's catastrophic defeat in the Dano-Prussian War, which had resulted not only in the loss of a large portion of the old homeland, but also, as the critic painfully articulates, Denmark's very sense of self-confidence and national destiny. The Brandesian concept of national sentiment is thus framed in the sense much less of a right than of a duty – a duty especially to the long-suffering Danish minority of Sønderjylland:

> And that effort, which has also been taken up by the Student Union, to establish connections between North Schleswig and the Kingdom in order to preserve the linguistic and cultural spheres of

Denmark, is for us Danes a cultural task of the highest order. We have a national duty to protect our language and to resist the loss of even an inch of that territory. The Germans themselves would look on us with contempt if we failed our *duty* in this respect. (Brandes 1902b:200)

The nationalist typically seeks to flatter the national audience at every turn, to indulge each of its vanities, and to insist that it is the rest of the world that must bow to the needs and the desires of the nation. National sentiment, in absolute contrast, places demands on the national community; it urges the citizen to seek continuously to close the gulf between lived reality and national ideality, and also constantly to re-evaluate and revalue those ideals. As stirring as this call was in 1894, the speech does not underestimate the challenges facing Denmark. Commenting on the meager reception of the Danish contribution to the 1878 Exposition Universelle, Brandes reports with alarm that one single sentence was on the lips of the Parisian attendees: "le Danemark s'efface" (Brandes 1902b:191). It was thus incumbent upon every Dane, especially young writers, to resist what seemed at the time to be a perilous slide into national extinction. Brandes himself would take the lead in this most essential national project, not only continuing his efforts to promote Danish literature abroad, but also issuing a steady stream of essays and stumping tirelessly on behalf of his embattled countrymen and women, all the way up until the matter was largely resolved after the Great War. His major writings on the Sønderjylland Question were in fact republished in the volume *Southern Jutland Under Prussian Pressure*, issued the year before the 1920 plebiscite that resulted in the return of much of the old North Schleswig territory to the kingdom.

Brandes' activities during the 1890s effectively served as dry run for his later, internationally oriented rights advocacy after the turn of the century – a kind of national dress rehearsal for his eventual entry onto the world stage. And yet his commitment to Denmark and Danishness is of further significance here in that it demonstrates that his foray into international affairs of state throughout possessed an equally important national component. That Brandes was sincerely dedicated to the cause of the Poles, the Armenians, the Finns, the Persians – all of the many oppressed peoples for whom he advocated – is beyond any measure of doubt. We need only look at how much his activism cost him; all the affection showered upon him by those whose cause he made his own was most certainly offset by the hostility it engendered in the major countries. This was most evident during his second phase of sustained activity, his principled and uncompromising opposition to the aims and conduct of the belligerent powers in the Great War. From October of 1914 through to the "resolution" of the conflict in the Versailles Treaty, Brandes consistently critiqued the allegedly high-minded ideals fueling the war from all sides. His impassioned defense of Danish neutrality, first against the repeated assaults of his longtime friend and ally, French premier Georges Clemenceau, and then against similar attacks from the Scottish translator and Scandinavianist William Archer, earned him the opprobrium of an entire generation of French and Englishmen. Indeed, the immense damage done to his international reputation by his wartime stance arguably contributed more than any other factor to his diminishment in world literary memory.

Despite the intensity of his commitment to the various oppressed peoples of the globe, Brandes' activity as international tribune was, as suggested, underpinned by a powerful national aspect, just as was the case with *Main Currents*. As Allen has demonstrated, he "believed that having the courage to protest injustice [in the larger world outside Denmark], even at great personal cost, was central to a grounded, enlightened Danish national identity as the development of the innovative literary culture to which his name had become so inextricably linked" (Allen 2012:91). His sincere hope was that the enterprise of national cultural modernization he had set in motion in the Modern Breakthrough might grow into an equally progressive and humane international orientation within his native land. Brandes seems to have believed, somewhat idealistically, that the particular historical experience of the Danes – their long period of national decline and descent into abject powerlessness on the world stage following the defeat of 1864 – ought naturally to inspire an inherent sympathy for all the similarly put-upon nations of the globe. He would render this national ideal imaginary in the powerful "Address on Møn" in 1904, asserting that a genuine, modern form of love of country is far more than the praise of its people, or the glorification of its past and present accomplishments:

> It is also more important to develop a sense of freedom and justice among the people, not just for its own use (…) Thus it was my ideal that it should be known that, despite the small size of our country, men lived here who felt sympathy with all wronged individuals or oppressed peoples across the world and who lifted their voices, spoke on their behalf. (*Samlede Skrifter* XV:443, transl. by Allen 2012:101)

Denmark, Brandes dreams, ought to come to be viewed as a kind of beacon of humane and just values, in natural sympathy and solidarity with all the oppressed peoples of the globe. That the Danes have historically failed to live up to this rather impossible standard is a matter of course. Indeed, and this would certainly be a source of immense sadness for Brandes, Norway and Sweden, those "humanitarian superpowers" and "regimes of the good," have most certainly come closer; for evidence of this we need only look to the dreadful images of a few years ago, when Danish state officials shamelessly harassed Syrian refugees simply transiting the country en route to safe harbor in Sweden. Yet the essentially Nordic idea that the national community might serve as a beacon of hope for the world arguably begins here, with Brandes.

Continuity in the Evolution of the Critic: Radicalism

In addition to his rather curious form of love of country, Brandes remained, as has been noted, a fundamentally *radical* thinker throughout his long career. It must be stressed here that the Danish noun *radikalisme* and adjective *radikal* are possessed of a historical trajectory fundamentally distinct from their counterparts in the Anglophone world. As such, a substantial philological interlude is necessary here.

The adjective "radical" first emerged in English in the Late Middle Ages within the domain of the natural sciences; clearly revealing its fidelity to the Latin root *radix* [root], the term connoted that which is "of, belonging to, or from the roots" (OED A.1.a). In its initial iteration it was wholly value-neutral; only in the later eighteenth century did it acquire a political and thus contested sense. It was first applied to politics in two related – but in fact distinct – usages. In the first, "radical" came to function as a descriptor for a minority faction within a larger political party that sought "thorough or far-reaching political or social reform," that is change that "goes to the roots" of existing forms of social organization (OED A.7.b). In Britain the Radical wing of the Liberal party sought the abolition of the property requirement for voting, while the Radical Republicans in the United States agitated for the abolition of slavery. Certainly these "radical" demands must strike us today as relatively modest; indeed, even within their respective historical contexts they would hardly seem to qualify as outrageous, given that universal (male, white) suffrage had largely been the norm in the U.S. since its founding, and that by the time of the Emancipation Proclamation, chattel slavery was a distant memory in the British Empire. Yet because these radical programs constituted an existential threat to established centers of power, the British and American radicals were of course denounced by their enemies in the second and deeply value-laden sense of the term, namely that of "representing or supporting an extreme section of a party." The evolution of the term since the nineteenth century has largely resulted in the collapse of this distinction, that is between change that is simply "thorough and far-reaching" and "goes to the roots," and change that is in its essence "extreme." In contemporary Anglophone political usage, "radical" is typically employed pejoratively against all those ideas deemed to be outside the domain of the permissible; in effect it is a weapon for the enforcement of ideological boundaries.

In Denmark the term first acquires a political sense in the 1870s and 1880s, always associated with Brandes and his circle, who were referred to as radical authors. These literary radicals were closely aligned with the political radicals, led by the critic's brother Edvard (1847–1931) and the politician Viggo Hørup (1841–1902), who together founded the daily *Politiken* in 1884 as an organ for radical commentary; the majority of Georg Brandes' political journalism, in fact, first appeared in this paper. While the radical movement did indeed seek change "at the roots" of existing social and political organization, they did not at all conceive of their program as "extremist" in nature. Certainly, their conservative enemies attempted to define them as such, but this largely came to nothing, as the radicals were almost immediately assimilated into mainstream politics, where they have remained ever since. In the domain of electoral politics, the Danish radicals, like their British and American namesakes, first emerged as a subset of a larger party of a decidedly *centrist* orientation, namely the Venstre, the descendant of the old National Liberal party that had played the central role in the mid-nineteenth-century transition to constitutional rule. On the right they were opposed by the Højre of J.B.S. Estrup (1825–1913), while the nascent left was occupied by the small but growing Danish Social Democratic party, founded by the postal worker Louis Pio (1841–1894) just weeks before Brandes' famous lecture of November 1871. The split within the Venstre that began to emerge in the 1880s should thus be viewed as a kind of "bourgeois intramural struggle," a fissure between the more conservative "national wing" of the party and its emergent "radical wing," who were also referred to as "the Europeans" for their generally internationalist orientation. This split would be formalized in 1905 – after Denmark transitioned from limited to full parliamentary democracy – in the founding of the Radikale Venstre party, which despite its name has remained up to the present a fixture of the political center, fully capable of forming governments with both the center left and the center right. While their platform has evolved over the years, the *Radikaler* have more or less consistently represented the core Brandesian values of the expansion of individual rights, vigorous internationalism, and opposition to any form of militarism or belligerent nationalism; today they are one of the few Danish parties committed to protecting the rights of Denmark's embattled immigrant communities. Their impact on Danish politics and culture has been immense; indeed the period between 1871 and the monumental elections of 2001, which brought the right back into power and marked the emergence of the far-right, anti-immigrant Danske Folkeparti [Danish People's Party], can aptly be described as Denmark's "Long Radical Century." As Hans Hertel has noted, the Danske Folkeparti framed the 2001 election as no less than the liberation of Denmark from "one hundred and thirty years of so-called cultural radical tyranny" (Hertel 2004:12).

The Danish radical movement was and is far more than the political party that bears its name; as the historian Leif Pjetursson has described, the original understanding of the term was largely identified with a particular *tankegang* or "manner of thinking" that "takes things at their roots" and is "penetrating and thorough," a "critical and analytic movement in which society is dissected" (Pjetursson 1984:7). The roots of this radical manner of thinking rested firmly within the eighteenth-century Enlightenment, as evidenced by Pjetursson's metaphor of dissection. Much as the eighteenth-century *illuminista* staked a claim to scientific rationality, so Brandes initially sought to bring literary praxis into greater accord with that of the natural sciences. As a political ideology, radicalism largely took its cues from the revolutionary and collectivist "humane" liberalism of Rousseau, which aimed to "cement together the singular will of the individual with the common will of society," in stark opposition to the strictly individualist "classical" liberalism of Smith and Ricardo, which claimed as its point of departure "the egoistic trait in human being" (Pjetursson 1984:13). As an essentially critical "ideal liberalism," Brandesian radicalism was in its essence an oppositional movement, situated firmly against the hegemonic ideology of the age – that which Johan Fjord Jensen has aptly deemed the *nationalliberale enhedskultur* [national, or perhaps more properly, bourgeois culture of national unity]:

> As culture it was hierarchical, built up on a series of institutions in which (…) the patriarchal family was central and holiest. It rested upon a fixed moral system, which through written and unwritten rules of propriety placed an endless series of limitations on human development. In its essence it was static and self-protecting. It was

pale and passionless in its understanding of life, except for when it was confronted with aberrant forms of culture that threatened it with rupture (…) against such threats it reacted with a passionate urge for self-preservation. (Fjord Jensen 1966:13)

As has been suggested, Brandesian radicalism did not in essence question the fundamental ideals of bourgeois civilization; in contrast, these ideals, at least in their original French revolutionary iteration, constitute the very model of humane social organization. Radical critique thus intended to expose the failure of the Danish bourgeoisie to live up to its own ideals, to peek beyond what Fjord Jensen terms its "façade morality." The emphasis on getting to the roots beyond this façade reveals both the Brandesianism of Ibsen and the Ibsenism of Brandes; as Franco Moretti has observed, Ibsen's cycle of 12 plays amounts to, in essence, a strikingly similar 20-year "settling of accounts" with the bourgeoisie (Moretti 2010:118).

At last we have arrived at a serviceable definition of Brandesian radicalism: it is a socially critical movement characterized by a manner of thinking that, more or less in tune with scientific inquiry, investigates society at its roots, beneath the veil concealing the actually existing bourgeois civilization of the late nineteenth century, in the effort to hold it to the high and humane ideals expressed in its initial, revolutionary phase. The apparent failure of the movement to produce concrete change in Danish politics and culture to a significant extent resulted in a certain measure of disillusionment for Brandes, yet his reinvention as a Nietzschean "aristocratic radical" in the 1890s was by no means a rejection of his earlier method. In absolute contrast, the thinking and praxis of the mature Brandes constitutes a deepening of the project of radical critique, as he came to an understanding that his earlier approach was no longer sufficient to meet the drastically changed political conditions of Europe and the larger world.

As has been previously noted, the change came about with the advent of Neocolonialism; the dialectical interplay between revolution and reaction that had served to structure *Main Currents* had been effectively undermined by the triumph of empire. It should be emphasized that both the theoretical models of the young critic – the Hegelian conception of history as under the guidance of abstract Absolute Spirit, as well as the Nietzschean insistence on the singular great individual – were firmly within the tradition of philosophical Idealism. In both views it is spirit, whether in the form of the abstract Idea or in the concrete heroic actions of the single individual, that moves history. Neither approach, as Olav Harsløf has illuminated, was sufficient in the changed circumstances of Europe at the turn of the twentieth century, for "the critical work could only continue through the analysis of the elements that make up the reactionary unity – racism, militarism, nationalism –, as well as their ultimate source, imperialism" (Harsløf 1973:136). In order to get at the roots of the imperial impulse, Brandes had to attempt something fundamentally alien to his nature, namely the materialist (although, of course, non-Marxist) analysis of the economic conditions of the Belle Epoque. This involved a complete reorientation of his critical perspective, from the "horizontal" *ideologikritik* of his early phase to the "vertical" understanding of the economic determinants of social organization and culture – and from "cultural politics" to a "more economically grounded social critique" (Harsløf 1973:137–138). As the new century dawned, Brandes was seized by a new and powerful sense of urgency; the old radical methodologies would no longer do, and he must make the fateful leap into direct intervention in affairs of state, lending his name and his formidable reputation to the cause of the manifold of oppressed peoples around the world.

Brandes as International Tribune of the Rights of Peoples: 1900–1925

As has been argued, the general ideological framework of the mature Brandes was riven with internal tensions, especially that between the seemingly unforgiving and anti-democratic leanings of his "aristocratic" proclivities and the much more generous spirit that characterizes his rights advocacy. With respect to the former, the political journalism of his final quarter century is replete with appeals to "the leading men" (as well as, occasionally, women) of one country or another, revealing his continued belief in the capacity of "men of influence" to produce real change. His 1904 call for a pan-European movement in defense of the university in Helsinki, which after the turn of the century was subjected to increasingly harsh measures of Russification, is a telling example:

> The student youth of the three Nordic countries, together with their university teachers, ought to express their sympathy with students and teachers at the university in Helsingfors and register their protest against the violence and abuse that is inflicted on them. We dare hope that the movement then spreads further, so that other countries' universities, first and foremost England's and Germany's, perhaps also France's, surely Italy's, attach themselves to the protest, and that it therefore rolls over the Earth, steadily more polyphonic. [Russian Interior Minister] Plehve should be made to understand that he cannot take lightly such a pronouncement from Europe's most enlightened class of men. (…) It is our purpose to bring the Russian government to perceive itself isolated, an isolation it more steadily begins to feel. (…) A similar sense of isolation ought to be instilled among Russia's leading men, the sense that they are set apart from European civilization by Europe's intellectual aristocracy. This government has expelled Finland's best men from their fatherland. In return Europe must expel Russia from its culture. (Brandes 1906b:63–64)

While collective civil disobedience is a critical component of this strategy, it is strictly limited to the educated classes; Brandes effectively hopes that pressure from Western Europe's university communities might provoke Russia's intelligentsia to apply similar pressure to the Czarist state, which would then lead to an easing of its repressive policies.

Yet the other side of Brandes – the critic as impassioned defender of the rights of whole peoples – is also capable of speaking directly to those same masses elsewhere written off as "the mob." Nowhere is this more apparent than in his 1916 "An Appeal," a call for peace talks distributed in the millions in both France and Germany (but not in England, thanks to the efforts of the propaganda bureau):

> In the war-making countries the armies naturally desire first and foremost victory, but most strongly they desire peace. The civilian population everywhere groans for peace. The governments who sit high in the saddle kick the spurs into the weary horse's flanks. (…) The cries for peace that soon shall arise in all states are called cowardly. But if the people keep silent then the stones will speak. Everywhere the ruins scream for peace, not for revenge. And where the stones remain silent, the fields and the meadows, drenched in blood and strewn with corpses, cry out. (Brandes 1916:256–257)

The "great men" of the twentieth century, if the perpetrators of the war could be called such, had failed entirely in their duty; indeed, it was one such "most enlightened man," the aforementioned William Archer, who had been primarily responsible for suppressing the appeal in the United Kingdom. In the absence of extraordinary individuals, only the people themselves could put an end to this "singular tragedy."

The general theoretical conception of the rights of peoples underpinning Brandes' praxis as international tribune is of immense complexity, but also possesses a strong measure of internal consistency. While an overview of its basic features is outside the scope of this essay, a detailed analysis of Brandes' thinking about rights – including a treatment of the essential question of whether his peculiar form of rights advocacy ought to be considered a precursor of the specifically *human* rights advocacy that would gain momentum in the decades after the Second World War – is provided in my volume, *Georg Brandes. Human Rights and Oppressed Peoples. Essays and Speeches*, which is briefly discussed below in section 6a.

With respect to Brandes' practice as rights advocate, as mentioned above, there were two periods of sustained activity, with the first beginning in the summer of 1900 and stretching forward through 1905, after which it tapers off before resuming in earnest with the outbreak of the Great War. Brandes' 25 years of advocacy work is characterized by its steadily expanding scope, although as noted he in fact began with a vigorous critique of the punitive campaign of the Eight Nation Alliance against the Boxer Rebels of China. For the most part, however, this first period was dominated by his concern for the subject peoples of Eurasia. Most prominent among them were of course the long-suffering Poles, with whom he had maintained close relations since his long journey through the old homeland in the 1880s, which he had chronicled in his 1888 volume *Impressions of Poland*. The appearance of this long-ignored book in German translation in 1898 invoked considerable ire in Germany, and thus it was only natural that he would come to take the lead in presenting the Polish civil struggles against both Germanization and Russification to Western Europe. Also of great significance to Brandes during this period was the fate of the Armenian population of the Ottoman Empire, of which he had become aware through his contact with the Armenian exile activists Avetis Nazarbekian (1866–1939) and Mariam Vardanian (1864–1941). His chilling accounts of the mid-1890s "Hamidian" massacres, the October 1900 essay "Armenia" and the February 1903 Berlin address "Armenia and Europe" are among the first Western European treatments of the initial mass killings in Eastern Anatolia that, despite the actions of Brandes and his pro-Armenia allies, did not awaken the continent to the impending and even greater catastrophe of 1915–1917. In addition to a miscellany of other European subject peoples for whom he advocated during this period, Brandes also addressed the rising specter of anti-Semitism in addition to the growing Zionist movement, with which he maintained difficult relations.

The eruption of the Guns of August in 1914 summoned him back to advocacy in earnest; he quickly emerged, along with the French author Romain Rolland (1866–1944), as a leader of the tiny anti-war movement. While his aforementioned feuds with Clemenceau in France and Archer in Britain amounted to direct confrontations with the allegedly high-minded war aims of the Allies, his wartime journalism was in general preoccupied with the fate of the neutral peoples caught up in the conflict – the Poles and the Armenians, of course, but also the Belgians and the Persians. As previously noted, it was this second period of activity, his principled opposition to the war aims and conduct of all sides, that cost Brandes most dearly; for a generation of Frenchmen and Englishmen, he would always remain "Mr. Facing-Both-Ways."

After the war Brandes' political journalism subsided again, although one effort, his 1922 Christiania address "Imperialism," deserves special mention here, as it sheds a great deal of light on the evolution of his thinking about the rights of peoples as well as, importantly, the relationship between his political activity and his better-remembered literary work. It can often seem, as has been stressed throughout this essay, that these two aspects of the mature critic's production were in some sense in tension with one another. Yet in one critical sense they were in fact mutually reinforcing. The key text here is Brandes' long, under-appreciated 1899 essay "World Literature," which due to a new interest in *Weltliteratur* in recent decades has finally begun to receive the attention it deserves. When Goethe first began to use the term in the late 1820s, he seemed to have had in mind something like convergence. Because of the long period of peace following the Napoleonic Wars, as well as, even more importantly, increased global exchange – not just of material goods but also of ideas and of literary works – the old form "of National literature means little now, the age of *Weltliteratur* has begun" (cited in D'haen et al. 2013:11). From Brandes' perspective at the conclusion of the nineteenth century, much of this is taken for granted, although, revealing his inherent sympathy for all small languages and literatures, he places all of the emphasis on the fundamental unfairness of the world literary system, in which "an author of the sixth rank in a widespread language, a world language, can with ease become more known than an author of the second rank in a language spoken by only a few million" (cited in D'haen et al. 2013:25). Further demonstrating his essential national cosmopolitanism, Brandes proceeds to attack those who, seduced by the prospect of world renown, "have begun to write for a general and unspecified public," those who – the specific target here is Zola – write "as Sarah Bernhardt acts when she performs in Peru or Chicago." In contrast to this new phenomenon of "writing for the world," the critic insists that the writer must "work in the land in which he was born and write for his countrymen," that the work might carry "the scent of the earth."

It is likely no coincidence that "World Literature" and "Thoughts at the Turn of the Century" were produced in the same year. Both are underpinned by a conception of the world system as an unequal struggle between major and minor powers, between colonizer and colonized, whether in the literary realm or in the domain of power politics. Brandes seems to have grasped intuitively what Benedict Anderson would later make explicit: that the fate of oppressed peoples the world over is intimately bound to language, and to national literature. He would make this clear in what is arguably the most stirring of his political works, the 1905 letter "To the Schoolchildren of Russian Poland," who had recently declared a national strike in protest against the banning of the Polish language in the school system:

> You have acted out of your best and surest natural instincts; out of enthusiasm for the most undeniable of human rights, that to speak and read one's language; out of enthusiasm for that language itself, in which immortal works are written; out of enthusiastic love of your people, your country and its history, but especially its future. (Brandes 1906c:43–44)

In one sense, then, Brandes' activity as an international tribune for the *rights* of peoples can be seen as a complement to, perhaps even a consequence of, his work as an international advocate for the *literatures* of (small) peoples. This is evident over and over again in his political journalism, as he constantly invokes the literary accomplishments of a given people as an argument in its defense. Julie Allen has astutely identified this uniquely Brandesian form of "cultural defense," noting that his work on behalf of Armenia:

> does not invoke sympathy as the sole or even the primary rise for coming to the aid of the Armenians, but rather culture, both

admiration for the cultural wealth created by Armenians over the past four thousand years and fear of the destructive effect of tacit complicity on European culture. (Allen 2012:110)

At times, indeed, this overwhelming preoccupation with literature can strike the contemporary reader as at least somewhat strange, even after all Anderson has taught us. In his May 1917 essay "The Armenians," written after the mass murder of hundreds of thousands, Brandes is still, for example, at pains to remind the reader that "in our time the Armenians have upheld their old reputation as poets and artists," and that no less a Brandesian luminary than Lord Byron had been motivated to study their language and literature (Brandes 1917b:365).

As has been suggested, Brandes' employment of his form of "cultural defense" and the pronounced bias towards literary culture it reveals raises a critical question regarding his theoretical conception of the rights of peoples, namely that of whether he had a civilizational bias. The absence of remark in his political journalism on the untold millions of indigenous peoples who came under the European thumb during his lifetime is indeed conspicuous, although it can at least in part be explained by the fact that, since so many of the newly colonized were preliterate, he simply lacked his best means of defending them. The two non-European peoples for whom he did advocate extensively, the Chinese and the Persians, were furthermore possessed of ancient cultural traditions far older than those of Europe; just as importantly, the efforts of European Orientalists have of course led to a profound appreciation of these peoples' cultural achievements, though they were seen as located in the distant past rather than the present. Whatever doubts might persist regarding the universality of Brandes' conception of the rights of peoples, however, are dispelled entirely by the aforementioned 1922 address "Imperialism," delivered in Christiania rather than in Copenhagen, likely as an acknowledgement of Denmark's colonial entanglements that continue to this day. He begins by recalling a previous visit to the Norwegian capital, shortly before the outbreak of the war he had long foreseen. At that time, in a distant echo of Nietzsche, he had asserted that the coming catastrophe would necessitate a revaluation of all values. Eight years and millions of deaths later, the critic laments, little has changed:

> The wish I had expressed in my final sentence, that "the old ideals must be replaced with new ones," has by no means come true. The old ideal, imperialism as the expression of nationalism, is at the moment dominant in all the countries whose attitude means something for the population of the world, the unfortunate mass of humanity. (Brandes 1932:158)

What follows is an impassioned and scathing indictment of persistent European imperialism, planetary in its scope and breathtaking in its indignation. Most importantly, the old practice of "cultural defense" of oppressed peoples is entirely absent, as the critic forcefully and without reservation asserts the right of all peoples, regardless of their "level of civilizational accomplishment," to self-determination and to dignity. Even at the age of 80, it seems, Brandes remained fully capable of self-reinvention and renewal.

Bibliography: Brandes' Political Journalism

Relative to his literary work, Brandes' rights advocacy journalism was characterized by a greater sense of urgency; indeed, a great many of these speeches and articles were produced on request, from representatives of the various oppressed peoples he encountered during his European travels and through his extensive correspondence. Since Brandes served as the editor for his own *Samlede Skrifter* (as well as the additional collections published after the completion of the *Samlede Skrifter* in 1910 and before his death in 1927), he typically produced revised versions of the original newspaper and journal articles, intended as authoritative editions for purposes of future scholarship. In preparing my volume, *Georg Brandes. Human Rights and Oppressed Peoples. Essays and Speeches* (Wisconsin, 2020), I have therefore chosen to honor's the critic's wishes by using these "posterity versions" as the source texts for my English translations.

The critical edition includes all of Brandes' major works on oppressed peoples, in total 35 essays and addresses, produced between 1900 and 1925. The following list includes titles (in English), original publication dates (for the Danish versions; many of these appeared simultaneously abroad in other languages), original places of publication, and the locations of the posterity versions used as source texts.

Title	Date	Venue	Source
The Hun Speech	7/28/1900	POL	SS17
Armenia	10/8/1900	POL	SS17
Missionaries	8/12&15/1900	POL	SS17
A Chinese Letter About the War	8/19/1901	POL	SS17
Chinese Letters	8/26/1901	POL	SS17
Contemporary Civilization	12/16/1901	POL	SS17
The Women of Poland	12/30/1901	POL	SS17
Macedonia	10/27/1902	POL	SS17
The Agony of a People and Utopias	1/26/1903	POL	SS17
Armenia and Europe	2/2/1903	TIL	SS17
Mano Negra	2/16/1903	POL	SS17
The Georgian People	6/29/1903	POL	SS17
Transvaal	10/26/1903	POL	SS17
The Ruthenians	3/14/1904	POL	SS17
Finland	10/1/1904	POL	SS17
To the Students of Germany	10/1904	FADS	SS17
The Rights and the Duties of the Weaker	5/16&17/1905	POL	SS17
The Aryan Race	6/25/1905	POL	SS18
To the Schoolchildren in Russian Poland	8/15/1905	POL	SS17
The Future of Russian Poland	12/5/1905	POL	SS18
Zionism	12/12/1905	POL	SS18
The Jews in Finland	6/14/1908	POL	SS18
The Fourth Partition of Poland	8/18/1909	POL	SS18

Race Theories	2/19/1912	POL	FP
Conditions in Russian Poland	10/25&26/1914	POL	VK
	2/28/1915	POL	VK
The Great Era	5/1915	VV	VK
The Great Nations' Concern for the Small	10/1915	TIL	VK
Poland	11/23/1915	POL	VK
Introductory Words for the Polish Evening	3/13/1916	POL	VK
An Appeal	5/17/1916	POL	VK
A Response to Mr. William Archer	6/28&29/1916	POL	VK
Persia	11/29&12/1/1916	POL	VK
The Armenians	5/17/1917	POL	VK
Imperialism	11/29/1922	SAM	KB
Europe Now	2/1925	TIL	US9

Original Venues:
POL = *Politiken*
TIL = *Tilskueren*
FADS = *Freier Almanach deutscher Studenten*
VV = *Verden og Vi*
SAM = *Samtiden (NO)*

Translation Source Texts:
SS = *Samlede Skrifter*
FP = *Fugleperspektiv*
VK = *Verdenskrigen*
KB = *Kulturbilleder*
US = *Udvalgte Skrifter*

Because the volume is limited to Brandes' writings on international political affairs, it does not include his extensive advocacy journalism in the national sphere. These essays on the Sønderjylland Question, produced between the mid-1890s and the resolution of the conflict, are collected in Danish in the volume *Sønderjylland under Prøjsisk Tryk* (Gyldendal, 1919).

The volume also excludes much of his writings on the Great War, which after first appearing in newspapers and journals around the world were collected in the volume *Verdenskrigen* (4 eds, Gyldendal, 1916–1917), as well as the totality of his commentaries on the peace, *Tragediens anden Del: Fredslutningen* [The Tragedy's Second Act: The Peace Settlement] (Gyldendal, 1919). I have included only those essays from *Verdenskrigen* (marked VK above) that have direct bearing on the general theme of the volume, that is Brandes' advocacy work on behalf of oppressed peoples, in this context the neutral nations (Poland, Belgium, Persia, and so on) caught up in the maelstrom of the conflict. The entirety of the first edition of *Verdenskrigen*, however, was superbly translated by the American peace activist Catherine Groth, appearing in the U.S. (but not Britain) as *The World at War* (Macmillan, 1917).

EMIGRANT LITERATURE (1872)

Torben Jelsbak

Introduction

"A book for me is an act," says Brandes in the afterword to *The Romantic School in Germany* (Brandes 1873:379). No other book in his authorship manages to live up to this declaration as thoroughly as *The Emigrant Literature*, the first in the series of lectures that constitute *Main Currents in Nineteenth Century Literature*, delivered at Copenhagen University in November and December of 1871 and published a month later, on February 3, 1872. *Emigrant Literature* was, as the Danish literary scholar Paul V. Rubow has put it, "the bravest action" taken by Brandes in his life as a public figure (Rubow 1976:21), but for the same reason it was also the single work that for better or worse came to seal his fate and his ensuing career as a literary scholar, critic, and intellectual.

Main Currents is an ambitiously designed comparative history of the major lines of development in nineteenth-century European literature and identity. It chronicles how the worldly ideals of freedom of the French Revolution of 1789 turned into their opposites, thus leading to European Romanticism, a Catholic renaissance, and empire, and ultimately how reason and freethinking overcame this reaction in a new movement leading onward toward the European revolutions of 1848, which function as the historical turning point. *Emigrant Literature* is the first movement – the first act – in this historical drama, which played out among the French émigré authors driven into exile by the repercussions of the French Revolution.

Emigrant Literature explores the connections and exchanges between literature and social development, and as such was innovative and provocative in that it introduced a modern and scientific vision of human beings and of history, inspired by Darwin's theory of evolution. But in order to understand the "bravery" and the consequences of publishing the book, it is necessary to view it in the local Danish context in which it was conceived.

Emigrant Literature was not only literary history, but also a cultural-political intervention: an act of rebellion directed at contemporary Danish literature, which according to Brandes had become mired in Romanticism and thus now found itself in a state of lethargy – 40 years behind Europe. But at the same time it was also an attack on what may be characterized as the dominant national self-understanding of Denmark itself, more closely defined as the National Liberal synthesis of Christianity, conservative sexual morality, and love of fatherland.

Brandes' program of comparative literary study was meant to "correct" established national orientations by promoting an international outlook (Brandes 1872a:15), and its famous battle cry that literature should "provoke debate" (Brandes 1872a:15) made the critic himself the standard-bearer of a process of historical development that concerned not only literature, but the entirety of the social order and the modernization of the culture in a broad sense. The overarching plot of *Main Currents* is the narrative of the individual's emancipation from traditional institutions of society and its authorities, such as Christianity, marriage, and the nation. This narrative acquired an especially inflammatory character in Denmark – a small, culturally homogeneous national state on the cultural and political periphery of Europe, which after its defeat by Prussia in the Schleswig War of 1864 found itself in a kind of spiritual state of shock.

The story of *Emigrant Literature* is also the story of an academic career plan that went awry. The lecture series was conceived as a part of a plan that would make the brilliant young doctor in aesthetics a professor at the University of Copenhagen, but instead it ended up provoking a public scandal that effectively foreclosed a promising academic career. The public lectures filled up university auditoria, yet also gave Brandes the reputation of rabble-rouser and blasphemer, which was the very reason that a majority of conservative professors in the faculty of philosophy opposed his appointment to the vacant professorship in aesthetics, for which he was otherwise the obvious candidate (see Larsen 2016).

Brandes thus had to bid farewell to his plans for a secure and respectively bourgeois livelihood as a state-appointed professor. The affair was a decisive factor in his career in that it compelled him to make his living as an independent journalist in the German press, from his base in Berlin, for the period between 1877 and 1883. But through the German-language literary market, he was also able to secure, over the following decades, the status of a leading European literary critic and cosmopolitan mediator between European literatures – a "guter Europäer und Cultur-Missionär" [a good European and cultural missionary], as the philosopher Friedrich Nietzsche called him in a private letter of 1887 (Brandes 1966:441). *Emigrant Literature* is thus also the gateway to an expansive contribution to criticism that encompasses not only the six volumes of *Main Currents* but also a long series of portraits of modern European and Scandinavian authors, politicians, and cultural personalities, written for an international readership.

That *Emigrant Literature* acquired this peculiar fate is also attributable to the fact that the man who led the relentless assault on Danish national self-understanding was himself of a mixed cultural background, as an assimilated Danish Jew. The Jewish component of Georg Brandes' thinking has traditionally played a lesser role in interpretations of *Emigrant Literature*, even though it is certain that his double identity manifests itself in various ways – both in his cosmopolitan perspective on literary history and in his profound empathy for the emigrant experience of homelessness and alienation. This openness to the alien is at the same time a part of what makes Brandes' method of literary and cultural criticism relevant – and controversial – to this day.

Background and Genesis

The most important elements and events in Brandes' intellectual trajectory and formation as a critic prior to the publication of *Emigrant Literature* have been outlined in the first chapter of this book. In January 1870, he successfully achieved his doctoral degree in aesthetics with a dissertation dedicated to the work of the French philosopher and literary historian

Hippolyte Taine (1828–1893). After the defense of his dissertation, in April 1870 Brandes departed on his Grand European Tour, or *Bildungsreise*, which came to last 16 months and was to leave a thoroughgoing influence on him.

Most important perhaps were his encounter and conversations with the English philosopher, economist, and liberal politician John Stuart Mill (1806–1873), whom he met in Paris and later visited in London in July of 1870. Mill was a modern liberal thinker, versed in the empiricist tradition in English philosophy and social science. On this basis, he had developed a modern social and moral philosophy, so-called "utilitarianism," which proceeded from the principle that every human action must be evaluated based on its sum usefulness to society – and not according to the degree to which it accorded with preordained principles, whether derived from religion or from natural rights. Mill's utilitarianism was critical to Brandes in that it established a modern ethics founded not in religious but in worldly principles. Furthermore, Brandes was also drawn to the practical dimension of Mill's philosophy, which brought together liberal ideas of freedom and the social and political reform movements of the age.

At the end of July – just as the Franco-Prussian war broke out – Brandes continued his travels southward from Paris over the Alps to Geneva and from there on to Italy.

During his stay in Italy, Brandes' spiritual development and political awakening were further stimulated and radicalized by his acquaintance and interaction with two quite distinctive personalities: the Italian law professor and later politician Giuseppe Saredo (1832–1902) from Rome, and the 24-year-old French art connoisseur and aesthete Georges Noufflard (1846–1897).

Saredo was an impassioned patriot, a supporter of the young independent Italy and a dedicated advocate of J.S. Mill's philosophical and political thought. When, in November of 1870, Brandes contracted typhus, an infection which nearly cost him his life and consequently confined him to four months of bedrest, it was Saredo who was his daily conversation partner through the winter, helping to keeping his nose to the grindstone with hours-long exegeses on liberal progress in the modern world.

Noufflard was Saredo's diametrical opposite: a distinguished aesthete who settled in Rome in 1871 to begin studies for a never-realized book on the monuments and artworks of the city. Brandes and Noufflard met at the Scandinavian Club in Rome at the beginning of April 1871, just as Brandes had risen from his sickbed, and the two spent a few intense months together, with excursions to art museums and churches in Rome, Sorrento, and Naples that became decisive in the development of his understanding of art.

If it was Noufflard who taught Brandes about the aesthetic perception of art, then it was Saredo who taught Brandes to politicize and to polemicize it. For Saredo the future of Italy and Europe was to be determined by politics, and to the degree he was interested in aesthetic questions, he was, in the pattern of Mill, in favor of a firmly utilitarian point of view, which both provoked and incited Brandes the aesthete:

> He endorses and adores all tendentiousness. He says: for you a book is a work, or rather a work of art; for me it is an act. The idea of literary immortality no longer has any meaning, a book only sticks around until a better one comes along, no measure of artistic perfection will save it from being swallowed up by what comes after. Let it be an act, a weapon. In all worthy books there is a hidden polemic, and it is the polemic that makes them worthy. (Brandes 1978, II:182–183)

In 1873, in the afterword to *The Romantic School in Germany*, Brandes summarized his understanding of the literary work as an act, showing the influence of Saredo; it is also tempting to see the Italian ideologue as the last stop on the process of intellectual radicalization and political awakening that was his European *Bildungsreise*. To sum up, the various impulses Brandes absorbed during the journey had more to do with his *Weltanschauung* and "the education of the heart" than with academic learning. "I cannot take pride in a direct scientific output," he confesses in a letter of May 23, 1871, to his academic mentor, the philosophy professor

Hans Brøchner (Brandes, Georg and Edvard 1939–1942, I:148). But his encounter with Italian art and folk culture, which for Brandes amounted to a continuation of the heathen and natural ideal of humanity of antiquity, had in combination with Saredo's political reform ideas implanted a rebellious and anti-clerical attitude in the young doctor, which came to expression in an oft-cited letter to his family written upon his departure from Italy on July 9, 1871:

> What is generally not expressed too loudly, I express here: the liveliest hatred of Christianity; from my very heart I shall always strike up Voltaire's "Écrasons l'infâme." I hate Christianity in my gut and in my bones. (Brandes 1978, II:431)

Brandes' Grand Tour was brought to an end in July of 1871; he returned home to find his place within a Nordic Lutheran society that, because of his impressions of Italy, he found utterly barren and hostile to art and humanity. After his return and in consultation with Brøchner, he planned the series of lectures that was meant to position him for the soon-to-be-vacant professorship in aesthetics at Copenhagen University. Brandes initially thought that the lecture series should concern modern French drama – a topic he knew thoroughly and on which he could have lectured without difficulty. Yet here a second surprising and fateful incident took place in Brandes' intellectual biography, for it was actually Brøchner who recommended that he embark on the grand project of six related series of lectures on the three major European literatures of the first half of the nineteenth century (Fenger 1957:211–212). It was also on Brøchner's recommendation that the project was titled "Main Currents."

An Expedited Work

When evaluating *Emigrant Literature* (1872), it must first be kept in mind that the work process itself was expedited. And when we consider how little Brandes knew about the literature that would constitute the theme of this first lecture series, it can perhaps best be described as a hazardous experiment. The aspiring professor's knowledge of early nineteenth-century French so-called emigrant literature was in reality limited to quite a small number of books, the majority of which he knew only second-hand or in any case did not have time to reread before the 12 lectures that were delivered twice weekly between November 3 and December 16, 1871.

As a kind of literary and intellectual historical prologue to the theme, Brandes addressed Jean-Jacques Rousseau's epistolary novel *Julie ou La Nouvelle Héloïse* (1761) and Johann Wolfgang von Goethe's debut novel *Die Leiden jungen Werthers* (1774). Thereafter the literature of the French émigrés is illuminated by reducing it to five works: François-René de Chateaubriand's short autobiographical novel *René* (1802), Étienne Pivert de Senancour's related hermetic novel *Obermann* (1804), Benjamin Constant's love novel *Adolphe* (1816), and two novels of Madame de Staël, *Delphine* (1802) and *Corinne ou l'Italie* (1807). As laconically noted by Henning Fenger, this was "by no means an impressive list for a seeker of a university chair in the scientific study of poetic art" (Fenger 1955:390). Compounding this problem was the fact that time did not permit Brandes to conduct any deep or independent reading of the works, which is why his characterizations rely heavily on observations from other critiques – especially Sainte-Beuve's literary portraits of the French Romantics.

A Hegelian Drama

But Brandes compensated for his lack of knowledge of his topic with his grandiose oratorical framing of the project. The introductory lecture alone is a rhetorical demonstration of power – a hybrid of a political manifesto and a theatrical stage setting that demanded attention not only because of its impertinent and flagrantly unnuanced attacks on Danish Romanticism and Golden Age literature, but also because of its self-confident presentation of the revolutionary main current in nineteenth-century European literature as an inescapably Hegelian process that sooner or later would reach and overwhelm the sleepy little peripheral nation. Without a quiver in his voice, Brandes cast his plan for the coming six lecture series as a "grand drama" in six acts (Brandes 1872a:12–13) about the realization of human freethinking and its ultimate triumph in history – with 1848, the year of revolutions, as the historical turning point.

The introductory lecture, like *Emigrant Literature* as a whole, is speckled with pregnant images and emphatic assertions. For example, Brandes compares Danish literature to a small chapel in a grand church that has its main altar elsewhere (Brandes 1872a:10). Similarly, he employs Aesop's fable of the fox and the stork, who respectively serve each other delicacies on a flat plate and in a tall, narrow-necked vase (Brandes 1872a:8–9), to reflect the nationalist orientations and lack of communication between European literatures and thus the need for the comparative approach that would constitute the literary-critical program of his lectures.

The starting point for this is the Taine-inspired view of literature as a historical-psychological document: "when a people's literature is fully developed, it represents the entire history of that population's thoughts and feelings" (Brandes 1872a:9). Thus Brandes introduces *Emigrant Literature* as an investigation of the historical types in literature that incarnate the great intellectual and literary-historical epochal change from Voltaire and the rational philosophy of the Enlightenment toward the breakthrough of feeling and passion in Rousseau and his descendants in European Early Romanticism. "What I seek to portray for you is the spiritual state, at once powerful yet unhealthy, the peculiar upsurge and the peculiar sickness of soul that characterized the beginning of our century" (Brandes 1872a:74).

The main event, or Hegelian "action," that sets in motion this development is the "great revolution in the human spirit" (Brandes 1872a:74), which Brandes views as a two-pronged movement: "the individual is emancipated … and thought is liberated" (Brandes 1872a:74, 76). He conceives of the revolution as the psychological and emotional process that came into being as human beings freed themselves from traditional societal authorities and seized the power that previously had been the preserve of gods and kings. Yet just as the French Revolution resulted first in the Terror and then in the reconsolidation of the empire, the emancipation of the individual led to new sicknesses of soul and anomalies. The individual asserted himself and the right to freethinking, yet the new sense of possibility was not coupled with a corresponding power, so the result was disappointment, melancholy, and – in the most extreme cases, like that of Goethe's Werther – suicide.

The fact that it is Werther who functions as the first figure in this literary- and intellectual-historical typology renders it clear that the revolution and the emancipation under discussion relate not so much to revolution as a social or political phenomenon. It is the emotional aspects of the revolution and the modernization of European society during this period that interest Brandes. The story of Werther's unhappy love for Lotte is in his view not just a story of the passion of one individual, but an expression of "the passions, longings and agonies of a whole epoch," more explicitly of "the misrelation between the infinity of the heart and the strictures of society" (Brandes 1872a:51, 55).

In order to analyze this problematic, Brandes relies on a typology of figures from nineteenth-century French emigrant literature. In the first place this involves disillusioned young men such as Chateaubriand's René, Senancour's Obermann and Constant's Adolphe, who as disciples of Rousseau and Werther are governed by an excess of dreams, feelings, and passions that cannot be realized. Second, a series of modern and otherwise vigorous female figures appear, in the form of Constant's Eleonore and Madame de Staël's Corinne. The story of emancipation that unfolds in *Emigrant Literature*, in other words, also concerns gender. The French Revolution and the human conception of freedom constitute the overarching historical frame of investigation, but an important secondary motif is the emancipation of women in intellectual and literary history.

A Love Story

Thus we are at the same time on the track of the story that constitutes the almost melodramatic plot of Brandes' lecture series. As scrupulous as *Main Currents* is as a whole, *Emigrant Literature* is also constructed as a drama with a reversal at the midpoint of the story. And just as Brandes in the introductory lecture could point to the hero of freedom Lord Byron as "the one man [who] brings about the reversal in the great drama" (Brandes

1872a:13), so is *Emigrant Literature* equipped with a hero – in fact a heroine – namely Madame de Staël. De Staël appears here in the role of the author who through her modern female figures and her own life example brings forth the epochal change in French and European literature, by introducing a new perspective on love as passion and marriage as social institution.

The reversal in *Emigrant Literature* is heralded by the long and detailed treatment of Benjamin Constant's autobiographical novella *Adolphe* (chaptors 8–10), based on the unequal and unhappy love relation between the author and Madame de Staël. For Brandes, *Adolphe* constitutes a revolutionary experiment and a new departure for conceptions of love and passion by virtue of its unconventional staging of a love story between a young man and a mature, married woman. Brandes' reading focuses on the female protagonist Eleonore, who sacrifices everything – her home, fortune, and bourgeois standing – in favor of her impassioned yet impossible love for Adolphe.

Brandes was especially drawn to the norm-defying elements of this arrangement. Whereas the traditional portrayal of romantic relationships in literature presumed the man to be older than the woman, in that such women were tied to the portrayal of the young girl who was herself the incarnation of innocence and chastity, Constant's experiment proceeds from a more complex understanding of love, as a "mixed composition" of variegated feelings and passions (Brandes 1872a:98–99).

The historically groundbreaking and profoundly intriguing aspect of *Adolphe*, for Brandes, is that it describes a fleeting romantic relationship conducted with passion as its driving force and with the woman as the active instigator. In this reversal of traditional gender roles, he sees a critical and revolutionary potential that allows for a new mode of thinking about love and passion – outside of bourgeois conventions and free of the traditional literary understanding of womanhood as the incarnation of virtue and innocence.

By staging this non-traditional love story, *Adolphe*, in Brandes' view, does not just pave the way for a new and more objective understanding of the complex psychology of love. The novel was at the same time epochal in that it anticipated a new type in literature: the mature and experienced woman – "the woman of thirty" [la femme de trente ans], who is first mentioned in Balzac's novel of the same name, written between 1829 and 1842. But it was equally important that the novel also appealed to Brandes' taste for gossip and personal stories, insofar as the fascinating modern female type of Eleonore was based on a real model in the form of Madame de Staël, "that woman who fought the greatest battle ever fought by a woman in all world history using purely intellectual weapons" (Brandes 1872a:125).

Madame de Staël

Brandes' analysis of *Adolphe* serves as the bridge to his ensuing lectures, which are devoted to the heroine de Staël. First he offers a focused discussion of the epistolary novel *Delphine* (1801), which continues the theme of *Adolphe* by addressing the contradictions between the individual and society and between passionate love and marriage as an institution. It tells the story of two lovers, Delphine and Léonce, who cannot be together because the latter has been tricked into an unhappy and disharmonious marriage with another woman (of a wholly alien nature), and because the law in Catholic France forbids divorce. The book, which was published a year before the later Emperor Napoleon entered into the Concordat with the Pope in Rome, can be read as an attack on indissoluble marriage as a religiously and juridically founded social institution – a theme that fitted Brandes' emancipatory agenda. *Delphine* furthermore provides Brandes with the occasion for a longer excursus on the status of marriage in the northern European and Protestant societies in which divorce was not forbidden by law but where, according to Brandes, societal morality, public opinion, and fear of judgment function as a guarantee of the inviolability of marriage.

It is within this context that Brandes flings his famous grenade in the form of his Taine-inspired analysis of the Danish and Nordic concept of "the home" and its implicit ideal of women as creatures of it. This moral doctrine, he argues, can be traced back to "one singular, cruelly simple, cruelly base climactic necessity," namely the frigid Nordic climate and "the necessity of artificial heating" (Brandes 1872a:151). Thus Brandes plays his trump card: "without artificial heating, in the full magnificence of sunlight, all the beautiful ideals, duties and virtues reveal themselves to be – not untrue but relative" (ibid.).

The excursus on the home within the lecture, however, also functions as part of the demonstration of Brandes' grand idea: that the comparative approach to literature can lead to national self-critique and to emancipation from national prejudices. This theme is at the center of the following lecture, which concerns Madame de Staël in her role as critic and cosmopolitan mediator between European cultures – with special emphasis on her main work *De l'Allemagne* (*On Germany*, 1810, published in London in 1813). In this book de Staël made the case for the bold point of view that France could learn from the recent literary renewal in Germany. While French literature and intellectual life had, according to de Staël, hardened into barren rationalist philosophy and classicist enslavement to rules, she saw in soulful German Sturm-und-Drang poetry and the idealist philosophy of Immanuel Kant a more fruitful model for literary renewal. In Paris, however, de Staël's effort to import the spirit of German Romanticism was viewed as an attack on the hegemony of French literature in Europe; the book called down the wrath and censorship of Napoleon, and its author had to go into exile at the family château, Coppet, located by Lake Geneva in Switzerland. Brandes here compares de Staël's role as a critical, exiled author with Voltaire's struggle for freedom and tolerance from exile in Ferney during the previous century.

There may also be an element of self-identification on the part of Brandes in his profoundly sympathetic description of de Staël as a critic and cosmopolitan, exiled author. In a variation of the basic formula of his reading of *Delphine*, he summarizes her efforts as "rendering the national poetry of the French relative to the nation" (Brandes 1872a:167–168) – in other words, the same operation Brandes had taken on himself with respect to the relation between Danish literature and national identity.

Corinne ou l'Italie – or the Conquest of the Autonomy of Art

The high point of *Emigrant Literature* is Brandes' commentary on de Staël's novel *Corinne ou l'Italie* (1807). Again the starting point is a romantic novel about two lovers who cannot be together, because moral and cultural norms raise obstacles between them. The young poetess Corinne is a modern type of mixed nationality, half Italian and half English. She loves the young Englishman Oswald, and this love is reciprocated, but in the end their relationship cannot come to anything, because Oswald cannot fit the independent and impassioned Italian into his image of womanhood. Brandes calls *Corinne* "a poem on national prejudices" (Brandes 1872a:199), first and foremost here Oswald's Protestant sexual morality and patriarchal view of womanhood. But Oswald's attitude to life also reveals itself in another manner that acquires a decisive significance in the novel, namely his total lack of receptiveness to art and the role of the aesthetic in existence, which makes him unable to understand Corinne.

The novel takes place in Rome, where Corinne tries in vain to open Oswald's eyes to the joys of the senses and the aesthetic experience of art. Brandes' reading of the novel proceeds like a stroll around the cultural and architectural sites of the city, which he supplements with memories of his own Italian travels. The lecture is noteworthy not only for its personal and subjective quality, but also and perhaps especially by virtue of its surprising embrace and celebration of "the liberal relationship between Catholicism and art" (Brandes 1872a:219), which Brandes sees manifested in Italian Renaissance art and architecture. With this inclination toward Catholicism, Brandes almost seems to set aside his anti-clerical agenda in the service of a higher cause. But what cause is this?

For Brandes, the great artistic and architectural works of the Italian Renaissance – such as Michelangelo's frescoes in the Sistine Chapel and St. Mark's Basilica in Venice – are monuments to an aesthetic sensibility and emancipated humanity that constitute a total contrast to Nordic asceticism, which is inherently hostile to art. Yet at the same time he attempts to argue for a connection or a historical parallel between the fifteenth- and sixteenth-century Italian Renaissance and German Romanticism at the dawn of the nineteenth century, which turned away from the Enlightenment's strict faith in reason and once again reoriented itself toward Catholicism. In de Staël's novel it is Corinne who promotes this Catholic orientation for its generosity, moral tolerance, and aesthetic liberality. Brandes sees this openness to the aesthetic culture of Catholicism as an expression of the influences on de Staël of the brothers Schlegel and of Immanuel Kant's aesthetics, which conceived of art as an independent and self-contained domain of human cognition that should not be subordinated to moral or social demands. His reading of *Corinne* thus at the same time develops into an object lesson in the aesthetic observation of art.

In the novel, de Staël has Oswald express moral outrage over the physical nakedness and sensuality in Michelangelo's images of God and the prophets in the Sistine Chapel, and it incenses the Protestant northerner that the Italian Renaissance artists could attempt to adorn Christian buildings with figures from the heathen pantheon of antiquity. Yet Brandes sees a significant sign of the dawning of modernity precisely in the free painterly treatment of religious motifs and the liberal intercourse with different pictorial traditions. At another point in the novel Corinne leads Oswald into the Colosseum, in which the moralistic Englishman can feel nothing other than indignation at the thought of all the Christian blood that has been spilled there. This scene is also construed by Brandes as an example of how Protestantism lacks a sensibility for art. He paraphrases Kant's division of human cognition into three separate spheres or domains – the practical-moral, the theoretical, and the aesthetic – and can thus conclude that Oswald is a man who lacks an aesthetic disposition: "he has no eyes, his reason and his morality has deprived his senses of vitality. Thus he cannot manage to forget content in favor of form" (Brandes 1872a:209).

The forgetting of content in favor of form thus becomes the surprising final salute in *Emigrant Literature* – surprising not least in light of the opening lecture's demand to submit content and "problems" to debate. Brandes' enthusiasm for the aesthetic culture of Catholicism is a facet of his revolt against the Protestantism of his homeland, which had been nourished by the impressions gathered from his stay in Italy. Even the idol of Brandes' youth, Søren Kierkegaard, must now account for his lack of "artistic cultivation" (Brandes 1872a:212). Yet the aesthetic disposition and the ability to evaluate art as art simultaneously becomes a litmus test of modernity for Brandes. When at the end he illustrates his idea of Catholic liberality in relation to art, he relies on his own observations of St. Mark's Basilica in Venice, which is depicted as a veritable bombardment of the senses, a "painterly" architecture in colored marble and gilded ornaments. Playing his trump card by emphasizing the point about how artistic form has here freed itself from religious content and the function of the building, he compares the church to a woman in a harem, "a lovely, harem beauty in repose, heavily loaded with gold, pearls and shimmering diamonds, with the richest brocade covering her Moorish sofa" (Brandes 1872a:221). He finds support for this interpretation by citing a Latin inscription on the building, in which, according to Brandes, the two architects, Francisco and Valerio Zuccato, challenge us to view it as a work of art.

Quite surprisingly, *Emigrant Literature* thus concludes as an apologia for the autonomy of art and for the aesthetic legacy of German Early Romanticism. It amounts to an impassioned defense of a kind of "l'art pour l'art" (Brandes 1872a:210) that Brandes believes to have located in the artistic freedom from religious dogma characteristic of Catholic Renaissance art, and which he saw as reemerging on the doorstep of the nineteenth century in the insistence of Kant and the German Early Romantics of the Athenaeum circle that art and aesthetic taste constitute a distinct domain of human cognition, with its own peculiar laws.

It is worth dwelling on the overwhelmingly positive view of Romanticism that marks *Emigrant Literature* and thus stands in stark contrast to the perspective of the following volumes of *Main Currents*, which adopt a much more combative attitude toward Romanticism in its later manifestations in Germany and France. The literature of the French émigrés was for Brandes the "healthy" part of the reaction to the eighteenth century, "a form of Romanticism before Romanticism" (Brandes 1872a:227), that is, before Romanticism subjected itself to the old authorities in the form of the church and the monarchy, and before it devolved into hegemonic schools in the various national varieties.

Comparatism and Cosmopolitanism

Emigrant Literature thus interprets Early Romanticism as an essentially cosmopolitan enterprise – a blended European culture that emerged from the meeting of peoples, nationalities, and cultures after the French Revolution. Employing a concept from late twentieth-century postcolonial theory, it can be said that Brandes emphasizes the inherent "hybridity" of the cultural poetics of Romanticism, which comes to expression in the paradox that in France it was viewed as too German and in Germany it was seen as overly "French." It is according to this perspective that Madame de Staël, the cosmopolite and the first lady of the revolution's intellectuals, can be assigned the role of the great literary historical mediator and reformer, whose historical mission was to foster a dialogue and synthesis between the apparently irreconcilable European cultural and intellectual traditions – between South and North, between Catholicism and Protestantism, and between the eighteenth-century faith in reason and the new aesthetic sensibility of the nineteenth century.

Rendering national poetics relative to the nation was Brandes' way of summarizing the lesson and legacy of de Staël with a formulation that could in reality also be applied to his own critical project. With his comparative method and his insistence on treating the major European literatures as a complex whole, Brandes made a pioneering contribution to the emergence of a new field of comparative literary studies, which in the following decades would develop into an autonomous discipline with its own journals, professorships, and scientific standards – distinct from the national philologies that had contributed to the emergence of nineteenth-century European national states. Yet when Brandes is referred to as the "père du comparatisme" (Madsen 2004:65), it is also important to keep in mind a critical difference between his methodology and that of later comparativists. The form of comparative literature that would be practiced and institutionalized as an academic discipline in the following decades was first and foremost a method of investigating and demonstrating *influences* between various literatures – a mode of perceiving that has no relevance to Brandes, for whom the comparative perspective always serves a different purpose. Lars Peter Rømhild has summarized the distinction in this manner: "He [Brandes] made comparisons to stimulate thinking and sometimes to *produce* influences, but in most cases not to show former influences and explain them genetically" (Rømhild 1980:286).

In other words, Brandes' comparatism was subordinated to his essentially extrinsic approach to literary criticism – to his interest in literary texts as psychological documents of the thoughts and feelings of various nations and changing epochs. Toward the end of *Emigrant Literature* he summarizes his programmatic point of view with a polemical address directed at the speculative Hegelian aesthetics he had been taught as a young student at the University of Copenhagen: "it was believed that poetic forms and works of poetry grew out of each other like the branches of a tree, instead of studying their connection to culture, to the whole of life" (Brandes 1872a:269). Brandes' conception of the comparative method was possessed of a vision that literature and literary criticism could function as a tool for cultural criticism and exchange between peoples and nations. Literary criticism should provide the reader with a kind of telescope, "one end of which magnifies, while the other shrinks" (Brandes 1872a:8), thus serving as an instrument for rendering national poetics relative to the nation. But as we shall see, such an agenda was not acceptable in the cultural climate of Denmark 1872.

Reception and Afterlife

The Contemporary Reception

The 12 public lectures given in November and December 1871 filled up the auditorium of Copenhagen University, making Brandes the leading subject of conversation around the city. In a November 17 letter to Georges Noufflard, he is able to report triumphantly on the tumultuous scenes at the fourth lecture, at which nearly 400 people – according to Brandes around 150 of them women – had to press themselves in close, many finding a place on the stairs or in the snow on Vor Frue Plads outside the auditorium before they were allowed inside (Brandes 1952:39). Rumors swirled in the press about the young rebel who from his perch at the university lectern launched his volcanic attacks on the social order, the nation, Christianity, and marriage.

As Brandes rather more humbly writes in the brief foreword to the first edition of *Emigrant Literature*, it was in order to avoid "the misunderstandings, distortions and exaggerations" (Brandes 1872a:5) then in circulation that he chose to publish the lectures. But his desire to dampen the mood and thus escape scandal was not fulfilled by publishing them. The publication of the lectures instead became a media event that mobilized the tone-setting segment of the Danish intelligentsia to engage in a purposeful campaign against Brandes, who was subjected to charges of indecency, unscientific practice, and socialism. This campaign destroyed his chances of his expected appointment to the professorship in aesthetics and further resulted in a years-long virtual blockade in leading Copenhagen newspapers and journals, at which he had previously earned a living as a literary critic and theater reviewer.

As Beth Juncker has demonstrated, the critique of and debates about *Emigrant Literature* can be categorized into three related themes: the literary, the moral-religious, and the social (Juncker 1980). The first concerned *Emigrant Literature* as a work of scholarship, that is, the scientific quality (or lack thereof) of Brandes' methodology. The moral-religious critique addressed Brandes' atheism and agitation for "freethinking," as well as his rejection of Christianity as the ultimate authority of existence. The social critique especially targeted the socially destructive element in Brandes' program, as well as its affinities with contemporary socialism.

That a literary treatise by a liberal freethinker such as Brandes could be likened to socialism reveals something about the nervous and perplexed attitude in Denmark in the aftermath of the Paris Commune of May 1871. In the summer of 1871, Copenhagen had witnessed its first tender suggestion of socialism with Louis Pio's founding of Denmark's first worker's newspaper, *Socialisten*, and with the organization of the country's first strike, at the Burmeister & Wain shipyard in September. Fate would also have it that the Danish chapter of the First International would come into being only the month before Brandes began his lecture series. The proximity of these events explains why socialism became the political context in which *Emigrant Literature* was read – though the deliberate efforts of Brandes' opponents to lead the public astray should not be underestimated.

The campaign was led by the two National Liberal newspapers, *Fædrelandet* and *Dagbladet*, as well as by the Grundtvigian organ *Hejmdal*. *Fædrelandet*, the flagship of National Liberalism, devoted no less than nine long articles (of which seven were on the front page) to the matter, while *Hejmdal* issued a series of five front-page articles, indicating the seriousness of the Brandes "problem."

The first reaction came from *Fædrelandet*, and it is conspicuous that the National Liberal camp viewed Brandes as a turncoat who had gone to war with the National Liberal education that had fostered him. It is likewise clear that the debate over *Emigrant Literature* was to a high degree a political debate, not least in the fact that two of the most articulate voices of the critique belonged to two of the period's highest-profile National Liberal politicians and personalities, the poet and *Fædrelandet* editor Carl Ploug (1813–1894) and the theologian Bishop D.G. Monrad (1811–1887), who as Council President in 1863 and 1864 had borne the chief responsibility for Danish politics during the war of 1864.

Carl Ploug set the tone in a February 17 editorial in which he discussed Brandes as an "ill-mannered fool" and a "petroleuse" – the term employed during the Paris Commune for the female terrorists who used petroleum as a means of setting fires. The accusation that Brandes was in league with socialism came in the form of the following chain of associations. First Ploug took exception to Brandes' imprudent discussion of suicide (in the case of Senancourt's *Obermann*) as the ultimate form of the emancipation of the self from Christian ethics; then he turned on Brandes' irreverent dissection of the concept of "home," which he saw as disdainful of family life and thereby of one of the loadbearing pillars of the National Liberal cultural synthesis. Hereafter Ploug discusses Brandes' trope of the individual's struggle against society, which he asserted acquires a peculiar meaning when it is proclaimed "in cold blood" from the university lectern "to a mass of impressionable and easily roused young people" and "at a point in time when disruptive forces had begun to stir." It is clear from this that it was the timing itself of Brandes' lectures that made them controversial. The fact that a group, especially of young people, had been gathered to hear a series of lectures designed to agitate was enough to associate Brandes with socialism. Ploug concluded his intervention by calling the young firebrand to order with a reminder of his Jewish ancestry, challenging him to proceed with greater gratitude toward "the society that had provided his forefathers with hospitable shelter."

Brandes attempted to respond to Ploug's accusations and anti-Semitic attack on his right to express himself, but was now subjected to the bitter experience that the newspapers and journals in which he had earlier published his literary criticism and theater reviews were now closed to him, such that it was necessary for him to publish his response to Ploug as a paid insert in *Dagbladet* (on February 22). In the meantime, *Fædrelandet* continued its campaign, as the critic Rudolf Schmidt raked him over the coals in two front-page articles (March 9 and 11), which criticized his subjectivity and lack of scholarly originality as well as, once again, repeating the accusations of socialism. "Behind Hr. Brandes' showcasing of aesthetic bric-a-brac," concludes Schmidt, "there lurks a fundamental dismay with societal organization as a whole, a fanatical desire to reorder it from the ground up" (*Fædrelandet*, March 11).

Another important target in the National Liberal critique was Brandes' critical methodology itself; *Emigrant Literature* was neither aesthetics nor science, but "a socially tendentious intervention," as another critic, Peter Hansen, registered in his *Dagbladet* review (March 27). The National Liberal politician D.G. Monrad repeated this objection in a series of articles on "Freethinking and Dr. Georg Brandes' Lectures" (*Fædrelandet*, April 4–6). Monrad rejected Brandes' call for a literature that debates social problems by virtue of a principle of the autonomy of art: "naturally art has its own problems, but they are purely artistic" (*Fædrelandet*, April 4). Like Peter Hansen and Rudolf Schmidt, Monrad calls for aesthetic evaluations of the works treated by Brandes. In other words, *Emigrant Literature* itself was evaluated according to the speculative Hegelian aesthetics Brandes had abandoned in favor of his comparative method of cultural criticism.

The Grundtvigian opposition to Brandes was registered by the author and lawyer Carl Rosenberg, who in a series of articles entitled "'Freethinking' and Danish Intellectual Life in the 19th Century" (*Hejmdal*, March 11–15) responded to Brandes' affirmation of the decline of Danish literature. There was no such decline, argued Rosenberg, who instead set himself to showing how in the nineteenth century Danish literature had experienced a productive and flourishing period on the basis of the Grundtvigian trinity of the Nordic, the popular, and the Christian. Danish literature had no need to seek "foreign" nourishment from Europe. For the same reason Rosenberg found it wholly unnecessary to provide a closer description of the theme of *Emigrant Literature*, "the insane asylum into which the author leads us" (*Hejmdal*, March 11).

By more or less vulgar means the campaign against *Emigrant Literature* thus managed to create an image of Brandes as persona non grata, an enemy of established society who was thus unsuited to holding an office as a servant of the state.

Reception in Germany

The opposition that marked the Danish reception of *Emigrant Literature* is set in relief by the way the work was received in neighboring countries. Swedish and Norwegian reviewers were positive, praising its originality and its lively and engaged manner of presentation. The contrast is still stronger for the book's reception in Germany, where it was published in September 1872. Here Brandes had a fine advocate in the translator Adolf Strodtmann, who in his favorably disposed introduction to the German edition and his somewhat valorizing discussion of Brandes in his book *Das geistige Leben in Dänemark* (1873) ensured that the Dane received the best possible introduction to the German literary market (compare Bruns 1977). Brandes was therefore received in Germany as the daring young freethinker who had challenged Danish orthodoxy and consequently been cut down by reactionary public opinion. The German reception was in a sense no less political than the Danish, but the evaluation of the work was the opposite, in that Brandes was received with open arms by liberal German critics and reviewers.

It is evident from the positive and receptive reviews and discussions of *Emigrant Literature* in the German media that German reviewers were well informed of the work's fate in Denmark. In *Das Magazin für die Literatur des Auslandes* (No. 49, 1872:640), Theodor Storm loyally referred to Brandes' revolt against "die Versumpfung" [quagmire] of Scandinavian intellectual life, and predicted that *Emigrant Literature* would acquire an epochal significance for the diffusion of European ideas of freedom and progress in the Nordic countries – "Eine bittere Medizin zwar, aber hoffentlich von heilsamen Folgen" [a bitter medicine, but hopefully with healing effects] (ibid.).

An anonymous reviewer in *Literarisches Centralblatt* similarly lauded Brandes for his uncompromising attack on Danish self-absorption and self-satisfaction. The review focuses especially on Brandes as rhetorician and agitator: "Ein literarischer Gambetta proclamiert Brandes darin die geistige Revolution" [Like a literary Gambetta, Brandes proclaims the intellectual revolution in Denmark] (Anon. 1873:820). The lectures are praised for their intellectual riches and elegant art of characterization, and Brandes is likened to a physician who enters a closed-up and foul-smelling sickroom, peeling back the shutters and opening the windows so that air and sunlight can enter. The reviewer takes exception to the reliance on simplified oppositions in *Emigrant Literature*, while commending its penetrating analogies between different cultural traditions. The conclusion is that Brandes' reform program has Germany's fullest sympathies.

Robert Waldmüller (the pseudonym of the author and painter Charles Edouard Duboc), in *Blätter für literarische Unterhaltung* (Waldmüller 1874:92–93), extolled Brandes as a lone fighter for freedom and modern science in the Scandinavian countries, yet noted also that "Er hat bei diesem Kampfe die liberalen Elemente aller Nationen auf seiner Seite" [in these struggles he has the liberal elements in all nations on his side] (Waldmüller 1874:93). Brandes is again praised for his refreshing and lively form of presentation, and Waldmüller deems *Emigrant Literature* as a work of interest to all Europe.

These three examples demonstrate that, unlike in Denmark, there were favorable conditions in Germany for a liberal and cosmopolitan critic and mediator like Brandes, and this measure of positive interest was influential in Brandes' decision to pursue a career in Germany in the years following. Thanks to Strodtmann, the subsequent volumes of *Main Currents* were published almost simultaneously in German editions (Brandes 1873, 1874, 1876), and in 1874 Brandes was retained as a staff writer for Julius Rodenberg's newly founded liberal journal *Deutsche Rundschau*, for which over the course of the next 15 years he produced a series of important treatises on European authors and cultural personalities, culminating with the long text on Friedrich Nietzsche in 1890.

The same year that Brandes became affiliated with *Deutsche Rundschau*, a review of the first three volumes of *Main Currents* by Friedrich Kreyssig appeared in the October–November issue. Kreyssig also celebrated the cosmopolitan ambition of the work, praising Brandes as a progressive advocate of freedom and modern science, additionally pointing to the disciplinary innovation in Brandes' methodology. *Main Currents* is not literary history in the traditional sense; it is neither biographical-genetic author portraits nor bibliographic annals nor aesthetic art criticism. "Wer also das Buch zur Hand nähme, um etwa auf eine Prüfung über Literaturgeschichte sich vorzubereiten, der ginge gewiss an die falsche Adresse" [Thus he who would take the book in hand to prepare for an exam in literary history would get lost in the trees]. In contrast, Brandes illuminates the mental labor of literature and the great transformations in the "psychology" of German and French society during the period (Kreyssig 1874:140). At the same time Kreyssig notes that Brandes does not shrink from slogans and anecdotes, but that this trait also constitutes an example of his originality and degree of emancipation from the speculative Hegelian school of aesthetics.

When *Emigrant Literature* was issued in 1882 in its revised German second edition (Brandes 1882), there followed yet another favorable review in *Blätter für literarische Unterhaltung* by Otto Weddingen, focusing on Brandes' work as a pioneering contribution to comparative literary studies. Weddingen further identifies Brandes' cultural-historical and psychological view of literature as the great merit of the work: "Es ist kein Buch in dem gewöhnlichen Sinne unserer Literaturgeschichten, es ist kein Sammelsurium von Namen und Daten, sondern ein Erzeugnis, welches die Literaturen vom psychologischen Standpunkt aus betrachtet" [it is not a literary history in the conventional sense, not a medley of names and dates, but in contrast a product of the psychological observation of the literatures] (Weddingen 1882:750).

These later reviews give witness to Brandes' rising reputation in Germany as a literary critic and cosmopolitan mediator – "a good European and cultural missionary", as Friedrich Nietzsche summarized his role in the aforementioned private letter of 1887 (Brandes 1966:441). During this same period Brandes also came to play a main role in the introduction of modern Scandinavian writing, for example by Henrik Ibsen and Bjørnstjerne Bjørnson, to Germany. The status and prestige enjoyed by Brandes in the young radical literary milieu of Germany is apparent in the following character sketch by the theater critic, dramatist, and founder of the Berlin-based Naturalist theater Freie Bühne Otto Brahm, published in *Frankfurter Zeitung* on March 3, 1884, on the occasion of a staging of Ibsen's *Ghosts*:

> We Germans cannot look on the development of Nordic poetry without envy … a cohesive literary movement … which aims at the liberation of the mind from the depths of darkness … It is with a "golden recklessness" that Ibsen and Bjørnson and the youth of Scandinavia, who have a leader in Georg Brandes, fight against the medieval oppression that burdens the minds of these bishop-ruled countries … When Georg Brandes some fifteen years ago awakened his countrymen by telling of the "main currents" of modern

literature, a new epoch broke out; just as the classical period in our literature emanated from Lessing and Herder, this breakthrough occurred at the urging of a purely critical intellect. (Brahm 1913:74)

Riding the Scandinavian wave and the fame of Brandes in Germany, a series of new collected editions of *Main Currents* were published in the 1890s, and thus a new round of reviews followed, in which the continued acknowledgment of Brandes as the leading figure of the Modern Breakthrough in Scandinavian literatures was blended with new critical voices. One example of this new engagement is Franz Mehring's review of the collected edition of *Main Currents* in *Die neue Zeit*, in which Brandes meets with criticism for his bourgeois and idealistic conception of history: "Als bürgerlicher Schriftsteller bewegt sich Brandes immer auf idealistischem Boden; er behauptet zwar gelegentlich überall ins Leben zurückzugreifen, aber die Erkenntnis, dass sich die literarische Bewegung in letzter Instanz aus der ökonomischen Entwicklung erklärt, ist ihm fremd" [As a bourgeois author Brandes treads always upon idealistic ground; sure enough he occasionally asserts that he reaches back toward life in all areas, yet the awareness that the literary movement in the end is a mirroring of economic development is alien to him]. Yet Mehring concludes by praising Brandes for his lively and intellectually abundant style, which "schmeckt wie feuriger Wein, verglichen mit der faden Limonade der preussischen Literaturgeschichte" [tastes like a fiery wine when compared to the flavorless lemonade of Prussian literary history] (Mehring 1893–1894:311).

Reception in France
The favorable German reception of *Emigrant Literature* can be compared to the book's fate in France. Such a comparison is of particular interest not only because the book was about French literature, but also because France at the time enjoyed status as the first nation of the world literary republic. Paris was the cultural center of artistic and literary innovation in Europe and the world – the place from which new literary and artistic movements emanated and in which the criteria of literary quality and

modernity respectively were set (Casanova 1999). For these reasons the French market, for Brandes and successive generations of Scandinavian authors, constituted the promised land: the place where more than any other it was desired to have one's texts published and evaluated (Briens 2010). Yet as we shall see, out of all the European countries Brandes had the greatest difficulty in establishing a name for himself in France.

Emigrant Literature was substantially introduced in France as early as 1873, in the form of an article of upwards of 30 pages by Henri Blaze de Bury in the November issue of the leading cosmopolitan journal of the age, *Revue des deux mondes*. The article contains no critical evaluation, instead consisting of a congenial and gripping summary of the main ideas of *Emigrant Literature* (based on Strodtmann's German translation from 1872), supplemented by a series of original French citations from Chateaubriand and Madame de Staël. The Francophone world thus had an early opportunity to become acquainted with Brandes' comparative understanding of literature and his principal literary-historical thesis on the main current in nineteenth-century European literature as an interplay between the spirit of Voltaire and the spirit of Rousseau.

Nevertheless, 10 years would pass before the French public would again hear of Brandes, this time in the form of a critical profile by Arvède Barine (the pseudonym of Madame Charles Vincens) in *La Revue Blanche* (Barine 1883). This article is of particular interest in that it contains a morally and ideologically grounded critique of Brandes' vision of humanity and society in *Emigrant Literature*. Barine characterizes Brandes as a "sectarian" disciple of Rousseau, asserting that his temperament was carried away by his passionate struggle for natural rights and individual freedom, at the expense of "civilization" and social morality. As a counter argument, she argues that the laws of society and moral rules of conduct in a modern civilized society also and especially serve the function of protecting people against infringement. Barine thus contests the democratic starting point of Brandes' radicalism, suggesting that the consequence of his struggle for the emancipation of the individual in reality would lead to a legitimization of the right of the stronger.

Despite these and other more literary-historical objections, Barine concludes by expressing her fervent acknowledgment of Brandes' bold attempt to present a synthesis of this chaotic chapter in French literary history using the opposition between Voltaire and Rousseau, predicting a grand career for the Dane in the future. At the end of the review it is evident that Brandes' work appealed to a certain form of national sentiment among French critics, which is underscored by their gratitude for the Dane's immense service in having demonstrated how the main currents of nineteenth-century European literature originated in France. "We are no longer pampered by these kinds of compliments," the review concludes (Barine 1883:764).

This formulation provides a glimpse of the national attitude of defeatism that marked the cultural climate of France after its defeat in the Franco-Prussian War of 1870. This defeatist attitude was also an important aspect of the relative insularity of the French literary market of the time – in comparison to developments in the contemporary German book market, which was characterized among other things by a burst of translation activity, not only of Scandinavian literature. There were thus also historical and structural reasons that the diffusion of *Main Currents* proceeded sluggishly in France, where only one of the six volumes, namely the fifth, *The Romantic School in France*, was published in French translation at the time.

While Brandes had established for himself a position as a European literary critic in Germany during his Berlin exile (1877–1883), it was a great disappointment to him that there was minimal interest in his works in France. His disappointment comes to expression in a letter to his friend Noufflard, dated January 26, 1888. The ironic twist here was that two English journals, *The Spectator* and *Saturday Review*, had just discussed the *German* Georg Brandes as "the greatest living critic," which provided Brandes with the opportunity to offer a few observations regarding power relations in the world literary republic:

> Je lis toujours beaucoup de Français. J'aime votre littérature plus que toute autre. J'ai écrit plus de livres sur la France que sur tout autre pays et pourtant je suis parfaitement inconnu en France.

Quand j'avais écrit un seul article sur les Flamands on était prêt à m'ériger des statues en Flandre; tout les poètes m'envoyaient leurs œuvres, tous les journaux parlaient de moi. Quand j'ai écrit deux petits articles sur les écrivains Russes sans même savoir leur langue, on a été tellement touché de mes connaissances qu'on m'a loué, m'a traduit, m'a fait venir. Sur la France j'ai écrit plus de volumes que je n'ai écrit d'articles sur la Russie, et on sait à peine que j'existe. Un certain Charles Simond veut me traduire; depuis deux ans il cherche en vain un éditeur, bien que Paul Bourget m'ait offert d'écrire une introduction. Cela m'attriste un peu, car une réputation n'est pas consacrée aussi longtemps que la France n'a pas dit son mot.

[I constantly read French. I love your literature more than any other. I have written more books about France than any other country, and still I am altogether unknown in France. When I had written a single article on Flemish literature, they were ready to erect a statue of me; all their poets sent me their works, all their newspapers talked about me. When I had written two short articles on Russian poets, without even knowing the language, they were so moved by knowledge of them that I was praised, translated and invited to visit. I have written more books on France than I have articles on Russia, and still the French hardly know I exist. A certain Charles Simond wants to translate me; for two years he has searched in vain for a publisher, even though Paul Bourget has for a long time promised to write an introduction. It irritates me, for the measure of an author has not been established as long as France has withheld its judgement.] (Brandes 1952:131–132)

In the meantime the judgment of France arrived in 1893 in the form of a new, 20-page article in *Revue de deux mondes*, in which the critic Jean Thorel examined *Main Currents* on the occasion of the newly published, collected German edition of *Die Litteratur des neunzehnten Jahrhunderts in ihren Hauptströmningen*, issued by the Leipzig house Veit & Co. (1882–1892).

Thorel begins by affirming Brandes' rising reputation as a European literary critic in Germany, and by contesting the view that French national chauvinism explains why his work has been ignored in France. According to Thorel, this lack of acknowledgement in France is due more to the fact that Brandes is not a literary critic at all, but first and foremost a polemicist whose chief cause from the beginning had been to fight against and ultimately destroy every form of religion. Brandes' anti-clerical agenda was however of less relevance in the French context, and what the Danish critic had to say about French literature in *Emigrant Literature* did not impress Thorel. Brandes' tiny selection of authors and works from the period was "wholly insufficient" and all too selective to fulfill his ambition of portraying the main currents of nineteenth-century psychology (Thorel 1893:343). Thorel further opposed the simplified scheme itself that undergirded Brandes' dramatic arrangement of nineteenth-century European literary history as an interplay and a synthesis between the spirit of Voltaire and the spirit of Rousseau, in that he could not comprehend what kind of common "liberal" spirit could be attributed to the intellectual essences of Voltaire, Rousseau, Lessing, and Schiller.

At the same time Thorel pointed out an internal contradiction in Brandes' comparative method, which consisted on the one hand of affirming the prior lack of exchange between European national literatures, and on the other of asserting that the literary works and types in the different literatures were causally connected and determinative of one another. If one wanted seriously to study the deeper and lasting influences between the literatures, then according to Thorel one must abandon the politicizing contemporary perspective on literature, instead going to the sources themselves. Evident in this objection is the influence of contemporary comparative literary studies, which had set new scientific standards for literary criticism according to which a positivistic interest in *influences* between works and authors had supplanted the older literary-historical romantic-idealistic doctrine of a universal spirit in history. From this perspective Thorel also criticizes the construction of the six volumes of *Main Currents*, arguing that the book on German Romanticism should have come before the volume on French emigrant literature. De Staël continued the work of the German Romantics, not vice versa. Again the problem was the politicizing Hegelian scheme that placed the abstract main currents and the oppositions between action and reaction over and above literary-historical fact and chronology, thus leading to an artificial division of the literature of the period.

At the conclusion of his review the French critic marshals all of his weapons in order to deprive Brandes of any claim to legitimacy or originality as a literary historian. Brandes' work was nothing other than "a long, confused and indirect defense [plaidoyer]" of political ideas that were alien to literature, and as such would have demanded a wholly different approach than that pursued in the work. From the point of view of literary history, Brandes' efforts amounted to nothing other than ephemeral compilation:

> quelque bruit qui ait été fait autour de son nom et de ses livres, on s'aperçoit, le premier moment d'étonnement passé, qu'il n'y a là rien qui mérite d'arrêter l'attention plus qu'il ne convient de le faire pour une compilation, momentanement utile à cause de la masse des materiaux qui y sont rassemblés, mais que demain le premier compilateur venu pourra refaire avec plus de méthode et de clarté, ce qui rendra tout de suite inutile, – même comme compilation, – toute l'œuvre de M. Brandes.

> [regardless of all the hubbub surrounding his name and his books, as soon as the initial bemusement has passed, one discovers that there is nothing in his work that deserves attention other than that it is passable as a kind of compilation, which at the moment is useful because of the great mass of material collected within it, but which tomorrow will be able to be reworked with more methodological skill and greater clarity than the initial compiler has exhibited, which will immediately render Mr. Brandes' entire work obsolete, even as a compilation.] (Thorel 1893:358)

Thorel's severe criticism of Brandes may also be seen as part of an ongoing debate in 1890s literary France about the proper attitude to the new and foreign literary expressions and influences that had recently been introduced to the country. Like Germany, France was also witness to a Scandinavian wave that manifested itself in translations and in Parisian productions of modern Scandinavian drama by writers such as Ibsen, Bjørnson, and Strindberg (Segrestin 2010; Rogations 2016). Yet at the same time the French literary public was also capable of exhibiting an equally fervent opposition to the present "Scandophilia" or "Nordomania," articulated by nationally oriented literati and theater critics who desired to protect France's national poetics and its hegemony in the world literary republic against foreign influence. Thorel's attempt to deprive Brandes of his status as a leading European literary critic also follows this pattern.

Given the positive reception of Brandes in Germany, it is interesting that it was in republican and secular France that Brandes' work encountered the most engaged moral and ideological opposing voices. It is also noteworthy that the majority of the objections to Brandes in French criticism (such as the charges of politicizing art and disavowing religion) were the same as those he had encountered in the National Liberal Danish public of 1872 – but with the important difference that French critics understood the difference between liberalism and socialism. As in Denmark after the defeat of 1864, France's defeat in the Franco-Prussian War in 1871 had rendered political and literary opinion in the country more national and thus less receptive to a cosmopolitan critic like Brandes.

Taken together these examples demonstrate how international politics impacted the reception of *Emigrant Literature*.

Later Scholarship
Paul V. Rubow is correctly viewed as the founder of scientific Brandes scholarship, by virtue of his treatise "Georg Brandes' Forhold til Hippolyte Taine og C.A. Sainte Beuve" (published in *Edda* VI 1916 and *Litterære Studier*, 1928), which outlines how Brandes' earliest practice as a literary critic took shape under the influence of his two French models. Rubow set the direction

for early Brandes scholarship, which was first and foremost comparatively oriented, that is it sought to show the decisive literary, philosophical, and theoretical influences that shaped Brandes as a critic. In *Georg Brandes' Briller* (1928), Rubow accentuates his relationship to the philosopher Søren Kierkegaard as critical to the development of Brandes' combative personality.

A necessary supplement to Rubow is Gunnar Ahlström's dissertation *Georg Brandes' Hovedstrømninger* (1937), which examines the influence of Hegel and German post-Hegelianism as the essential ideological and historical-philosophical inspiration for *Main Currents*.

Henning Fenger's dissertation *Georg Brandes' Læreår* (1955) outlines the entirety of Brandes' literary and scientific education up to the breakthrough of *Emigrant Literature*, with special emphasis on the inspiration he took from French Romanticism. A main point in the dissertation is expressed in the pregnant characterization of Brandes as "a Romantic who spent his life fighting against Romanticism" (Fenger 1955:407).

In *Den unge Brandes. Miljø. Venner. Rejser. Kriser.* (1957) – the follow up to his dissertation – Fenger proposes an alternative background for *Emigrant Literature* by seeking the cause of Brandes' combativeness and critique of marriage in biographical circumstances: Brandes' impossible, yet no less impassioned love affair with the (unhappily) married Caroline David, 12 years his senior. "We cannot understand much of Brandes in the years 1867–72 if we are not aware of this relationship, which functions as the secret code of his critical writings, not the least the lectures of 1871 and 1872" (Fenger 1957:119–120).

The biographical approach to Brandes is followed to its fullest extent by Jørgen Knudsen in *Georg Brandes. Frigørelsens vej. 1842-77* (1985), which constitutes the first of the eight volumes of his grand Brandes biography (1985–2004). A condensed version of this biography was published in 2008 under the title *GB*.

Bertil Nolin's monograph *Den gode europén* (1965), subtitled *Studier i Georg Brandes' idéutvekling. 1871-1893*, covers Brandes' activity and development as a critic during the 20-year period in which *Main Currents* was produced. The treatise takes its title from Nietzsche's previously mentioned famous characterization of Brandes as "the good European and cultural missionary," and outlines how Brandes wrote his way to this status through his broad orientation in contemporary German, English, Slavic, and French literature. Nolin is also the author of the short English-language introduction *Georg Brandes* (1976).

A central direction within Brandes scholarship since the 1970s has focused on the political and activist dimension of Brandes' work. On the hundredth anniversary of Brandes' lectures on emigrant literature, Copenhagen University hosted a series of lectures published in 1973 under the title *Den politiske Georg Brandes*, edited by Hans Hertel and Sven Møller Kristensen. In 1978, Hertel and Kristensen further organized an international symposium with around thirty participants from eleven countries, which in 1980 resulted in *The Activist Critic. A Symposium on the Political Ideas, Literary Methods and International Reception of Georg Brandes*, which constitutes a milestone in modern Brandes scholarship, both by analyzing Brandes' efforts as a liberal and activist critic and by tracing the reception of his works across Europe and the rest of the world.

In the twenty-first century three international conferences have been dedicated to the topic of Georg Brandes as international literary critic and intellectual. In 2002 a conference with the title *Georg Brandes og Europa* was organized in Florence, Italy, resulting also in a volume of proceedings (Harsløf 2004). In 2008 another conference was held in Nancy in France. This conference resulted in the publication of the book *Grands courants d'échanges Intellectuels: Georg Brandes et la France, L'Allemagne, L'Angleterre* (Bourguignon et al., Eds, 2010), which likewise contains a series of interesting contributions with a special emphasis on *Main Currents*. Most recently, in 2019, a conference was organized in Copenhagen on the topic of *The Global and Digital Georg Brandes*.

In the same period, three doctoral dissertations containing analyses of *Emigrant Literature* have been published in Denmark. Svend Skriver's *Europæere i 1800-tallets danske litteratur: Om Jens Baggesen, P.L. Møller og Georg Brandes* (2007) contains a literary historiographical analysis of the narrative devices and "strategies of internationalization" in *Emigrant*

Literature, without however addressing Brandes' strategies of international publication and the transmission of the work abroad.

Pelle Oliver Larsen's *Professorat. Kampen om Det Filosofiske Facultet 1870-1920* (2016) provides a detailed sociological investigation of the course of events surrounding the denial of the professorship in aesthetics at Copenhagen University to Brandes after 1872. The dissertation outlines how moral and religious concerns, rather than scientific arguments, were the reason that a majority of the professors on the faculty opposed Brandes.

Finally, Georg Brandes' conflicted relationship with Judaism and Jewish culture has been made the object of an independent investigation by Søren Blak Hjortshøj in *Son of Spinoza. Georg Brandes and Modern Jewish Cosmopolitanism* (2021). His thesis is that even though Brandes often distanced himself from Judaism, throughout his whole authorship he is interested in the role of the Jew in history and the Jewish contribution to the development of Western civilization. Hjortshøj thus argues that there is a connection between Brandes' cosmopolitan vision of literary history and his own particular experiences as a Jew. Through an analysis of the topos of exile in Brandes' early authorship, Hjortshøj demonstrates how Brandes saw the modern European Jew as a historical type that, precisely by virtue of his "cultural hybridity," homelessness and lack of anchorage in a national tradition, was especially disposed to play the role of cosmopolitan bridge-builder and pioneer of Europe's cultural and political modernization.

Concluding Perspective

Thus we arrive back at the question of Brandes' relevance to the twenty-first century. As suggested many times along the way, both Brandes' cosmopolitan vision of European literature and his profound sympathy with the emigrant experience can be brought into dialogue with the views of late twentieth- and early twenty-first-century postcolonial theory. A fundamental idea in postcolonial theory is that modern Western identity has been decisively shaped by European nations' histories as colonial powers and the various long-term effects of these histories. Thus postcolonial criticism accentuates European and Western culture and identity as a phenomenon that has come into being through mobility, migration, and cultural encounters, and which thus has the experience and the homelessness and foreignness of emigrants and the exiled built into it.

As the Palestinian-American professor of literature Edward W. Said has emphasized, modern Western culture is to a great extent a product of the exiled, the emigrant, and the refugee (Said 2000). In the same place Said stresses how exile and emigrant literature can articulate "a contrapuntal consciousness" (Said 2008:148), or an awareness of difference and openness to the alien that renders us able to consort with people and cultural forms of expression that are different from our own. Another central voice of postcolonial theory, the Indian-English scholar Homi K. Bhabha, has with his concept of "hybridity" identified the mixing of races and the meeting of cultures as the very space of creativity and innovation in a globalized culture (Bhabha 1994).

Such ways of thinking can almost sound like the Romantic music of the past in light of our age of the global movement of refugees and migrants and reawakened nationalism, but they also provide the opportunity to reassess the contemporary relevance of Brandes' comparative and cultural-critical methodology.

THE ROMANTIC SCHOOL IN GERMANY (1873)
Anna Sandberg

Introduction

Georg Brandes' second volume of *Main Currents* was on German Romanticism. Published in 1873, it is characterized by a discordance between judgment and understanding. He is possessed of a peculiar sense of the Romanticism toward which he directs all his critique; indeed, a segment of Brandes scholarship considers him to be an outright Romantic anti-Romantic. He shares this equivocal stance with his model, Heinrich Heine, who was a part of the "Young Germany" in the decades before the 1848 revolutions. Both criticize Romanticism and yet – if the period is defined elastically – belong to it: Heine is a part of Late Romanticism, while Brandes is situated in the middle of a still later age's artistic and philosophical reception of Romanticism, represented by, among others, Richard Wagner (born 1813) and Friedrich Nietzsche (born 1844).

It is not, however, this later iteration of Romanticism that Brandes describes in this volume of *Main Currents*. He views German Romanticism as a closed historical phase situated between the French Revolution of 1789 and the July Revolution of 1830, while Danish Romanticism, on the contrary, was still an influence on Danish cultural life at the time Brandes was writing – an influence that according to him should be resisted. Against this Romanticism's idealism and its tendencies toward flight from reality, he advocates a liberal activism and a faith in the rights of the individual. Contemporary literature, with Romanticism as its contrast, should be mobilized in the service of progress and democratization. Romanticism thereby serves as the point from which a new orientation in Danish culture is to be launched.

How does Brandes conceptualize Romanticism? His approach is twofold, in that on the one hand he describes "the Romantic school" as a group of authors and works, and on the other "the Romantic" as a psychological-mental phenomenon and a variegated art form. Both approaches reveal that he does not intend to write a well-ordered and historically exhaustive literary history, but rather to paint a portrait, at the same time political, intellectual-historical, and psychological, of that which is uniquely German.

The title's phrase *The Romantic School* is not of Brandes' invention. It was a widespread designation in nineteenth-century German literary criticism, from Heinrich Heine's *Die romantische Schule* (1836) through Hermann Hettner's *Die romantische Schule in ihrem inneren Zusammenhange mit Goethe und Schiller* (1850) to Rudolf Haym, whose *Die romantische Schule* (1870) marks the beginning of modern scholarship on Romanticism (Ansel 2003:247; Huggler 2006). The designation "school" suggest both a unity and a common program in German Romanticism, which in contrast to later literary historiography does not take account of the multiplicity of the period and its various phases, from an Early Romanticism toward a National Romanticism and then a Late Romanticism.

Brandes is especially preoccupied with authors from before 1800, that is the Early Romantics: Novalis, Friedrich Schlegel, Ludwig Tieck, and W.H. Wackenroder, together with the Romantic women authors Dorothea Schlegel and Caroline Schlegel-Schelling. The so-called national phase of Romanticism after the turn of the century is represented by Heinrich von Kleist and Zacharias Werner, the late period by E.T.A. Hoffman especially, but also Joseph Eichendorff and Friedrich Fouqué. Achim von Arnim and Clemens Brentano are mentioned sporadically, and a transitional author between Classicism and Romanticism, Jean Paul, is viewed negatively as a forerunner of Romanticism. This text corpus is limited, but is later widened in Brandes' second edition. His canon still has relevance to an extent, but today his work should not primarily be read as a literary history. The book has value – like *Main Currents* in general – as a literary psychology and history of mentalities typical of the age, as a work with a particular reception history, and as an especially significant contribution to the cultural conflict in Denmark at the time.

Background and Genesis

The German Reich was young in 1873, having been established in 1871 by virtue of Prussia's three "wars of unification" against, respectively, Denmark (1864), Austria (1866), and France (1870–1871). It was in the midst of the so-called *Gründerzeit*, experiencing economic growth and industrial expansion.

During his stay in Germany in 1872, Brandes quickly become enthusiastic about the country, and he settled in the German capital in 1877 and stayed until 1883. He begins *The Romantic School in Germany* with a portrait of the country at present, which contrasts both with German society in the age of Romanticism around 1800 and with the Danish small state after 1864. Berlin was a big modern city marked by its industry, military, and rationality, in a country staunchly led by the "Iron Chancellor," Otto von Bismarck. Through his characterization of a disciplined and future-oriented Germany, possessed of a common cause (also in literature), Brandes sought to rouse his fellow Danes and to mobilize a new energy and force amidst the national decline that followed the defeat of 1864. His portrait of the German faith in freedom and progress is clearly idealized. In other places, not least in his substantial work *Berlin as the German Capital*, Brandes presents a more nuanced and more critical vision of German political development and of Bismarck.

In Denmark there had been gradual liberal reform of society after the introduction of the constitution in 1849, but after 1866 parliamentary rule had been scaled back following a constitutional revision in July of that year. Even after the failure of their Greater Denmark program in 1864, the National Liberals in alliance with the Conservatives fought to preserve their power and limit the influence of the new Venstre [Left] party. The period between 1870 and 1901 was defined politically by constitutional struggle and democratization. In this political landscape, in which the modern party system was established, Brandes formulated a wholly new radical liberal position. Even though his program largely cohered with that of the Venstre (Thomsen 1998:51), his *Main Currents* created a platform of argumentation from which he participated in the so-called culture wars, setting himself up as a contrast to the bourgeois Conservatives and the new Social Democrats, as well as the Grundtvigian project of enlightenment that was especially influential in the folk high school and cooperative movements.

During the summer and fall of 1872, Brandes sought refuge in Dresden and Berlin from the commotion resulting from his first series of lectures on "emigrant literature," and from the denial of the professorship in aesthetics at Copenhagen University that he had expected to receive. It was here that he prepared the second installment of his lecture series, on German Romanticism (Nolin 1965:56). The following year, in a six-week period between February 2 and March 27, Brandes delivered the 12 lectures. In this relatively brief period he not only managed to write and give the lectures, but also deliver the completed manuscript to the publisher (Knudsen 1985:303); in May of 1873 it appeared in book form.

Very little scholarly material exists on this process (Bjerring-Hansen 2008:151), and the published volume received far less attention than *Emigrant Literature* had. Its later publication history, on the contrary, was rather dramatic. Brandes initially revised the first German edition of the volume, which had also appeared in 1873, publishing a second German version in 1887, which served as the foundation for the Danish second edition, released in 1891. The second edition contains 15–20 per cent more material (Bjerring-Hansen 2008:153), adding new German Romantics in new chapters: W.H. Wackenroder, A.W. Schlegel, Friedrich Hölderlin, Adelbert von Chamisso, Achim von Arnim, Clemens Brantano, and Joseph von Görres. Brandes further adds a section on the Danish poet Schack von Staffeldt and another on Scandinavian Romanticism at the end (Knudsen 1994:407–408). He tones down his judgmental rhetoric, for example changing the chapter headings on the "negative" and "positive" pioneers of Romanticism to merely "The Pioneers of Romanticism." Likewise, the most radical assertions – for example that "Romanticism was poisoned by its sources" (Brandes 1873:21) – are removed. A few altered descriptions, for example of Novalis (Bjerring-Hansen 2008:156) and of Heinrich von Kleist, can be identified. Through the use of author names as chapter headings, the presentation in general becomes more biographical, more monograph-like, and Brandes draws to a greater degree on authorial biographies as source material. The work's character as a document of the culture wars is lessened, and it becomes less a local Danish work and more broadly European in its perspective. These differences will be addressed in the following (see also the section 4, "Reception and Afterlife").

Main Currents describes a macro-historical, spiritual, and intellectual-historical course of development toward reason and freedom. This historical vision is inspired by G.W.F Hegel, whose philosophy had exerted immense influence on Danish cultural life in the decades before Brandes began his career. Brandes' reception was marked by German Young Hegelianism, which in the 1830s and 1840s continued Hegel's method of dialectical thinking, politically and socially radicalizing it in the struggle for social change in conservative Prussia. Brandes' periodization is determined by the dialectical relation between political action and reaction.

In the second volume of *Main Currents*, German Romanticism functions negatively as a period of reaction following the French Revolution, which only gave way to new action in the July Revolution of 1830. Brandes' critique is strongly inspired by G.W.F. Hegel and Heinrich Heine, but in Germany after the failure of the bourgeois revolution in 1848–1849, a new and more moderate, liberal, and nationally oriented form of criticism took hold. Brandes employs the pre-1848 aggressive rhetoric of the Young Hegelian Arnold Ruge as well as the more tempered critique of the liberal Hettner and his contemporary Haym (Nolin 1965:57–59). The different tendencies of these writers sporadically manifest themselves as ambiguities in Brandes' evaluations.

Methodology, Concepts, and Themes in *The Romantic School in Germany*

This section first sketches out Brandes' methodology (a) and his cultural-political employment of Romanticism (b). Next, his complex conception of modernity is characterized (c). Brandes works with both a social and an aesthetic conception of modernity, closely tied to his critique of idealism and his portrait of Goethe, which also contains a definite conception of form (d).

Central to *The Romantic School in Germany* is Brandes' thesis on the Romantic and specifically German mentality, which is charted in the three middle chapters on soul [gemyt], longing, and reflection (e). Brandes discusses Romantic individualism in a dialogue with both Goethe and Søren Kierkegaard (f). Finally, an investigation is made of how Brandes views the themes that are important to his program for the Modern Breakthrough, namely love and gender (g), along with politics (h). These topics correspond to those of the chapters in *The Romantic School in Germany*, which are regularly referenced and cited.

Brandes' Organizing Principle and Methodology
Brandes does not arrange his material chronologically, but thematically, into areas such as sociality, music, art, nature, politics, and central Romantic concepts such as psychology, soul, and longing, all of which are categories in which the anthropological-social and poetological-aesthetic are combined. A timeline is still established, however; in the first two of the book's three sections Brandes places the main emphasis on the Early Romantic phase around 1800, and then concludes with the Restoration after 1815. He sees a certain revolutionary potential in Friedrich Schlegel's novel about free love, *Lucinde* (1799), but he fundamentally understands Romanticism from its point of conclusion, in that he projects the conservative tendencies of Late Romanticism back onto the early Universal Romanticism, which is also rooted in his biographical approach to the literature. The same early work of Schlegel is accordingly negatively evaluated when it is viewed in light of the author's later conversion to Catholicism and his ultra-conservatism during the Restoration, after the Congress of Vienna. Romanticism in toto thus comes to be portrayed as politically reactionary.

Brandes describes his particular method in the introduction as that of seeking the connection between biography and work. He designates "the anecdote" as his principle (Brandes 1873:4), understood as the illustrative microhistory, which is supplemented by topicalizing commentaries, which at certain points are expanded into programmatic declarations of a modern view of life. "Real life" is the object of investigation (Brandes

1873:5); Brandes' interests are in the psychology, palpitations of the soul, and feelings (Brandes 1873:5–6) that form the basis of the literature. At the same time he stylizes his own role – in the spirit of Naturalism and Positivism – as that of the natural scientist and physician (Brandes 1873:6). This thus suggests a duality of the scientific and the vitalistic, understood as the non-material forces of life. This interest in individualistic aspects results in certain fissures in Brandes' negatively determined view of Romanticism: he is concerned with that which deviates from normality, with the transgression of boundaries, the mystical, the unexplainable, and the ingenious. Such ambivalence, between social-political condemnation and psychological-aesthetic fascination, is an important thread in *The Romantic School in Germany*.

Brandes' Cultural-Political Employment of German Romanticism

The timely nature of his political and literary criticism is clearly evident in Brandes' comparison of German and Danish Romanticism in the introductory chapter. Even though the feudal, absolutist, and divided Germany of 1800 precluded political influence, German authors created no less than a wholly original Romantic literature. The second-hand Romanticism of the Danes, on the contrary, was to a high degree built upon impulses from outside. Brandes does refer to a "Nordic vein" (Brandes 1873:8), but mainly views Danish Romanticism as a German import. The German literature is a genuine expression of life and of life experience, demonstrating a "poetic-philosophical total vision of life" (Brandes 1873:11). The German authors have sophistication, experience, and spirit, and are furthermore extreme, consequential, and sickly, while the Danes, who have not produced ideas themselves, are on the contrary moderate, even-keeled, harmonious, healthy, and vigorous. These are not only personality traits, but also formal artistic characteristics, and the works of the Danish Romantics are said to be more rounded and more elegant than those of the Germans.

Here, in a gesture typical of his form of presentation, Brandes employs two metaphors that show that these fundamental differences cannot be valorized purely negatively or positively. On the one hand he deems German

Romanticism to be a "hospital" full of "eccentric personalities," while on the other he describes the Romantics as bold and daring mountaineers. The Danes are neither sick nor mad, yet consequentially lack the courage and desire for conquest: "we have left to others the scaling of Montblanc. We have avoided breaking our necks, but we have left standing the Alpine flowers, which only bloom atop the highest mountain peaks and at the edge of the precipice" (Brandes 1873:15). In this image of the new extreme sport of the era, alpinism, Brandes makes it clear that the literature in this book should be viewed as action, energy, and the manifestation of life, and not as a museum piece.

In relation to Danish institutionalized literary history writing in the nineteenth century, Brandes departs from the three-phase model of Romanticism after 1800, which was held to constitute a new period of flourishing and of golden ages. This model was introduced by N.M. Petersen's *Contribution to Danish Literary History* (1854–1861), and consolidated in the decades after Brandes (Conrad 1996:305, 311–319). Brandes does not dwell significantly on the idea that Nordic and popular Romanticism constitutes something especially valuable in Danish literature.

But while Brandes is frequently critical of the Danish Romantics, he should not be understood to be anti-national. On the contrary, he would gladly strengthen the national literature, inaugurating a new period of greatness under the sign of realism together with a new political future for Denmark, yet in so doing he would dispense with the Romantic Golden Age as an ideal. In contemporary German literary-historical writing, for example in the prominent figure of Rudolf Haym, Romanticism is reevaluated in attunement with Germany's political unification, and is read integrally with the Weimar Classicism of Goethe and Schiller as a part of the national canon (Hohendahl 1985:184). In Brandes these German texts collide to a certain extent with his employment of Arnold Ruge's Young Hegelian, anti-Romantic cultural critique from the 1840s.

These partially conflicting sources also manifest themselves in a contradictory image of Goethe and of German Neoclassicism in *The Romantic School in Germany*. The negative climax in the introduction is Brandes' radical rhetoric of contamination: "Romanticism was poisoned by its sources" (Brandes 1873:21). The main sources for Danish Romanticism were Henrich Steffens and his teacher F.W.J. Schelling; Brandes identifies their philosophy of nature and of identity with opportunistic conservatism and a Christian life view. In later Danish literary history writing, the role of Steffens is otherwise regarded as positive, as the inspiration for Oehlenschläger and therefore for Danish Early Romanticism – the Universal Romanticism of 1800–1807. For Brandes the freethinker, the orthodox Christianity (in both Lutheran and Catholic variants) and the orientation toward the past and the Middle Ages characteristic of Early Romanticism constitutes a point of attack in the following chapters of the book.

Brandes' Conception of Modernity
Brandes' conception of modernity is complex. In a continuation of Left Hegelianism, he maintains a social-philosophical understanding of modernity as defined by reason, freedom, emancipation, and progress, but simultaneously operates with an aesthetic-literary modernity that is less unequivocal. The German critic Karl Heinz Bohrer has analyzed this tension between a social and an aesthetic conception of modernity, identifying it is as distinct thread in the German critique of Romanticism during the nineteenth century. Bohrer's thesis is that the dominant Hegelian reception of Romanticism effectively blockaded the new culturally critical and aesthetically radical concept of the modern that was in fact formulated by the Romantics in the form of a new understanding of subjectivity, as well as new literary categories such as the "fantastic" and the "evil" (Bohrer 1999).

This analysis may be applied to Brandes' critique, which on the surface condemns the Romantic experience of modernity and its literary expressions, yet at the same time captures it precisely. During the 1870s Brandes maintained an optimistic view of the liberal social-philosophical conception of modernity, yet soon found himself on the threshold of the artistic transitional phase toward post-Naturalist currents in art and literature. It is common to place a "breakthrough of the soul" in Danish literature around 1890, characterized by a new understanding of art and an interest in the subject and the psyche, which has affinities with the splintered and fragmented aesthetics of Romanticism. This literary and cultural-critical paradigm shift becomes evident in the reworking of *The Romantic School in Germany*, and in its impact and reception history.

Another tension in Brandes' aesthetic conception of modernity is that on the one side he proposes an understanding of literature and art within a frame of a Realist-Naturalist conception of art and literature, while on the other he affirms an aesthetic ideal and conception of form that points back to Weimar Classicism and the time of Goethe. This is not obvious, however, in *The Romantic School in Germany*, insofar as Brandes expends much energy criticizing the Idealism dominant around 1800 in Classicism, as well as in Romanticism. His critique of Idealism will be explained in the following.

There are two constants in Hegel-influenced, nineteenth-century literary history writing: the charge that the Romantics were overly subjective, and the analysis of their lack of anchoring in reality (Bohrer 1999:142–; Ansel 2003:273–). These are both present in Brandes. Subjectivism – that is to say the philosophical doctrine that our knowledge of the world is conditioned by consciousness – is negatively associated with Romanticism by the Hegelians, and designated as arbitrariness, egomania, self-reflection, solipsism, and so on. J.G. Fichte's radicalization of Kant's theory of perception in his *Wissenschaftslehre* (1794–1795) is viewed as the source of Romantic Subjectivism, and many Hegelian critics do not distinguish between Fichte's doctrine of the I and Romantic poetry, especially with respect to Romantic irony (see below). In the same manner Brandes conceives of the Romantic period as "what is called Subjectivism and Idealism, the avoidance of historical external reality" (Brandes 1873:43), and like the Hegelians he identifies Fichte as the spokesperson of this tendency:

> By the absolute I it was understood, by Fichte himself in a foundational yet varied manner, not the idea of divinity but the human, the thinking being, and the new desire for freedom, the self-willfulness

and the self-satisfaction of the I, which with the arbitrariness of the absolute monarch allowed the external world to vanish in relation to the self. This intoxication with freedom comes to a head in a peculiarly arbitrary, ironic and fantastical band of young geniuses. (Brandes 1873:43–44)

Looking closely at Brandes' utterance, in the first part there is a suggestion of the acknowledgment of the revolt against the metaphysical as a constricting program of interpretation, but in the second part he turns 180 degrees toward a negative analogy between the perceiving subject and political absolutism. In the first edition Brandes identifies two early Romantic *Künstlerromane*, Ludwig Tieck's *Die Geschichte des Herrn William Lovell* (1795–1796) and Jean Paul's *Titan* (1800–1803), as exemplary of Romantic Subjectivism and Idealism.

Properly understood, these novels are not well suited as ammunition in the war between action and reaction, because both were more differentiated than appreciated, and they directly address the post-Kantian philosophy and Fichte's Subjective Idealism. Brandes acknowledges Jean Paul, but does not entirely comprehend that through his figure of Roquairol in *Titan* he demonstrates both the psychological possibilities and the risks of the autonomy of consciousness, including in varying degrees those of melancholy, self-destruction, the fragmenting of the self, and madness (Schulz 1983:356–357). On the contrary, Brandes sees the novel as a celebration of the Romantic illness of reflection and its lack of capacity to master reality (Brandes 1873:56–57). It is furthermore a historical distortion on the part of Brandes when he designates the two works as "pioneers" of Romanticism; *Titan* was published only after Schlegel's *Lucinde*, which for Brandes marks the beginning. In the second edition Brandes demonstrates greater attention to chronology by moving this analysis to later in the book, to a dedicated chapter on Jean Paul, yet the negative evaluation of him remains unchanged.

Not only Fichte's philosophy and literary Subjective Idealism, but also the Objective Idealism and the imitative Classicism of Goethe and Schiller are included in Brandes' characterization of the "negative" pioneers of Romanticism. The two German poets flee from a society that has removed the possibility of citizen participation (Brandes 1873:29), and their retreat from reality leads to a polarization of literary life, between an elite poetry of cultivation and a literature of popular entertainment. Here Brandes reasons democratically and sociologically, from the idea that literature constitutes an important element of the new public around 1800.

There is in Brandes a kind of double argumentation that is also typical of contemporary German criticism (Hohendahl 1995:129–131). On the one hand he subscribes to an understanding of literature as autonomous and set apart from societal interests and politics, although it can also be a countervailing force against these factors, a role which had been adopted in seriousness by Romanticism. On the other hand he holds that works of literature should possess a distinct function, as calls to action and as political documents. This tension reveals itself in Brandes' treatment of Goethe, who is described strikingly critically in the introduction (Rømhild 1996:46–47). Here Goethe is accused of creating an abstract and de-individualized, ahistorical art. Brandes thus takes up a thread from the final part of *Emigrant Literature*, where he describes German Romanticism as a natural counter-reaction to the strictness and universality of Classicism. Brandes acknowledges Goethe's passionate youthful poetry, especially the novel of *Werther* (1774), and otherwise praises only his idyllic epic of the revolutionary years, *Hermann und Dorothea* (1797).

In the second edition, however, the view of Goethe is far more positive; he is described along with Herder and Lessing as part of a new cultural departure, in which the Sturm und Drang, Classical, and Romantic periods are viewed in a dynamic interplay. But even in the first edition, Brandes' view of Goethe had slowly changed, as throughout the work he eventually reconciles with the German "poet prince." He employs Goethe's conceptions of form and of *Bildung* as an antidote to the Romantics, especially how they reveal themselves in the novel of *Wilhelm Meister*. The main character Wilhelm manages to form his ideal in tune with experiences of the world (Brandes 1873:252–253). Goethe's conception of *Bildung* becomes the positive counterpart to that which Tieck, Wackenroder, and especially Novalis exhibit in their *Künstler-* and *Bildungsromane* (Brandes 1873:253–). According to Brandes, literature on the one hand should be in contact with modern life and be realistic, while on the other it should poeticize this reality and impact in an edifying manner, that is to say it should form positive images of existence. Romantic art, with its interest in the past and the Middle Ages, its fractured expression "without fixed forms" (Brandes 1873:19), its Romantic irony, its hybrid genres, and its antiheroes, does not achieve this. Strictly speaking Wilhelm Meister is also an antihero, and Brandes must take up its continuation, *Wilhelm Meisters Wanderjahre*, in which Wilhelm becomes a doctor, in order to legitimate Goethe on this point.

Brandes' Concept of Form: Romantic Music and Painting
In his critical praxis Brandes works fundamentally with a view of art that reaches back to a classical and idealistic aesthetics of wholeness. Goethe's harmonious conception of the work – which is tied to an image of the cultivated and autonomous individual (Sørensen 2017:79–80) – is the implicit norm against which Romantic art is measured. It is therefore both the form and the content of Romanticism that is critiqued. Brandes' conception of aesthetics and form becomes especially evident in the two chapters on music and painting, chapters VII and VIII (Brandes 1873:126–184), in which he demarcates Romantic literature in relation to the non-linguistic art forms.

Brandes' ideal is the plastic description, and he himself employs a pictorial language that is sensual, concrete, and comprehensible. By describing Romantic literature in relation to music and painting, he is able to isolate the various forms of representation. In its imitation of instrumental music Romantic literature loses its material reality and becomes "artistic moods" rather than "works of art" (Brandes 1873:136).

Romantics like Schlegel and Novalis valorize the musical principle in their works, that is euphony and beauty, at the expense of meaning. Brandes here reveals himself to be an aesthete of content, yet ultimately demonstrates an understanding of form and of Tieck, who ventures "wholly outward into his madness" (Brandes 1873:144). Illustratively, Brandes then imitates a Romantic text built upon the movements of a symphony with purely nonsense words. He bemoans how Romantic literature lacks "'tendency,' that is an orientation toward life and action" (Brandes 1873:149), yet at the same time reveals a sharp sense for the poetics of sound and for language as ornament – as arabesque. In the chapter on the Romantics' relation to art and to landscape, Brandes cites Goethe's writing on Winckelmann to criticize the so-called Nazarene painters, who in opposition to the Classicist norms of the academy around 1800 cultivated an inward and pious Romantic-religious art. They took inspiration from medieval Italian and German painters, from contemporary Romantic theories of art, and especially from Tieck's novel *Franz Sternbalds Wanderungen*.

But Brandes primarily employs the Nazarene phenomenon as a launching point for a critique of the later Catholicism of the Romantics, and of the older Friedrich Schlegel's interest in "lox, crayfish and wine" (Brandes 1873:167), as well as the Restoration politician Friedrich von Gentz's passion for "furniture, perfume and the refinement of the so-called luxurious" (Brandes 1873:167). This section particularly demonstrates Brandes' technique of representation. By going back and forth between Goethe's Winckelmann book of 1805 and Friedrich Schlegel's biography after the Congress of Vienna, Brandes manipulates the historical chronology and changes the causal context such that the decadent, the elitist, and the reactionary is already witnessed in the young Romantics' point of departure.

Brandes asserts that the Romantic understanding of nature displaces the emotional in favor of the fantastic. The Romantics favor the solitude of the forest and the moonlit night, the superstitious, intuitive, and mystical, but wholly lack mimetic description. Brandes thus criticizes the Romantic image of Italy for not representing the "real Italy with its powerful colors and lively movement" (Brandes 1873:154), but on the contrary "Italy as ruins" and "Catholicism as a mummy" (Brandes 1873:154). Brandes here tests out the connection between actual geography and the literary space of engagement, and between the authors' place of residence and their literary production, thereby entering into the domain of literary geography. This was doubtless inspired by Taine's theory of climate, race, and milieu, yet ultimately Brandes can be viewed as a pioneer, in that literary geography as an independent genre of criticism is normally dated after 1900 (Piatti 2008:68–70), before it was taken up again in the twentieth-century's "spatial turn" in literary studies. Brandes' approach is not systematic, but his prioritization of place and space over time is an important supplement to his historical-philosophical optics.

Ludwig Tieck is especially in Brandes' spotlight. Tieck's childhood in sandy Brandenburg and the "cold and clear days of Berlin along with his modern north German rationalism" (Brandes 1873:170–171) is said to explain why Tieck longs for nature yet does not manage to recreate it authentically in his works, instead portraying artificial landscapes that resemble stage scenery. Brandes puts his own nature program to the test in a travel account from Saxon Switzerland (southeast of Dresden in Saxony), filling many pages with realistic observations of nature. He contrasts his own report with that of an unnamed Romantic fellow traveler (which could have been H.C. Andersen but in the second edition is identified as M.A. Goldschmidt; see also Brandes 1907:106), which poetically transforms the landscape as night falls into a transcendent, ghost-ridden, gothic space. Brandes thus blends the fictive and the essayistic in his literary criticism. This spatial-concrete strategy of description, which demonstrates the opposite of the Romantic principle of form, is also employed by Brandes in his analysis of the Romantic mentality.

**The German Romantic Mentality: Soul [Gemyt],
Longing, and Reflection**

Brandes lays out the Romantic mentality in chapters IX, X, and XI (Brandes 1873:184–282), summarizing it with three dispositions: reflection, soul, and longing. In each chapter he employs a chief literary example that, in combination with biography and cultural history, describes the peculiarly Romantic anthropology that leads toward the modern, Brandesian ideals of personality and art. There are certain recurrent traits in this part of the book: Brandes addresses the reader almost in the manner of the tour guide, and he concludes each chapter with his own manifesto for the modern human personality. He especially cites Arnold Ruge (Brandes 1873:216, 219), one of the severest critics of Romanticism, and employs a vigorous pictorial language throughout that critically mirrors the stylistic traits of the Romantics.

Fruitfully, in the chapter on soul, Brandes zeroes in on the Romantic locus: the mountain and the mine (which in various forms connote mysticism, eroticism, and transformation in, for example, E.T.A. Hoffmann, Joseph Eichendorff, and later Richard Wagner's Venus Mountain), turning the pragmatic into a concrete locality of the German "soul." Instead of imparting a spiritual dimension to the typical materials of the Romantic strategy of symbolization, he moves in the opposite direction, interpreting something abstract and psychological wholly materially and physically. The plane of the image becomes the plane of reality when Brandes challenges the reader to go down into the mountain hollow that is the Romantic mind. This is made into an experiential discovery:

> Have you ever gone down into a mine? Have you ever been led by a man with a lamp down into a subterranean shaft, and by the uncertain light of that lamp gazed around at the expanse? . . . The shaft I challenge you go down into with me is the German soul, a hollow as deep, as obscure, as extraordinary as any other. (Brandes 1873:213–214)

"Soul" is a specifically German phenomenon that is fundamentally untranslatable, Brandes asserts. He places it between conviction and feeling, tracing a line from Goethe's warmth of soul toward the extreme, overheated emotionalism of the Romantics, who bottle themselves up in their faith in the right of the "world of inwardness" (Brandes 1873:216, 234). Yet whereas the French revolutionaries, along with Brandes, understand the right of the world of inwardness as reason that shall be realized, the ideal for the world-shy Romantics is equivalent to soul and thus becomes an internal phenomenon. This analogy, between French political revolution and the spiritual German Romantic revolution, is therefore purely psychologized in Brandes, which diminishes German philosophical Idealism.

Along with this German–French antithesis, a German–English antithesis is employed in a similar manner, by contrasting Novalis' "introspective soul-life" with Shelley's "practical enthusiasm for liberty" (Brandes 1873:244). Novalis and two of his works are at the center of Brandes' analysis of soul: first the cycle of poems *Hymnen an die Nacht* (1800), the six songs of which celebrate the night as a complementary, liberating, and redeeming space in a synthesis of Christianity, classical mythology, and the poet's own mystical vision; and second the address *Die Christenheit oder Europa* (1799). The latter is an oft-discussed vision of Europe's future after the French Revolution, which valorizes the Middle Ages as a time of European unity that will be recreated as a new golden age. This Romantic philosophy of history, with its three segments of past, present, and future, should be understood, however, as a fiction and a hypothesis. Both the poems and the speech entail a Romantic project of creating a "new mythology" that could provide a renewed sense of cohesion in a secularized and enlightened age.

Brandes considers this Early Romantic discourse both anachronistic and alien to reality. He does not accept the works' attempt to escape genre by blending poem, prayer, sermon, vision, prophecy, and meditation. He reads them referentially and according to content, dismissing the valorization of the night and regarding the sensuality as lascivious illness (Brandes 1873:218) and the mysticism as orthodoxy (Brandes 1873:224), yet nevertheless cites long passages of the hymns in both Danish and German. Likewise, he reproduces long excerpts from *Die Christenheit oder Europa*, from both the understanding of the past – not least Novalis' negative view of the Reformation and Protestantism – and the vision of the future. These expansive citations flow into Brandes emphatic demand for "Air! Light!" (Brandes 1873:233) and for emancipation from the German claustrophobia of the mountain hollow of soul toward the political and social realities of the external world.

Brandes introduces the chapter on Romantic reflection and psychology with the same performative zeal, inviting the reader into a mirror cabinet to experience the dizzying effect of seeing oneself infinitely reduplicated. The effect is likened to the manner in which Romantic irony punctures the illusion. Brandes identifies Holberg's comedy *Ulysses on Ithaca* (1723) as a forerunner to Tieck's drama *Der gestiefelte Kater* (1797), which is speckled with Romantic irony in the form of the characters' meta-commentaries on the action and in the segments framed within segments, in which the characters in the first segment act as observers in the next. Brandes illustrates this textual complexity by comparing it to a series of Danish theatrical works from Holberg through Oehlenschläger to Heiberg, before concluding with Shakespeare: "will you imagine such confusion? Think of *Jeppe of the Hill* written in such a manner, such that 'Jeppe' sits and watches *Hakon Jarl*, while *April Fools* is performed for Hakon and Thora, while *Hamlet* is played for Hans and Trine" (Brandes 1873:189). Brandes' psychological method of argumentation is on display here. He rejects the idea that an individual can transcend his own temporality and thus experience several centuries, as in Novalis' *Bildungsroman Heinrich von Ofterdingen*:

> Romanticism thus diffuses the I, spreading it over space, just as it stretches the I over time. It respects neither space nor time. The being of self-consciousness is self-duplication. But this self is sick, in that it does not manage to master this duplication. (Brandes 1873:198)

Brandes briefly identifies doppelgangerism and self-duplication in Jean Paul, Heinrich Kleist, and Achim von Arnim, but he dwells on it most in E.T.A. Hoffmann's Late Romantic, fantastical horror novel *Die Elixiere des Teufels* (1815–1816), which describes the monk Brother Medardus' struggle against his doppelgangers. Here he draws on Danish literature, showing how the theme of the fracturing of the personality is an inspiration for B.S. Ingemann. The crowning example of Romantic ironic psychology is identified, however, in Kierkegaard's double communication and his pseudonymous authorship (see below).

Finally there is the third category, Romantic "longing," which Brandes defines as "lack and desire in unison without the will or the decisiveness to acquire that which is lacking and without the choice of means to bring it under one's control" (Brandes 1873:247). This is illustrated by the central symbol of Romanticism, the blue flower that appears in Novalis' novel. The blue flower does not manifest itself concretely, but is glimpsed, sensed, intuited. Brandes thus critically attacks a characteristic of Romantic Idealism, namely its accentuation of becoming and process over result. Whereas Goethe's Wilhelm Meister, as noted, shifts his ideal as a result of his encounters with reality, Romantic heroes such as Heinrich von Ofterdingen, Franz Sternbald, and William Lovell do the opposite, in that reality dissolves and "the world in the end becomes soul" (Brandes 1873:257). Brandes further discusses Joseph Eichendorff's novel *Aus dem Leben eines Taugenichts* (1826), which is compared to the heroes in H.C. Andersen's *The Improvisatore* (1835) and *O.T.* (1836). In this chapter the telescope is turned against the Danish Romantics' variant of this world-denying poetry of longing, especially in Andersen and Ingemann, but also in M.A. Goldschmidt, Poul Møller, Christian Winther, and J.C. Hostrup.

Soul, longing, and reflective fragmentation constitute the contrasting pole to Brandes' own ideal of personality and art in the name of social and philosophical modernity. Yet he neither dismisses psychological complexity nor defends a trivial and flat understanding of existence, but acknowledges the extreme state of dreaming, hallucination, and madness (Brandes 1873:206–207) as well as loss, sorrow, and pain (Brandes 1873:207). With reference to Taine he conceives of the personality as an association of ideas that creates cohesion between the experiences of the I and finally is held together by the identity, whose minimal definition is "the name" (Brandes 1873:207). The healthy personality must constantly assert itself against attacks from external conditions, just as with illness, and he summarizes his program in the well-known dictum of the trinity of freedom, will, and decision: "if man is multi-faceted and of necessity divided by nature, then he is made fully human through freedom, will, and decision" (Brandes 1873:213). In a similar manner, Brandes rejects the Romantic faith in pleasure and happiness through his Mill-inspired, utilitarian moral philosophy. Lack is an unavoidable fact of life (Brandes 1873:281), but pain and suffering can be alleviated. Brandes concludes this section with a challenge to emancipate the pent-up and suppressed part of humanity from "ignorance, dependency, foolishness, and the chains of slavery" (Brandes 1873:282). The task of the new man and the modern poet is not to long or to dream, but to act:

> The child of the new age will not gaze up into the heavens in search of his stars, nor off into the horizon in search of the blue flower. Longing is idleness, but he wants to act. He wants to understand what Goethe meant when he had Wilhelm Meister end up as a doctor. There is nothing else: we must all become doctors, the poets too. (Brandes 1873:282)

This intellectual historical sketch, in its antithetical style and its translation of aesthetic-literary categories into psychological-mental ones, is of a pace with a broader cultural reception of Romanticism that would produce offshoots in the twentieth century. The analysis of the Romantic as an especially German intellectual tradition bounded against those of France and England is later taken up by Thomas Mann (see section 4, "Reception and Afterlife").

Brandes' Conception of the Individual: Between Goethe and Kierkegaard

Brandes expounds his conception of the individual in dialogue with Goethe and Kierkegaard (Rømhild 1996:48). While he engages with Kierkegaard regularly in the first three volumes of *Main Currents*, in *The Romantic School in Germany* this discussion of his compatriot is intensified. Only a few years later, in 1877, Brandes would produce the first Kierkegaard biography, which marked the beginning of scholarly investigation of the Christian existentialist philosopher as both literary figure and theologian. As Finn Hauberg Mortensen argues, this biography can be seen as an examination of how Kierkegaard fit into Brandes' Modern Breakthrough (Mortensen 1993:47). Furthermore, Kierkegaard appears in *The Romantic School in Germany* as both opponent and ally. He is cited liberally in the first three chapters on Romantic pioneers, in the material on Schlegel's *Lucinde*, and in the chapter on Romantic reflection and psychology. Brandes discusses Kierkegaard's treatise *On the Concept of Irony* (1841) and his *Either-Or* (1843), especially "The Seducer's Diary," which he had read in 1860 during a religious crisis that concluded with his embrace of atheism (Fenger 1980:50–53).

Kierkegaard's *On the Concept of Irony* is an investigation of irony in three parts: first as concept and praxis in Socrates, next in German Romanticism and finally in Kierkegaard's own doctrine of "controlled irony." On the surface Kierkegaard adopts Hegel's critique of the Romantics, similarly asserting that Fichte's subjective philosophy sidelines the objective sphere, that is, tradition, society, and external, historical reality. Fichte's doctrine in both Hegel and Kierkegaard is placed alongside Schlegel's irony and is viewed as a destructive power (Stewart 2015), which Kierkegaard designates as "infinite, absolute negativity" (Kierkegaard 1997:309).

Schlegel's irony was a target of critique throughout the nineteenth century, and thus it is necessary here to briefly sketch his conception of it, which is as something more than a rhetorical figure or literary concept. It encapsulates his philosophy in the form of an "ironic idealism" (Oesterreich 1994:355–356) that is diametrically opposed to that of Hegel. Schlegel's irony, which is developed on the basis of both Socrates and Fichte, emphasizes that thinking is a process that is never completed, which occurs in the interplay between extremes. It is variously defined as, for example, an enthusiastic "*Selbstschöpfung*" [self-creation] or a skeptical "*Selbstvernichtung*" [self-destruction] (Schlegel 2000:97), these terms revealing that irony is possessed of both artistic and existential implications and is closely bound up with Schlegel's conception of *Bildung* (Zovko 2017:310). Whereas Hegel's idealistic philosophy is teleological and operates with a final aim in sight, no endpoint can be fixed in Schlegel's thinking. Kierkegaard reads Schlegel's irony as leading to nihilism, positing in opposition "irony as the controlled moment" (Kierkegaard 1997:352–). This suggests a break with the Hegelian system (Oesterreich 1994:362), and thus in the course of Kierkegaard's analysis of Schlegel he moves from critique toward positive reception, in that his reading of *Lucinde*, in the words of Ernst Behler, becomes a singular "literary delirium" that anticipates the modern subjectivity of the aesthete in his later authorship, thereby nearly annulling the moral and ethical condemnation of Schlegel (Behler 2011:27; Bohrer 1999:69–72). Kierkegaard summarizes Schlegel's doctrine as "living poetically" (Kierkegaard 1997:316) and "poeticizing the self" (Kierkegaard 1997:318), yet on ethical grounds rejects the idea that an aesthetic mode of possibility can support a mode of reality.

Brandes is fundamentally in agreement with Kierkegaard on his critique of irony, which he attacks throughout the book. Yet Brandes does not distinguish between Kierkegaard's early treatise on irony and "The Seducer's Diary" in *Either-Or* (1843). It is difficult to extract a positive or unequivocal result from this text on *Bildung* and eroticism, which in its complex form and narrative structure includes the voices of a publisher and several narrators, yet Brandes sees an equivalence of the whole text with Johannes the Seducer, as well as with Schlegel's *Lucinde*. Both works are for Brandes examples of the Subjectivism of Romantic irony:

> At the deepest level of *Lucinde* lays the Subjectivism, the self-willfulness that as arbitrariness can become all that is possible, revolution, audacity, dogmatism, reaction, because from the very first it is not bound to any power, since the I does not work in the service of the only idea that provides a striving with foundation and worthiness: that of progress and freedom. (Brandes 1873:74)

Brandes cannot come to terms with the dangerous and indeterminate space of communication that irony discloses. For Brandes Kierkegaard's subjectivity, which expresses itself in paradoxes and asserts a "freedom from prejudices," simultaneously exposes itself to these same risks (Brandes 1873:75–76). "The Seducer's Diary" thus constitutes the completion of

Romantic irony and its conclusion in Danish literature (Brandes 1873:49); its only reconciliatory component is that it is held in check by the ethical in the novel's "schema" (Brandes 1873:49). Brandes' use of Kierkegaard is dubious, in that through lengthy citations he in part affirms Kierkegaard's cultural-critical characterization of the bourgeoisie, conventions, and quotidian morality of the Romantic era (Brandes 1873:68–69, 81), and in part rejects his Christian understanding of Schlegel's *Lucinde* (Brandes 1873:73). This same duality characterizes his Kierkegaard biography, in which he identifies with Kierkegaard's polemic against society, his passionate combativeness, and his feud with the national church in his final years, yet criticizes him for remaining within the strictures of religious thought, with which Brandes had previously broken (Mortensen 1993:51).

Another liberation Brandes acknowledges in Kierkegaard is the emancipation of language from tradition and systems of genre, in the establishment of a new literary-philosophical discourse (Lundtofte 2003:210). Kierkegaard's fluid pictorial style constitutes a foundational inspiration for Brandes; he adopts it himself in the biography, which can be viewed as the adoption of the Romantic anti-mimetic aesthetic he otherwise opposes (Mortensen 1993:50; Lundtofte 2003:210).

In *The Romantic School in Germany* Brandes asserts an understanding of individuality grounded in both his own social-philosophical conception of modernity and in Goethe's concept of *Bildung*. He demands a concentrated personality of "unity, will and freedom," but also accepts an openness in the form of idealistic striving and a processual synthesis between the individual and the environment, as in Wilhelm Meister. Kierkegaard's radical subjectivity and his concept of "that single individual" presents a third model, which in its modern expression is of a pace with Romanticism and points forward to later aesthetic modernism as introduced by Symbolism. This modern conception of the individual, marked by loss of identity, fragmentation, and conflict, goes beyond Brandes' horizon of understanding in *The Romantic School in Germany*; Annemette Lundtofte illuminates the paradox that Brandes chooses Kierkegaard, who challenges the idea of a cohesive identity, as the object of his first biography (Lundtofte 2003:190–).

Brandes scholars normally date the change in his understanding of the individual to his "aristocratic radical" phase in his later authorship, which was closely connected to his discovery of Nietzsche at the end of the 1880s (Mortensen 1993:52), yet it is already foregrounded here in his struggle against Romanticism.

Brandes rejects the Kierkegaardian and Romantic conceptions of the individual subject, but is sympathetic to the social project that is found in Schlegel's only novel and especially in the women of Romanticism.

Schlegel's *Lucinde*, Love, Women, and Gender
In the chapter "Romanticism's Social Experiment" Brandes addresses the themes of marriage, eroticism, women, and gender. Equality was an important point in Brandes' emancipatory program, and *The Romantic School in Germany* was published between his translation of Stuart Mill's *On the Subjection of Women* in 1869 and the "Nordic War over Sexual Morality" that played out in the 1880s. At the center of the chapter is both the Romantic conception of love, as found in Friedrich Schlegel's novel *Lucinde. Bekenntnisse eines Ungeschickten* (1799), and the Romantic praxis of life with special focus on the biographies of women authors.

Freidrich Schlegel's novel caused great offense, specifically in its suggestion that marriage should be grounded in passion. The idea that both the man and the woman should be active in a spiritual and physical romantic relationship was met with immense moral condemnation by his contemporaries. In addition to its status as a scandalous novel, *Lucinde* was read biographically, as a portrait of Friedrich Schlegel's out-of-wedlock relationship with Dorothea Veit and against the background of her divorce from her husband, and yet it was not just the content but also its experimental form that earned it condemnation. Nineteenth-century criticism of *Lucinde* is marked by its skepticism, apart from that of Friedrich Schleiermacher, who wrote a continuation of the story in his 1800 *Vertraute Briefe über die Lucinde* (which was reissued with an enthusiastic afterword by the Young Germany poet Karl Gutzkow in 1835). In the early twentieth century the novel was positively reevaluated, and in the 1960s, in connection with the historical and critical edition of Friedrich Schegel's works (ed. by Behler and Eichner), a rising tide of interest in *Lucinde* was evidenced in German literary studies (Polheim 1999:213–215).

Brandes' assessment can be positioned somewhere between the Young Germany movement's celebration of *Lucinde* as an erotic manifesto and the critical reservations of contemporary German literary historians. Yet he reads Schlegel in his own manner, in dialogue with both Schleiermacher's early appraisal and Kierkegaard's later views in *On the Concept of Irony*. There are thus three layers of reception and three horizons of understanding that Brandes attempts to weave together. He is sympathetic to Schlegel's project, but critical of its execution. He affirms the revolt against the bourgeois conception of rational and compulsory marriage, yet criticizes the novel's presentation and language. It is "pale and doctrinaire" (Brandes 1873:72), artistically impotent, and filled with "false starts" and "feeble self-worship" (Brandes 1873:74). Brandes' physical, even corporeal pictorial language and his suggestion of impotence negatively reflects the erotic theme, yet he does not deliver a substantial analysis of the novel's form. *Lucinde* is a heterogeneous collection of textual parts in various genres such as letters, diary entries, dialogue, and aphorisms. Today this is viewed as Schlegel's ambitious attempt to realize his philosophical program for a Universal Romantic poetry of modernity in a new Romantic novel, which also contains its own theory and reflects on its own construction.

Brandes does not, however, address Schlegel's fragments, *Über das Studium der griechischen Poesie*, *Athenäeum* (1797), and *Lyceum* (1798) – just as, because of his Hegel-influenced philosophy of history, he lacks a sense for how Schlegel emphasizes the processual as both means and end. Although Schlegel shares a faith in the ideality of art with Weimar Classicism, his concept of form is in contrast open and disharmonious. Since art should point forward to a yet unrealized ideal, which could be called his utopian dimension (Dehrmann 2017:172), its form becomes complex and fragmentary. Kierkegaard had a greater understanding of this than Hegel, and as is apparent Brandes was blind to it. He does not continue the discussion taken up by both Schopenhauer and Kierkegaard on the relation between the aesthetic and the ethical, for instance concerning whether *Lucinde*'s hypothetical model of reality could be applied to real life (Dierkes 1983:432). Brandes rejects the philosophy of life of the protagonists Julius and Lucinde and thus also "the Romantic doctrine of identity as life and poetry" (Brandes 1873:73), but he only selectively addresses the middle section of the novel "Lehrjahre der Männlichkeit." This section resembles an epically narrated novel and describes Julius' process of *Bildung*, from being a libertine to finding true love with Lucinde and becoming a father. Brandes does little to document his analysis, only quoting single sentences spoken by Julius and Lucinde, which are employed as the launching point for a critique of the regressive Romantic historical vision and the Romantic philosophy of life, summarized as "Idleness, lawlessness, enjoyment!" as well as "purposelessness" (Brandes 1873:79). Yet he also defends Schlegel by way of Kierkegaard, who is drawn in as a critic of the social conditions that have rendered love "as tame, as well-trained, as shambling, as lethargic, and as utilitarian as any domestic animal, in short, as unerotic as possible" (Brandes 1873:80).

Brandes agrees with Schlegel in opposing an old-fashioned conception of womanhood, gender, and love, yet he is not content with *Lucinde*'s failure to work out "any social result" (Brandes 1873:83). Whereas Schleiermacher and Kierkegaard, both as theologians and as philosophers (and Schleiermacher as a clergyman), were anchored in a fundamentally ethical and religious, specifically Lutheran, vision of existence, and in their readings of Schlegel proceed to a defense, albeit with quite distinct implications, of the bourgeois institution of marriage (Dierkes 1983:434, 442–443), Brandes maintains his social critique, positing George Sand and Shelley as opposing figures to Schleiermacher. Thus he expands the spectrum of the Romantic discourse on love to France and England. In contrast to Schleiermacher's idealization of love as a "*Bildung* force," George Sand, according to Brandes, sees it as a force of nature and a strong yet mercurial passion that does not correspond to the fantasy of "the one true love." She would therefore dissolve marriage as an institution (Brandes 1873:119–120). Brandes finds the same program in his hero of freedom

Shelley, who would emancipate erotic love from compulsion and ways of life from religion and empty morality (Brandes 1873:121–124).

This section of *The Romantic School in Germany* – the treatment of *Lucinde* and the comparative analysis of love – anticipates the Nordic conflict over the sexual double standard and equality. In opposition to Bjørnstjerne Bjørnson's call for chastity and restraint, which applied to both women and men, and both before and during marriage, Brandes' camp advocated for "free love." While the feud also involved the new political women's movement, the Nordic dispute over sexual morality should be viewed – as Annegret Heitmann has critically discerned – primarily as a men's debate that reflects the insecurity born of maintaining privileges in a time of change (Heitmann 2006:204). A disruption of the male dominance of literature can be witnessed in the numbers: in the years between 1870 and 1890, 70 Danish and 148 Swedish women made their debuts as authors (Heitmann 2006:203).

In this section Brandes is especially interested in women as cultural personalities, portraying both Dorothea Mendelssohn-Veit-Schlegel (married to Friedrich Schlegel) and Caroline Böhmer-Schlegel-Schelling (married to A.W. Schlegel and later to F.W.J. Schelling). These series of last names show the women's maiden and then married names, and it had long been a convention in German literary history to refer to female authors by their first names. Both women were active as translators and reviewers, and as editors and secretaries of their author husbands, as it was difficult at the time to publish as a woman. The publication of their collected letters later in the nineteenth century led to the beginning of a new literary-historical interest in female authorships. Brandes cites liberally from these letters and can be viewed as a pioneer in the critical reception of these women, even though he adopts certain characterizations of their personalities from Rudolf Haym (Haym 1870/1961:663–). Dorothea Schlegel is one of the few who wrote and published a novel, *Florentin* (1801), although Friedrich Schlegel is listed as its publisher. Brandes was not fond of the work, yet asserted that it demonstrated greater poetic talent than Friedrich Schlegel possessed (Brandes 1873:94). He empathized with her plight and presented her as an example of how the Romantic women were "manlier and possessed more undivided power" (Brandes 1873:95) than the men, and also how they were engaged with social conditions: "they feel more deeply the oppressiveness of the conditions, they are less weakened by bookishness, and they have more practical sense and vision then the men around them" (Brandes 1873:95–96). The women's critique of Fichte especially demonstrates much clearer vision than the men, he argues (Brandes 1873:96–97, 104). Brandes illuminates Caroline Schlegel-Schelling's role as an inspiration for the whole of the Romantic circle with citations from A.W. Schlegel and Schelling, as well as references from her anonymous review of the former's drama *Ion*. He dwells especially on her dramatic biography, particularly her sojourn with the Jacobin Georg Foster in Republican Mainz during 1792–1793, which upon recapture by German troops resulted in her imprisonment. He is fascinated by the freethinking that marked the Romantic milieu, with its ever-shifting romantic couplings and mutual acceptance of new marriage alliances, and yet despite this "complete spiritual freedom from social bonds" (Brandes 1873:109), he pronounces a harsh judgment on the men, whose women were superior to them and whom they had destroyed: they "have dragged them down, have denied them their full attention and their most tender sympathies, providing only bits and scraps instead" (Brandes 1873:111–112).

Brandes' feminism can be characterized by contrasting it with that of Friedrich Schlegel. *Lucinde* – despite its utopia of free and equal love – tends toward essentializing the feminine as the natural, spontaneous, and emotional in contrast to masculine rationality, reflection, and understanding. Brandes does not dispense with this gender binary, but transfers the positive masculine qualities over to the women. By quoting them at length he gives women a voice, making them active discussion partners in his literary history. In this sense Brandes is ahead of German literary history writing, which only in the final two decades of the nineteenth century, commensurate with Germany's first women's movement, began to address the women of Romanticism (Becker-Cantarino 2000:262). Yet the liberal Vormärz writers had treated Rahel Varnhagen and Bettina von

Arnim as iconic poetesses of freedom (Becker-Cantarino 2000:262–263), and while Brandes discusses the former with enthusiasm (Brandes 1873:90), he does not mention the latter (who is however treated in the volume *Young Germany* of 1890).

This gender-determined optics changed in the twentieth century, as real scholarship on female Romantic authors began. Yet the female authorships are typically not included in the Romantic canon, instead forming a separate canonical body, and they are continuously under-represented in accounts of German Romanticism (Becker-Camarino 2000:260–261). In Danish literary history Lise Busk-Jensen's vital work is the first account of Danish women authors in European Romanticism (Busk-Jensen 2009).

Romantic Politics
In the final section on Romantic politics, which includes an inset chapter on the drama, Brandes addresses the national phase of Romanticism after 1806. In the second edition the two nearly identically titled chapters are combined into one reduced and rewritten chapter. In both editions Brandes adopts Arnold Ruge's negative view of Romanticism as anti-Enlightenment and anti-Humanist (Brandes 1873:344). Brandes employs the "fateful year of 1806," in which Napoleon defeated Prussia and dissolved the Holy Roman Empire, as the point of departure for his analysis of German national culture, which is presented as a consequence of the antagonistic Franco-German relations. He addresses the German national ideologues Fichte, Arndt, and Körner, but also mentions the liberal reforms of Prussian society instituted by Karl Freiherr vom Stein and Karl August von Hardenberg. Brandes remains critical in principle of the so-called Wars of Liberation in 1813, in that while Germany is no longer occupied by the French archenemy, that enemy had however represented the Revolution of 1789.

Brandes asks what freedoms were in fact brought about by the wars. They only paved the way for a new system of oppression: "they had fought against the revolutionary tyranny on behalf of the reactionary principalities" (Brandes 1873:291). Perhaps inspired by Ernest Renan, Brandes sees clearly that national ideologies and the national cultural interest in language, history, folklore, and fatherland emerge against the image of the enemy, and that German national character was cultivated in opposition to France. At the same time he himself engages in cultural stereotyping by contrasting French frivolity and freethinking with German morality and Christianity: "since the religion of the enemy had been humanity, the human spirit in its clarity and freedom, the national religion [of Germany] became Christendom, the Christian spirit in its obscurity and compulsion" (Brandes 1873:294). In this volume Brandes reduces National Romanticism to a feudally oriented "knightly Romanticism" represented by the German writer Friedrich Fouqué and the Dane B.S. Ingemann, whose trivial literary characteristics Brandes satirizes as "the psychology of the nobility or of horses, which in any case come off as one and the same" (Brandes 1873:306). In the second edition Brandes exhibits a greater openness to the national and folkloric stream in Romanticism, for example by identifying Richard Wagner as a part of the revitalization of the Middle Ages and by writing favorably in the new chapter on Arnim and Brentano of their collection of folk ballads in *Des Knaben Wunderhorn* (1806).

That the chapter on Romantic drama in the first edition constitutes an interlude between the political sections can be attributed to Brandes' Hegelian understanding of the dramatic genre as the synthesis of epic and lyric, and as an expression of freedom and of spirit (Brandes 1873:308). Brandes employs Heinrich von Kleist and Zacharias Werner as examples, and is especially preoccupied with the former. The difficulty of placing dramatists and poets between Classicism and Romanticism is a result of the literary historical canon of the late nineteenth century, and is defined both negatively and positively by Brandes. Kleist's formal abilities and character portraits are, unlike those of the Romantics, not "spongy" or "blurred," yet "are penetrated by the Romantic-poetic madness" (Brandes 1873:312). Kleist exhibits Romantic individuality in radical form, in that he sends "his probes deep into the points of illness, where the intellect loses its mastery over itself: somnambulism, animal ecstasy, distraction, cowardice in the face of death" (Brandes 1873:312). Yet at the same time the pathological fascinates Brandes. He goes through all the dramas and some of the short stories, most substantially *Das Käthchen von Heilbronn* (1810), in which passion is presented in a compound "that indiscriminately contains much that is laughable, offensive and sublime" (Brandes 1873:314). He rounds this out with a sympathetic portrayal of Kleist's malaise and the circumstances of his suicide together with Henriette Vogel.

Brandes chooses to illustrate "Romantic politics" with individual histories, namely in the form of a biography of the German-Austrian writer and politician Friedrich von Gentz (1764–1832), who later also served as a theme for prominent historians and philosophers such as Golo Mann and Hannah Arendt. To begin, Brandes cites a total of three sources: Karl Mendelssohn-Bartholdy's biography of Gentz; his correspondence with Adam Müller; and two volumes of his posthumous papers. To the Young Hegelians, Gentz, because of his extravagant life and his impact – as Metternich's close adviser, First Secretary of the Congress of Vienna, and coauthor of the repressive Karlsbad Decrees of 1819, which limited rights in the German states – was the very incarnation of the restorationist regime (Bohrer 1989:188, 213–). Gentz translated Edmund Burke's *Reflections on the Revolution in France* (1790) into German in 1795, which would exert a strong influence on the German Romantics' skeptical reception of the Revolution. Brandes does not discuss this, however, though he was – as a comparative critic and literary mediator – cognizant of the intellectual significance of the translation.

In portraying the life of Gentz, Brandes manages to encompass three important phases in Romantic political thought: the reaction to the French Revolution and its after-effects (in Early Romanticism); the national mobilization during the Napoleonic wars and the occupation of German territory (in National Romanticism); and finally the circumstances of the Restoration after 1815 (in Late Romanticism). One must distinguish the three phases from one another, as well as between Romantic political thought and actual political engagement.

Later scholarship on Romanticism has investigated the contemporary implications of, for example, the German Romantics' interest in the concepts of republicanism, peace, and freedom, which were discussed in both fictive and non-fictive texts, such as letters, treatises, and essays. It is difficult to maintain a sharp distinction between conservative and liberal positions among the Romantics of the Restoration period (Schwering 1994:494–495), so the image is much more diffuse than that given by Brandes. In looking more closely at the actual political action of the Romantics, it must be taken into account that Friedrich Schlegel's appointment as Austrian counsellor to Prince Metternich lasted only three years (1815–1818), because his ultraconservative papal vision of recreating a Catholic empire was out of step with the politics of the allied powers (Schwering 1994:480–481). On the contrary, Adam Müller and Franz Baader, alongside Gentz, can be counted among the active Romantic politicians of the Restoration, and through Gentz as the chief representative of the political dimension of Romanticism, Brandes is able to portray its anti-French, reactionary, and monarchical threads without difficulty.

Brandes concludes this chapter and thus the volume by illuminating the merger and climax of the German and French reactions in Joseph de Maistre, in order to be able to proclaim his critique of the contemporary reaction in Denmark and also the transition to the theme of the third volume of *Main Currents*, titled *The Reaction in France*. In the second edition this last chapter is rewritten. The French ultraconservative thinker is left out, and in his place Brandes provides an overview of the three main groups of European Romantics: the French-German-English, the Scandinavian, and finally the Slavic.

Reception and Afterlife

On the Editions

The first edition of *The Romantic School in Germany* came out in 1873 in both Denmark and Germany. In 1887 Brandes published a revised edition in Germany, which became the basis for the Danish second edition of 1891. The history of the work's reception and impact thus has a number of phases, stretching over three decades through the epochal shift from the Modern Breakthrough to the fin de siècle. Jens Bjerring-Hansen has diligently described the complex historical process of its publication and republication, as well as analyzing the context, in part with respect to Brandes' own development and changing conception of Romanticism and in part with respect to the sociological, market, and publication rights circumstances (Bjerring-Hansen 2008). His account is briefly summarized here.

One important reason that Brandes rewrote *The Romantic School in Germany* was the nature of the German book market. When after the first edition he switched to a new publisher, Veit & Co. of Leipzig, the rights to *Main Currents* were not secured, instead passing to a competitor, Barsdorf, also based in Leipzig. Barsdorf capitalized on Brandes' rising popularity, issuing the first edition in three printings, which dominated the market, even after Brandes published the second edition in 1887. Brandes failed to claim his publication rights in a court case at the time (Bjerring-Hansen 2008:158–161). This is the reason that the first edition of *The Romantic School in Germany* is most prominent in the German reception, whereas in Denmark it is the second edition of 1891, which is also included in Brandes' *Collected Writings* and in Jespersen and Pio's 1960s edition of *Main Currents*.

Danish and Scandinavian Reception
The appearance in Denmark of *The Romantic School in Germany* in 1873 garnered little attention. No major Copenhagen newspaper reviewed it, and as Jørgen Knudsen notes, Brandes suspected that he was being silenced unto death (Knudsen 1985:308). The few mentions in the media pointed to the difference between the controversy occasioned by the first volume and the silence that greeted the second, which would seem to suggest that Brandes' was no longer a factor in the Danish cultural scene. These comments also give witness to a polarized climate.

The anonymous reviewer of the Højre-aligned *Dags-Telegraphen* polemicized against Brandes' style of debate, which it was argued rendered his "freethinking" doctrinaire. In keeping with the conservative rhetoric of the time, the reviewer offers words of warning against the looming threats of socialism and communism, asserting that radical freethinking – if put into practice – would be equivalent to "revolution, socialism and atheism, societal collapse and blasphemy" (*Dags-Telegraphen*, November 17, 1873, No. 311:7).

Jyllandsposten turned Brandes' critique of Romanticism back on itself and all of "today's men of progress and freedom," who like the Romantics would take down social institutions such as marriage by defending the idea of free love. Brandes is accused of being foreign to Christianity and the fatherland; he does not understand "Danish spirit, Danish feelings, Danish intellectual life" (*Jyllandsposten*, October 3, 1873).

Lollands-Falsters Stifts-Tidende (July 29, 1873), however, took exception to the harsh press treatment of Brandes, but from the point of view that it could risk making him a martyr, which would only help his cause. Denmark should not antagonize Brandes like the Norwegians did Henrik Ibsen, since a "ruthless manner of treatment" would only win Brandes an all too large measure of local influence.

Fyns Stiftstidende (December 18, 1873), however, defended Romanticism against Brandes, finding fault with his lack of acknowledgment of Oehlenschläger and Steffens as well as his selective portrayal of Tieck. This article is the only example of contemporary scholarly critique of the work, and demonstrates both first-hand knowledge and experience of German Romanticism. A positive review in *Dagens Nyheder*, which otherwise consists purely of citations from *The Romantic School in Germany*, makes the same point about Tieck, noting that the book appeared "just as the hundred-year anniversary of Tieck's birth was being celebrated" (*Dagens Nyheder*, July 6, 1873, n. 177).

It was not until 1876 that the first four volumes of *Main Currents* were reviewed positively, in the new Venstre main organ *Morgenbladet*, which from 1874 had employed Viggo Hørup and a little later Edvard Brandes. The review appeared in a feuilleton published over the course of three days. The occasion was the renewal of discussion over the professorship of aesthetics at Copenhagen University, and the review functions like a partisan brief, introduced with a demonstration of Brandes' scientific credentials.

The Romantic School in Germany is referenced continuously over many pages; the words of the anonymous reviewer can hardly be distinguished from those of Brandes (*Morgenbladet*, February 12, 1876).

The reviews in the newspapers and journals of the other Scandinavian countries were longer and more substantive. They informed Swedish and Norwegian readers about Brandes' lecture series, as well as his modern program of ideas and the circle around it. The debate culture of Denmark is presented as rather more lively than that of its sister countries; in Denmark a book can "just as much" be an "event as political conflict can" (*Aftenbladet*, Kristiania, January 3, 1874), writes the Norwegian author Kristian Elster. These reviews take Brandes seriously as a literary historian, examining his methodology and argumentation as well as, despite sympathy for him, defending Romanticism against an overly narrow and historically unnuanced reading. Elster asserts an idealistic understanding of art against Brandes' utilitarian orientation, suggesting that his Neo-Rationalism, by virtue of its negation of "that which is deepest and most beautiful in human nature" (*Aftenbladet*, Kristiania, January 3, 1874), will inescapably end in reaction. He protests against Brandes' intolerance of Christianity; as does Karl Warburg, who asserts that it blinds him to Grundtvig and leads him to overlook the positive impact of the folk high school movement (*Göteborg Handels- og Sjöfarts Tidning*, August 22, 1873).

Whereas Warburg compared Brandes' work to Hermann Hettner's literary history, finding the latter more balanced, the reviewer in *Sydsvenska Dagbladet* (September 5, 1873) suggested that Brandes had exceeded Heinrich Heine in wit and satire. A substantial academic critique was provided by C.R. Nyblom in *Svensk Tidskrift for Literatur, Politik och Ekonomi* (Stockholm 1873: 401–422), in which he rejects Brandes' blending of psychology and reflection and critically identifies patriarchal formulations in his discussion of the Romantic women. The Swedish writer Arvid Ahnfelt, known for his biography of the Swedish Romantic Carl Jonas Love Almqvist, in his *Aftonbladet* review (July 3, 1873) enthuses that Brandes reads German Romanticism through the lens of Kierkegaard, who shares a number of common traits with Almqvist. In his "Bref från

Köpenhamn" (*Göteborg-Posten*, June 25, 1873), Paul Pry (the pseudonym of Richard Kaufmann) discusses Brandes alongside a book by his German translator, Adolf Strodtmann, *Das Geistige Leben in Dänemark* (1873), which paints a quite negative portrait of stagnation in Danish cultural life. The circumstances surrounding this book cannot be described here, but it can briefly be noted that Brandes himself was a coauthor, in that he contributed a whole section during its production in 1872, when he lived with the Strodtmanns in Steglitz outside Berlin (Knudsen 1985:310–313).

Some years later, in 1877, on the occasion of Brandes' lectures on Kierkegaard in Norway, a longer review of the first four volumes of *Main Currents* as well as his Kierkegaard biography appeared in *Norsk Tidsskrift for Literatur*. It is quite critical of Brandes' view of literature, especially his North–South dualism, manifested in his distaste for "Germanic stove heat and Germanic soul" and his preference for "the south's playful sunbeams and vigorously outward turned way of life" (*Norsk Tidsskrift for Literatur*, July 29, 1877). It is noteworthy that the reviewer posits a contrasting valorization of northern European intellectual history, viewing the "Germanic-Nordic" countries – that is England, America, and the Nordic countries as the true birthplace of the liberal ideas of freedom.

English and German Reception

Two positive reviews appeared in 1873 in the London journal *Athenæum*. Edmund W. Gosse identified Brandes as the finest Scandinavian critic of the age and was in agreement with his view of Danish and German Romanticism, yet he includes a critical commentary suggesting that Brandes overlooks the immense impact Jean Paul exerted on Germany (Gosse in *The Athenæum*, No. 2406, December 6, 1873:727–728). Edwin Jessen also defended Brandes as a religious, national, and personal freethinker against the Danish Christian critique (Jessen in *The Athenæum*, No. 2409, December 27, 1873:847).

Thanks to Strodtmann's quick translation, *The Romantic School in Germany* came out in German in the fall of 1873, and was immediately discussed in *Magazin für die Literatur des Auslands* and *Literarisches*

Zentralblatt. Longer reviews of the first four translated volumes as a unit appeared some years later. These reviews share three key characteristics: the sense that the work's genre is not that of typical academic literary history but of cultural critique; the reception of Brandes' methodology as a new kind of literary psychology; and, finally, an awareness of the different status of Romanticism in Germany and in Denmark. In Germany it was no longer viewed as an ongoing cultural period, but seen more in a fading historical light. A number of the reviewers were well informed about the impact of the Copenhagen lectures and sympathetic toward Brandes regarding how he was misunderstood at home. The review in the inaugural issue of *Deutsche Rundschau* was especially positive. The reviewer, F. Kreyssig, writes about the professorship denied Brandes and expresses sympathy toward his "Modern Breakthrough." He singles out Brandes' methodology as original, in that it demonstrates "die Physiologie der Literatur" [the physiology of literature] underlying the investigation of "Gedanken- und Empfindungs-Symptome" [symptoms of thought and feeling] (Kreyssig in *Deutsche Rundschau*, Vol. 1, No. 1, October 1874:140). Despite certain lacunae and a measure of overlap due to the division of the material into political phases, Kreyssig endorses Brandes' critical view of Romanticism. *Deutsche Rundschau* would in the following decades become Brandes' most important German platform in his roles as publicist and critic. His German career and service as a German–Danish cultural mediator is summarized and analyzed by the Danish Germanist Klaus Bohnen in numerous publications (for example Bohnen 1980; 2001; 2004).

In the 1870s and 1880s *Deutsche Rundschau* became the main cultural organ of the liberally oriented German bourgeoisie, which defined itself ideologically against the social democrats, the conservatives, and Bismarck. Bengt Algot Sørensen has noted that its founder Julius Rodenberg had already assigned the review of *Main Currents* to Kreyssig prior to his formal collaboration with Brandes (Sørensen 1980:133), because *Rundschau* could make common cause with Brandes' struggle for freethinking and free inquiry. Brandes wrote long annual articles in the journal in the years following: on Lasalle in 1875, on Heyse in 1876, introductions to French

Realism and Naturalism (Balzac, Flaubert, Zola, and others) in the 1880s, and finally, on Nietzsche (Sørensen 1980:134) in 1890. *Rundschau* then developed in a conservative direction in its rejection of Naturalist and Post-Naturalist literature, to which Brandes in contrast increasingly gravitated.

Two longer, negative reviews from 1876 distinguish themselves as defensive reactions to Brandes' image of German Romanticism. In Vienna, the literary critic and professor Emil Kuh argued that Brandes conducted his struggle from the antiquated bastion of "Young Germany." In his review he defended German Romanticism against the French variant, refuting all Brandes' characterizations of German authors from Goethe and Schiller forward. On the other hand, he dismisses "der schwächliche, verdächtig naïve Oehlenschläger" [the weak and hopelessly naïve Oehlenschläger] (Kuh in *Beilage zur Wiener Abendpost*, April 13, 1876). Brandes has furthermore, he writes, overlooked important late Romantics such as Eduard Mörike, Ludwig Uhland, Joseph Eichendorff, Robert Schumann, Achim von Arnim and Clemens Brentano, Heinrich Heine, and Jacob Grimm. Kuh's deeply conservative convictions reveal themselves when he finds Brandes' portrait of Dorothea Schlegel all too idealized: "eine widerwärtigere Grimasse der Weiblichkeit aber, als Dorothea schneidet, ist in der ganzen Hässlichkeitsgalerie der emanzipierten Frauenzimmer nicht anzutreffen" [a more disgusting figure of womanhood than that cut by Dorothea is found nowhere among the gallery of ugliness of emancipated women]. In 1877, Alexander Jung of Leipzig reviewed *Main Currents* over three issues of *Blätter für die literarische Unterhaltung,* praising Brandes for taking into account in his introductions the lack of knowledge of contemporary readers, but calling Brandes' treatment of the German writers irresponsible, citing especially Tieck and Jean Paul as examples. Tieck is in his "Allseitigkeit der Bildung, Phantasie, Virtuosität im Uebersetzen" [comprehensive education, imagination, virtuosity in translation] an intellect that Berlin can take pride in having produced (Jung in *Blätter für die literarische Unterhaltung*, Leipzig, No. 22, May 31, 1877:341), and Jean Paul cannot be periodized as either a Romantic or a father of Romanticism. Jung employs the complex figure of Roquairol in Jean Paul's *Titan* as an example of a poetry critical of idealism, which Brandes hardly has the capacity to comprehend (Jung 1887:342). He concludes his final installment with a defense of Henrich Steffens' authorship (Jung 1877:381–382).

Reception of the Second Edition and Afterlife
A new phase of reception began with the second German edition, which was issued with a declaration that it constitutes "an original German work." This is due to the nature of publication rights in the past, which did not protect authors' copyrights outside their homelands; such protection only began with the Bern Convention of 1886, which Denmark did not sign until 1903. Brandes thus did not publish the second edition as a revised and expanded version of the first translation from 1873, but as a newly written work, which should have secured the publisher exclusive rights for the first six years. It resulted in a court challenge from the publisher Barsdorf, to which Brandes responded by arguing that the two works were fundamentally distinct. Jørgen Knudsen reproduces Brandes' argumentation, which also appeared in *Politiken* in the summer of 1887: the first edition's attack on the German Romantics was directed against the Danish Romantics, while the second edition shifted focus from a religiously and politically determined critique to an interest in personalities (Knudsen 1994:405–406).

The question of whether Brandes was in the right was discussed at the time and has been since, and reviewers as well as scholars are divided on the issue. Jørgen Knudsen and Bertil Nolin incline toward viewing the editions as a single work, while Jens Bjerring-Hansen demonstrates that it constitutes an "unstable text" with two separate reception histories, one Danish and one German. As illuminated throughout this section, the second edition includes more authorships, arranges the material differently in partially new chapters, and employs a less polemical style. Romanticism is thus presented as more nuanced, also because it is viewed in interaction rather in conflict with the previous periods and because other dimensions, such as Romantic translation activity, are included. Yet neither the central thesis of a peculiarly German Romantic mentality nor the fundamentally psychological optics of understanding is undermined by this.

The German reviews of Brandes' second edition functioned as briefs in the case on German publication rights, and through comparison with the first edition critically put to the test the argument that the work was original. Whereas *Literarisches Centralblatt* (No. 17, April 23, 1887) ruled against Brandes, *Magazin für die Literatur des In- und Auslands* (1887, No. 4:55) came out in his favor. In 1888, one Dr. Puls published a comprehensive critique of Brandes' uses of sources and his working methodology. He shows that Brandes' citations are full of errors, that he does not indicate from which text edition he is citing, and, worst of all, that he does not cite his German secondary sources. Puls identifies a long series of passages in Brandes that are quite similar in wording and content to Rudolf Haym's *Die Romantische Schule* (1870) and Goedeke's *Grundriss zur Geschichte der deutschen Dichtung* (from 1857 forward), and his verdict is severe: Brandes lacks both honesty and scientific credibility (Puls in *Archiv für das Studium der neueren Sprachen und Lieraturen*, 1888).

Brandes had already before and would later again be accused of plagiarism, and this was employed against him in the Danish public sphere. His eclectic method of working entailed inherent risk (Nolin 1965:59; Knudsen 1985:306–308). *The Romantic School in Germany* should not, however, be judged against academic standards or compared with philologically and historically correct and acute literary histories such as Haym's, but instead be seen as a cultural historical work with a strong effect on its readers. This is also characteristic of the volume's impact on the world and its afterlife.

In 1891, when the second Danish edition appeared, the conjunctures of literary history had shifted. As Jens Bjerring-Hansen adduces, the revision of *The Romantic School in Germany* can also be viewed as grounded in Brandes' sense that a new cultural paradigm of modernity, that of Symbolism and of Neo-Romanticism, had emerged, and in his desire to make himself relevant to the new world literary order. This is clear, too, in Brandes' effort to get J.P. Jacobsen's *Niels Lyhne* translated into German, the results of which came out in 1889 (Bohnen 2013). A new sensibility toward Romanticism is evident in the two reviews of 1891, by the Swede Frederik Vetterlund and the Dane Johannes Jørgensen. Whereas Vetterlund sees more of the same in Brandes' negative view of Romanticism and – using the Swede Per Daniel Amadeus Atterbom as an example – defends Romantic longing as a legitimate desire for transcendence and spirituality (Vetterlund in *Nordisk Tidskrift for Vetenskap, Kunst and Industry*, No. 4, 1891), Jørgensen views the second edition as a breakthrough and a new vision of Romanticism. The youthful first edition was justified in its shock effect on the educated citizenry, which discovered that Romanticism in its "dissolute, fantastic and ironic spirit" was something other than that which they themselves cultivated (Jørgensen in *Kjøbenhavns Børs-Tidende*, August 14, 1891). The new edition, in contrast, illumines a more differentiated Romanticism, beginning with Herder and encompassing many more personalities than before. Brandes is further praised for discussing the translation activity and scientific side of the Romantics – as reflected in the establishment of mythological studies and comparative linguistics – and on the whole the work is characterized as "altogether deeply and clearly understood." Johannes Jørgensen wrote the review in *Kjøbenhavns Børs-Tidende*, whose editor was Brandes' brother Ernst. Jørgensen belonged to the cultural radical milieu, but with the foundation of his journal *Taarnet* in 1893 became the founder of Danish Symbolism, which built a bridge back to the Romantic vision of existence and art. This is perceptible in the last part of the review, which has the character of a poem:

> There are so many threads of the old Romanticism that are taken up in recent poetry. The Romantics' ironic attitude to society has well prepared the individual for the emancipation that is now underway. And the man of culture is still drawn away from the busy streets and daily noise toward the loneliness of the forest and the peace of night.

Brandes' second edition fitted well with the changed climate of the 1890s, in which the literary historians Valdemar Vedel and Vilhelm Andersen rehabilitated Danish Romanticism. Despite his revisions, however, it was Brandes' critical view of Romanticism that was inherited by twentieth-century

Danish literary criticism, all the way forward to the re-evaluation of especially German Romanticism in the phenomenological and deconstructive literary theory of the 1980s (Rosiek 2008:65–).

When *Main Currents* crossed the Atlantic in English translation in 1902, it also motivated reviewers in New York and Boston to reflect on the topicality of Romanticism. *The Independent* saw German Early Romanticism as a youth revolt with corresponding appeal to young readers (*The Independent*, New York, Vol. 54, No. 2800, July 31, 1902:1838–1839). *The Forum* emphasized Brandes' presentation of Romantic women as an example of his brilliant critique, and was in agreement that the women were much more heroic than the men, "as passion is greater than sentimentalism, life than literature" (*The Forum*, New York, July, 1902:81–84).

The Romantic School in Germany has had a peculiar afterlife in Germany. The history of its impact was established in the decades around the turn of the twentieth century. Although Brandes did not play any particular role in Germanistics (Bohnen 2004:157), there was an important contribution to German literary history writing in the figure of Wilhelm Dilthey, who reviewed the first volume of *Main Currents* positively in 1873 and again in 1882 (Bohnen 2001:189), showing interest in Brandes' literary-psychological approach. As argued by Klaus Bohnen, Brandes can in this respect be viewed as a forerunner of hermeneutic literary studies and intellectual history [Geistesgeschichte], as established by Dilthey.

As noted, it was the first German edition of the volume that was circulated in the German book market and read intensively in intellectual and artistic milieux, as amply attested by figures such as Arthur Schnitzler, Thomas Mann, Heinrich Mann, and Stefan Zweig (Bohnen 2001:198–199). Thomas Mann's artistic and cultural-critical reception of the volume constituted a center of gravity for this reception context. Hans-Joachim Sandberg has traced the significance of *Main Currents* for Mann's authorship from *Buddenbrooks* (1901) forward, while Steven Cerf shows that Mann was especially inspired by Brandes' suggestive description of Novalis during his work on the novel *Der Zauberberg* (1924). The Romantic preoccupation with illness and erotic cultivation of pain and death became a model for the figure of Hans Castorp

(Cerf 1981:124–125), and thus Brandes' mediation of Romanticism can be viewed as an important source of inspiration for Mann's ironic understanding of Romanticism. There is a certain parallelism between Brandes' portrayal of the peculiarly German in *The Romantic School in Germany* and Mann's influential work of cultural criticism *Betrachtungen eines Unpolitischen* (1918), with its positive configuration of (German) culture as incommensurable with (Western) civilization and thus with the democracies of France, England, and the United States. As is known, Mann changed his politics some years later, defending the Weimar Republic and thus the first German democracy in his 1923 address "Von deutscher Republik," but still with Romanticism and Novalis functioning as an important fulcrum.

Brandes' *The Romantic School in Germany* has been a powerful inspiration outside of the borders of Denmark, and in its defense of a literature of engagement and its condemnation of and fascination with Romanticism, a continual point of reference in Danish cultural life.

THE REACTION IN FRANCE (1874)
Anders Engberg-Pedersen

Introduction

Of the six volumes that constitute *Main Currents in Nineteenth Century Literature*, *The Reaction in France* is the least literary and most historically oriented tome. Nevertheless, it occupies a central position within Brandes' peculiar form of literary history. The reactionary currents of the Empire (1804–1814) and the Restoration (1814–1830) mark the negative pole in his portrait of the intellectual and emotional life of Europe in the first half of the nineteenth century. The first two volumes trace the steadily rising reaction against eighteenth-century ideals of freedom, first in the literature of French emigrés and then in German Romanticism. In the third volume, Brandes describes the triumph of the reaction. History winds its way from Voltaire's Kingdom of Reason through Rousseau's Kingdom of Feeling, only to end up in a delta of conservative, nationalistic, and repressive attitudes. This delta Brandes subsumes under the term "the principal of authority."

In his presentation of this historical development, especially in the first half of the volume, aesthetic literary criticism fades somewhat into the background in favor of a focus on historical fact and the history of ideas as they are expressed in the form of philosophical and social treatises. Yet this apparent shift in perspective points toward something more fundamental in his larger project. Brandes writes at precisely the moment at which comparative literature is about to establish itself as an independent discipline in Europe and in the United States. He has often been identified as a central figure in the development of comparative literary studies, or even more definitively as its principal founder. But how does Brandes understand what he refers to as a "comparative literary perspective" (Brandes 1872:8), and what role do "currents" play in it?

The theoretical frame of *Main Currents* is a peculiar construction blending together quite distinct theoretical positions. The influence of French aesthetic theory is palpable, particularly that of Charles Augustin Sainte-Beuve and Hippolyte Taine, whom Brandes had discussed in his 1870 dissertation. But Brandes supplements French aesthetic theory with a Hegelian frame, albeit in a modified form. Whereas Hegel had defined the motor of (literary) history as metaphysics, Brandes replaces this with an alloy of ideas, feelings, and moods. It is this alloy that constitutes the essence of Brandes' "currents," which determine history and whose character and development can be extrapolated from literature.

This composite theoretical construction manifests itself throughout on the plane of metaphor. Alongside concepts from the empirical sciences, primarily botany and zoology, Brandes employs a recurring metaphorics of water: ideas surge forth in torrents, moods ferment in the morass, and feelings are dammed up by dykes but soon flood the banks. Brandes develops a kind of hydraulic literary theory to represent the ebb and flow of the main literary currents, for the task of the comparatist is, according to him, to describe through literature the development and the movement of the ideas, feelings, and moods of a given historical period, and to channel their energies into the present.

In its comparative methodology and its peculiar metaphorics, *The Reaction in France* (and *Main Currents* as a whole) is thus simultaneously a history of ideas, a literary history, and a history of feelings of the first half of the nineteenth century.

Background and Genesis

1873 was a productive year for Brandes. In February and March he delivered 12 lectures on the German Romantic school, which were quickly published as the second volume of *Main Currents* on May 3. Now it was time to prepare for the next volume on the reaction in France.

In June Brandes left Denmark for Germany, where he remained for the next four months. Aside from shorter excursions to Dresden and Leipzig he was chiefly in Berlin and then Munich, where he wrote the first four lectures at the library. Since his student years Brandes' social life had vacillated between a gregarious desire for dialogue and debate, and a contemplative hermetic existence. That Janus-faced tendency revealed itself again during his sojourn in Germany. When he was not sequestered in the Munich library he often found himself in the company of the poet Paul Heyse, with whom he maintained a long written correspondence. Heyse's cheerful and optimistic disposition lifted Brandes' spirits, who, as he notes himself, had been in the habit of seeing only "how damned awful everything really was" (Brandes 1907:133).

Heyse and Brandes also had their intellectual differences. This became clear, for example, in their discussions of the relation between literature and the age in which it was written. As is evident from the first two volumes of *Main Currents*, Brandes subscribed to a strong historical determinism. No author existed outside historical circumstances, and literary works were directly conditioned by them. Heyse's response – that the laws which govern intellectual development are far more indeterminate and capricious than those that govern nature – began to weaken Brandes' fundamental understanding of the relation between the particular and the universal, and thus the status of the literary work in relation to broader historical developments. While this change was yet to manifest itself in the design of the third volume, Brandes did revel in the lavish praise Heyse had for *The Romantic School in Germany*, which had been subjected to harsh treatment in Denmark (Brandes 1907:127–133).

In Berlin Brandes vacillated between an almost ascetic existence and its opposite. "There is not much to report on my part," he wrote to his brother Edvard.

> Nothing terrible has happened to me. No one has the slightest thought of such. Moreover I have not visited anyone, which has been made all the easier, since all my acquaintances are away from Berlin such that no one knows I am here again. I read almost the entire day in preparation for my book. (Edvard and Georg Brandes 1972:83)

His German translator Adolf Strodtmann and his wife Henriette, however, also lived in the Steglitz district where Brandes was staying.

Their interactions during the summer developed into a stormy affair between Brandes and Henny, as Brandes calls her. A certain ambivalence was present on his part; nevertheless Brandes wrote to Heyse down in Munich: "I could well do without that person. But were I to succeed in breaking it off, I would lose all faith in anything solid here in the world" [Ich konnte wol [sic] dieses Wesen entbehren. Aber gelang es mir den Faden zu zerreissen, dann hätte ich allen Glauben an irgend etwas Festes in der Welt verloren] (Brandes 1966:67). Brandes initially tried to compel Henny to divorce, but she was reluctant. It was a precarious situation, hardly eased by the fact that Strodtmann had yet to finish translating *Main Currents*, and Brandes himself had not completed the project. They decided not to reveal their relationship until Brandes had finished the work and Strodtmann had translated it. But in the end the lovers could not wait that long. Just one year later the affair was revealed, and two years after Henriette Strodtmann became Gerda Brandes (Knudsen 1985:327–340). In the meantime Brandes left Germany alone on September 30, returning to Copenhagen to complete the lectures. He delivered the first of them on October 28, and *The Reaction in France* was published on February 13, 1874.

From the very beginning the reader is struck by the tone of the work. In *The Reaction in France* Brandes' usual confrontational style reaches its apex; he himself referred to it as "the most polemical of all my writings" (Brandes 1907:143). This is due not only to the theme – the powerful conservative forces he describes – but also to the political conditions of his own time, as well as his personal situation. The reactionary assault on Brandes by a segment of the Danish press, the dismissal of his application for a lectureship, and the monarchical and religious political tendencies present especially in France are distilled into a more combative attitude:

> I labored strenuously, plagued by dismay, poverty, and the hostility of my surroundings. This part of the work was according to the plan the most negative, in that it was the most fruitful opportunity

to give voice to the bitterness that had accumulated in my mind, to my hatred of those who would lobotomize humanity and of the very air breathed by the oppressors. I was thinking of the reaction in contemporary France while I wrote about the reaction of the past. (Brandes 1907:151)

The rejection the previous year of his application for an interim lectureship in aesthetics or general literary history also contributed to his bad mood, especially because no one on the selection committee doubted his scientific qualifications. The objection was to Brandes' progressive views with respect to established institutions such as society, the family, and religion. In his two-page opinion, the Slavicist C.W. Smith, the only member of the committee to have attended his lectures, wrote that while no one could require Brandes to be a Christian, "one can demand of a Danish man of conscience that he not desire to undermine the respect for the institutions considered holy by the nation among an impressionable youth (the majority of which are of the other sex)" (Larsen 2016:90).

Brandes was thus completely surrounded by reactionary forces, including those present in contemporary European politics, the newspapers, and the Danish university, as well as by the reactionary nature of the literary and historical material with which he was occupied. Together these forces incited his inner polemicist, sharpening his pen to produce barbed, uncompromising, and often remarkably well-written attacks on the authority principle and its advocates. *The Reaction in France* is therefore shaped by the dismay and bitterness that the age had inculcated in Brandes, which he tried to transform into a combative polemic against reaction and ignorance. In the afterword to the second volume, written to his teacher Hans Brøchner, Brandes had been very clear: "a book for me is an act" (Brandes 1873:379). This statement could serve as the epigraph of the third volume. With rhetorical excess and polemical sting, Brandes battles against the reaction not only in history, but also in his own time, on the political stage, in the newspapers, and at the University of Copenhagen.

What is a "Current"? Brandes' Methodology

Brandes as an Historian of Ideas

Literature seems to play a secondary role in *The Reaction in France*. In large sections of the volume literary works are notably absent in Brandes' portrayal of the development, triumph, and fall of an idea – the idea he calls the authority principle. He dives deep into the Empire and Restoration in order to identify manifestations of the principle in the historical circumstances of the Concordat of 1801 – that is, the acknowledgment and privileging of the Catholic Church by the French state – and in the conservative social-philosophical treatises of Joseph de Maistre and Louis de Bonald on matters such as religion and marriage. The authority principle has taken such a hold that it now constitutes the reigning idea of the era. For Brandes the Church is the central core of the principle, for in his words this was "the golden age of the priests" (Brandes 1874:337). Thus in the first part of *The Reaction in France* he interrogates the political and social ideas about religion, state, and marriage represented by the Church, as well as decisive historical events such as Napoleon's effort to employ a restored Church as a central power player. Only later does he concern himself with the literary works of the period. From these works he extrapolates the emergence of conservative ideas, after which he rounds out the volume with the overcoming of the authority principle both on the formal plane of literature and on the concrete plane of politics and society.

That Brandes is less occupied with literature in this third volume reveals a fundamental characteristic of *Main Currents* as a whole. He is interested in large ideas – freedom, emancipation, enlightenment – and in the zigzagging progress of these ideas in the struggle against their opposites – authority, reaction, ignorance. In the introductory lecture of 1871 he already declares this clearly: "the central subject of these lectures is the reaction in the initial decades of the 19th century against the literature of the 18th century, and the overcoming of that reaction" (Brandes 1872:7–8).

Brandes' literary analyses in *The Reaction in France* follow along in the slipstream of his account of the history of ideas. In this manner the status of literature as empirical material in the scientific project is made apparent. One of Brandes' central perspectives on literature is to view it as a symptom – a surface phenomenon from which one can extrapolate the more deeply rooted movement of the history of ideas. Because the idea "stamps" all literary genres, "the epic, the novel, the poem, the ode, even the theater, with its distinguishing mark" (Brandes 1874:122), Brandes can say of his approach to Victor Hugo:

> In these initial odes of Hugo let us study less the poet than the age in which he came into existence. They go through the whole of France's history from 1789 onward to 1825 and contain the entirety of the Restoration's official system of views. (Brandes 1874:276)

We might say that Brandes writes literary history in the service of the history of ideas. When he holds a literary text up to the light, it is the silhouettes of the ideas of the age that appear to his analytical gaze.

Brandes as an Historian of Feelings
However prominently ideas feature in the third volume of *Main Currents*, Brandes is not exclusively an historian of ideas. Literature also represents a different and more fundamental phenomenon. The works of Chateaubriand, Alfred de Vigny, and Victor Hugo are symptomatic not just of a series of clearly defined ideas, but also of more obscure and formless feelings and moods. As Brandes repeatedly notes throughout the six volumes, his primary task is "to provide an outline of the psychology of the first half of the 19th century" (Brandes 1890:570). By reading "literary history as psychologically as possible," he believes that he can "grasp the movements of the soul, which farthest back, deepest down and in every case, *prepare* and *bring forth* literature into existence" (Brandes 1873:4; italics mine). Brandes is once again reading literature symptomatically, but as empirical material it has precedence over the philosophical treatises and commentaries of Louis de Bonald, Joseph de Maistre, and Félicité de Lammenais. Whereas they provide access to the ideas, literature can provide insight

into the changing moods and feelings of the period. In his dissertation on *Contemporary French Aesthetics*, Brandes already asserts the privileged status of literature when he writes that "a superb poem, a good novel, the confession of a great man, all these are more instructive than letters of state or political treatises" (Brandes 1903, 13:247).

The aesthetic theory underpinning this conception of literature is the critical praxis of C.A. Sainte-Beuve. In a revolt against philosophical criticism, which had isolated the work from history and from the author just as the New Criticism of the twentieth century would do once again, Sainte-Beuve practiced a psychological criticism that traced the work back to the personality and the character of the author. For Brandes this constituted a wholly decisive shift that asserted the precedence of literature over ordinary historical inquiry.

> Thus Sainte-Beauve's reforms have made literary history, which before had been an adjunct to actual historical studies, into its trailblazer, the most soulful, most lively form of history, because literature constitutes altogether the most interesting and richest material with which the historian can grapple. (Brandes 1882:494–495)

Only in literature can we get a sense of the enthusiasm, the hatred, the erotic spark, the seraphic-platonic coldness, the languor or the downcast self-ironic attitude that an author has felt at any given point. Yet Sainte-Beauve's pointillist form of criticism of individual authors did not permit larger syntheses. Brandes takes the further step of expanding the psychological approach from the individual to the period. From the animating feelings of the individual work he infers the feelings of the author, from which he then infers a group of feelings, which together constitute the soul of the period (Brandes 1873:20). In *The Reaction in France* the poetic-religious spirit of the Restoration is incarnated in figures such as Chateaubriand and de Vigny, but especially in Madame de Krüdener, since, as Brandes asserts, "if as a rule the spirit of an age is typically mirrored in its most prominent figures, then it is doubly so with respect to those whose character is defined by being a convert to that spirit, especially if this personality is a woman" (Brandes 1874:203). In gathering together the isolated literary expressions of the era, Brandes is able to form the whole he seeks: a psychology of the first half of the nineteenth century. The fact that he found the Restoration authors mediocre and regarded the social commentators of the period as nothing short of criminals is of secondary importance in this context. They all, albeit in a mediocre and criminal manner, articulated the reigning ideas and feelings of the age. They must therefore be included, for otherwise Brandes' grand account of the psychology of European humanity would be incomplete.

From Voltaire to Rousseau
On the one side ideas; on the other, feelings and moods. These are the twin components of Brandes' system. In *Main Currents* they appear as two historical principles that feed into one another. The two principles are also baptized: Voltaire and Rousseau.

Employing his usual sense for synthesis and mediation, the intellectual life of the eighteenth century is boiled down to "the principle of freedom or of brotherhood," represented respectively by Voltaire's rationalism and Rousseau's feeling. In *Emigrant Literature* the reaction began with Madame de Staël's shift from Voltaire to Rousseau, with the reaction of feeling against reason (Brandes 1872:167). In *The Reaction in France* the development is completed with the Church's reaction against feeling. History thus winds its way through the Kingdom of Reason through the Kingdom of Feeling toward the authority principle (Brandes 1874:101).

It is important to take notice of the linear development of thought here. The authority principle asserts power and submission not merely in the world of ideas, but equally in the domain of feeling. The whole of the reaction is an attempt to contain an intense feeling, that of revolutionary enthusiasm:

> And now it is as if all that which the heroes of the intellect have thought and for which they have suffered martyrdom should be able to be shoved aside as useless and futile! As if that which had stirred up the noblest of hearts, that which had infused them with

courage on the battlefield and on the scaffold, all that enthusiasm should now be able to be bottled up anew like the genie in the bottle of the fairytale, and that the bottle could be permanently sealed by an Emperor and a Pope! (Brandes 1874:87)

The denial of the freedom to think by the Empire and the Restoration is just as much a denial of the freedom to feel. In Chateaubriand, Alfred de Vigny, and Madame de Krüdener, eroticism – for Brandes the most important literary sentiment – withers into a pale and prudish Platonism, or is moralistically repressed and manifests itself as sin and shame: Eros becomes Satan himself (Brandes 1874:260). In Brandes' view the renewed Catholic tendency either distorts the emotional experiential world of human beings into religious spiritualism or represses it entirely in the assertion of the authority principle. Whether in the form of active enthusiasm and warm-blooded eroticism or of the hatred and sin of the reaction, the spectrum of feeling is as important as the spectrum of ideas.

The Emotional-Ideological Basis of History
In Brandes' evolutionary history, ideas and feelings thus follow one another only to be suppressed by the authority principle. But his historical perspective does not stand alone. As already suggested, ideas and feelings constitute the two fundamental components of Brandes' system, fundamental components that together form a permanent matrix for historical development. Even when feelings are suppressed by the reaction they constitute an essential object of study, in that they represent that which is distorted, garbled, and subjugated. Conversely, Brandes criticizes German Romanticism for its moonshine mood and its wallowing in emotion (Brandes 1873:309, 215). He thus simultaneously seeks "the concealed feeling and the abstract idea underlying everything" (Brandes 1873:4). Here there is the suggestion not of transmission from the one to the other, but of the simultaneous existence of two modes of human psychology.

It is easy to read Brandes exclusively as an historian of ideas. Ideas have sharp contours. As a rule they have an origin that can be clearly identified and their development can be traced relatively easily. Feelings, on the contrary, are diffuse and frayed at the edges, and they morph imperceptibly into formless moods that cannot so easily be identified, localized, or traced. Here, for example, is the mood that reigned during the French reaction: "thus the mood of the period, worn out but complex, full of disappointments, expectations and an impulse toward personal reveries, is not a mood conducive to action, but to meditation and contemplation" (Brandes 1874:243). Despite its complex and fluid character, however, the emotional element has a decisive explanatory potential, for as Brandes continues: "it is this popular mood that *explains* how Lamartine's "Meditations" could become the most beloved poems of the age" (Brandes 1874:243; italics mine). But moods do not just explain the literary preferences of the period. They are often described as the actual subject of history. An author like Ludwig Börne, for example, is merely a passive medium through which a more foundational emotional energy is channeled: "Börne is here only an organ for a feeling that had seized the largest part of the many in Germany who were receptive to enthusiasm" (Brandes 1890:35).

In this manner, feelings and moods constitute the intangible yet effective raw material of history. It was not the soldiers who drove Napoleon out of Germany in 1813; it was "national feeling" (Brandes 1890:21). And when Brandes describes how Napoleon reestablished the Concordat in 1801, he does not first and foremost point to historical events. Rather, he seeks a psychological explanation:

> A change in external circumstances is always prepared by a change in moods and further brings forth still more moods that correspond to the new circumstances. The moods and ideas that prepared the ground for the Concordat were, when it was established, granted full freedom to speak and to call forth similar moods. And since these moods and ideas now expressed themselves in literature, a new literary movement emerged that corresponded to the Concordat, translating it, so to speak, into the language of literature. (Brandes 1874:93–94)

Both history and literature are surface phenomena that emerge out of deeper sources – the moods of the period. Brandes often speaks of moods, feelings, and ideas in the same sentence, but what is their internal relationship? They are almost always closely entangled with one another. A mood can be a symptom of a pantheistic mindset (Brandes 1875:62), but ideas can also be the product of feelings. Brandes cites the famous assertion by the English poet William Wordsworth that the "influxes of feelings are modified and directed by our thoughts, which are indeed the representations of all our past feelings" (Brandes 1875:72). Here moods exist at a deeper level in the chain of causation, for vague moods gradually take on form and become "more defined moods," which again crystallize in still clearer "ideas," which together constitute the conditions for the emergence of the Concordat. However fluid and vague feelings and moods might be, the alloy of emotions and ideas comes to bear a heavy explanatory burden as the ultimate ground of both history and literary hermeneutics. Taken together, moods, feelings, and ideas *create* history and *explain* literature. What, then, does Brandes call these alloys of emotions and ideas, these psychological forces that shape history and structure his entire work of literary history? He calls them "currents."

Streams, Rivers, Channels
The original title of the lecture series was *Fundamental Currents in Nineteenth Century Literature*. Brandes' teacher Hans Brøchner did not care for this title, and so Brandes replaced "fundamental currents" with the now well-known "main currents" (Fenger 1957:211–212). Brandes did not just maintain the metaphor; he also expanded its semantic field to a larger complex of metaphors. Moods, feelings, and ideas flow along in broad streams through rivers and thousands of channels; they break down into vortexes, ferment in swamps, and divide themselves into surface and undercurrents; they burst the dikes of the reaction or determine its countercurrent. Brandes speaks of "the revolutionary current" (Brandes 1872:14), "the mental current of the age" (Brandes 1882:448), and "the course of the intellectual currents" (Brandes 1882:50). Together this multitude of

currents makes up the fluid material that binds together Brandes' analyses and permits him to postulate connections between a series of often loosely related authors and events.

In the introduction to the second volume, *The Romantic School in Germany*, he explicitly formulates the premise and the approach of the work: "The method consists, as is known to the reader, in psychologically tracing the deeper movements in literature from country to country, showing how now and then the fluid material is compressed, crystallizing in one or another clearly defined type" (Brandes 1873:19). Here Brandes articulates a hydraulic literary theory, in which literature and its characters are manifestations in a more stable form of the moods, feelings, and ideas that flow across national boundaries. Thus he writes of Chateaubriand's German-influenced 1802 short story *René*: "again the thoughts and feelings flow back over the borders of France, and on French ground this river is called René" (Brandes 1872:38). Furthermore, the central object of Brandes' research – the literary schools – are themselves products of such aquatic convergences. The Romantic school in France, for example, emerges from the efforts of a number of authors "to exchange with youthful haste their ideas, inform each other of their hatreds, their sympathies and antipathies. And this profusion of feelings flows together in brooks that form a river" (Brandes 1882:22). The task of the comparatist – the new possibility offered by the comparative analysis of literature – is precisely to describe, through the crystallized material that constitutes literature and its schools, the currents that lie beneath them and that give them form and clarity.

So moods, feelings, and ideas flow. They flow together and form schools; they flow geographically back and forth between the European countries; but they also flow through time. The many intricate water metaphors are organized by an overriding historical-dialectical schema that is Hegelian in appearance. The question is how Hegel's philosophy of history coheres with the French aesthetics of Sainte-Beuve and Taine, and with the ontology inherent in Brandes' pervasive water metaphorics.

Metaphysical Water?

It is unsurprising that *Main Currents* has many Hegelian traits. Hegelianism predominated at the University of Copenhagen in the 1860s, and Brandes' teacher Hans Brøchner was himself strongly influenced by it. The degree to which Brandes' intellectual development during his student years was shaped by Hegelian ideas is most clearly apparent from a note in his diary on October 4, 1861, written after his first reading of Hegel's *Encyclopedia* (1817): "Blessed beyond compare to study this, to kiss this book, altogether intoxicated by it" (Dagbog 1861–1863:119). His enthusiasm cooled over the years, yet the historical-dialectical manner of thinking, in which actions lead to reactions and further to new actions and thereby drive forward the idea of freedom slowly but surely, is indeed employed by Brandes as the frame of *Main Currents*. In the sixth volume he describes Hegelianism as such: "world history was one continuous drama, one great drama of freedom" (Brandes 1890:310). It is precisely as a Hegelian drama of freedom that Brandes stages *Main Currents* from the very beginning. Actions and reactions contain their own antitheses, and when a movement becomes suitably strong it compels the reversal with the force of "historical necessity" (Brandes 1873:377).

As Gunnar Ahlström noticed early on, Brandes adopted the German historian G.G. Gervinus' *Geschichte des neunzehnten Jahrhunderts seit den Weiner Verträgen* (1855–1866) as a model (Ahlström 1937:46–54). Beyond borrowing the concept of "emigrant literature," Brandes appropriated – without acknowledgment – Gervinus' overall account of how revolutionary potential drowned in reactionary Romanticism, and how these circumstances prevailed until the Byronic reversal. But more than that: he also borrowed Gervinus' Hegelian scheme of literary-historical development, along with his metaphorics of water. As Gervinus writes in his introductory volume, *Einleitung in die Geschichte des neunzehnten Jahrhunderts*, which had appeared a few years prior, the macro-historical perspective provides insight into the fundamental patterns of movement in history:

> All history, when it is observed in a shorter time span, moves in a uniform manner formed by certain reigning influences. Looked

at in longer periods it draws a picture of continuous vacillation between incongruous driving forces that counteract every instance of the predominance of a single idea by virtue of a governing power or movement. When we look at entire centuries, a steady current in a specific direction, the unmistakable progress of a reigning idea, emerges out of this ebb and flow.

[Alle Geschichte, in kleineren Zeiträumen betrachtet, bewegt sich in einem gleichartigen Charakter, der von bestimmten vorherrschenden Einflüssen gestaltet wird. In grössere Perioden zusammengefasst, gewährt sie das Bild steter Schwankungen zwischen entgegengesetzten Antrieben, die allem Uebergewichte einer einzelnen Idee, einer leitenden Macht oder Bewegung zuwiderwirken. Ganz im grossen Verlaufe der Jahrhunderte überschaut, ist dann wieder in diesem Wechsel von Ebbe and Flut eine stete Strömung nach einer bestimmten Richtung, der Fortschritt einer herrschenden Idee ganz unverkennbar.] (Gervinus 1853:12)

There are indeed many ideas and metaphors that have flowed from Gervinus into Brandes' *Main Currents*. In Brandes, the bodies of water in his many streams, rivers, and channels even flow in precisely the same manner; he finds "the norm of the movements" in the "great rhythm of ebb and flow" (Brandes 1890:571).

Coupled with the teleological understanding of history as the revelation of the idea of freedom, one could therefore easily be lead to view all the metaphorical water that runs through *Main Currents* as a metaphysical entity, as Gervinus' and therefore also Brandes' visualization of the Hegelian Geist (see, for example, Lundtofte 2003:102). In a later newspaper article Brandes himself makes the link:

When I began work on *Main Currents* in 1871, I was still metaphysically minded in my intellectual orientation. I overlooked the personalities; they were for me only the organs of the ideas. As the title suggested, it was only the currents within the world of ideas that interested me. The individual personalities were carried by the currents, swept along by them; they were mouthpieces for the ideas. Their personalities were not of interest to the author. (Brandes 1887)

This is somewhat of a simplification. Because of a dispute over the rights to the German edition of *Main Currents*, it was now in Brandes' interest to draw the largest possible contrast between Strodtmann's original translation and his own later translation, in which he had made a number of revisions and toned down the Hegelian vocabulary. Moreover, in his dissertation from 1870, Brandes had devoted himself to recent French aesthetics and in particular to Hippolyte Taine's attempt to replace speculative metaphysics with an empirically based scientific approach to literature. Rather than a manifestation of a metaphysical rationality, literature, according to this understanding, was the natural product of three elements: "race," "milieu," and "moment." In other words, history was a product of a concrete culture – of the mentality that reigned at a given point in time. Literature, for its part, emerged as a monument to "the manner in which human beings have felt and thought many centuries prior" [la façon dont les hommes avaient senti et pensé il y a plusieurs siècles] (Taine 1866:iii). In his dissertation Brandes summarizes Taine's fundamental insight: "the purpose of literature is to sketch out and to preserve feelings," and thus "history is at its base an examination of the soul" (Brandes 1903, 13:247).

Brandes had his reservations, yet he was persuaded by Taine's more worldly approach to literature. In the place of speculative idealism, empirical science became Brandes' model. When in the final volume (*Young Germany*) he arrives at Hegel, he must demonstrate that Hegel's system "has collapsed and that the all too delicate instrument of its methodology has broken apart in our hands, such that only a few great fundamental thoughts remain" (Brandes 1890:310). In *Main Currents* Brandes thus modifies the Hegelian frame. On the one hand, he needs the Hegelian dialectic to bind the whole work together; hence the repeated invocations of actions and reactions and the internal necessity of development. On the other hand, Brandes' currents become steadily less commensurate with Hegel's ontology and metaphysics as the work progresses.

But not even in the first volume of *Main Currents* do we find a metaphysical rationality driving history forward. When Brandes states directly what the metaphor of the current refers to, he repeatedly points to the reigning moods, feelings, and ideas of a given period. In other words he appropriates Hegel's scheme as a formal concept – as a drama that provides him with a structure and a plot – but he empties it of metaphysical content which is replaced with emotions and concrete social and political ideas. The rhythmic ebb and flow of historical movement certainly recalls Hegel's dialectic, but in contrast to the metaphysical water in Gervinus the fluctuating bodies of water that flow through *Main Currents* consist of empirical individuals' natural psychology.

Metaphors Without Content

It is a curious theoretical construct: French content in German form, an empirical history of literature, culture, and mentalities encased within a historical-dialectical corset. Its complex nature also manifests itself on the metaphorical plane. Other metaphors taken from zoology and botany are quite frequently blended with the currents. Comparing his perspective to that of the "intrepid eye of the natural scientist and the physician," Brandes botanizes literature, describing the "soil" from which literary works sprout and employing literary works as a thermometer to measure "the temperature of the whole emotional life of an age" (Brandes 1873:6; 1875:31; 1874:251). Natural science is the model for the concrete praxis of literary analysis. Despite their larger movements, the streams, rivers, and channels are thus more important for the frame Brandes erects than for his analyses. As the work progresses, the water metaphorics are employed less and less, and when they do appear, it is typically in the introductions and concluding summaries. Thus the fourth volume concludes with an exercise in dizzying aquatic acrobatics:

European poetry was flowing on like a sluggish, smooth river; those who walked along its banks found little for the eye to rest on. All at once, as a continuation of the stream, appeared this poetry, under which the ground so often gave way that it precipitated itself in cataracts from one level to another – and the eyes of all inevitably turn to that part of a river where its stream becomes a waterfall. In Byron's poetry the river boiled and foamed, and the roar of its waters made music that mounted up to heaven. In its seething fury it formed whirlpools, tore itself and whatever came in its way, and in the end undermined the very rocks. But, "in the midst of the infernal surge," sat such an Iris as the poet himself has described in *Childe Harold* – a glorious rainbow, the emblem of freedom and peace – invisible to many , but clearly seen by all who, with the sun above them in the sky, place themselves in the right position. It presaged better days for Europe. (Brandes 1875:526–527)

The reader, who after 500 pages has forgotten the central metaphor of *Main Currents*, is here thrown into the river. It soon becomes clear, however, that Brandes is compensating for the absence of the water metaphorics throughout the rest of the work. In his literary analyses he is rarely interested in specific influences. When he occasionally points to concrete authors and works as sources of inspiration for the works of other authors, he often dissolves philological accuracy in the abstract concept of the current. The river that acquired the name of René in France, as noted above, is none other than Goethe's Werther.

Even though the current plays a wholly decisive role for the cohesion of Brandes' project, it is a category without much analytic value. The works are often analyzed as independent artefacts that may well provide an open window on to the general atmosphere of moods, feelings, and ideas, yet their specific referents and concrete connections to literary history rarely form a part of his large gestures. Chateaubriand's *Le genie du christianisme* [The Genius of Christianity] from 1802, for example, becomes "the book of the moment" in that it "in the wrappings of sentimentality smuggled in the authority principle that would soon mount the throne" (Brandes 1874:135).

But Brandes is not interested in substantiating his assertion of "its colossal success and immense influence" (Brandes 1874:134). Instead, he devotes 30 pages to a sarcastic critique of the Christian conservative ideas in Chateaubriand's epic *The Martyrs, or the Triumph of the Christian Religion* [Les Martyrs, ou Le triomphe de la religion chrétienne] from 1809, where Brandes, acting the role of engaged and polemic literary critic, is truly in his element (Brandes 1874:171–202). Accordingly, he viewed traditional philology with a skepticism bordering on arrogance. Through Paul Heyse he encountered the Professor of Literature Michael Bernays, whose career had been built upon the strictly philological method. It is difficult to miss Brandes' contempt in his characterization of him:

> He had cleansed Goethe's Werther of all original as well as later typographical errors, just as Madvig had cleansed Livius of scribal errors. He was the most passionate admirer of Goethe, and since he was equipped with the memory of a mnemonist, he could recite *Egmont* or *Iphigenie* by heart from end to end, not to mention the ballads or the lesser poems. He knew exactly where every sentence one might cite was found in Goethe. (Brandes 1907:136)

This kind of micrology was for lesser intellects than Brandes. He gladly left to others the arduous work of tracking down concrete connections, influences, and developments and documenting them with detailed empirical evidence and philological minutiae. The current is the category of macro-history and broad developments and as such it is best reserved for introductions and conclusions. In between lie the literary works, like well-demarcated islands on which Brandes can botanize.

The Current and the Genius

The relationship between the broad currents and the individual authors is therefore precarious. Do the authors exclusively articulate the feelings and ideas carried along by the currents? Or are they also autonomous individuals who themselves set the course? In other words, how strong is a current in Brandes' *Main Currents*?

In his correspondence with Heyse, Brandes, as mentioned above, had maintained that the currents were more important than the individuals, because every author is conditioned by the age. Yet Heyse's defense of the individual ultimately shook Brandes' philosophical determinism, awakening within him a slumbering yet passionate individualism (Brandes 1907:128). An account of this is found in the second volume of Brandes' memoirs; naturally it is written in retrospect. After his engagement with Nietzsche in the late 1880s, individual genius becomes much more prominent in his thinking, as evidenced in his later monographs on, for example, Shakespeare, Goethe, and Julius Caesar. In *Main Currents*, however, especially in the first volume, genius is pushed to the side. According to Kant's definition a genius is someone who breaks an existing rule and sets a new one (Kant 2001:193–194). But in Brandes authors are captive to currents, which are so strong that "even characters with such a natural inclination to revolt as Ibsen have been submerged in them" (Brandes 1872:25–26). The genius, who exists outside the artistic tradition and does not draw sustenance from it, remains isolated and wastes away. While Brandes acknowledges the singular artistic talents of Heinrich von Kleist and Percy Bysshe Shelley, they fall outside the history of ideas and feelings he outlines. Whereas Hegel's famous thesis of "the cunning of reason" asserted that reason allowed its battles to be fought out by individuals while it remained securely in the background, in Brandes it is the underlying currents of ideas and feelings that determine the emotional and ideological manifestations of the concrete literary work. Feelings are first experienced en masse, before they are experienced individually.

Nevertheless, the power of the current is limited. In his dissertation Brandes had already criticized Taine for "overlooking the remarkable spontaneous power of the individual genius" (Brandes 1903, 13:198). There is therefore a certain weakness in the argumentation of *Main Currents* when we survey the entire work: authors articulate the feelings of the period, but the period is possessed of precisely the feelings articulated by the authors. By means of this circular logic the historical representativeness of the literary feelings is simultaneously secured and undermined. Despite his programmatic theoretical proclamations, Brandes often formulates his thoughts ambiguously. Madame de Staël channels the moods and feelings of the period, yet she is also the literary source of the reaction in French intellectual life (Brandes 1874:350). The independent powers of the individual are seen most clearly in the position Brandes attributes to Byron. From the very beginning of the lecture series Byron functions as the decisive peripety of the grand drama, as Brandes later formulates it: "An Englishman such as Byron was required to single-handedly stem the tide flowing from the Holy Alliance" (Brandes 1875:20). The English poet is on the one side; the current of the reaction on the other.

That Byron was not just a medium for broader feelings and moods but himself produced them is clear from the analysis. Of all the oeuvres Brandes treats in *Main Currents*, no other encompasses the spectrum of feelings and the intensity of their articulation than that of Byron. Withdrawn melancholy vacillates with choleric explosions of ire and indignation. Of course Byron writes against the foil of the Greek Revolution, but it is by virtue of "the fearsome outburst of revolutionary anger" in his poetry that he inaugurates the counter-reaction that constitutes the turning point (Brandes 1875:515). Rather than being the product of a current, Byron himself sets a river in motion. Brandes compares him to the English philosopher Jeremy Bentham, who had tried to undermine the reaction by speaking to human interests. Byron is much more effective. Because he "let loose all the passions" he was able to "revolutionize minds" (Brandes 1874:349). The broad current again reveals its importance, but now it is the result of literature and not the other way around.

The Byronic reversal is therefore also a reversal in the relationship between literature and history. As Brandes writes of the reaction in the third volume, its literature could not cope with the powerful feelings the Napoleonic wars had awakened. The greatest *Iliad* of the age was Napoleon's series of victories and defeats; the invasion of Russia its greatest tragedy (Brandes 1874:163). With Byron, literature for the first time emerges as the source of feelings that can equal and even exceed those of history. The reversal thus marks the high point not only in the larger plot of the unfolding of freedom, but also in the theory that the individual and literature – in other words, the author – is possessed of an independent spontaneous power: that the author and not the current is the true subject of history.

Operative Literary History
In *Main Currents* Brandes is never able to escape the circularity between the authors and the currents, the particular and the universal. Literary works appear both as the encapsulation of the age and simultaneously as the source of new moods, feelings, and ideas. In different ways, Hegel and Taine had given him the tools that made it possible to erect the scaffolding of a grandiose comparative project, but its execution also revealed Brandes' increasing aversion to his own construction: to the main currents that organized European literature, consigning the literary work and the author to secondary roles as merely well-articulated but passive intermediaries.

Over time, his understanding of the relative strength of the current and the individual, as previously noted, evolved into "its opposite" (Brandes 1887), thus resulting in efforts to loosen the Hegelian corset. But this unresolved conflict is already present in the early volumes of the 1870s. As he was working on *The Reaction in France* in 1873, the tension between his philosophical and his political-aesthetic persuasions was palpable. From Munich he wrote home to Hans Brøchner, decrying that it was the lot of human beings to rise or fall on one of the waves of world history, especially if one found oneself atop a wave about to sink (Brandes 1907:143–144). But at the same time Brandes was troubled by the contemporary forces of reaction, and thus attempted to agitate against them in his merciless excoriation of the authority principle. The introductory lecture of *Main Currents* also makes clear the real aim of the entire project: "the major part of the work will involve opening up a multiplicity of channels through which can flow the streams and currents that have their origin in the revolution and the age of progress, thereby putting a stop to reaction in all those areas in which its task has historically come to an end" (Brandes 1872:28).

Brandes' version of literary history is not descriptive but operative. The role of the critic is not to describe, but to organize history productively in order to put it to use. Like the artist who gives form to the material or the engineer who builds dykes and dams, the critic must shape literary history into currents that flow so powerfully that they can break into the present and transform it. Brandes' hydraulic model now acquires a different function. Hydraulics is not only a technical discipline that describes the movement and pressure of liquids – as Brandes describes the movements in the energies of the European states of mind. It also denotes concrete technical contraptions, in which liquids are used to transfer pressure and energy. It is just such a technical contraption Brandes constructs in *Main Currents*. Despite the deterministic philosophy it is not the main currents in themselves but the *Main Currents* as written by Georg Brandes that must stem the tide of reaction.

The Reaction in France is – like *Main Currents* on the whole – an incitement to action. The model is precisely the poet who 30 years prior had set the reversal in motion. Just as Byron had revolutionized minds with indignation and enthusiasm in his literary works, so Brandes wanted to revolutionize his own age with his comparative literary history. And again, as with Byron, feelings are the means. When Brandes recounts 1848 he does not merely seek to describe "the emotional life and the wealth of moods of the revolutionary years." He also wants to "place the reader inside them" (Brandes 1890:563). According to an aesthetic theory Brandes sketches rather quickly in the final volume, the value of art rests on

> the originality and the strength of that inner life and those palpitations of the mind of which the work is an expression, combined with the capacity of the work to infect us with them. (Brandes 1890:50)

The measure of literary works as well as literary criticism is their capacity to infect the reader with feelings. Thus the metaphor of the drama takes on a different meaning than the purely plot-oriented and structural function.

As in Aristotle's theory of the impact of tragedy on the spectator, the six acts of *Main Currents* must provoke in the reader a number of feelings – if not fear and pity, then contempt for the reaction and enthusiasm for the idea of revolution and its realization in the present. *Main Currents* is itself a balancing act between historical-dialectical teleology and individual autonomy: the work channels the currents of the past into the quagmire of the present, but Brandes must at the same time actively shape history in opposition to the feelings and ideas of his own age, in order to effectuate the revolution of the mind *Main Currents* is intended to bring about. The reader can already sense the enthusiasm for this revolution toward the conclusion of the third act of Brandes' drama, for in *The Reaction in France* Brandes channels the idea and the feeling of freedom safely through the dark years of the emergence, diffusion, fall, and dissolution of the authority principle. "Finally this principle falls, never to rise again," Brandes proclaims in conclusion (Brandes 1874:352). The way was paved for Byron, for English Naturalism, and for the great reversal in Europe's political, emotional, and literary currents.

Reception and Afterlife

Denmark
If Brandes had believed that the publication of *The Reaction in France* constituted an action that would revolutionize the Danish public, he was disappointed. He did have good reason to expect a certain amount of attention, however. Leading journals in Germany, England, and France had discussed the first volume quite positively, and he himself felt that recognition would be forthcoming in his homeland. But when the third volume appeared on February 13, 1874, it was largely greeted with silence. Only two reviews appeared in Denmark. In April the critic at *Berlingske Tidende* praised the book for its lively presentation, for its wealth of detail, and for its review of the literature, but politically he cannot sanction Brandes' critique of the authority principle. "No state, not even the freest," according to the reviewer, can "do without authority," and thus Brandes' book constituted

an incitement to "anarchy" and "terrorism" (Anon. 1874:1–3). Six months later the second and last contemporary Danish review appeared in *Fyens Stiftstidende*. It follows in the footsteps of the critic at *Berlingske*, acknowledging Brandes' immense knowledge, but distancing itself from his – in the opinion of the reviewer – one-sided and superficial characterization of the authority principle. Nearly 20 years passed before Sophus Schandorph attempted to push back against this unfavorable critical reception with a highly descriptive but hardly insightful, yet at the same time effusive review of the second revised edition in *Tilskueren*. Schandorph, who "in all essence shares the author's view of literature," painstakingly goes through the content of the volume and Brandes' formulations in an effort, through the power of repetition, to overcome "all the resistance this work has faced" – a resistance he chiefly ascribes to narrow-mindedness "and that sweet Danish preeminent characteristic: envy" (Schandorph 1893:490).

Abroad
Once again Brandes drew greater attention outside of Denmark. Whereas the Danish Brandes was jeered at for his politics or passed over in silence, the European Brandes was of a different stature. In Sweden he was praised for his presentation (see Anon. 1874, *Aftonbladet*; Anon. 1874, *Ny illustrerad Tidning*), while in Norway for his method that breaks with speculative criticism and places the work in its historical context (see anon. 1877). The largest measure of attention, however, came from Germany. Despite his painful marital situation Strodtmann was hard at work, and in April the first three volumes appeared in German as a single edition. The journal *Deutsche Rundschau* was the first to publish a complete review, praising not just the presentation but also Brandes' distinctive method – his wholly original manner of writing literary history. Instead of approaching the works bibliographically or employing philology and genealogy to trace their internal development, the reviewer writes, Brandes focuses on the "restless mental labor" and "the main changes in moods and mental currents" that condition the development of literature ["rastlose Gedankenarbeit," "die maßgebenden Stimmungswechsel und Geistesströmungen"] (Kreyssig 1874:140).

Despite the accolades there were also critical voices. Overall the German critics praised *The Reaction in France* at the expense of the previous volume on German Romanticism. Brandes was accused, not entirely incorrectly, of a thinly veiled Francophilia that disfigured his reading of German literature. Moreover, it was noted that he took much of his inspiration from other critics and historians, such as Gervinus (see Anon. 1874; Jung 1877; Kuh 1876).

Later Reception

A second wave of reviews appeared in the 1890s, this time of all six volumes. These reviews were written in retrospect and are just as concerned with the historical impact of *Main Currents*. There is general agreement on the enormous significance of the work in Germany. It is presented as an epochal work, decisive for the introduction of Taine's methods in Germany and the best guide to the European literature of the first half of the nineteenth century (see Anon. 1893; Anon. 1894; Morgenstern 1894; Sauer 1898). Especially interesting, however, is Franz Mehring's judgment in *Neue Zeit* that the overarching construction of the work does not hold up to closer scrutiny (Mehring 1893–184:311). Some years later, the German literary scholar Samuel Lublinski followed up with a devastating critique of Brandes' methodology. In 1899 and 1900 Lublinski published *Literatur und Gesellschaft im 19. Jahrhundert* – the first systematic sociological literary history. Having read reviews that elevated Brandes at the expense of his own work, Lublinski was quick to respond. He levels his accusation in no uncertain terms: "I contend that Georg Brandes doesn't know the slightest about *fundamental* currents. What he does know something about is precisely the opposite – *superficial* currents" [Ich behaupte, Georg Brandes hat von *Grund*strömungen keine Ahnung. Was er kennt, ist das Gegenteil davon: die *Ober*strömung] (Lublinski 1900:872). In other words, Brandes only observed the superficial currents as they appeared in literary-political salons. The moods of the salon were all he analyzed. A fundamentally sociological literary history like Lublinski's is, on the contrary, concerned with mass phenomena. It dives deep into the intellectual mass psychology of the age in all its manifestations. Lublinski asserts that he himself presents empirical material en masse, while Brandes offers close readings of only a handful of authors and then supplements his readings with anecdotes. Brandes' conception of Romanticism is thus "as if it had been shot out of a pistol" [Freilich ist bei ihm die Romantik wie aus der Pistole herausgeschossen] (Lublinski 1900:873). Brandes never shows what the currents actually consist of, how they are connected, or how they develop. They remain empty postulates and the slogans of an exclusive group of authors tell us nothing about them.

Brandes and Comparative Literature
The critique of the current as a concept and thus of Brandes' methodology points both sideways and forward. The long gestation period of *Main Currents* between 1871 and 1890 coincided with the institutionalization of comparative literature as an independent discipline. In 1877 in Hungary Hugo Meltzl founded its first journal, *Comparative Literary Journal* (after 1879 *Acta Comparationis Litterarum Universarum*); in 1886 H.M. Posnett's book *Comparative Literature* was published; a year later in Germany Max Koch founded *Zeitschrift für vergleichende Literaturgeschichte*; and in France the first professorship in Littératures Modernes Comparées was established in 1896 in Lyon. On the other side of the Atlantic a professor at Cornell taught "General and Comparative Literature" from 1871, just as Brandes delivered his first lectures in Copenhagen. And in 1890, the same year the sixth and final volume appeared, the first American Department of Comparative Literature was founded at Harvard University.

Given the transnational perspective and broad international impact of *Main Currents*, Brandes was therefore counted among the founders of the discipline, if not "le père du comparatisme" – the father of comparative literature (Madsen 2004:65).

Yet the ambivalence that characterized the contemporary reception of Brandes' methodology also manifested itself later on. On the one hand, his originality and ingenuity is credited with opening up a wholly new manner of reading literature. On the other, his concept of the current is criticized as empty and incoherent. Upon Brandes' death in 1927, Fernand Baldensperger wrote that his work was obsolete "because of the superficial level of its information and because of the all too fragile structure" [par sa superficialité d'information et par la structure trop légère de sa bâtisse] (Baldensperger 1927:370). And in an echo of Lublinski, René Wellek wrote in 1955 that the sociology of literature did not lose much with the passing of Georg Brandes. While he possessed a large measure of psychological insight and "a power of marshalling currents and movements," Wellek's final verdict is that Brandes was merely "a middleman without originality and substance" (Wellek 1955:368–369, 357).

Brandes remains an ambiguous figure in the history of comparative literature. However much he was fêted internationally in his time, he and his *Main Currents* quickly vanished into thin air after his death. Nevertheless, Brandes' method, with the current as its central element, at once maligned and admired, demonstrates an aspect that has remained essential to the field: the necessity of methodological experimentation.

When Erich Auerbach, upon the publication in 1946 of his *Mimesis: Dargestellte Wirklichkeit in der abendländische Literatur*, assumed the status of the central figure in the history of comparative literature, it was by virtue of a work that in various ways differs significantly from *Main Currents*. Auerbach's focus is stylistics, and he operates with neither a concept of the current nor an overarching historical-dialectical frame. Yet like Brandes he lifts his gaze from the national state and adopts a European perspective, and in his own way he attempts a coupling of minute *explications de texte* with the contextualization of social history and the history of ideas. And as with Brandes, Auerbach's key concepts, such as mimesis, representation, and reality, are vaguely defined, shape-shifting entities. Nevertheless *Mimesis* remains a standard reference in the history of the discipline. Auerbach managed to transform the problem of method into a hitherto undiscovered opportunity, namely the synthesis of European literary history across language, geography, and time. With this ingenious maneuver, he and comparative literature have an important forerunner in Brandes' currents.

NATURALISM IN ENGLAND (1875)
Robert William Rix

Introduction

Naturalism in England, the volume on literature in the English language as it had developed at the beginning of the nineteenth century, was published at the end of 1875. While the title might suggest that the theme is "English" literature, it is in fact more broadly the literature of Great Britain, since in addition to the English poets Brandes includes in his analytic portraits the Scottish author Walter Scott and the Irishman Thomas Moore (Ireland having been ruled by Westminster until 1922). Since Brandes places much emphasis on the national strain in the authorships he treats, it is thus more correct to refer to the volume as an analysis of *British* literature, as shall be maintained hereafter.

Of the six volumes of *Main Currents*, three are concerned with French literature, two with German and only one with British. Thus, there appears to be an imbalance in the respective significance attributed to the three national literatures. That the *Morgenbladet* reviewer (perhaps Edvard Brandes?) can ultimately assert that *Naturalism in England* is the "fourth, greatest, and most important volume in Brandes' work" is attributable to the fact that it contains the portrait of George Gordon Byron (after 1798 Lord Byron), the hero of freedom who constitutes the culmination of the movements in European intellectual life that Brandes had described in the earlier volumes. This is already anticipated in the introductory lecture to *Emigrant Literature* (1872), in which Lord Byron's works are said to mark a turning point.

In the 1923 edition of the first volume of *Main Currents* (*Emigrant Literature*), Brandes reflects on his entire project as constituting a "piece of the history of the European soul" (Brandes 1923:3) as anchored in politics. Already in the original edition of 1872 he makes it clear that the literary production of the era must be seen as the decisive factor in "the final victory of freethinking" (Brandes 1872:7). Byron's poetry is an important part of this development, since it was published at a time in which religion and authoritarian ideas had trampled revolutionary sentiments under foot, thus once again establishing a dominant position. Byron signals the return of freethinking, after which the continental revolutions of 1848 put an end to tyranny and to captive intellectual life in many places across Europe. Only Denmark remained unchanged and thus weighed down by reactionary sentiments.

"Naturalism," the unifying principle in the volume, is Brandes' name for a literary orientation that breaks with the traditions that constantly limit the possibilities of human development and novelty (it is in the natural landscape, at sea, and among the animals that we can distance ourselves from society and reconstruct the subjugated self). The Anglophone authors are treated not just for their literary qualities but also for their indirect as well as direct political engagement.

As much as *Naturalism in England* is a literary history, it is also a defense of engaged and socially critical poetry, which serves as an example that may move the Danish reader to employ literary art in a new manner.

Background and Genesis

Agony and Inspiration

The lectures that formed the basis of *Naturalism in England* were given in the spring of 1874 and, after a stay in Germany, in April and October of 1875; the volume appeared on November 12, 1875. Brandes himself relates that his collection of the material took place under "unfavorable conditions," as he was staying with his parents in Krystalgade, Copenhagen, in a little room with a view of a garden wall and with the constant "hellish racket" of a piano teacher in the background (Brandes 1907:154). 1875 was a year in which Brandes' marital agonies worsened and he was plagued by several small ailments, such as diphtheria and a paralysis of the palette that made it difficult to speak (Brandes 1907:174). There was briefly hope of an opening in the impasse concerning Brandes' application to the university when a new Minister of Culture, J.C.H. Fischer (1814–1885), was appointed to serve in J.B.S. Estrup's government. Because Fischer was in an unmarried relationship he was considered a "freethinker," yet any possibility of a more tolerant attitude toward Brandes and his application was soon extinguished when one of his old opponents, Hans Lassen Martensen, Bishop of Sjælland, intervened in the matter.

There was, however, a silver lining. While Brandes was working on the English-language material, Frederik Hegel, director of the Gyldendal publishing house, arranged for him to found the cultural journal *Det nittende Aarhundrede: Maanedsskrift for Literatur and Kritik*, which was published between 1874 and 1877. Brandes and his brother Edvard became the editors of the new periodical, which was intended to be a channel for the liberal and anti-clerical side in the culture war that was also written into the fabric of *Main Currents*. In one of the issues, Brandes published an essay on the English poet Percy Bysshe Shelley (Brandes 1875b), who was presented as a forerunner of such progressive attitudes. The essay was based on the two-hour lecture on the poet that Brandes had delivered at the Studenterforening in April. While most Danish readers were aware of authors like Walter Scott and Lord Byron, Shelley remained as good as unknown, as only a few sporadic examples of his poetry had been translated into Danish. Brandes' Studenterforeningen lecture was thus erroneously billed as an address on "Schelling" (Brandes 1907:174), the German Romantic and philosopher much better known in Denmark.

It is evident that Brandes had only become acquainted with many of the poems treated in *Naturalism in England* shortly before the publication of the volume. Yet he was already familiar, to greater or lesser degrees, with many of the authors themselves. An 1861 note in his diary, for example, indicates that he had read a biographical article on Shelley in *Fædrelandet* (Dagbog 1861:100). But it was the personal meeting with the English critic and author Edmund Gosse (1849–1928) that proved decisive in the shaping of *Naturalism in England*. Gosse, who had learned Danish and was interested in Scandinavian literature, visited several Danish authors, making contact with Brandes in May of 1874. Brandes ascribes great significance to the meetings in his *Memoirs*: "Gosse's visit provided a new opening for my study of English poetry. His enthusiasm struck a chord with me" (Brandes 1907:157). The two men arranged to read their respective national literatures aloud to one another. Gosse relates that during their morning meetings he recited, among others, Shelley, William Wordsworth, and A.C. Swinburne. He especially recalls an episode in which he read Shelley's "Ode to the West Wind," which was unknown to Brandes at that point. During the recitation Brandes "shivered with pleasure," and upon its final line fell back on the sofa, entranced by the beauty of the poem (Gosse 1911:288–289). Brandes would later refer to this ode as Shelley's "mightiest poem" (Brandes 1875a:324–325).

It was Gosse who provided Brandes with insight into how British authors were generally viewed and judged. He also gave Brandes the incentive to revise the canon. Thus, in his *Memoirs* Brandes writes that Gosse "was the first who taught me how much more highly the artists of modern England esteemed Shelley, Keats and Coleridge than Byron, and how strongly the bourgeoisie preferred Wordsworth to him" (Brandes 1907:157). In the revolt against petit bourgeois values that is writ large in *Naturalism in England*, it is precisely Byron who comes to the forefront and Wordsworth who is downgraded.

The English Language
If the analysis of the British material receives less attention from the author – measured in terms of page count – than German and French literature, it is partly due to the generally lesser impact English literature exerted in Denmark of the 1870s. Yet in the second half of the nineteenth century a rising number of Danish translations from English were published, both of Romantic and of contemporary literature (see Downs 1948).

One unavoidable question in this context concerns Brandes' reasons for writing *Naturalism in England*. His knowledge of English was limited. English teaching had not been a part of his schooling, as French and German were the common foreign languages of Denmark. Yet there was a rising acknowledgment of the importance of English. Copenhagen University established a professorship of English in 1851, which was occupied by the eccentric George Stephens, and in 1864 it first became possible to choose English as an elective in the school system (Rasmussen 2003:83–84). Even though Brandes had acquired solid competence in reading English, his command of the spoken language was lacking. During a three-week visit to England in 1870 when he had met the utilitarian philosopher John Stuart Mill, whose *The Subjection of Women* he had translated into Danish, they spoke French together.

Gosse recalls from his time in Copenhagen that "Brandes had a good knowledge of literary English and was accustomed to the pronunciation, but he did not trust himself to talk." Therefore they spoke Danish when they met. Gosse also mentions that Brandes had difficulty grasping the metrics of English poetry and was especially tone deaf to one metrical foot, the anapaest. In an 1895 appearance at the London Author's Club, 20 years after the publication of *Naturalism in England*, Brandes acknowledged that: "Although I, as you can hear, speak English quite poorly, I can reassure you that I read it with ease" (Brandes 1905:428).

In the volume on British literature, it can be observed that the section that had been used as the basis of the Shelley lecture at the Studenterforening primarily provides the readers with Danish prose renderings or paraphrases of the poems so that Brandes would not have read aloud too many direct quotations from the English. In his correspondence with his soon-to-be wife, Henriette Strodtmann, Brandes noted that he had used a German translation of Shelley's works, but had found that the poet was awful in this language (cited in Nolin 1965:195).

Method, Canon, and Conceptual Apparatus

A Characterization of Naturalism in England

In *Naturalism in England* we witness the culmination of the thinking Brandes set out in the previous volume, *The Reaction in France*, in which he discusses the return of authoritarian ideas. Naturalism is the literary mode Brandes sees as the means of realizing freethinking. He thus begins the volume by describing the political situation in Britain at the beginning of the nineteenth century: the tyranny of the Church and the monarchy, the fear of revolution among the establishment classes, and the imperialistic tendencies. Political domination and cultural stagnation function as the point of departure for the selection of authors to be treated in the volume. The authors are evaluated according to their ability to reflect how the dominant class exerts political power.

As noted, Brandes attributes great political and cultural significance to Byron's works, which were published between 1807 and his death in 1824. Yet the subtitle of *Naturalism in England*, "Byron and his Group," is misleading, since the poets were not a cohesive group and many of the older authors were deeply critical of George Gordon Byron. But with his chosen title Brandes signals his underlying agenda: the nature-oriented literature from the beginning of the nineteenth century can be understood as an overture to Byron, whose poetry constitutes the climax of the book. This model of analysis, which has a clear goal in sight, appears to justify Brandes holding up Byron's poetry as a yardstick for the other naturalistic authors in the volume in a manner that is always unfavorable to them.

The material in *Naturalism in England* falls into two sections, although with respect both to page count or to Brandes' judgment they are hardly equal. The first and shortest section addresses the first generation of nature poets, the so-called "Lake Poet School," as they were dubbed by the influential Edinburgh critic Francis Jeffrey. This group includes William Wordsworth, Samuel Taylor Coleridge, and Robert Southey, each who were connected to the Lake District of northwest England. In reality they never constituted an actual "school" with a common program, but in Brandes' view they all shared a decline from radical sympathies in their youth toward a later conservative ideology. Brandes also sees the Scottish writer Walter Scott as belonging to this old guard.

Despite the immense literary significance of these authors, they are for Brandes political apostates, and discussion of them functions in part as a prelude to the second half of the volume, in which the younger generation of poets is addressed. The first of these young poets is John Keats. He is followed by a chapter on the Irishman Thomas Moore, who is viewed as an erotic poet but whose political rebelliousness provides Brandes with an occasion for a long historical commentary on Irish Rebellion at the turn of the nineteenth century. The cultural-historical development that Brandes describes builds to a crescendo via the controversial poet Shelley, after which the volume culminates in a 170-page treatment of Byron. That Byron would be placed so prominently in *Main Currents* had already been presaged in *The Reaction in France*:

> In Napoleon positive greatness had fallen, the real hero of an age vanished from the Earth. Human admiration was as empty as a pedestal from which the statue had been removed. Lord Byron occupied the empty space anew with the fantastical greatness of the hero. Napoleon had replaced Werther, René and Faust; the promethean and desperate heroism of Byron replaced Napoleon. He was marvelously attuned to the needs of the age. (Brandes 1874:348)

Literary-Historical Methodology: Hippolyte Taine

A general tendency in the nineteenth century was to tie literary studies to historical empiricism and to leave aesthetics to philosophy. Brandes' method of literary criticism incorporates that of the French critic Charles-Augustin Sainte-Beuve (1804–1869), who is especially associated with a biographical approach to literature. Yet with respect to Byron, Brandes cultivates an exorbitantly admiring approach that is thus distinguished from his attitude to Sainte-Beuve.

The other great source of inspiration is Hippolyte Taine (1828–1898), whom Brandes had addressed in his dissertation of 1870, and with whom he had both corresponded as well as met personally. In the fourth volume of Taine's *Histoire de la littérature anglaise* [The History of English Literature], published in 1864, early nineteenth-century literature is described as a part of "l'âge moderne" [the modern age], which involved not only a break with

Neoclassical forms in poetry but also a flourishing of new revolutionary thoughts. It is this same frame of understanding we find in Brandes' writing. Many of the literary figures are also the same, and the greatest poet, toward whom all early nineteenth-century poetry pointed, is Byron – the only figure to warrant his own chapter in Taine's account of the period.

The systematic method of literary criticism that Brandes implicitly employs in his analysis can also be traced back to Taine, including the three main principles of the understanding of literary production: "race" (national character), "milieu" (the author's environment), and "moment" (the historical circumstances). It is within these three parameters that the author should be understood, as well as the national tradition of which the author is a part. Yet Brandes broadens the literary-critical scope, for whereas Taine sees the literary product as the final result of the three conditions, Brandes emphasizes how the work is subsequently transmitted, and how it influences and inspires later authors. Brandes judges works according to their ability to inspire political debate, which is the criterion that distinguishes him from Taine's more apolitical criticism (see Levin 1963:13–14; Wellek 1968:359).

Taine's concept of "race" receives a measure of special attention from Brandes. Thus, he suggests that Walter Scott, through his "detective's gaze," attempted to capture in his historical novels concepts such as the "natural substance" and "psychology of the folk" (Brandes 1875a:183). These national traits are in part the result of climactic and hereditary circumstances. Taine describes, for example, Byron's rebellious instinct as springing from the cold northern climate: it affected his pride, gave his powers of representation a wildness, sharpened his appetite for destruction, and fostered the kind of frenzy in him that had driven the Scandinavian berserkers, who had conquered and settled England (Taine 1864:528–529). Brandes also refers to Byron's Scandinavian ancestors, when he infers that the poet chose to become an officer in the Greek War of Independence, because "the Viking blood in his veins could not give him peace until he himself had become a Viking king just the like the Normans from whom he descended" (Brandes 1875a:479–480).

Taine received some attention in Denmark during the second half of the nineteenth century. His analyses of Alfred Lord Tennyson and Alfred de Musset were translated by Rudolf Schmidt and published in the anthology *Stories and Sketches* in 1867. And as Brandes began writing *Naturalism in England*, H.S. Vodskov's translation of Taine's *The History of English Literature* (4 vols, 1874–1877) was already in the works.

On the whole, literary histories like Taine's were much appreciated in late nineteenth-century Denmark. Julius Paludan, for example, published *A Sketch of the History of French National Literature* in 1874, and part of the same period is covered in *French Literature of the 18th Century* (1876), which is an excerpt H. Schwanenflügel had translated from Hermann Hettner's highly esteemed *Literaturgeschichte des achtzhenten Jahrhunderts* (1856–1870). Methodologically, Taine also inspired writers other than Brandes in Denmark, including the professor of literary history Valdemar Vedel (1865–1942) and especially those who worked on the cultural ideals of the Middle Ages.

The Physiognomic Approach

Another largely overlooked strand that Brandes borrowed from Taine is the physiognomic approach to the analysis of authorships. This is the idea that the physical appearance of a poet will be reflected in his work. *The History of English Literature* begins with a long passage on how the inner man can be extrapolated from the outer, which leads to a formulation of the three elements of literary analysis described above.

Physiognomically-oriented literary criticism is not limited to Taine, but was a theme within French, German, and English criticism throughout the nineteenth century (Tylor 1982:82–122). Brandes many times introduces his author portraits with a description of the poet's external appearance in order to understand the anatomy of his work. For example, we learn that Keats' "appearance corresponded to the impression we now receive from his poetry." Brandes describes the "earthy and heavy-footed Keats" as having "a broad and powerful chest with strong shoulders (…) eyes large, glowing and dark blue and glinting with strong palpitations of the mind"

(Brandes 1875a:203–204). This can be compared with Brandes' portrayal of the "sensuality" in Keats' poetry, which stands out as "sturdy and heavy" (Brandes 1875a:208) and expresses the enjoyment of all the impressions the physiological senses can discover (Brandes 1875a:210–212).

In contrast to Keats, we encounter "the ethereal and feminine Shelley," who is a "slender, delicate and small-shouldered figure" (Brandes 1875a:203), and whose eye is "womanly and almost seraphic in its gaze" (Brandes 1875a:307). This coheres nicely with his poetry, in which his hero Alastor is "the spirit of the wind and the air with luminous eyes, refreshing breath and a light gait" (Brandes 1875a:315). Yet, as Brandes wrote in the preface to Johannes Magnussen's translation of Shelley's play *The Cenci*, there is a contradiction between the physical poet and the inspiration he uses to change the world: "Shelley's delicate and brittle body" could not "bear his exalted powers of imagination." This renders Shelley unsuitable to carry the banner of the political transformation the world had been expecting, and thus he goes to ruin as a "martyr of the imagination" (Brandes 1878a:iv).

There are, however, further examples in *Naturalism in England* of strong poets who are possessed of robustness and flair. The brow of the Irish national-political poet Thomas Moore, for example, is described as "large and radiant" and "so interesting that it would send a phrenologist into convulsions" (Brandes 1875a:238). The portrait of Byron, whose poems heralded a coming cultural and political storm over an ossified Europe, begins with a reference to Bertel Thorvaldsen's 1821 bust of the poet, about which Brandes notes that the sculptor had provided a brow on which "clouds might gather (…) and lightning flash from the clouds, and from something violent in the gaze" (Brandes 1875a:358).

With Taine as his intellectual mentor, Brandes emphasizes that the life of the author is the chief source for understanding his work. When it comes to the judging of the literary quality of an authorship, Brandes invariably links this with an evaluation of the author's biography. Since it is Brandes' aim to construct an image of the great poets as castigators of society who – according to the nature of the matter – must necessarily be controversial in their own age, he almost draws an equivalence between the adversity encountered by each author and their ability to create great art. The primary examples of this are Shelley and Byron, who had to struggle against the condemnation of their surroundings, as well as Keats, whose lovely verses were written "amidst great agony" (Brandes 1875a:221).

In the other camp are Coleridge and Wordsworth, whom Brandes desires to pull down from their pedestals. Coleridge was "will-less" and "like a child allowed his life to be preserved by others" (Brandes 1875a:131); his poetry is therefore not ultimately successful. Wordsworth is portrayed as a poet who lived an "idyllic and protected life" (79) devoid of any external events that might "inflame the passions in his poetry" (80). Yet here Brandes leaves out Wordsworth's sojourn in France during the Revolution, as well as the financial problems that forced him to return home. It can thus be said that there is a certain selectivity in his arrangement of the biographical material; and it is no accident that Brandes chooses to focus on anecdotes about the conservative Wordsworth's obstinate self-absorption and various caprices. It borders on character assassination that in turn functions to legitimize Brandes' critique of the limited literary merits of his work. In this endeavor Brandes was assisted by the Edinburgh professor David Masson's *Wordsworth, Shelley, Keats and Other Essays* (1874), from which he borrowed many of the anecdotes that are repeated in *Naturalism in England*. Like Masson (Masson 1874:34–35, 68), Brandes also compares Wordsworth negatively with the much more rebellious Byron.

A distinguishing characteristic that seems to render Brandes' text different from modern critical praxis is that at times he borrows literary themes and images from the works he discusses. An example of this is the transition he makes from the first generation of poets, who had sold themselves to social and political conservatism, to the young and rebellious poets (Brandes 1875a:196). This is laid out in a reading of John Keats' unfinished epic *Hyperion* (1818–1819), from which Brandes cites the tribute to the god Apollo. Here a new era is heralded for the Gods of Olympus after the fall of their old overlord Saturn and his titans; Brandes appropriates this as a relevant image of the inauguration of a new age in nineteenth-century literature. Brandes also allows the voice of the literary critic to blend in with the object of analysis, as when he describes Keats as the nightingale, which had intrigued the poet in the famous "Ode to a Nightingale": Keats is like a "radiant bird that rises high up into the air from Wordsworth's ancient many-leaved oak" (Brandes 1875a:201). This undeniably introduces a certain form of pathos into Brandes' criticism, which Jørgen Knudsen characterizes as the "exaggerated language" of the volume that constitutes "glaze atop the viscous cake" (Knudsen 1985:387). An example of Brandes' penchant for metaphorical formulations can also be seen in the reference to Byron's *Childe Harold's Pilgrimage*, Canto III, in which the reader becomes an observer of a waterfall, which "in the raging white froth, swirled into the maelstrom, split (...) everything that stood in its way, indeed in the long run hollowed out the rocks" and yet in its middle brought forth "a magnificent radiant rainbow, a sign of harmony and peace and the love of freedom." This kind of nature description is read allegorically as a portent of the "better days for Europe" that will follow in the wake of Byron's powerful poetry (Brandes 1875a:527).

Naturalism as Concept
The various authors addressed in *Naturalism in England* would be placed under the category of "Romanticism" in modern textbooks. Yet Brandes wishes to group them under the concept of "Naturalism." Of all Brandes' literary terms this is the one that has most often raised eyebrows, and it always demands explanation when mentioned. This is because "Naturalism" is today almost automatically associated with the literary approach of Émile Zola, as expressed, for example, in his 1881 *Les Romanciers naturalistes* [The Naturalist Novelists], in which modern literature is characterized as the presentation of realistic social and psychological sequences of events. That such a connection has come about is related to the fact that Naturalism was later tied to the Modern Breakthrough in Scandinavian literature after 1870, in which Brandes was a key figure.

But what did Brandes mean by the concept when he originally used it? In *The Men of the Modern Breakthrough* he notes that Naturalism is a "quite comprehensive word" and can connote both the "most delicate elven melodies" of Shelley as well as the prosaic scenes of Zola (1883:398). Yet as Zola's conceptual explanation took hold and gained dominance, Brandes sharpened the distinction between these poles. In the preface to the fifth edition of *Main Currents* he writes that the concept of Naturalism "was shaped by me a decade before Zola introduced it into France in an entirely different sense than I had given it: the love of nature" (Brandes 1923:4). Bertil Nolin has suggested that Brandes' conception of Naturalism is borrowed from the German literary historians Rudolf Haym, Hermann Hettner, and Julian Schmidt, to whom he refers in *The Romantic School in Germany* (Nolin 1965:192). In *Naturalism in England*, however, Brandes focuses on "the love of nature" as an opposing pole to the artificial order of established society and to political repression. In this sense he recalls Jean Jacques Rousseau's idea that humanity is at its best in the natural state: "applied to society Naturalism becomes, as it already was for Rousseau, revolutionary" (Brandes 1875a:19). Nature becomes the vehicle of free-thinking, by which Brandes' concept of Naturalism can acquire a series of overlapping meanings. Toward the end of the volume he notes in summary that the British authors "prefer the forest to the sea, natural man to salon man, and the original expression of passion to its artificial language" (Brandes 1875a:483). It is worth briefly attending to these three elements in order to understand the significance Brandes attributes to Naturalism as a literary orientation.

Whereas German Romanticism was marked by the supernatural and the Danish iteration was centered on the rediscovery of the Scandinavian and Old Norse past, its national character in Great Britain was that of "worshipping (...) nature" (Brandes 1875a:12–13). This involved an interest in landscape and in the sea (not unnatural for a seafaring nation), as well as a warm affection for the animal world (Brandes 1875a:12–25). But this entails more than just a reproduction of physical objects, as in landscape painting. The observation of nature is filtered through the form of highly developed "sensibility" (that is, the ability to feel and to sense) that Brandes sees in Moore and Keats. He further identifies an over-imaginative "pantheism" in Wordsworth (62–63), Keats (Brandes 1875a:210), and Shelley (Brandes 1875a:307). Thus, in Wordsworth there is a suggestion of the reactivation of the mystical understanding of "the poetry of nature" (Brandes 1875a:87). This is the result of the displacement of traditional Christianity by nature mysticism, which Brandes traces back to Spinoza and Jakob Böhme (Brandes 1875a:55). This reading had already been introduced in *The Romantic School in Germany*, in which Brandes describes how nature replaces religion (Brandes 1873:124–125, 239–240). This displacement would later be mapped out by the American critic M.H. Abrams under the heading of *Natural Supernaturalism* (1971), the title of his influential thesis on both German and English Romanticism.

Brandes' designation of "natural man" is perhaps best understood through his description of Wordsworth's "naturalistic passion" for the "peasants and rural folk," who live with and through nature (Brandes 1875a:103). As Wordsworth expresses in his landmark "Preface" to *Lyrical Ballads* (1802), it is the rural population who are the real philosophers of the age, in that they are in close contact with nature and learn from it. Wordsworth therefore imitates a "natural prose dialogue" (Brandes 1875a:58), which (in modified form) resembles the language spoken by "the common people of the countryside." Brandes designates the dismantling of the artificial and stilted Neoclassical style as "the most extreme literary consequence of Naturalism" (Brandes 1875a:105). He sees a common thread in the various authors treated in *Naturalism in England* in the fact that each breaks with the salon style and the rigidly Neoclassical rhyming pattern that dominated the poetry of Alexander Pope (1688–1744) and the "stiff school of art" that had "perfumed the air with affectation" during the eighteenth century (Brandes 1875a:314). Continuing in this vein, Brandes at times allows his ideas about the Naturalist love of nature to be reflected in an author's aesthetics: Thomas Moore's *Irish Melodies*, for example, are described as poems that can "murmur like the waves of the sea and with the overwhelming force of a natural element" (Brandes 1875a:263). On the other hand, Brandes also insists that the portraits of nature created by the Naturalist authors are not only illustrations of feelings, but also true to nature – indeed even scientifically accurate. Thus, in Walter Scott's works he observes "portraits of nature" so accurate that "a botanist could well familiarize himself with the vegetation of the area from them" (Brandes 1875a:13).

Even though Brandes later insisted on distinguishing his conception of Naturalism from Zola's hyperrealism, he still understands the British authors as advocates of realism in nature. With respect to Wordsworth's "She was a phantom of delight," for example, he praises its presentation of an "authentically naturalistic ideal of the English female type" (Brandes 1875a:78), that is to say, her beauty is not mythologized or unnecessarily embellished. Brandes also alludes to realism in literature when he adopts the skepticism Taine reserved for Scott's popular historical novels. Brandes thus cites the novel series *Tales of the Crusaders*, and specifically *The Talisman* (1825), as works that are not faithful to truth, but "popular fictions about the fairytale world of the crusaders and their wondrous deeds" (Brandes 1875a:193). The contrast here is Byron, whose "direct clear vision" was capable of "grasping all that science seeks and demonstrates" even in an age before the natural sciences had truly triumphed (Brandes 1875a:195–196). Science, as Brandes understands it, is bound up with the inclination to revise hallowed yet incorrect understandings of the world. Here he is thinking not least of Byron's distancing himself from Christianity (Brandes 1875a:447), which chimes with his own hard stance against the religion.

In Brandes' conceptual usage, the term "Romantic" is reserved for the literature that takes inspiration from the Middle Ages and its magical romances. Thus, for Brandes it is "the truth of nature" in Wordsworth that distinguished him and the other British authors from the German Romantics, who revel in the "supernatural or fantastic" (Brandes 1875a:88). Yet examples of the supernatural can be located in the English material, such as in Scott's semi-gothic *Lay of the Last Minstrel* and in the enchanted dreams of Coleridge's unfinished *Christabel* (Brandes 1875a:118). Brandes views Coleridge as the chief exponent of "romantic-fantastic" poetry, which "neither presents an energetic, lively and personal life of a soul nor reproduces observations of the surrounding world" (Brandes 1875a:128).

Coleridge borrows from the German Romantics, whom Brandes had criticized in a prior volume of *Main Currents*, thereby registering "an abstract scientific protest against the Enlightenment." Brandes views rationalism as a distinguishing characteristic of the English national spirit, of which the empiricist philosopher David Hume (1711–1776) is the doyen. Within this frame, Coleridge's poetry is designated as downright "unenglish," in that he makes himself the "representative of the German philosophy of the past," which is "in opposition to the experimental character of English science" (Brandes 1875a:11). Scott's dreams and prophecies in the same way belong to the "Romanticism of the Uncanny" as it is found in Germany in the writings of Novalis or Hoffmann (Brandes 1875a:175).

Brandes is also skeptical of Southey's "exterior Romanticism," which makes use of "all the superstition of Arabia and all the most fantastic dreams of the Orient" (Brandes 1875a:144). Brandes' specialized employment of the term "Romantic" is not unusual for his time, but it departs from Taine, who refers to the same group of authors treated by Brandes as "L'école romantique" [the Romantic School]. Brandes also distances himself from his Danish predecessors, such as the critic Knud Lyne Rahbek, who for example in an 1820 *Tilskueren* article had designated Byron, Scott, and Moore as "Romantics" in contrast to the "classical poets from the age of Queen Anne" (cited in Nielsen 1976:281).

Even though the authors all adhere to the practice of describing nature in a manner faithful to reality, Brandes evaluates them differently, depending on what they esteem in the natural landscape and how they communicate it to the reader. For example, he ties the rebelliousness of Byron's temperament to his landscape portraiture in *Childe Harold's Pilgrimage*. According to Brandes, these passages demonstrate how Byron loved nature for its wrath, which stands in contrast to Wordsworth's affection for nature in its peacefulness (Brandes 1875a:423). Brandes points to a distinction here that could have been further supported by citing Byron's lines from Canto II: "she [nature] is fairest in her features wild" (Byron 1833:81). Yet Brandes' distinction between the two poets ought to be qualified by the fact that Canto III, 65–109, also contains a philosophical appraisal of nature in its peacefulness, and that often in Wordsworth we find descriptions of wild and sublime landscapes.

If we are to understand Brandes' volume as a general overview of British writers at the beginning of the nineteenth century, then "Naturalism" is too narrow and too politicized a frame to fully represent the literature of the age. As a literary concept it is more properly understood as a carefully selected focus that represents only a portion of the authors' total production. "Naturalism" is an ideal Brandes employs in order to pass judgment according to how well the writers fulfill its potential. At the same time, he outlines a developmental history that points to Byron as the literary figure against which all early nineteenth-century literature should be measured.

The Grand Narrative of Freethinking

In the introduction to the first volume of *Main Currents* Brandes had employed the classical metaphor of the *teatrum mundi* to describe the shift heralded by Byron: the Napoleonic Wars are the stage on which this poet "brings about the reversal in the great drama," and when he fell in the Greek war for freedom, his "hero's death" makes "an enormous impression on all the writers of the continent" (Brandes 1875a:13). Byron's poetry, especially *Don Juan*, is the culmination of Naturalism – a trumpet fanfare for the awakening that brings back the lost spirit of rebellion to European cultural history. A Hegelian manner of thinking can be discerned in this drama (Ahlström 1937:36–37), and the direction is clear: it is a movement toward freethinking. It is this grand narrative that shall be discussed and evaluated in the following section.

In *Main Currents* we follow the European spirit that moved from revolution at the conclusion of the eighteenth century toward counter-reaction at the beginning of the nineteenth and so turned back again toward an intuition of freedom. Brandes illuminates the same movement in miniature in British literary history. The early Lake Poets started out with radical intentions but quickly became anti-revolutionary and reactionary. The author of the Lake Poet School who receives the severest treatment is

Robert Southey. Brandes begins with a characterization of his early years as "free-minded" (Brandes 1875a:141), but this freethinking is silenced, not the least because he accepts the position of Poet Laureate, which meant that he was employed to compose "poems of adulation" for the royal house (Brandes 1875a:51). The year 1822 is a turning point, in which Byron through his biting satire *The Vision of Judgement* came into the public eye, delivering a "divine counter parade" to Southey's servile poetry (Brandes 1875a:149). Southey was an obvious victim of Brandes' critique of hirelings who serve the elite. When Brandes remarks that Southey was "reduced to living by his pen and thus necessarily wrote too much," his judgment is not far from that of the reception of the poet following his death. Around 1900, for example, the famous English critic Leslie Stephen spoke positively of Southey's character, but criticized him for being too mechanical in his poesy, which meant that his works were possessed of neither profound reflection nor much artistic merit (Stephen 1902:45–85).

Among the older generation of writers in the volume, it is Walter Scott who achieved the widest commercial success, and he alone acquired his renown through prose writing. His novels were translated into most European languages; in Germany translations were made in virtual "translation factories." In Denmark Scott's novels were published in competing translations, and they were reissued numerous times. *Naturalism in England* is wedged between two bursts of Scott novels in Danish translation, the first between 1855 and 1871 and the second in the 1880s (Eriksen 1976:108–112). Yet Brandes writes at a time when Scott's reputation as a serious writer was in decline. His popularity had made him the property of the masses, and as writers of serious literature turned their backs on Romanticism to embrace realism, Scott's novels were viewed as at best suitable for cheap entertainment. Brandes is clearly supportive of this development, yet it is Scott's conservatism that he finds most repulsive. Scott wrote historical novels that perhaps well enough addressed the violent religious and political conflicts that had marked Scotland's past, but the sequence of events focuses on reconciliation and marks out a road toward the peaceful present. Scott's support for the contemporary government, the Church, and the union between Scotland and England appealed to a broad readership and conservative critics.

Such glorification of the political status quo is in conflict with Brandes' ideal of literature as polemics: Scott had "still not, in the religious, political and poetic senses, reached the point of emancipating the personality from the peculiar traditions that hold it captive from birth." Thus, his novels succumb to the Brandesian "law" according to which what is not controversial in its own time inevitably will come across as "trivial and narrow-minded" to the next generation. Since Scott's stories invoke universal "jubilance" rather than rebellious reflection, he must therefore leave for the "younger generation of poets an unresolved, yet from the historical perspective clearly defined task" (Brandes 1875a:190–191). Brandes thus does not regard Scott's immense popularity and his many imitators as something that moved culture forward in either Denmark or Europe. In *Emigrant Literature* Brandes attacks B.S. Ingemann's historical novels, which he designates as belonging to "an unsuccessful and now renounced genre imported from Scotland, the historical novel, which was instigated by a full-blooded Tory emanated from an intellectual state that found all its ideals in the past, just like ours" (Brandes 1875a:22). Brandes' irritation at the popularity of the historical novel evidently stretches further back than *Main Currents*, for already in October 1867 he made his acceptance of a dinner invitation from the author Rinna Hauch conditional upon a promise that Scott would not be discussed (Fenger 1955:308).

English-language Romantic poets have traditionally been grouped into a canon of "the big six": Wordsworth, Coleridge, Keats, Shelley, Byron, and William Blake. This canon (which has come under significant pressure in the twenty-first century) is practically the same as is found in Brandes, with the exception of the English poet and painter William Blake (1757–1827). This is hardly surprising, for despite the increased attention devoted to Blake's authorship in his homeland and through the second half of the nineteenth century, he was peripheral until the early twentieth century, when his authorship was canonized. The first Danish translation of Blake appeared in 1897 (comprising three nature poems), and a sustained critical interest in him first began to manifest in Denmark in the 1930s (Rix 2018). It would have been interesting to see how Blake's lifelong radicalism would have shaken up Brandes' distinction between the first and second generations of poets, since Blake debuted before Wordsworth and outlived Keats, Shelley, and Byron. Yet it is likely that Brandes (parallel with his analysis of Shelley) would have found Blake's prophetic style too ethereal and his poetry too unknown to play any larger role in *Naturalism in England*.

In Brandes' view, it is John Keats (1795–1821) who is first among the younger generation to lead the way forward toward what will become Byron's revolt against petit bourgeois values. Yet it no easy matter for Brandes to fit Keats into his historical scheme, since his poetry is "l'art pour l'art" (Brandes 1875a:22), and a special kind of "pure art" that delivers sense impressions almost devoid of meaning. As Keats died young, Brandes is unable to say in what direction his politics would have evolved had this "world-shy child" reached manhood (Brandes 1875a:220–222). Yet Brandes does mention Keats' embittered poem "To Hope" as well as his relationship with English radical circles, including the journal editor and radical Leigh Hunt (Brandes 1875a:220). At Brandes' time, Keats' political and social engagement was rarely touched upon and would only receive real critical attention much later, as in for example Marilyn Butler's landmark *Romantics, Rebels and Reactionaries* (1981) and Jack Siler's *Poetic Language and Political Engagement in the Poetry of Keats* (2008).

The next poet in the chronology is the Irishman Thomas Moore (1779–1852), who is not read much today but whose works awakened some interest in Denmark. Several of his poems were translated into Danish (see Eriksen 1976:146–147). Brandes presents Moore as a political poet, indeed the first to "lead English poetry, then recumbent in the contemplation of nature, into the camp of freedom, thereby signaling the poetry of political engagement" (Brandes 1875a:227). This provides Brandes with the opportunity to begin the chapter with a long description of how English domination oppresses Ireland, especially with respect to the execution of the rebels in 1803 (Brandes 1875a:224–228). This digression distracts from the literary focus, but is justified by Brandes in that "it furnishes an idea of the impressions received by Moore during the years when he was ripening into manhood" (Brandes 1875a:233). In this context it is interesting to note that Brandes indicates his intention to work against the grain of current historical accounts of the Rebellion and its suppression. Thus, a note indicates that his account of the events "is founded upon descriptions given by English patriots" (Brandes 1875a:228). This assertion of a critical approach to the source material ought to be taken with a grain of salt. The historical work Brandes cites here is William Nathaniel Massey's *A History of England under George III* (4 vols, 1855–1863), a moderate liberal interpretation of the period with little sympathy for the King's politics.

Under the chapter heading "Republican Humanism" Brandes provides space for the poet Walter Savage Landor (1775–1864), whose works he had become acquainted with through his contact with Edmund Gosse (Brandes 1875a:292 note). Landor is portrayed in *Naturalism in England* as a "friend and intellectual soulmate of the great European revolutionaries" (Brandes 1875a:294). In the same manner that the critic esteems Byron, Landor is praised for building a bridge between poetry and political activism, as he travelled to Spain to fight against Napoleon in 1808 (Brandes 1875a:23, 284). Yet Brandes finds Landor's poetry stodgy. His Latinate vocabulary clearly falls outside the smooth and immediate style Brandes points to as a persistent and positive trait in the writings of the other Naturalist poets of the era. For Brandes Naturalism is synonymous with an anti-elitist orientation and a universal accessibility in the poetry that does not require the knowledge of the Classical tradition, which was limited to the privileged classes. Landor's most well-known poem, the heroic-orientalist *Gebir* (1798), is described as "stiff and inferior" in spite of its "powerful republicanism." Thus Landor is not the poet who can "bring about a free-thinking rupture in European public opinion" (Brandes 1875a:298–299).

Shelley

Another politically engaged poet for whom Brandes provides more space is Percy Bysshe Shelley (1792–1822). Brandes had already held up Shelley's ideals of freedom and vision of love as a positive contrast to the German poetry and philosophy addressed in *The Romantic School in Germany* (Brandes 1873:121–122, 124–125, 239–240, 244). His literary acquaintance with the poet went back many years. The Royal Library's records show that Brandes borrowed *The Poetical Works* in 1864 (Fenger 1955:118), after he had read a biography of the poet in *Fædrelandet*. In this context he notes that Shelley's "unreal life" had made a "powerful impression" on him (Dagbog 17.9.1861:100). In *Naturalism in England* Brandes also emphasizes the resistance Shelley encountered in his life in the form of censorship and legal prosecution. In this way Shelley is made a supporter of Brandes' idea that engaged art is born in opposition: Shelley's fearless radicalism and atheism mandates that his "political poetry is written in his blood" (Brandes 1875a:335).

All through the nineteenth century there was a split between those critics who saw Shelley as a dedicated political poet and those who viewed him as a lyrical dreamer (Morton 2006:36). Brandes sees both possibilities. He notes in his travel essay "Impressions of London" that "Shelley is the brightest, finest expression of English freethinking, and for freethinking especially in the areas in which the English otherwise are typically unfree," and yet at the same time he is also "the expression of pure lyricism" (Brandes 1896:307). Shelley's lyrical grace is praised time and again in *Naturalism in England*, yet Brandes never lets his political side out of sight. In an acute formulation he writes that Shelley's poetry had "greater and more varied significance for the spirit of human emancipation than anything written in France in August of 1792 [when the monarchy was abolished]" (Brandes 1875a:302). It is his admixture of revolutionary spirit and lyrical virtuosity that is attractive to Brandes, and as the reader gradually begins to comprehend, Shelley functions as the very ideal of poetic art that Brandes seeks to define in *Naturalism in England*.

According to Brandes, Shelley sensually and passionately seeks in nature a refuge from the world of human beings. Brandes reads Shelley's poetic treatments of nature's movements, destruction, and rebirth to a large measure as metaphors of social and cultural renewal. Shelley sees nature through his "world-dominating imagination" or with "the eye of his soul," thus elevating it into a stomping ground for Greek mythological figures such as Prometheus and Jupiter (Brandes 1875a:326–327). The Danish critic Aage Kabell has found such a reading to be incompatible with Brandes' own idea of Naturalism in the period. It is "a bad joke," he writes, when Brandes praises the eyewitness accounts and scientific nature of Naturalism other places in the volume and yet insists on incorporating Shelley, who barely delivers "any precise study" of the immediate physical world (Kabell 1944:204–205). Yet despite Kabell's objection it is not difficult to see how Shelley must be included in order that Brandes' continuous narrative of Naturalism as a progressive, freedom-seeking movement can reach its conclusion. Shelley's poetry was in fact a direct source of inspiration to Byron – a connection that had already been underlined in Grimur Thomsen's 1845 Danish biography of Byron, to which Brandes also refers (Brandes 1875a:432 note).

For Brandes, Shelley is not just a unique talent (as he also finds Moore to be), but "a genius (…) with all the powers of such" (Brandes 1875a:354). The presentation of Shelley as an enfant terrible, the untimely genius who cannot find a place in the prosaic world, introduces a familiar mythical construction of Romanticism to the analysis. Yet the fact that the ideals of this genius are ethereal and otherworldly is also Shelley's weak point. For example, Brandes describes *Revolt of Islam* as "imprecise and vague, abstract and metaphysical" (Brandes 1875a:355), and thus lacking in social impact. If Shelley had played a fine violin, says Brandes, a trumpet was needed to provide the "call to arms" against Europe's intellectual tyranny (Brandes 1875a:356).

Byron

As many critics have noted, Brandes' grand cultural narrative with Byron as its finale resembles the presentation of the German critic Georg Gottfried Gervinus (1805–1871). Byron is inserted into history as a catalyst for the renewal of the revolutionary spirit, or as Gervinus describes it (in a work that was translated into Danish), it was believed that "the excesses of the revolutionary spirit" had been halted forever, when it suddenly appeared that "American republicanism, German freethinking, French revolutionary enthusiasm, and Anglo-Saxon radicalism seemed all to have been brought to life in this single intellect [Byron]" (cited in Elze 1876:449).

Byron's mature poetry is inscribed in Brandes' literary-historical narrative as "The Culmination of Naturalism" (the title of the last chapter of the volume). In the writings of the mature Byron one finds a trinity of characteristics, according to Brandes, for which the highest form of poetry ought to aim: the realistic portrayal of things, the perfection of aesthetic form, and an active political vision in the direction of human emancipation (see Kristensen 1980:17). Revolutionary poetry comes into its own in *Manfred* and is sharpened in *Cain*, but it is not until *Don Juan* (the great, incomplete opus magnum) that Byron is "completely himself" (Brandes 1875a:503). Brandes believes that it was Byron's earthbound style that paved the way for the immense influence he had. In his later study of the British reformer Benjamin Disraeli (who was prime minister twice, in 1868 and 1874–1880), Brandes notes of the statesman's revolt against his hidebound homeland that "Disraeli believed that Byron was an intellect on the same level as himself; Shelley was too ethereal" (Brandes 1878b:165).

That Byron was the epitome of rebelliousness was also asserted by British critics in Brandes' own time, including Matthew Arnold, W.E. Henley, and A.C. Swinburne (see Rutherford 1995). Yet there is a difference between how positively Byron's literary achievements were received in Britain and on the continent. Brandes quite correctly notes that Byron was not buried in Poets' Corner, Westminster Abbey (a memorial stone was not erected until 1969). Yet his poetry had taken root in "the intellectual life of Russia and Poland, Spain and Italy, France and Germany" (Brandes 1875a:524). Byron's participation in the Greek War of Independence and his struggle on behalf of oppressed nations resonated across Europe. For Brandes, Byron is a beacon rising above the national. Whereas Wordsworth, Moore, and Scott had each given their respective lands a national song, Byron's focus on the I brought forth a newer and deeper understanding: "Byron's I is the universally human, (and) its sorrows and hopes those of all humanity" (Brandes 1875a:432). Many years later Brandes writes that "Byron's poetry [illustrates] the despair and the desire for freedom common to all Europe," and further notes that he was a decisive influence on Slavic literature, since its brightest lights, Poland's Adam Mickiewicz and Russia's Alexander Pushkin, both began as Byronians (Brandes 1888:203, 49).

Byron's poetry was debated assiduously in Denmark, yet as Brandes observes the reception was often cold and, according to him, the meaning often misunderstood. His old enemy Hans Lassen Martensen had in his *Christian Ethics* (1871) argued that Byron was the exponent of a pessimism that rendered impossible "the realization" of the "ideal of freedom" and the "consolidation of true progress." Brandes cites this attack (Brandes 1875a:433) as a starting point for a lengthy revision of this common interpretation. His reading of Byron seems to be more in harmony with that of the Italian patriot and writer Giuseppe Mazzini (1805–1872), who in a famous 1839 essay had declared Byron to be the author who would lead Europe forward toward political freedom and democracy (Mazzini 1970).

Byron had been translated into Danish numerous times, making it possible for contemporary Danish readers to assess Brandes' readings against the primary texts. Knud Lyne Rahbek translated Byron as early as 1817, while the first Danish translation of one of Byron's major works was of *Manfred* in 1820. Simultaneously with *Naturalism in England*, Edward Lembeke's two-volume selection of the author's poems and stories (1873–1876) was published. Byron was viewed as a subjective poet, hence Brandes devoted much ink to excerpting from his biography. The chief references for Brandes' presentation are well-known works on Byron's life: Thomas Moore's *The Life of Lord Byron* (1835), Grimur Thomsen's university thesis *On Lord Byron* (1845), and the Halle professor Kristian Elze's extensive German monograph *Lord Byron* (1870), later published in Danish translation by Kristian Kroman in 1876. These biographies paint a picture of an apostle whose alternative lifestyle and ideas upset the sanctimonious self-satisfaction of the bourgeoisie. Brandes views the agonies suffered by Byron at the hands of establishment England as mirrored in the sufferings endured by the heroes of his poetry. This supports the connection between life and work that is postulated in *Naturalism in England*. Brandes writes about Byron both as a writer and as a celebrity. With respect to the latter, interest in Byron's escapades and public scandals was widespread in the European press. As early as 1815 a Danish newspaper commented on Byron's private life, and parts of Thomas Moore's *Letters and Journals of Byron* were published in Danish journals (Nielsen 2003:366).

Byron was by no means a new acquaintance for Brandes. We know that he read *Manfred* in 1860 (in Lembeke's 1843 translation), commenting on that occasion that he found the final scene "absurdly ingenious" (Fenger 1955:11). Thereafter he read *Sardanapalus*, *Heaven and Earth*, *The Two Foscari*, and *Beppo*, but in the Byron chapter it is primarily *Childe Harold*, *Manfred*, *Cain*, and *Don Juan* (in C.V.A. Strandberg's translation) that are addressed in depth. It is these latter poems, with their focus on the individual and singular hero and his world-encompassing agonies, that make possible Brandes' thesis of the defiant subject's emancipation from norms. Byron stands out as the incarnation of what makes a modern figure in literature, an archetype that Thure Stenström (1961) has identified as the "solitary one." This positive reading of Byron's subjectivity stands in contrast to the charges of egotism that have often been registered against him. Taine, for example, views Byron as so self-centered as to be incapable of falling in love with another (Taine 1863:540). This was a critique that Danish critics had expressed earlier, for example Adam Oehlenschläger, who spoke of Byron's "monotonous proud egotism" (Oehlenschläger 1833:109), and Johan Ludvig Heiberg, who held that Byron had allowed himself to be ensnared "within the web of his own dialectic" and thus could not "reach the unity" that was the idealistic poet's true goal (Heiberg 1833:43). For Brandes, it is Byron's courage in embracing the subjective – the I that frees itself from the yoke of tradition – that constitutes his genuinely heroic achievement.

Reception and Afterlife

Editions and Changes

The second edition of *Naturalism in England* bears the publication year of 1892, but in fact appeared in April 1893. Many small changes were made, among others the addition of new sections on Keats' letters to his beloved Fanny Brawne. These were first made public in 1878 and thus not included in the original edition. Also added was a longer section on the Scottish-born poet Thomas Campbell (1777–1844), who is best known for his long poem *The Pleasures of Hope*, in which he reflects on political themes such as the French Revolution, the partition of Poland, and slavery. Yet even though Brandes refers to Campbell as a political poet, he is most assiduously cited in the chapter on "Erotic Lyricism."

Perhaps most noteworthy is the supplementary material on Shelley now included. The volume's epigraph, which in the first edition had been from Johann Peter Hebel's writing, is now exchanged with a citation from Shelley's notebook poems: "I am as spirit." This indicates that Brandes' interest in Shelley remained ardent and even seems to have grown. In the book *Impressions from Poland* Brandes comments, quite significantly, that few had paid much attention to Shelley "while the name of Byron was on everyone's lips." This is stated in order to point, in his eyes, to an injustice he goes on to describe as "the general belief in all seriousness that Byron was England's greatest lyricist" (Brandes 1888:201). This is most of all a comment directed against the technical virtuosity of Byron measured against that of Shelley. Yet in the context of the 1892 German edition of *Main Currents*, Brandes composes a poem in which he comments on *Naturalism in England* in this manner: "In faith and blood red zeal it was written. / Shelley! Its spirit belongs to you. You I have lived" (cited in Brandes 1908:284). This upgrading of Shelley's significance does not cohere with the actual content of the first edition of the volume, which undeniably stands under the sign of Byron (see Nolin 1965:198). Further documentation of Brandes' reevaluation of Shelley in relation to Byron is found in his *Memoirs*, in which Brandes reflects on how, in spite of his respect for Byron, "it was at that time Shelley who moved me, through the unselfish rebelliousness of his being against every contemptible rule in custom as in dogmas, that rebelliousness in irreducible unity with the purest poetry" (1908:383).

The third edition was published as a volume in Brandes' *Collected Works* (1900). There were few changes in comparison to the second edition. New bibliographic references were added, and Brandes included a reference to Shelley's "Song. Sorrow." One of the changes worth noting is that many of the English citations are now translated into Danish verse (in the first edition the preference was for prose reproductions). This change had a mixed reception. Adolf Hansen commented specifically on a translation of Keats, asserting that Brandes just about "mutilates" the meaning with his erroneous translation (Hansen 1876:25–26). Otto Jespersen, the world-renowned grammarian, who took a special interest in the English language, praised the new renderings (Jespersen 1912:94), noting only a single exception that he found unsuccessful. Much later, Aage Kabell suggested that the translations are often brilliant, but in other places lack metrical sensibility (Kabell 1944:191–193).

The fourth edition from 1906 is identical to the third edition.

The fifth edition was published in 1924. With respect to the content it was more comprehensively revised, especially the Byron material. Otto Jespersen has suggested that already in the fourth edition Brandes had come to look more unsentimentally at Byron's private life and "the lack of conscience in his behavior" (Jespersen 1912:91). This is taken a step further in the fifth edition. Many of the women are now discussed, which means that Byron's love life and gender ethics are given greater emphasis; among other changes, a few pages are added on his incestuous relationship with Augusta Leigh. Brandes was perhaps reacting to the complaints that he had painted too ennobled a portrait of Byron. There is also more material on the poet's time in Switzerland and Venice. That the biographical material was expanded is commensurate with Byron's reception in the 1920s, when critical treatments focused more on his life and his morality than his poetry (Stabler 2013:1–3). One change of a certain significance here is that many citations are now in the original language, especially with respect to verse lines from Shelley's works.

The sixth edition from 1967 is a reproduction of the fifth edition but with modernized orthography, and the Danish translations of the poems are reinserted.

Danish Reception

That the publication of *Naturalism in England* did not receive much attention in the Danish press is surely a consequence of the fact Brandes was seen as persona non grata by the Copenhagen media, which was still dominated by National Liberal ideas. Yet there were reviews in *Morgenposten* and *Lolland-Falsters Stiftstidende*, both of which had connections to Brandes.

Only a week before *Naturalism in England* appeared, Brandes published a translation of the literary realist Gottfried Keller's *Swiss Stories*, which were regarded as daring and risqué. The reaction to what was interpreted as a commercial venture for Brandes may have functioned as a lightning rod for the polemic *Naturalism in England* might have provoked. In Carl Ploug's review of *Swiss Stories* in *Fædrelandet* (November 20, 1875), Brandes is called a "literary businessman" who preaches "*the gospel of pleasure*" and contributes to the degeneration of youth; Vilhelm Topsøe accused him in *Dagbladet* of introducing the Danish reader to erotic scenes that would take root because of their "impurity and corruption" (December 13, 1875); and *Dags-Telegrafen* (November 21, 1875) published a sarcastic review which bemoaned Brandes' decision to translate so base a work (cited in Friis 1965:59–61 and Knudsen 2008:137–138).

The lack of press reviews of *Naturalism in England* was compensated for to a certain degree by the critic Adolf Hansen, who published a 49-page review of the volume in pamphlet form in 1876. Hansen praises Brandes for his profound insight into British literature, not least for his clear descriptions of Scott's and Wordsworth's contrasting views on nature. While it is evident that Brandes confers the poetic laurels on Byron and Shelley at the expense of Wordsworth, Hansen devotes much space to persuading the reader that Brandes actually views Wordsworth's works positively; they were, after all, generally viewed as the masterpieces of the period. This was clearly important in order to avoid Brandes being accused of lacking critical intelligence. Hansen's review functions most of all as a kind of defense of Brandes in the Danish debate about him, and thus further concludes with an expression of anger that he had not been given the professorship that was his due. Even though Hansen disagrees with some of the details, his general praise of *Naturalism in England* is unaffected, since he maintains that Brandes' criticism is correct in its broad outlines and his observations accurate.

The English-Speaking World

Brandes was known abroad for, among other things, his readings of European authors, for his support for Nietzsche, and for having introduced Scandinavian literature, especially Henrik Ibsen, to the English-speaking public (see Waller 2008:322–323). But most of all it was his three-volume study of Shakespeare (1895–1896, ENG 1898) that made his name in the Anglophone world and paved the way for the translation of *Main Currents*. The volume on *Naturalism in England* appeared in English during the first half of 1905 (New York, Macmillan Co.; London, W. Heinemann) and was a translation of the second edition. Yet even when the first Danish edition was issued a review was published in the well-known London journal *The Spectator*. The review primarily consisted of a summary of Brandes' main points as well as excerpts of his descriptions of Scott and Byron, here translated into English. The reviewer begins by calling Brandes "one of the most eloquent and enlightened of modern critics," and even though the volume contains much that is generally known, the judgment nonetheless is positive: "his knowledge and accuracy are surprising, and (…) – except misprints of English words, which are too common – there is hardly any misstatement of fact upon which we have been able to lay our hand" (*Spectator* 1876:17).

When the English translation appeared the journalist and author Elia W. Peattie wrote an equally positive review in the *Chicago Daily Tribune*, which gives the impression that Brandes was already a known quantity:

"never was Brandes more delightful. What gossip – what knowledge – what comparison – what deductions" (Peattie 1905:9). Peattie sees Brandes' commentaries as a refreshing alternative to English-language criticism; the latter directed its attention toward the abstract as if literature were music or pictorial art, whereas the Dane, according to his nature, demonstrates a protestant preoccupation with morality and an emphasis on the good and the orderly in the literature. Yet not everyone esteemed Brandes' radical freethinking when it came to the evaluation of English literature. Walter Raleigh, Professor of Literature at Oxford, thus wrote in a private letter in 1905: "There's nothing in Brandes; he's just a Continental Jew culture-monger. He doesn't know what poetry is. Keen about his sawdusty creed, namely rationalism, progress, enlightenment – all perfectly abstract" (cited in Waller 2008:323).

Both in Denmark and abroad the tendency among later critics is to comment on Brandes' quite heavy-handed evaluation of the British poets. In a festschrift for Brandes, Otto Jespersen notes that while Brandes had perhaps taken sides in the volume, his "partisan judgment had only in exceptional cases damaged the presentation and never resulted in a distorted or stunted image of the personalities of the authors" (Jespersen 1912:87). Jespersen thinks that Brandes is perhaps hard on "a great poet like Wordsworth" but that Southey's "lack of talent" receives its proper treatment, and that "this occurs in the most enjoyable manner and the finest form" (Jespersen 1912:88). Others were not so convinced of Brandes' powers of judgment. It was especially his affection for Byron at the expense of Wordsworth that occasioned commentary. The politician and later Minister for Irish Affairs Augustine Birrell appreciates Brandes' "hearty, honest delight in Byron's beauty and daring and rank and reckless wit" (Birrell 1916:211), yet contends that Brandes is unjust in placing him above Wordsworth. The Norwegian-American critic Hjalmar Hjorth Boyesen had already contributed an even more skeptical position. The lionization of Byron's rebellion against the authorities is cause for special concern: "Dr. Brandes has so profound an admiration for the man who dares to rebel that he fails to do justice to the motives of society in protecting itself against him" (Boyesen 1895:205). The English literary critic George Saintsbury writes in the same vein on the hundredth anniversary of Byron's death: Brandes was wrong about Byron and never managed to understand how destructive an influence the poet had been on the morality of his homeland (Saintsbury 1924:50–51).

In Scandinavia, it was especially the analysis of the atheist and freethinker Shelley that drew attention. The Norwegian bishop Johan Christian Heuch thundered against Brandes' attack on Christianity (which he saw as part of a Jewish plot). The assertion is that Brandes promotes Shelley for his anti-Christian attitudes rather than for his poetry (Heuch 1877:67–72). Brandes' quite out-of-hand dismissal of Southey further drew censure from the author, nationalist, and anti-Semite Harald Nielsen. In an essay he refutes Brandes' critique of the English poet, concluding with a castigation of *Naturalism in England*, which he argues does not deserve to be viewed as literary criticism because of "his cock and bull characteristics, his flagrant absurdities and psychological self-contradictions" (Nielsen 1922:83). Nielsen was the center of a "new youth movement" whose goal was to create an alternative to Brandes' radical understanding of culture.

Brandes' politically motivated attempt to revise the British canon provoked sharp commentary throughout the nineteenth century. His quite severe and personal critique of Wordsworth incited Aage Kabell to call his treatment of him "a masterpiece of perfidy" (Kabell 1944:205). Kabell also questions the use of biographical data in the context of Shelley's flight from England. He argues that Brandes overplays the role of the social persecution of the poet, when there were other reasons for his journey to Italy, such as his miserable health (1944:189). Further skepticism of Brandes' powers of judgment is to be found in the tone-setting literary critic René Wellek, who in his *A History of Modern Criticism* argues that *Naturalism in England* provides "a completely distorted picture" of the early nineteenth-century poets (Wellek 1968 [1955]:360). That on which other critics are in agreement is not appreciated by Brandes: Wordsworth's merits are undervalued, Coleridge as a philosopher is practically never mentioned, Moore receives more attention than Keats, and so on. Another misstep is that the impact of

Byron is presented as the beginning of a new era, which in a literary-historical sense at least is not the case (Wellek 1968 [1955]:360–361). Brandes' fulsome praise of Byron also motivated the Swedish critic Gunnar Ahlström to point out a contradiction: how can Brandes praise the individualism of Byron when he had condemned precisely the same attitude among the German Romantics? (Ahlström 1937:97). Yet Thure Stenström argues that Brandes, when addressing Byron, establishes a separate and more action-oriented ideal of individualism than the empty reveries upon which the Germans fall back (Stenström 1961:99ff).

As mentioned above, Edmund Gosse believed that Brandes saw something of himself in Shelley. Later critics have read the portrait of Byron with its focus on the persecuted loner as a mirror of Brandes' own position in Denmark at the time *Naturalism in England* was written. Paul V. Rudow also offers a biographical interpretation of the material, referring to the analysis of Byron as an example of Brandes' "characterization of the poets in which he mirrors himself, so that the critic and his object are blended together" (Rubow 1934:634). A similarly biographical observation is offered by Jørgen Knudsen, who writes that a more fully formed image of Byron – as a poseur defined by ennui – is underplayed by Brandes because it was evidently too uncomfortably close to the traits he could recognize in himself (Knudsen 1985:388–390).

Influence and Afterlife

One reason why *Naturalism in England* had a relatively meager impact is because it did not bring anything decisively new to the treatments of the individual authors in relation to the existing English-language criticism. Wellek thus formulates his status abroad: "the oblivion which has overtaken him is deserved, as he was only a middleman without originality and substance" (Wellek 1968 [1955]:357).

One less agreeable consequence of making use of the ideas of others is accusations of plagiarism. As early as 1876 Brandes was accused of borrowing from Elze's Byron biography in "the sloppiest manner," such that for example he reproduces a translation error when he does not check the original text against Elze ("S" 1876:3). Aage Kabell (1944:206–209) demonstrates that Brandes plagiarizes from William Michael Rossetti's essay "A Memoir of Shelley" (1870).

If, from the perspective abroad, *Naturalism in England* was felt to lack originality, it was still important for the reception of British literature in Scandinavia. In connection with Edward Lembeke's Danish translation of Thomas Moore's great frame story *Lalla-Rookh: An Oriental Romance* (1878), for example, one reviewer refers to Brandes' reading of the text as an analogy of the subjection of Ireland – a reading with which, incidentally, the reviewer (writing under the pseudonym "B") is in disagreement ("B" 1878:2–3). Yet it is especially Brandes' interest in the rebel poets Shelley and Byron that can be traced in his successors. A similar interest in the relatively unknown Shelley can be observed in the Danish critics Karl Gjellerup and Valdemar Rørdam, in Viktor Rydberg in Sweden, and in Herman Wildenvey in Norway (Engelberg 2008:159–160).

Under the influence of Brandes, Adolf Hansen published translations of Shelley's poetry in *Poems Translated from English* (1884) and provided a version of *Prometheus Unbound* (1892); he also translated Byron's *Childe Harold's Pilgrimage* under the title *Junker Harold's Pilgrimsfart* (1880). In his grand English and *North American Literary History in Outline*, Hansen closely follows Brandes' analysis of Byron as the active poet who stood "alone against scorn and hatred, held his head high, recklessly spoke what he saw as the truth, and made his words into action" (Hansen 1902:139).

Alfred Ipsen, an English language teacher, published Byron's poems *Manfred* (1888) and *Beppo* (1891) in Danish translation. Since he originally gravitated toward Brandes' revolt against Christianity, it is natural to assume that his interest in Byron was influenced by the analysis of *Cain* in *Naturalism in England*. Yet later Ipsen turned away from Brandes when he rediscovered his Christian faith. In one of his attacks on Brandes, he describes how the portrait of Byron as well as several others in the volume on British authors are consciously distorted and selective in order to "underpin precisely those facets and characteristics of their personalities and production that cohere with the tendency and plan of the work"

(Ipsen 1902:103). Brandes' good friend Holger Drachmann (1846–1908) achieved his literary breakthrough with a volume of poems dedicated to Brandes, *Poems* (1872), in which many of the verses express an interest in England's revolutionary movements. This is particularly evident in "English Socialists," in which he hopes that England will take lessons from the revolutionary Paris Commune. Drachmann also translated Byron's *Don Juan* into ottava rima (published in eight parts in 1890–1891 and as a complete edition in 1902). Brandes perhaps also inspired August Strindberg to read Byron's *Manfred* (see Nielsen 2004:384), and it has been suggested that the concept of the superman in the Swedish poet Gustaf Fröding (1860–1911) can be traced back to Brandes' interpretation of Byron (Sjöholm 1940:188ff).

Brandes suggests in *Naturalism in England* that the poet Frederik Paludan-Müller wrote "imitations" of Byron's *Beppo* (Brandes 1875a:468) at the beginning of his career. This was, however, denied by the author in a reader letter published in the Brandes-edited journal *Det Nittende Aarhundrede*. Paludan-Müller protests that he had not read Byron's poem (Paludan-Müller 1876:471–473). Brandes published an apology in response, yet at the same time argued that influence can be indirect, exerting itself intangibly through "the poetic atmosphere of the age" (Brandes 1876:474).

The German edition of *Naturalism in England*, which was reissued many times, played a certain role in discussions of nineteenth-century British literature in non-English-speaking countries. It is referenced, for example, by the literary historians Carl Bleibtreu (1887) and Ika A. Thomése (1923), but is also taken up as late as 1963 by the Slavicist Karel Krejöi. In conclusion it should also be noted that Brandes has had an influence in China, not least in the wake of the translation of his book on Shakespeare in 1935 (see Jensen 1980:233–234). Yet before that translation, Brandes made an impact on the productive translator of Western literature and later Chinese communist leader Zhang Wentian (1900–1976), who nourished a profound fascination with Shelley and Byron. On the occasion of the 100th anniversary of Byron's death (1924), he translated a chapter on Byron from Brandes' *Naturalism in England* into Chinese (see Gamsa

2010:22). A translation of the whole book by Han Shih-heng (from the English edition) followed in 1939, together with the first three volumes of *Main Currents*. The key word "Naturalism" was again taken up in the 1950s by the literary critic Li Zhichang in his essay "Naturalism in Chinese Literature," which concerns a literary wave in China that had gathered inspiration from Japanese models. In this context, Brandes' conceptual apparatus and his treatment of British authors are referenced (see Shotung 2002:299). Brandes thus seems to have set forth certain foundational principles in the love of nature that resounded in the understanding of literary movements outside the immediate circle of poets he wrote about.

THE ROMANTIC SCHOOL IN FRANCE (1882)

Carsten Meiner

Introduction

Georg Brandes' *The Romantic School in France*, the penultimate volume of *Main Currents in Nineteenth Century Literature*, appeared in Copenhagen in 1882.

It is a "cheerful" volume, in which much of the work is driven by enthusiasm both for French Romanticism and for its own methodology. At the same time, it is characterized by the wealth of learning exhibited, acquired through many years of reading – in contrast to the first volume, *Emigrant Literature*, which also treated French literature but was based on a small handful of novels and a good measure of polemical ideas. The fifth volume is on the contrary less polemical, which was reflected in its complimentary (and less critical) reception. The volume also distinguishes itself in other ways. There is, for example, no real central figure, like Byron or Heine in the corresponding volumes on the English and German schools. Even though the writings and person of Victor Hugo form a natural focal point in the French Romantic school, he does not receive his own chapter in the book. Most importantly, Brandes seems to have developed, or was in the process of developing, a new understanding of the central concept of all six volumes: the "main current."

The following presents the process of composition of the volume, after which its contents are discussed. Georg Brandes' presentation of the ideas and aesthetics of the French Romantics centers on three characteristics which a reader versed in French Romanticism will readily recognize. Brandes combines them in a new manner so that they are in conflict with one another, rather than serving as organizational components of a Romantic program. Thereafter Brandes' argumentation shall be analyzed with a special focus on a distinguishing feature of the volume, the admixture of on the one hand a detail-heavy and sober, yet hardly arid literary historiography, and on the other, a successful metaphorics. Finally, the literary-historical "methodology" shall be discussed in relation to a series of contemporary French literary historians who resemble Brandes, or at any rate are analogous to him, in their experiments with otherwise time-honored literary historical categories such as work, author, causality, the spirit of the age, nation, and so on.

Background and Genesis

Brandes in Berlin and Paris

The fifth volume of *Main Currents*, *The Romantic School in France*, was released in 1882 as a kind of final portrait of the French Romantic movement, with which Brandes had been occupied for a long time. During his stay in Paris in 1866–1867 he had read Victor Hugo, Alfred de Musset, and George Sand, and before the publication of the first volume of *Main Currents* in 1872 he had already written on Prosper Mérimée and Charles-Augustin Sainte-Beuve. In the fall of 1871 he had planned to lecture in Copenhagen on French drama with an emphasis on French Romanticism, an idea that ultimately transformed into the lectures on emigrant literature which became the first volume of *Main Currents*.

During the brief and productive period between 1872 and 1875, Brandes managed to publish the first four volumes of *Main Currents*, after which fully seven years would pass before the fifth volume appeared. The reasons for this pause are many. In the first place, certain biographical circumstances intervened. These years are appropriately designated as his "period of exile," for he travelled much, especially to Germany, where he settled in 1877. He managed to hold three lectures on French Romanticism in Copenhagen in September 1877; after a farewell celebration he left for Germany in October, where he remained for the next five years. This self-imposed exile is distinguished by an extraordinarily immense production of lectures, articles, and no fewer than four biographies: Søren Kierkegaard and Ferdinand Lassalle in 1877, and Esias Tegnér and Benjamin Disraeli in 1878.

In 1879 Brandes took a kind of research trip to Paris, consequentially delivering eight lectures on French Romanticism in Copenhagen in November. In 1880 he gave lectures on the subject in Berlin as well as Christiania (Oslo) and Bergen, publishing some of these at the time in reworked versions. In a September 8, 1879 letter to his mother, Brandes describes how rather remarkably, in the midst of all this productivity, he found himself unable to write (Brandes 1994, 1:249).

This leads us to the second reason for the long gestation period of *The Romantic School in France*. Brandes lectured and wrote on French Romanticism in diverse contexts, but could not gather his collected material into a monograph, because according to his biographer Jørgen Knudsen he "continuously and tirelessly added to the growing stable of manuscripts" (Knudsen 1988:199).

Personalities and Schools

There could have been a methodological reason for this blockage, namely that Brandes was preoccupied with two factors that could not easily be reconciled. The author's biography was for him a wholly necessary element in the understanding of literary works. This is attested by the publication of the four previously mentioned biographies in 1877 and 1878, and especially so with respect to the important episodes and psychological phases in the life of Søren Kierkegaard; Jørgen Knudsen thus notes that "here in the fifth volume of the work Brandes has reached the point in his own development at which the biographical is truly essential as the key to the poetic work, and this creates problems he is unable to resolve" (Knudsen 1988:201). The problem concerns how his interest in the biographical, which had acquired the status of a methodological conviction, should be related concretely to another and evidently equally pressing methodological question, that is the literary-sociological question of the formation of schools.

There is nothing new in the fact that during this period Brandes was preoccupied with literary schools; the second volume of *Main Currents*, after all, was titled *The Romantic School in Germany*, while the fourth was named

Naturalism in England: Byron and his Group. Yet the idea of a German Romantic school in the second volume was quite vague in comparison to Brandes' conception of a school in 1880. Likewise, the designation of a "Naturalist group" in England seems almost disingenuous in the sense that it is bound up to such a high degree with a single person, George Gordon Byron, who sits atop the hierarchy and consumes fully one half of the volume, just as Heinrich Heine takes up half of the last volume of *Main Currents*, *Young Germany*.

There are signs that, while working on *The Romantic School in France*, Brandes was in the process of rehabilitating the idea of literary schools. This impulse came in part from the French material, which was not dominated by a single figure to the same extent, like Heine in Germany or Byron in England. Victor Hugo is important, but it is clear in Brandes' account in *The Romantic School in France* that he does not play the same role as Heine or Byron, nor that he would later attribute to Goethe. This interest in reevaluating the idea of the literary school can also be seen in *The Men of the Modern Breakthrough* of 1883, which was conceived and written at the same time as *The Romantic School in France*. Here Brandes writes: "it has been my intention to characterize a larger group of men who here in Norden have promulgated and furthered the modern literary movement" (Brandes 1883:[v]). But it is a group without a leader (Bjørnstjerne Bjørnson, Henrik Ibsen, J.P. Jacobsen, Holger Drachmann, Edvard Brandes, Sophus Schandorph, and Erik Skram): a collection of Scandinavians who formed a school only by virtue of having felt the same impulse to import and to disseminate the modern literary movement from abroad. Moreover, Brandes writes in the introduction that the aim of the book is to communicate to young people the particular literary "constellation" under which they were born (Brandes 1883:[v]).

A final reason for this concern with the formation of schools could be that, in the various Romantic schools, Brandes saw something of his own role as a central figure in his own movement, particularly regarding the exposure he had experienced as a consequence of this. He was in many ways a father figure, and thus exposed to the less savory side of the group dynamic; just as his own group had formed itself spontaneously, as the French school had, it was also, in 1882, in many ways in the same state of dissolution he describes in the Romantic school: "and there was, moreover, a certain amount of weariness and discouragement in the new camp after the first great intellectual effort. The combatants were young; they had fancied that one mighty onslaught would be sufficient to capture the fortifications of prejudice; and it was with a feeling of disappointment that they found themselves after the attack still only at the foot of the redoubt, with their numbers greatly reduced. They lost patience and ardor for the fight" (Brandes 1882:144–145). The circumstances of his own group in the year 1882 were not dissimilar.

Furthermore, Brandes speaks in *The Romantic School in France* of "a psychological motive of a nobler nature that contributed to the dissolution of the group, namely the writers' sense of independence" (Brandes 1882:145), which leads back to the question of the biographical. Brandes fought to hold his group together, but his strategy changed. At times he was tyrannical – one author (Karl Gjellerup) should be held by the ears, he writes in a letter; at other times he released his grip: "NB – we permitted the individualities within our camp to develop themselves completely freely. Only in this way does each do his best work," he writes in another letter to V. Pingel (Georg and Edvard Brandes 1940, 3:344). Of his concern for groups and schools at this time, Brandes notes how the Germans, whose contemporary literature in his estimation was nothing special, compensated for their shortcomings with "modern" Russians and Scandinavians: "no literary schools," he noted in 1882 (cited in Knudsen 1988:291).

There are thus a good many reasons that it took Brandes a long time to prepare and write this volume. The process was, all in all, painful for him: "November 24th. After a dreadful night – without effect I took four measures of potassium bromide and drank more than half a flask of port without getting more than three hours sleep –, a day of exhaustion" (Dagbog, 24.11.1882).

A Positive Current

Nevertheless, the fifth volume is remarkably uplifting. Against the background of the previous volumes in Brandes' *Main Currents*, which had possessed a critical and at times spiteful tone toward the literary reactions to the French Revolution and the emergence of the new Europe, *The Romantic School in France* is marked by the flame of enthusiasm. That flame is the result of the appearance around 1830 of a particular generation of authors, pictorial artists, sculptors, and composers which, almost unconsciously, gathered together and united around the will to criticize the political and social situation in France. In his conclusion, Brandes details what each of the Romantic authors had contributed:

> In every one of these domains the generation of 1830 has produced imperishable works. The French Romantic school may therefore, without exaggeration, be called the greatest literary school of the nineteenth century. (Brandes 1882:593)

Thus the book's charting of the most important main current of European literature comes across as uplifting, precisely because it demonstrates that the French school was a current in the dynamic sense of the word: a current that left lasting and productive traces in that it split into new rivers that later would gather in the revolutions of 1848. The opposite of this positive reading of the concept of reaction is the current that "stagnates," which according to Brandes is the case with Danish literature as it is presented in the first volume of *Main Currents, Emigrant Literature*:

> A true, appropriate, correcting reaction is progress. But such a reaction is powerful and short-lived and does not stagnate (…) When a stick has been bent in one direction, one straightens it out by bending it in the other direction—but one does not keep doing this. (Brandes 1872:12)

This is what happened in Denmark: whereas the revolutionary currents in the major European literatures first were dammed up but later broke through the dykes that had been erected, the Danes, according to Brandes, still worked to keep the revolution in the "swamp of Reaction" (Brandes 1872:14). As has been noted, it was different with the generation of 1830.

The Romantic School in France

Framework and Selection
The Romantic School in France is organized into two sections of unequal length. The first part lays out the different political, literary, and artistic preconditions, French as well as European, of the French Romantic school. First Brandes describes the internal political situation during the restoration of the monarchy between 1815 and 1830. Thereafter, in the chapters "The Generation of 1830" and "Romanticism," he relates how the Romantic authors quickly formed a kind of brotherhood that reacted with a critical attitude toward the reinstitution of the monarchy and its bourgeois traits. Here Brandes describes how the Romantics also rejected political reality in a kind of self-imposed exile. The principal characteristics of the school are then illuminated. He asserts that the French Romantics wanted to represent reality, both its political and psychological dimensions, in all its complexity and natural contradictions, rather than draw out its truest or most pleasing sides as morally worthy. Brandes further contends that the school has a talent for the supernatural, and that this can be observed among virtually all the involved authors, from Charles Nodier to Victor Hugo to Honoré de Balzac. Finally, Brandes maintains that the French Romantic school is in a stylistic sense not Romantic, but Classical, since the authors subscribe to stylistic ideas that can be traced back to the seventeenth century.

These ideas form the threads of the book's second section, the longest, which consists of a series of portraits with equal weight placed on biography and works. The author Charles Nodier is deemed the pioneer of the Romantics and is presented as the writer who introduced the fantastic and the gothic to literature, while the poet Andres Chénier is also identified as a pathbreaker, insofar as his poetry is Romantic in content but composed according to Classical ideals. Thereafter follow portraits of the most important members of the school. The titles of the chapters, characteristically, are the names of the authors rather than literary themes or ideas, which had been the norm in earlier volumes of *Main Currents*, as for example in the chapters on "British Freethinking" or "Republican Humanism" in *Naturalism in England*. Each chapter is laid out biographically, with details on upbringing, education, travels, and romantic life, and further contains a description of the author's temperament. Only after this does Brandes begin describing selected works.

Another characteristic of these chapters is that they are subdivided. First he describes how Victor Hugo found success with his poems and how his theatrical works were banned, but he also relates how a young man of nineteen years visited him at home and showed him a selection of wholly modern poems. This was Alfred de Musset, whose youthful work forms the center of the second half of the chapter. Thus the portrait of Hugo slides into a portrait of Musset. This occurs several times: the Musset portrait is shared with a portrait of George Sand, and Henri Beyle (Stendhal) is paired with Prosper Mérimée, who is coupled with Théophile Gautier. This is a means for Brandes to uphold his two intentions: to describe both a school and a series of an author's individually determined works.

There is no doubt that Brandes covered all the most important authors of the period, and that they are treated in detail. There are chapters on Musset, Sand, Balzac, Beyle, Mérimée, Gautier, and Sainte-Beuve, and there are partial chapters in which two or more authors are compared internally. Finally, there are chapters on the Romantic drama and on Sainte-Beuve and literary criticism. When compared with contemporary literary histories, this selection of authors is relatively canonical. But it is still a selection, and it is only in the conclusion that Brandes explains his reasoning: "as a rule, I have only been able to present the typical main figures in relief" (Brandes 1882:590). Continuing, he notes that "there are however in the generation of 1830 two groups of authors, a small one that has written for the whole world, and a larger one that has written for France, and it is only the first group that I have wanted to depict in its full light" (Brandes 1882:591). The first criterion for selection is that they be "typical main figures," but typical of what? They must be typical of the Romantic school, which explains why an otherwise tone-setting author like Alphonse de Lamartine does not receive his own chapter. His *Méditations poétiques* of 1820 was a colossal success, and was widely viewed as the beginning of Romanticism in France because of its dominate poetic I and its personal and often melancholic landscape of feeling. In the meantime, however, Lamartine entered into the French Academy in 1829, and in 1833 the National Assembly. This political activity did not fit into Brandes' image of the Romantic school as a rejection of the political world, which is why Lamartine is presented as an author who was drowned out by the emergence and triumph of Andre Chénier's poetry. The absence of Alexandre Dumas the Elder's historical novels is also noticeable, which likewise can be explained with reference to certain – according to Brandes – atypically Romantic characteristics in his literary production: rapidly written historical works for the masses with financial reward rather than participation in the Romantic program as the final goal. Thus in one place Brandes refers to Dumas' authorship as "literary industry" (Brandes 1882:25). That Gérard de Nerval and Eugène Sue are not treated can however rather be attributed to their anchoring in the local, such that they do not meet the otherwise slightly unclear demand of "writing for the whole world."

Regarding Brandes' selection of authors, only one woman, George Sand, is presented in *The Romantic School in France*. Marceline Desbordes-Valmore published *Elégies et poésies nouvelles*, *Poésies inédites*, and *Les Pleurs* to great success in 1825, 1830, and 1833 respectively, that is in the middle of the period that is the focus of Brandes' book. Louise Colet, who was closely associated with both Alfred de Musset and Gustave Flaubert, published the poetry collection *Fleurs du Midi* in 1836; Delphine Girardin, so central to the Romantic milieu, published *Poésies* in 1836. None of them receive independent treatment, and neither is Flora Tristan's *Pérégrinations d'une paria* from 1838 named. Brandes can only confess that "the period's great female figure, George Sand, must stand as the representative for the women of the age, however entertaining it would have been to portray many of the others, the spiritual Madame de Girardin, the elegiac Madame Desbordes-Valmore, or the two free living authoresses Madame d'Agoult and Madame Allart" (Brandes 1882:590). That Brandes refers to the potential treatment of them as "entertaining" could be an expression of a derogatory attitude toward the literary production of women. He also writes that "nearly every one of George Sand's novels bares the mark of one or another manly influence (…) Again and again she makes herself the organ of the ideas of others" (Brandes 1882:29). In any case it is clear that his reasons for excluding Lamartine also apply to these women: by virtue of their (gendered) political engagement they do not fit into Brandes' idea of French Romanticism as a school that rejects political reality, the bourgeoisie, capitalism, and working life. He sees them as spiritual and free living, but he cannot see them as both politically engaged and a part of the Romantic school.

Comprehensiveness was not Brandes' working principle. He had a great deal of material with which to work in *The Romantic School in France*, and as noted he waits until the end to address his sins of omission. Brandes' work on the volume is marked by another interest, namely his eye for how a school – in a short time and against the background of a miserable political situation – emerges as an exuberant fellowship and yet relatively quickly dissolves into individual careers. Between the two parts of the work we can already sense one of the methodological tensions in his project: the relationship between, on the one side, historical determinism and its consequentially impersonal metaphorics of currents, movements, and fields of force, and on the other, Brandes' biographical orientation, with detailed portraits of a comprehensive series of authors' origins, lives, and genius.

In the following, Brandes' account of the political background of French Romanticism shall be presented. Here there will be special focus on how the Romantic school overcomes the reactionary political, religious, and economic forces that dominated the country in 1830. Thereafter, Brandes' form of argumentation shall be analyzed, as his style, metaphorics, and pathos also play an important role in his argument for the Romantic school as a "proper" reaction. Finally, certain literary-historiographic perspectives shall be identified, in comparisons of Brandes' work with current experimental versions of French literary-historical writing.

The Political Situation in France around 1830

The point of departure for Brandes' literary-historical tableau is fundamentally political. In his conclusion he notes that "we have seen how the Restoration and the *Juste milieu* regime formed the historic background from which Romanticism projected itself, and without which it cannot be understood" (Brandes 1882:591). He singles out the years 1825–1835 as the period in which French literature reacted to the political situation, which was relatively complex. Brandes, who was of course historically closer to the events, thus provides a kind of insider perspective; a more comprehensive account is therefore necessary here.

After the Empire of Napoleon I (1804–1815), France returned to monarchy in 1815, which lasted until 1830. This period, the Restoration, is generally divided into two sub-periods, including in Brandes. The first ran from 1815 to 1824, with the relatively reconciliatory, or at any rate prudent, Louis XVIII as king. Upon his death in 1824, Charles X ascended the throne, pursuing in contrast an ultra-royalist and quite repressive political program of tightening laws and censorship, as well as compensation for the returned nobility; in general, he sought to return France to the absolute monarchy that had been abolished by the Revolution of 1789. After six years of this very Catholic and anti-democratic regime, and various gratuitous changes in key governmental posts, the July Revolution followed in 1830. In the French context this is called *Les Trois Glorieuses*. In contrast to the great revolution of 1789, which properly understood lasted 10 years and was only concluded with Napoleon's coup d'état in 1799, the 1830 revolution played out over only three days in late July. Over and beyond the dearth of bloodletting, the hasty conclusion of this revolution meant that the republican forces, paradoxically enough, were not organized enough to enact the change in regime they desperately desired.

The opportunity was taken by moderate royalist forces (among them the journalist Adolphe Thiers, who in 1871 would become president of the Third Republic) to install Duke Louis Phillipe, who was not of Bourbon stock but of Orléans, as king. Louis Phillipe, who had participated in the revolution of 1789 on the side of the rebels, and who in the 1830s was called the "Bourgeois King," instituted reforms, but rather quickly lost popularity. Brandes refers to him as the "Umbrella King," painting a portrait of a monarch whose good sense and efforts to ingratiate himself with the people was necessary enough as a beginning. Contemporary Frenchmen, especially Parisians, however, viewed this "hunt for popularity" (Brandes 1882:12) as disgraceful, self-abasing petit bourgeois sniveling.

Under this pseudo-royal order French society was divided. The court stepped back, thus vanishing in a series of hitherto prominent cultural patterns of behavior, while the banking and financial worlds, governed by new and less noble social practices and ways of life, took over power. It was no longer traditional values, but capital and industry that governed the interests of the ruling class. At the same time the cultivated portion of the upper bourgeoisie, which earlier had held salons for artists and intellectuals, attempted to gentrify into a new nobility. According to the artists all of this was shameful, irritating, and mediocre – nothing other than a juste milieu kingdom, a society of drabness. Brandes concludes:

> Little wonder that the umbrella soon became the symbol of this monarchy, and the expression *Juste-milieu* — which the King had once cleverly used in speaking of the policy that ought to be employed — became the nickname for everything weak and inefficient, for a power without luster and dignity. (Brandes 1882:14)

Literary History Between Main Current and Historical Electrical Field

Brandes' diagnosis of reaction is interesting on the level of argumentation. He notes how "art for art's sake" becomes the watchword of the age: "during the Revolution the youth worshipped freedom, under Napoleon the glory of war, now they sanctified art" (Brandes 1882:16–17). With the political events of 1830 and the financial bourgeoisie's seizure of power, art became the watchword of the youth. When Brandes asserts that art is a reaction against the hypocritical and money-grubbing bourgeois society, he notes that it is no longer about formal rule-boundedness and symmetry or idealized content. Art means the presentation of the natural, the sensual, the lucid, and the passionate. The artist orients himself against existence and movement and has contempt for sensible rules of style and poetological principles.

The quality of Brandes' argumentation in this critical part of the work is, on closer inspection, due to seemingly objective description rather than a stylistic dramatization of an historically thrilling situation: "all the conditions were present in combination which were certain to impel, with *force*, young and restless minds towards romantic intoxication"; "*enthusiasm* for liberty in art"; "art was the highest," "its natural antipathy to utilitarianism and plutocracy managed to compel in the intellectual *current* (…) a *turning* in the direction of antagonism to everything existing and accepted, and at the same time mightily increased the *force* of the current" (Brandes 1882:15); "a *movement* within the mind had begun that recalled the Renaissance" (Brandes 1882:18). This state of affairs is asserted by Brandes as fact, but he provides no actual examples in support of it. This may be because Brandes' interests lie elsewhere than in demonstrating his assertions through evidence. He is less interested in documenting the literary-historical causal relations than in characterizing the concept that already figures in the title, which is introduced at the beginning as something that is of concern to him during this period: the Romantic *school*.

The traits that occupy Brandes are located less in the diachronic perspective, which incidentally figures prominently later in the work, than in a characterization of the selected decade as a dynamic continuum. The terms Brandes employs in determining the emergence of the Romantic school reveal this clearly: "movement," "force that compels," "restless," "turning," "force," "current." There is thus much more a sense of a field dominated and animated by physical forces than a historically determined reaction to previous events. This is the central idea in Brandes' larger project on reaction, which has now received a supplement: this group of authors' interests and ideas are of course a reaction to a political situation, but the reaction also overcomes its initial negativity, insofar as it takes place upon an electrical field that is perceived to be common to all:

> Their meeting is electric; they exchange ideas with youthful haste, impart to each other their hatreds, their sympathies and antipathies, and all these well-springs of feeling flow together like the streams that form a river. (Brandes 1882:22)

The recurrent river metaphor is supplemented here with a metaphorics that makes it prudent to conceive of Brandes' chosen decade as an electromagnetic field. Electrically charged particles, in this case the authors' and artists' "hatreds" and "sympathies," are impacted by the force of the field, and the movement of these particles in turn impacts the field. It is decisive for Brandes that the Romantics were united in opposition against the money-mad bourgeoisie, yet their unity came from a common movement – an electrical force – rather than clear ideas or a Romantic program. It is electricity, currents, and exchange rather than ideas and thoughts. Brandes points numerous times to Hugo's preface to his drama *Cromwell* as a critical text for the school, yet he also notes that it is not entirely clear to the members of the Romantic school, indeed even to Hugo himself, what these pages actually say:

> They may be only half true, they may be vague, but they have this remarkable quality that, in spite of more or less indefiniteness, they affront all traditional prejudices and wound the vanity of the day where it is most vulnerable, whilst they ring in the ears of the young generation like a call, like a new, audacious watchword (…) So it happens that first one man, then another, then a third, comes to be a spokesman of the new tendency, each with his own standpoint, his own past, his own revolt, his ambition, his need, his hope, his resolve. (Brandes 1882:21–22)

Victor Hugo's unclear yet seductive prose pages function, to continue the metaphor, more like an electric coil that conducts the electrical field. As Brandes emphasizes in the passage quoted above, it is crucial that the charges of the Romantic electrical field are, outwardly speaking, critical and spiteful, but inwardly the field is fundamentally ethical. Thus after 1830 the mere reaction to a political disappointment is overcome by a positive ethics held in common: admiration for that which is worthy, which provides meaning for the electricity, the forces, the current. Brandes repeatedly notes that the distinguishing mark of the school is the immeasurable regard of its members for each other: the security of a brotherhood that provides the field with its power of cohesion. One example of this is that the authors share the feeling of being outside of society as authors, not because they have yet to write themselves into social status, but more because they cannot understand themselves to be a part of the new financial bourgeois society. Such a reaction seems to them wholly natural, and thus self-imposed exile necessary, yet it is in their meeting and in their common feeling of this necessity that their reaction leads to the formation of a school. According to Brandes, it is the experience of this shared fate that transforms the Romantic school from being a negatively oriented and merely reactionary circle to a self-reinforcing and centrifugal electric force in the literary and political landscape.

Three Main Ideas of the Romantic School

That such a fellowship – which had first been a reaction against petit bourgeois values, capitalism, and a normative understanding of art – could emerge and consequently produce important literature is the result of another circumstance. This electromagnetic field consisted, as previously mentioned, of many kinds of artists – writers, musicians, pictorial artists, and composers – as well as critics, but they did not possess a common program. They found one another and worked together out of a will to break with society and to rebel, and their self-understanding was rooted in an idea that being an outcast is an essential part of being an artist. They were not creatures of the court (as Racine and Molière had been in the seventeenth century) or of the world (as Voltaire and Diderot were in the eighteenth century), but rather shut out from the start. They would rather not curry favor with the public's miserable taste and preconceived ideas. Brandes notes that the artists of the Romantic school would be artists in themselves and no longer follow along with the "surface current" of the age, which consisted of opinion, prejudice, and convention. They allowed themselves to be driven by the undercurrent of the age: a "class of urges that had yet to take shape, but were in the air" (Brandes 1882:30). This was the "unifying element in their efforts" (Brandes 1882:30). Once again, Brandes thus characterizes the Romantic school in natural and physical terms: currents, elements, formlessness, air, and so on are the conditions for an artistic fellowship out of which, in time, individual artistic personalities would be distilled.

Literary Contrasts

It becomes clear that the school's desire for solidarity came before its ideas when Brandes takes up the task of recounting what actually crystallizes in and through this school. He identifies three characteristics of the Romantic school, of which the first acts programmatically, while the second and third act to annul the first. The first, which stems from Victor Hugo, involves a new definition of the content of literature. Literature should integrate contradictions and no longer portray types. It should no longer be built on the plausible and the credible, but on the true and the natural. In his famous preface, Hugo says that the real should be called forth from immediate contrasts and contradictions such as beauty/ugliness, virtue/depravity, and good/evil. Literature should not distinguish these in a moral sense and should not identify the good and the beautiful as higher than the wicked and the ugly, but represent them in integrated form: Caesar can thus be nervous that his triumphal carriage might tip over. Similarly, a judge may become so hungry that his sense of justice wavers. Such is the nature of man in reality, and it is as such that literature ought to present it.

The Supernatural

Brandes, however, identifies a characteristic of Romantic literature that de facto detaches its poetics from the naturalistic register. In the first place these contrasts in Romantic literature are exaggerated, and involve more the relation between the natural and the supernatural than pinpointing and classifying contrasts in human nature. It is difficult for Romantics to manage prosaic and quotidian contradictions, and Brandes provides a series of persuasive examples to argue that they are most interested in presenting the contrasts between the mundane and the supernatural. Texts by Sand, Hugo, and Balzac are cited to demonstrate that the fantastic is an important element as an opposing pole to the miserable reality of 1830.

A novel that demonstrates this configuration of the supernatural and the fantastic amidst the new social and political reality is Balzac's *La Peau de Chagrin* of 1831 (Brandes 1882:245–248). It begins with a young man, Raphäel, who has lost his money gambling, wandering despairingly along the Seine and considering drowning himself. He absent-mindedly enters an antique shop, coming into possession of a magic piece of shagreen that grants all wishes. The price, however, is that each time a wish is granted, the young man's life is shortened. The first thing Raphäel wishes for is a sumptuous dinner, and immediately he is met with a series of journalist friends, whom he invites to a grandiose and Dionysian banquet with a wealthy financier. The novel takes place in October 1830, that is several months after the July Revolution, and its young men are thus all marked by the political confusion and disillusion over the "new" regime, while at the same time enjoying the temptations of the Upper Seine, that is the riches of the city's actual new center of power. After having lived his life, becoming wealthy and successful in fashionable Paris, Raphäel grows old rapidly, renounces everything, and in a kind of paradox of biological desire, dies of his only remaining wish: the wish to live. The novel exemplifies Brandes' diagnosis of French Romanticism in depicting a quotidian existence against a backdrop of a politically unsatisfying reality that is at the same time governed by a fantastic and supernatural element.

The Romantic School and the Classical Style

There is something persuasive in Brandes' analysis of how certain weighty Romantic works go beyond (or forget) the very poetics that otherwise serve as their point of departure. He identifies a further characteristic that acts not to transgress but rather to denaturalize Romantic poetics. This deserves notice in that it can evidently explain Brandes' description of the Romantic school as an electrical field. He asserts that the contradictions the Romantics seek out are in reality Classical antitheses, and that they maintain these contradictions in strictly Classical forms: they are Romantics, but Classical in form. In the second part of Goethe's *Faust*, for example, the powerful content overflows the form, while among the French Classical forms and structures are upheld. Brandes compares Victor Hugo to none other than Pierre Corneille, the chief exponent of the Classical drama in France (Brandes 1882:39). While the identification of the supernatural and fantastic element in literary works is a corrective to the self-understanding of the Romantic school, it is quickly abandoned by Brandes. His point about the stylistic and formal strictness of the Romantics, however, is one he returns to again and again throughout his review of the authors of the Romantic school. Of Charles Nodier, who together with André Chénier was a source of inspiration for the Romantics, Brandes notes:

> However eager he was to defend the new tendencies in literature, he remained conservative in the matter of style, expressing the 19th century fantastic in the strict and perspicuous style of the 17th. Frenzied in his fancies, he is prudent and clear in his form. (Brandes 1882:59)

To Nodier and the other source of inspiration for the school, Chénier, Brandes thus attributes a "chastity of style" and a "sober clarity of presentation." Together they therefore provided for the school the following stylistic point of departure:

> It was a foundation of this kind the new Romantic school would build upon — the noblest simplicity of language, correct drawing,

a Grecian rhythm in all the transitions, the beautiful lines of the bas-relief, pure color, and strict form. (Brandes 1882:111)

Brandes proceeds right from the start to characterize the style and form of virtually all the Romantics according to this idea of the Classical. Of George Sand:

She is romantic in her enthusiasms, in the way in which she yields her personality unresistingly to her feelings, which defy rules and norms, but she is in a strict sense classical in the rule-boundedness of her periodic structures, the abstract beauty of her forms, and the sobriety of her coloring. (Brandes 1882:206–207)

Mérimée receives a corresponding characterization:

Without difficulty it can be said that Mérimée, despite the restraint and strict classicism of his style, is in many respects an outstanding representative of the French Romantic tendency. (Brandes 1882:347)

Brandes continues: "Mérimée's restraint and discretion receives its final testimony in the classical and elegant strictness of his style" (Brandes 1882:411). Of Stendhal (Brandes uses his birth name Henri Beyle), he says by way of introduction that his intention was that "one ought to be 'Romantic' with respect to the ideas, for that is 'the challenge of the century,' yet one ought to remain classical in manner of expression, in the form of language and turn of phrase (…) one ought to strive to write like Pascal, Voltaire, La Bruyère" (Brandes 1882:72–73). And Brandes concludes with Stendhal by noting that "it is clear enough that happiness for Beyle consisted of clarity" (Brandes 1882:325). With respect to Théophile Gauthier, Brandes speaks of "the perfection of form and of refinement, the strict purity of rhyming and proportionality of harmony" (Brandes 1882:433).

Brandes sees this Classical quality of style in all the authors with which he is occupied. Moreover, he had bombastically announced as much in his introductory characterization: "all the French Romantics are Classicists. Mérimée is a Classicist, Gautier a Classicist, George Sand a Classicist, even Victor Hugo is a Classicist" (Brandes 1882:39). Paul V. Rubow argues that the idea of the Classicism of French Romanticism was already present in Brandes, but it was only after studying German and English Romanticism that he could with certainty ascribe this peculiar stylistic trait to it (Rubow 1932:15–17). This is a valuable insight; one can also tie the idea of the Classicism of Romanticism to the description of the literary electrical field noted previously.

It is striking in itself how stringently Brandes applies the same concept to denote the style of the Romantics: purity, clarity, strictness, symmetry, and sobriety. Yet it is still more striking that this characterization, which acts both apodictically and unsupported, seems to be in conflict with what Romantic style is universally regarded to be. Brandes expresses this as follows: "if by Romantic, as is customary, we understand an excess of content over form, content not subordinated to recognizable form (…) then all the French Romantics are Classicists" (Brandes 1882:39).

From this it can be concluded that within the Classical style there is a more determinate relation between content and form, and that form dominates content. More precisely formulated and with a nod to Aristotle, it can be said that the two qualities that should be determinative of the Classical style are clarity and deviation. Thus Aristotle writes in his *Poetics*:

> The perfection of style is to be clear without being mean. The clearest style is that which uses only current or proper words; at the same time it is mean (…) Lofty and elevated is that style which dispenses with all too familiar words and employs rarer ones (…) Yet if one exclusively uses such expressions, the language will be either inscrutable (a riddle) or barbaric (…) One thus ought to employ a mixture. (Aristotle 1999:51–52)

Aristotle's qualification of Classical style (*lexis*) is thus double: it should be clear and sharp and at the same time possess something distinctive, a foreignness that distinguishes it from ordinary speech. It can be said that the Classical style is itself conscious of the poetic effects of deviation, yet at the same time is also aware that this deviation must not exceed the boundaries of immediate understanding. It is necessary to distance the thought from its customary and trite expression, on the condition that clarity is in equilibrium with the stylistic deviation and, like a stylistic superego, binds it to the thought, whose expression thus avoids becoming "barbaric" or "inscrutable."

Style and Field

If we now place Brandes' designation of the Romantic style in France together with Aristotle's definition of the domain of style via deviation from the coordinates and clarity, a particular perspective comes to light. When Brandes constantly characterizes the style of the Romantics as Classical through predicates such as clarity, purity, sobriety, symmetry, and so on, we should not understand this as a demand for a normative style. For Aristotle clarity was a kind of stylistic relay that kept an eye on deviation, which could come forward if the style risked becoming overwrought. Logic dictates, then, that if there is a high degree of clarity, purity, and sobriety among the Romantics, then it is precisely because there is a powerful tendency toward deviation in their works. Or to continue this line of thought: if there is a high degree of tension in Romantic content, then there should also be a highly functioning and proven relay that is on a level with the charges of the field.

Thus clarity is not just a quality of syntax, diction, genre, and ideal type. It is operative. It is a purifying and cleansing force that does not impact the historical norms of what literature ought to be. If the Romantic style can in the sense of its obstinateness be said to be the expression of complex emotional, social, or political experience, then the clear and pure expression can be understood as a clarification and purification of such complex Romantic experience. Thus there is no invocation of a governing tradition according to whose particular rules one must write, and respect certain normative demands of style. Stylistic clarity is instead operative as continuous linguistic clarification and revelation of the emergence of a complex new reality within language.

Brandes notes that the program of the Romantics was not particularly clear from the beginning, and that it was only after the school dissolved and the individual authors embarked on their independent careers that clear ideas took shape. Thinking in terms of justice, equality, the truth, and politics amidst the new tumultuous reality thus presumed, according to Brandes, that the ideas were guided through the initial powerful tension within the electrical field (affection and admiration), thereafter acquiring form. It is here that clarity as an operative element is important, because it is this – not accordance with the normative – which guarantees that the extraction of the new ideas respects the new political reality of the thinking, its empirical conditions of possibility. It is in this manner that the unity between thought and stylization should be clarified, every time the thought of the new is extracted from the ideal, secure sphere in and of itself, with its point of departure in the new sensibilities, new political conditions, and new social practices. Clarity becomes the operative element that guarantees the confused and emergent ideas of the electrical field will be crystallized, continually revealed, and purified, so that they can remain faithful to their dynamic nature in their further development within the various careers of the authors. These originally unclear yet commonly held ideas are the content of the electrical field that Brandes calls the Romantic school, and when he notes that a proper reaction is "short and powerful" in contrast to the Danish "swamp," it could be asserted the proper form of reaction in France is precisely the form of clarification. The Romantic school identified a long series of ideas that had yet to become norms or ideals, but which were still coming into being; it is in the individual Romantic authors' own careers that they would ultimately be implemented.

Reception and Afterlife

Local Reception
After the intense debate around the lectures and the person of Georg Brandes at the start of the 1870s, *Main Currents* did not attract much attention in Denmark. Brandes' polemical and aggressive, ad hominem

style had been noted abroad, but in Denmark it led to a kind of generalized retreat from *Main Currents*, indeed almost a kind of non-reception regarding its ambition and quality. With the appearance of the *Romantic School in France* in 1882 this seemed to change. Sophus Schandorph reviewed the book quite positively in *Ude og Hjemme*, remarking that Brandes was no longer an "agitator" (Schandorph 1883:197), and in *Illustreret Tidende* H.S. Vodskov concludes correspondingly: "the transition from polemicist to man of science is in all essence complete" (Vodskov 1882:271).

The National Liberal *Dagbladet* was also remarkably complimentary toward the book (Knudsen 1988:210), as was *Sydsvenska Dagbladet Snällposten*, published in Malmö, which discussed the work in its "News from the New School" section. This latter review emphasized the change in attitude from the previous volumes, for example in the observation that while Brandes was still not free of "fanaticism," he was, however, in his basic approach "more mature and more thorough than ever before" (*Sydsvenska Dagbladet Snällposten*, 1883). One gets the sense that his longer stay abroad rendered Brandes' need to polemicize against Denmark less pressing, at the same time that, returning home, he was perhaps interested in being received as a less combative type of critic.

Reception in France
It was Brandes' grand dream to be acknowledged in France. In an 1888 letter to Georges Noufflard, an art connoisseur, he writes:

> Je lis toujours beaucoup de français. J'aime votre littérature plus que toute autre. J'ai écrit plus de livres sur la France que sur tout autre pays et pourtant je suis parfaitement inconnu en France. Quand j'avais écrit un seul article sur les Flamands on était prêt à m'ériger des statues en Flandre; tous les poètes m'envoyaient leurs œuvres, tous les journaux parlaient de moi. Quand j'ai écrit deux petits articles sur les écrivains Russes sans même savoir leur langue, on a été tellement touché de mes connaissances qu'on m'a loué, m'a traduit, m'a fait venir. Sur la France j'ai écrit plus de volumes que je

n'ai écrit d'articles sur la Russie, et on sait à peine que j'existe. Un certain Charles Simond veut me traduire; depuis deux ans il cherche en vain un éditeur, bien que Paul Bourget m'ait offert d'écrire une introduction. Cela m'attriste un peu, car une réputation n'est pas consacrée aussi longtemps que la France n'a pas dit son mot.

[I constantly read French. I love your literature more than any other. I have written more books about France than any other country, and still I am altogether unknown in France. When I had written a single article on Flemish literature, they were ready to erect a statue of me; all their poets sent me their works, all their newspapers talked about me. When I had written two short articles on Russian poets, without even knowing the language, they were so moved by my knowledge of them that I was praised, translated and invited to visit. I have written more books on France than I have articles on Russia, and still the French hardly know I exist. A certain Charles Simond wants to translate me; for two years he has searched in vain for a publisher, even though Paul Bourget has for a long time promised to write an introduction. It irritates me, for the measure of an author has not been established as long as France has withheld its judgement.] (Brandes 1952:131–132)

It was only in 1902 that Brandes' *The Romantic School in France* became the sole volume of the six to be translated into French. Moreover, it was translated from a German edition and not the Danish original, and while the introduction is quite laudatory, it was written by the less well-known (compared to Paul Bourget) aesthetics professor Victor Basch (Basch 1902). There had been a longer and quite critical French reaction to Brandes' *Main Currents* in 1893, from the critic Jean Thorel. Thorel begins by asserting that Brandes is a polemicist and a partisan for an anti-religious and anti-clerical party, and that it was this positioning that initially established his success and reputation among the youth of Denmark. Thorel next argues that Brandes' *Main Currents* is hamstrung by the author's commitment to a doctrine from the Enlightenment. In the first place, there is an internal contradiction between the idea and the main current, and in the second, from the very first pages Brandes limits his corpus to *certain* central groups and *certain* significant movements.

The problem for Thorel is that Brandes' selection criteria are based on neither the formal determinations of literary genre nor the intellectual-historical content, which objectively can be said to have determined the European main currents. The main currents he addresses are those that point forward to 1848, the year of the great European revolutions, which are important in that they contribute to the literary development he traces. But Brandes, according to Thorel, defined his project before he even began his analyses according to the scheme of revolution, reaction, and the overcoming of reaction, which is then filled out with suitable works, without however providing space for works, genres, authors, or ideas that do not fit the scheme. The concept of the main current is thus not only tautological, but also ideological. Brandes, states Thorel, decided ahead of time that those who overcame the reaction could be designated as main currents, such that he presupposes what he then proves. Brandes had likewise predetermined that this overcoming should point forward to the revolutions of 1848, which according to Thorel is an ideological decision and justifies calling Brandes, who seeks to be acknowledged as a man of science, a polemicist instead.

Thorel further criticizes Brandes' conception of literature as an art form that submits problems to debate, by inquiring as to how we should analyze and interpret those quieter canonical works, that is those that are not possessed of such urgency yet are still read. Thorel furthermore points out that the drama in six acts that Brandes had announced in the first volume is in fact of faulty construction. His focus on the Revolution of 1789 necessitated that the émigré literature (for example, Chateaubriand and Madame de Staël) came first, followed by German Athenaeum Romanticism. But the revolt against Weimar Classicism in Jena and Berlin, as a defined literary period, was already concluded by the time the French émigrés began to write. Thorel concludes his critique with the following:

> Un avocat ayant une cause à défendre: en résumé, c'est là tout M. Brandes, et c'est ce qui fait, selon nous, tout le vice de son œuvre. Elle n'est qu'un long plaidoyer, confus et indirect, en faveur d'une cause, et d'une cause étrangère à la littérature. M. Brandes a déclaré lui-même qu'il n'a eu en vue, en composant cette histoire dite des principaux courans [sic] de la littérature, que le progrès des idées libérales.
>
> [A lawyer defending a case. That is the whole of Brandes' work, and in my reckoning my problem with it. It is just a long, grubbing and indirect defense of a case that is alien to literature. Mr. Brandes has himself declared that in his presentation of the so-called main currents of literature, his only concern has been the progress of liberal ideas.] (Thorel 1893:358)

That Brandes is a polemicist, or simply polemical, is hardly a new statement. Nor is the assertion that this fifth volume could be seen to be apologetic. The majority of Thorel's objections are fair, but the question remains what consequences they ought to have for the evaluation of Brandes' work. Thorel seems piqued at Brandes' methodological liberties and determines from the start that the work suffers under these to such a degree that it cannot be taken seriously from a scientific perspective.

If, however, we view Brandes' work as what it is – a literary history – then it appears inspired and "elastic," as William Barry wrote in a 1904 review in *The Bookman* (Barry 1904:97). It could also be said that it is independent, in a double sense of the word. First, it is autonomous and individually secure in itself, which in the scientific context thus means isolated. Brandes' work stands on its own, but therefore also stands alone from the perspective of science. That this independence was a problem at the time is understandable, as attested by Thorel, but from a modern perspective it is instead interesting. If we follow along, point by point, Thorel's objections, then his disqualification of Brandes as literary historian by virtue of his overly independent methodology seems to us old-fashioned.

Turned on its head, it could be seen as meaningful in identifying a potential scientific modernism in Brandes' project.

Experimental Literary History Writing
Brandes can be compared to newer and distinctive experiments in French literary historiography. Since around 2000, especially in the Anglo-Saxon academy, efforts have been made to formulate new versions of French literary history, including the placing of parentheses around otherwise classic and – one might think – more or less unavoidable categories such as period, style, historical background, and author.

The first in this series of experimental literary-historiographic efforts appeared in 1998, bearing the appropriate title of *A New History of French Literature* (edited by Denis Hollier). Through a long series of short-form chapters (the work counts 165 contributors), the book identifies what could be called "literary events" that are not, on first sight, recognizable to the reader in the context of overarching categories such as period (for example Classicism, Romanticism, or Naturalism), genre (for example novel, tragedy, or sonnet), or historical situation (for example political regime).

The chapters are most often anchored in a date, an unknown person, or a social-historical anecdote that conventional literary history has overlooked. One chapter, which addresses Voltaire's dramatic production and aesthetic taste during the Enlightenment, is thus titled: "1759, 23 April. The Duc de Lauragais pays the Théâtre-Francais an Indemnity of 12,000 Livres to Remove Spectators from the Stage." The chapter details how the actor who played the king in Voltaire's *Sémiramis* had stumbled over the privileged spectators who had leave to purchase side seats on the stage, and who had proceeded in the closest quarters (and quite loudly) to express their amusement at what otherwise was a moment of seriousness in the tragedy. The Duke of Lauragais thus paid the theatre to move all these seats for the remainder of the performances, thus creating a wholly new understanding of the work of art as autonomous fiction, which the new bourgeoisie should observe at a distance and with respectful seriousness. Aside from the surprising yet persuasive connections between unnoticed events and significant new literary forms and ideas, it is interesting that works – in this case Voltaire's – are treated from different points of view by other chapters (as is also the case with Marcel Proust and Surrealism, for example), such that the work or the period emerges as a cross-thematized tension rather than, in light of its unity, being bound up with a priori categories such as authorial intent, time, and genre.

The second example of experimental literary historiography is called *French Global. A New Approach to Literary History*, and was edited by the Harvard professors Christie McDonald and Susan Suleiman. Published in 2011, it was informed by the awareness that French literature had come into being not within a geographical and political continuum – a nation – but in the meeting of and exchange with other cultures. French literature is a "literature of interaction," whose most important works, each in a wholly distinct manner and to varying degrees, were conditioned by meetings and negotiations with other political, geographical, linguistic, ethical, and aesthetic conditions, from Montesquieu's Persians to the Irishman Samuel Beckett, who wrote his works in French; from Pierre Corneille's *Oedipus* to contemporary African Francophone authors; from Honoré de Balzac and the conquest of Algeria in 1830 to Gustave Flaubert's Orientalism; and so on. To a great degree and in varying ways, all came into being in the encounter with one or another form of cultural "otherness." This concept does not just allow the identification of a series of exchanges between the French canon and a generalized cultural otherness; it also serves to demonstrate that the porousness of national borders, historically viewed, is both a recurrent and productive characteristic of a literature that otherwise is often viewed as both self-sufficient and proud of its national self-understanding. *French Global* is thus also logically organized into larger parts whose titles (*Spaces*, *Mobilities* and *Multiplicities*) are a far cry from the typically temporal and aesthetic literary-historiographical categorizations such as genre, style, period, and century.

These new literary histories, each in its own iconoclastic manner, both surprise and persuade, if the premises with which they are conceived and written are accepted. Both share a clear sense that a de-sacralization of the above-mentioned literary-historiographical concepts, from organized categories to ad hoc analytical tools, will permit new and unappreciated problematics to emerge. These new efforts thus conceive of the object of literary historiography as dynamic, in tension, and in conflict, in that they mobilize a series of new concepts to coordinate and identify these tensions and conflicts.

Turning back to Brandes, we may rediscover a measure of the elements of these new literary histories. As noted, Brandes also wanted to analyze conditions that had not been charted out beforehand: a polemical scheme of the configurations of the reaction and its overcoming during the nineteenth century. If *French Global* challenges the national understanding of French literature, and if *A New History of French Literature* challenges the logic of causation and turns anecdote and determinism upside down (and neither of these things is innocent), then it seems that what primarily provoked Jean Thorel is that Brandes had no methodology, and thus no corresponding concepts or categories with which to administer his big idea of reaction and overcoming. As a result his project appears tautological.

Brandes' work is of course in the main a long series of author portraits, which do not in this manner feed into or "prove" the thesis. But Brandes, in his lack of a recognizable methodology, did possess – and this is perhaps what most provoked Thorel – two quite effective metaphorical registers with which to dramatize the material in relation to his idea. Instead of concepts and categories to identify the content of his literary history, Brandes develops two figurative registers within which to position the events and structures that are decisive in his grand literary-historical scheme. In the first place, he employs the water metaphorics: main currents, tributaries, dykes, swamps, and so on are concepts that recur in the majority of the volumes and are employed to illuminate the complexity of the diachronic course of reaction that functions as the point of departure for *Main Currents*.

In the second place, in *The Romantic School in France*, Brandes develops a metaphorics taken over from physics, according to which the Romantic school is portrayed as a magnetic field that rejected the new capitalist market economy, the political conservatism, the financial bourgeoisie, and the new opportunistic art, yet wholly naturally maintained the similarly charged elements that consequently acclaimed and strengthened one another's productions. This pictorial language was Brandes' method of grasping the *synchronic* aspect of the overcoming of reactionary and reactive France: a positively charged field, which in a few years gathered authors and artists into a school that consequently dissolved into individual careers, which correspond to the portraits that take up the second half of Brandes' fifth volume of *Main Currents*.

In other words, Brandes has both a (polemical) idea of literary-historical development in Europe and a stylistic method of dramatizing this idea. He can be called modern for two reasons: first because he conceives of the important points in literary history as problems, conflicts, and tensions (rather than as new ideas or genres), and second because he is aware that this new conception of the conflict-ridden gravitational points of literary history requires something more than the kind of scientific methodology Thorel demanded. For the decisive problems and conflicts to become comprehensible in their historical development, a series of stylized images are required – images that reveal the lines and patterns for which there are no corresponding scientific concepts.

As mentioned, Brandes had already announced in the first volume of *Main Currents* that the work would be a drama in six acts, yet in these final remarks on the modernity of Brandes we have a different and deeper variant of this initial pronouncement: namely that this drama is not just a manner of organizing the historical development of an immense amount of material, but also a stylistic method. With a little audacity, it could be concluded that *Main Currents* constitutes the first foray of literary studies into not comparative literary history, but experimental literary history, which would examine the potential and the boundaries of an idea that cannot be identified by classical literary historiography. In *Main Currents*, Georg Brandes found a style that would permit literary history to reveal itself as a drama.

YOUNG GERMANY (1890)
Adam Paulsen

Introduction

Young Germany – the sixth and final volume of *Main Currents* – was nearly as long in the making as the first five volumes taken together, and one can well understand Brandes' sense of relief when at long last in 1890 he was able to complete the work that had occupied him ever since he had presented its ambitious plan in the introduction to *Emigrant Literature* in 1872.

Young Germany is at once the lengthiest and the least homogeneous of the six volumes. While the previous five volumes were each possessed of a delimiting theme around which the narrative was structured, there is something unfocused and disjointed about the sixth volume, as if the author found it difficult to determine what should be included and which story he would tell. No doubt some of this is due to the material, which not only proved to be more difficult to shape and to synthesize than expected, but also contained fewer essential authorships than that which constituted the foundation of the other volumes. Part of the explanation why the content of the final volume did not have a greater impact, and why Jørgen Knudsen deemed it "the dullest of the six" (Knudsen 1994:379), is presumably to be found in the nature of the subject matter.

However, the author who had initially launched such an ambitious project was not the same person on all accounts as the one who would now bring it to completion. The material did not captivate him in the same manner as before; other authors and projects demanded attention, and his youthful faith in the political-ideological program that underpinned the formation of the original plan had, if not entirely vanished, at least been partially overlaid by the skepticism of middle age. Whereas for the younger Brandes a poetic work stood or fell by virtue of its inherent political tendency, the older writer valued the great personality alone, regardless of the presence of particular political attitudes – indeed even regardless of whether the poet was interested in politics at all.

Finally, the world at the conclusion of the 1880s was very different from that at the beginning of the 1870s, and not the least to the south of the Danish–German border. In the course of the nearly six years he had lived in Berlin, Brandes had had ample opportunity to observe up close the cultural and political development of the new German Reich, and conditions seemed to him to be far from encouraging. In Brandes' view, the Germany that took form under the leadership of Bismarck was a military and police state modeled after Prussian ideals, defined by subservience and cultural stagnation. He certainly acknowledged the greatness of Bismarck, especially in foreign policy, but it was a concern to him that the German Chancellor, by concentrating power in his own person, kept the population in a state of political infancy and immaturity.

All these circumstances, to greater or lesser degrees, were significant in the crafting of *Young Germany*.

Background and Genesis

Periodization, Selected Authorships, Omissions

Despite the 18 years between the publication of the first and sixth volumes of *Main Currents*, Brandes proceeded in almost all essentials according to the plan for *Young Germany* he had presented in the introduction to *Emigrants Literature*:

> the sixth and last group of writers is inspired by the ideas of the Greek war and the July revolution and, like the French writers, in Byron's shade sees the leader of the movement for freedom. The most important of these young writers are of Jewish descent: Heinrich Heine, Ludwig Börne, and later Berthold Auerbach. (Brandes 1872:13–14)

Upon close examination of *Young Germany*, one discover that Berthold Auerbach is barely mentioned, and that the shadow of Byron does not loom as large as it did for the young Brandes. Yet the central idea did not change, and both Heine and Börne maintain their narrative centrality as initially planned.

"Young Germany" is a designation for a relatively small group of authors whose central core includes, in addition to the aforementioned Heinrich Heine and Ludwig Börne, Karl Gutzkow, Heinrich Laube, Theodor Mundt, and Ludolf Wienbarg. They were connected by a more or less directly expressed critique of the Metternichian system, as well as corresponding agitation for political reforms, liberal conceptions of freedom, and anti-clericalism: in short, an emancipatory program that broke with the abstraction and unworldliness of late idealism and the political conservatism of the Restoration (Hermand 1974:370–372). Literature should keep abreast of the age and engage with social and political questions instead of seeking refuge in a lofty kingdom of allegedly eternal values. For the same reason the poets of Young Germany did not have much regard for the national hero Goethe, who was viewed as the chief representative of the political impotency of the Restoration – a "fool for stability" and a "servant of the princes," who handed over an unfree people to the pleasure of the prince (Hermand 1974:372). These writers were not equally thorough in their critique, however, and they differed significantly when it came to the national and political implementation of their liberal ideas. Some agitated for a republic, in Börne's case even with a cosmopolitan bent: "I hate every society that is less than the whole of human society" [Ich hasse jede Gesellschaft, die kleiner ist als die menschliche] (Börne 1964a:625). Others contented themselves with a constitutional monarchy within the national boundaries. And while all were capable of intervening on behalf of the cause of political liberty and especially freedom of expression, only Börne and Georg Büchner were seriously preoccupied with the social question (Hermand 1974:384–385).

This variety in attitudes is in part explained by the fact that the above-mentioned authors did not have all that much to do with one another (Hohendahl 2004:568–569). Strictly speaking, they first became a distinct group when the Federal Diet in Frankfurt in 1835 – after a previous smear campaign against especially Gutzkow, led by Wolfgang Menzel, a litigious and at the time influential newspaper publisher with whom Gutzkow had earlier collaborated – instituted a total ban on the writings of Heine, Mundt, Gutzkow, Laube, and Wienbarg across the German Confederation, claiming that the mentioned authors "under the name 'Young Germany' or 'Young Literature'" "openly (…) attack the Christian religion in the most brazen manner, disparaging existing social conditions, and undermining all discipline and decency" [unter der Bennenung "das junge Deutschland" oder "die junge Literatur" (…) unverholen (…) die christliche Religion auf die frechste Weise anzugreifen, die bestehenden sozialen Verhältnisse herabzuwürdigen und alle Zucht und Sittlichkeit zu verstören] (*Verbot der Schriften des 'Jungen Deutschland'*, December 10, 1835).

It is this little and relatively heterogeneous group of authors who make up the nucleus of *Young Germany*. Aside from the fact that the central figures of Young Germany can be counted on one hand, this brief era in German literature did not encompass much more than the five years or so between the July Revolution in France and the ban of 1835. Brandes solved the problem in the most obvious way, namely by letting the volume continue up to the revolutions of 1848, which thus comes to serve as the vanishing point not only of *Young Germany* but of the entirety of *Main Currents*. In addition, the volume contains a series of perspectival chapters on, among other things, the philosophy of the period (G.W.F. Hegel, Ludwig Feuerbach) and its most prominent female figures (Bettina von Arnim, Rahel Varnhagen, Charlotte Stieglitz), which are perhaps not equally necessary for the context. Finally he also includes the ubiquitous Goethe, who serves as a continual point of connection and comparison for the majority of the main figures of Young Germany, and alongside Heine is the single most important figure in the volume.

The main problem for Brandes was, however, that neither the authors of Young Germany nor the political literature of the period up to 1848 are particularly interesting from an artistic point of view. And even though he is undoubtedly correct in his assertion that Heine's declining popularity after the unification of Germany in 1871 was predominantly due to political concerns, the same does not apply to the rest of the Young Germany authors, none of whom have a prominent place in German literary history and did not have it in Brandes' own time either. He was not successful in finding a satisfying solution to this problem, though numerous possibilities were available. The most natural solution would have been to include Biedermeier literature as a contrast to the political literature. But Brandes leaves it at a short and idiosyncratic chapter on "Neutral Literature," which is limited to the authors in which the Prussian King Friedrich Wilhelm IV was interested and with whom he associated during his rule (Alexander von Humboldt, Ludwig Tieck, Friedrich de la Motte Fouqué, Friedrich Rückert, Hermann von Pückler-Muskau, and Ferdinand Freiligrath). He does not, however, seem to be aware of the most important German-language poets of the period, the Biedermeier figures Eduard Mörike and Annette von Droste-Hülshoff, and two of its great dramatists, Friedrich Hebbel and Franz Grillparzer, are mentioned only in passing.

Even stranger still is that Brandes fails to pluck two particularly low-hanging fruits who were additionally closely associated with Young Germany: Georg Büchner and Christian Dietrich Grabbe. The canonization of Büchner – along with Heine the only one of the period's political poets who is still read outside German Studies – first began to gather steam in the course of the twentieth century, but his name was known in the relevant literary circles long before then. This was due in large part to Karl Gutzkow, who saw him as a political ally and among other things published his revolutionary drama *Dantons Tod* in his journal *Phönix* as early as 1835, albeit in a more palatable version for fear of the censors (Borgards 2009:318–319). That Büchner was already included as an independent entry in the 1838 *Conversations-Lexikon der Gegenwart* can thus be attributed to Gutzkow's legwork in the preceeding years. There is probably no doubt that Brandes was aware of him, he may even have read *Dantons Tod*

(Knudsen 1994:380). Why he does not mention him thus remains something of a mystery. Even in Johannes Prölß's more orthodox contemporary account of the movement, *Das junge Deutschland*, Büchner is discussed in detail in numerous places (Prölß 1892:34, 585–587). Compared to Büchner, Grabbe is a significantly more peripheral figure, yet it is at least conspicuous that Brandes also fails to mention one of the period's great renewers of the historical drama.

This all helps to explain why the discussion of Heine consumes nearly a quarter of *Young Germany*. With respect to quality, one can do no better than Heine, particularly if Büchner, Grabbe, and the Biedermeier poets are passed over. Brandes himself addresses this problem in the prelude to his commentary on Heine: "this literary group includes no poetic spirit of the very first order and only a single one of a quite elevated rank: Heine. It has not left us with much in the way of the positive, as it functions mostly through negativity, through its capacity to release tension and to clear the air. It is strong in its skepticism and in its hatred of servitude, and in its individualism" (Brandes 1890a:51). But Heine's central placement in *Young Germany* also has an autobiographical component, for few poets played such an important role for the young Brandes. From Brandes' first acquaintance with *Reisebilder* (1826–1830) as a 14-year-old in 1856 until he began his *Main Currents* lectures at the University of Copenhagen, Heine functioned again and again as his literary guide and companion (Dahl 1985:92–93). It was Heine who introduced him to Hegelianism, and who just as importantly acquainted him with the Hellenistic cult of beauty as an opposing pole to the asceticism of Christianity. Through Hippolyte Taine, who considered Heine to be among the greatest of poets, his enthusiasm was later strengthened (Dahl 1985:94). In May of 1871, during his grand tour of Europe, he wrote home to his parents from Napoli:

> I came home from the theater and read through the night a part of Heine's 'Reisebilder' in French. Décidement, Heine is one of the greatest writers the world has produced. The older one gets the more one admires him as a writer. As I have said and thought

for more than two years, he is the only one of Germany's authors who will endure after Goethe. He is the only one of all of them who in certain respects has approached him. I want to reread him methodically. (Brandes 1978:285–286)

The thorough treatment of Heine in *Young Germany* may thus be understood as the fulfillment of a promise to reread Heine "properly."

'An Arbeit klebt Blut': *Young Germany* in the Melting Pot

Work on *Young Germany* stretched over the majority of a decade, with long interruptions along the way. As early as November 1882, when the fifth volume on French Romanticism was completed with "passionate fervor," Brandes resolutely embarked on "the reading of the innumerable books" that had to be studied before the concluding volume could be written (Brandes 1908:46). At this point he had been living in Berlin for more than five years, and thus he found himself not only temporally but also geographically closer to the sources than he had been in producing the previous volumes. How much of this material he had already digested before he began his preliminary studies for the sixth volume is evident from the notes and travel letters from Berlin which were later collected in *Berlin as the German Capital* (1885). When Karl Gutzkow died in 1878, for example, Brandes used the occasion to draw a portrait of the author who "felt himself alienated from the era of Bismarck, unappreciated and forgotten" (Brandes 1885:249–250). And in an 1881 note on "The Movement Against the Jews in Germany," Brandes provides perspective by pointing to Börne and Heine, whose critique of Prussia and "bloody satirical verses about Frederick the Great," according to Brandes, had fueled the fires of anti-Semitism (Brandes 1885:372–374). Still other notes contain more or less detailed remarks on Feuerbach (p. 108), Auerbach (pp. 131–132, 262), Gottfried Keller (pp. 258–260), Rahel Varnhagen (pp. 289–290), and many of the other persons who appear in *Young Germany*.

Beyond functioning as a kind of unintentional preliminary study, Brandes' Berlin years undeniably provided a more sober, not to say disillusioned view of the immense distance between the consciousness of the 1848 revolutions and the new German Reich. In the same note that memorialized Gutzkow, we thus find a fierce critique of the liberal bourgeoisie, which according to Brandes had not only forgotten everything about its own part in the 1848 revolutions, but moreover no longer even understood it. In contemporary literature, Brandes asserts, a 48er appears as either a naïve idealist "or as a giddy rebel, a traitor against fatherland and king." And for the few remaining protagonists from that era, matters are not more favorable: if they are not in exile, they "have either denied their past or remain silent or have fallen into powerless opposition" (Brandes 1885:253).

That Brandes judges the liberals so severely is, of course, a reflection of how high he had set the ideals now being betrayed – and perhaps also indirectly a kind of admission that he had been rather naïve to see in contemporary liberals the inheritors of the generation of 1848. His verdict on the occasion of the 30th anniversary of the revolution – delivered in March 1878, a few months after his arrival in Berlin – suggests as much: "What a vigorous and enthusiastic generation it was, how not vainly it risked blood and life for its hopes, its delusions, its designs. The newly created German Reich owes everything it has in freethinking and faith in ideas to it" (Brandes 1885:107). Only half a year later Brandes no longer maintained any delusions that the German Reich was in any manner indebted to the freethinking of the 48ers. It was now on the contrary clear to him that modern Germany was patterned on Prussian militarism, and that the lack of freedom in Bismarck's military state was a reflection of "the German people's political immaturity" (Brandes 1885:168).

Back in Copenhagen Brandes continued work on *Young Germany*, which took place in close engagement with the capital's literary-minded citizenry. Barely had he returned home from Berlin before *Dags-Avisen* noted that "yesterday evening Dr. Georg Brandes gave his first public lectures on 'Young Germany'" before an enthusiastic audience "of five hundred" (*Dags-Avisen*, February 27, 1883). A few days later this success was repeated with an equally large turnout, again remarked upon by *Dags-Avisen* (March 2, 1883). The next lectures followed in April, and the quick tempo was continued through the year with addresses in October and December. Thereafter he apparently ran out of steam, occupying himself with other more pressing projects. As can be gathered from his library records, which are a barometer of his shifting interests, in 1884 he was particularly occupied with Holberg, while his borrowings in 1885 were dominated by literature on Poland (Nolin 1965:116). In 1886 he borrowed a series of titles by Schlegel, Novalis, Brentano, Hölderlin, and Chamisso for use in revising the German edition of volume two of *Main Currents, Die romantische Schule in Deutschland* (Nolin 1965:116–117). Only in 1887 was study for *Young Germany* resumed, and this time it continued consistently until the completion of the manuscript, with parallel lectures on Heine and his contemporaries from the beginning of November through to mid-December of 1887. A longer preliminary study on Börne and Goethe was published in the journal *Tilskueren* (I, 1884:1–19), a shorter piece on Heine and Rembrandt in *Jule-Kalender* (III, 1887:21–26), and still another on Heine in Peter Nansen's journal *Af Dagens Krønike* (I, 1889:50–63), for which Brandes served as collaborator for a brief period.

In October of 1890, after 10 years of labor, he was at long last at the end of the road. Just how unbearable the last few months in particular had been is evident from his memoirs:

> I was immeasurably burned out and exhausted with the last part of *Main Currents*. I had dragged it along with me since the beginning of 1883, gasping, cursing it, suffering through the execution of an old plan devised by the person I had been in 1871. I recalled the words: *An Arbeit klebt Blut* (work costs blood). I had as mentioned allowed eleven of its sheets to be printed. Now it was impossible for me to remain occupied with it. I felt like a clipped wild goose. (Brandes 1908:273)

Thus was his relief all the greater at having crossed the finish line, completing not only this volume but the entire work. His joy at seeing the last printed sheet of *Young Germany* laid out before him resulted in a poetic look back at the entire work in the form of a distich for each of the six volumes:

I
A war of all wars it was, meant to arouse, to call to arms –
It awakened hatred, that became my fate.

II
A time for spears – and while all around me they rained
to the wall my old specter was nailed.

III
A time for swords – I did not feel myself hard pressed,
I lived young and strong and despised and suffered and longed.

IV
In faith and blood red zeal it was written.
Shelley! Its spirit belongs to you. You I have lived.

V
See how fate turns! Hear its clear tones
A time of triumph! a long, rich, melodious fanfare.

VI
Out of steady defiance and bitter life experience
the final volume of the work is a revelation.
(Brandes 1908:284)

Later Revisions to the Text

Brandes continued to make more or less sweeping changes to the individual parts of *Main Currents* long after 1890. The second, completely rewritten edition of *Emigrant Literature* had been released in 1877, which was followed in 1891 by a rewritten second edition of *The Romantic School in*

Germany. Immediately after the completion of *Young Germany* it was time for a re-inspection of volume five, after which "a fundamental reworking of the third part" (Brandes 1908:352) was expected, and also a re-visitation of volume four, which was to be "revised" and furnished with "individual additions," and so on. It is, explains Brandes, like the "fortifications surrounding a city. As soon as the work is completed, it must be taken up again and spread outward" (ibid.).

In light of the considerable extent of this mania for revision, it is striking how few changes were made to later editions of volume six, and this despite the fact that its first edition was more than double the length of the first edition of volume one. There are hardly any changes in the second edition of volume six in 1898; in the third they are limited to seven in total; and in the following editions there are none at all. Given how difficult this last volume was for Brandes, it is reasonable to presume that the explanation was a lack of desire to engage further with the material. That this factor played a role cannot be denied. But presumably more importantly, *Young Germany*, as the final volume to be written, was significantly closer in form to the author's initial goal as set out in the first volume. Characteristically enough, the changes to the third edition do not seem to be segments of a larger reappraisal. For the most part they consist of the additions he made to his separate monograph on Heine from 1897, on the occasion of the centennial of the poet's birth. Compared to the substantial reworking of the other volumes, this relative lack of revision could indicate that there were no weighty political or aesthetic concerns behind the changes to *Young Germany*.

The most substantial additions to the Heine material include a brief digression on the affection of German composers for him, as well as a fuller portrait of the woman with whom Heine lived during his final years (Brandes 1900:372–373, 500–501). The most interesting addition, however, is a new summary and evaluation of the poet, which after a lyrical ode to the cosmopolitan Heine uniting "Germanic emotional romanticism with French esprit and Jewish inwardness" delivers a kick in the teeth to both the German and the French neglect of Heine:

> the new German Reich has refused to raise the monument to Heinrich Heine his admirers have sought and which he himself could well do without (…) Even in the little provincial city in which he was born, no statue of him has dared to be erected. And opposite the attitude of the German Reich, the Frenchmen of our time have not at all had the thought or the courage to raise a monument to him in the Paris he loved so dearly and in which he lived the second half of his life. (Brandes 1900:503–504)

If German narrow-mindedness and chauvinism on the one side and French cowardice on the other has meant that Heine has not been honored for his services either to Germany or to his second fatherland of France, he was according to Brandes still more popular outside of Germany than any other German-language author, indeed even "Byron himself has hardly impacted the nineteenth century as profoundly as him" (Brandes 1900:504). Given the central place occupied by Byron in the overall architecture of *Main Currents*, this is a noteworthy addition. As if to emphasize this point, Brandes concludes the new section by reeling off a list of Heine-inspired poets in other parts of Europe, especially in the Nordic countries.

Finally, Brandes made a small but not uninteresting change to the final lines of the third edition, which in the first edition is directed at the voices who over the years have criticized him for being too selective in his choices and compared him to Procrustes. "Herein lies the answer," says Brandes with a certain pride in 1890, "namely that the true Procrustes" who had selected and grouped "is nothing other than the power we are otherwise in the habit of calling art" (Brandes 1890a:572–573). Polemical to the last, sharply and tersely formulated and as such wholly commensurate with the original sting of the work – and yet it might not have seemed entirely worthy to Brandes as a conclusion to 10 years of labor. At any rate, both the polemical tone and the reference to Procrustes were removed from the third edition.

Main Themes and Ambivalences

Between "Hero-Worship" and Emancipatory Struggle

Main Currents is in all respects a work that is marked by its long period of genesis, and it could hardly be otherwise, Procrustes or not. Brandes did not remain the hothead he had been when as a 29-year-old he had so forcefully introduced his plan for the work, and the world was not the same in 1890 as it had been in 1871. There was obviously no one more aware of this than Brandes himself, who not only rewrote and reworked the early volumes beyond recognition, but took various other opportunities to let it be known how his aesthetic and political views had changed in the intervening years. Not everyone understood or accepted this, which irritated Brandes, who often felt that his opponents lumped the older homme de lettres in with the young radical when they criticized points of view that did not seem to him to accord with his actual position. In a characteristic passage from his memoirs, Brandes explains how his radicalism over time slowly came to find a natural counterweight in "a strong historical sense of the connection between the times and a consciousness of the impossibility of working from scratch. From the end of the 1870s onward, my writings and opinions came more and more to be defined by a certain equilibrium of rationality" (Brandes 1908:384). But this flew right over the heads of his opponents, who continued to portray him as a "blind, fanatical partisan" (ibid.).

Sympathetic readers had a more acute understanding of the development of and the internal tensions within the work. Brandes refers to a letter he received after *Young Germany* had been published, in which the anonymous correspondent expresses his indignation at the role Goethe is assigned in the final volume: "thus, the letter bitterly laments, the whole spiritual revolution runs its course in the deification of Goethe!" (ibid.). Brandes categorically denies that his enthusiasm for Goethe is of a more recent vintage and points to his unrestrained praise in *Goethe and Denmark* (1881). Yet since he quotes from the letter and highlights the correspondent's acumen in contrast to the lack thereof in his other opponents, this is also a kind of confession.

However, Brandes had provided the clearest description of his understanding of the development of *Main Currents* long before the completion of the final volume and in a quite different context. In a letter to his German publisher that he had published in *Politiken* in July 1887, he briefly described the development the second volume had undergone between the first edition in 1873 and the second in 1887. Although this account only concerns *The Romantic School in Germany*, at the very least it is just as relevant to *Main Currents* as a complete composition and work. Brandes begins by stating that the first edition of *The Romantic School in Germany* was a "polemical exercise" that "attacked the dead German Romantics in order to locate behind them the living Danish Romantics." Next he asserts that his present foundational aesthetic understanding is quite different from what it was in 1871. Whereas then he judged individual works according to the "religious and political attitudes" of their authors, now, in 1887, he understands the art of poetry as the mirroring of "the whole and full life of a people and age." Finally, there is the question of style and method: "when I began work on *Main Currents* in 1871," Brandes explains, "I was still not metaphysically minded in my intellectual orientation. I overlooked the personalities; they were for me only the organs for expressing ideas (…) The individual personalities were held aloft by the currents, split apart by them; they were mouthpieces for the ideas. Their personalities were not of interest to the author." In the first edition of the second volume the biographical portraits are included as brief and incomplete supplements following after the review of the individual works, as a kind of "necessary evil." Only much later, after he no longer presumed there to be "an abstract world spirit" that had produced the works, did he begin to immerse himself in "the historical personalities, demonstrating *how their production emerged out of their lives*." In summary, the 1873 and 1887 editions of *The Romantic School in Germany* are significantly distinct from one another in at least three respects:

> while the original task of the work was to agitate, in the second edition it became purely scientific; it was thus conceived as national and Danish and then became universal. In the beginning my

understanding of poetry and art was conditioned by tendentiousness; it is now otherwise. Ultimately my understanding of the relation between ideas and personalities was turned on its head, resulting in a correspondingly different conception of the composition of the work. (Brandes 1887)

In fairness, it should be noted that Brandes' account was in fact a brief in a pending German court case. Because Denmark was not a signatory to the Berne Convention on literary copyright, and thus Brandes could not claim copyright abroad, his German publisher, after the publication of the second edition of *The Romantic School in Germany*, stood accused for technical and juridical reasons of having unlawfully republished a partially existing work (Bjerring-Hansen 2016:127–134). In other words, Brandes had an obvious interest in the first and second editions being viewed as two different books. That said, it is still difficult to disagree with the characterization that precisely summarizes the most important differences between the two editions, and more importantly in this context points to a more general tendency across the entire work. The latter point is most easily illustrated by comparing the volumes furthest apart from one another in time, that is the first editions of *Emigrant Literature* and *Young Germany*. While the former – as Brandes points out – emphasizes currents and ideas and is strong in its faith in enlightenment and progress in history ("Faith in the right of free inquiry and the final triumph of free thinking," Brandes 1872:7), the latter is significantly more concerned with the biographical material of "the great personalities" and correspondingly less occupied with the "emancipatory struggle of humanity" (Brandes 1890a:38), which characteristically is wholly eclipsed when he turns his gaze on the present age and the contemporary generation ("what we call progress is a sickly snail," Brandes 1890a:536). But this tension is also repeatedly found within the individual sections of *Main Currents*, to greater and lesser degrees. Even in the original introduction to *Emigrant Literature*, by far and away the most agitational and programmatic passage in the entire work, it is far from the case that everything is dominated by currents and ideas. Even here we can without great difficulty locate traces that anticipate or in any case hint at the "hero worship" (Brandes 1908:151) of the later authorship, such as for example when Brandes – in a formulation that could be inspired by John Stuart Mill's *On Liberty* (see for example Mill 2003:76–77, 128–138) – points to the conflict between "the personalities" and to the tyranny of public opinion.

"The Great Personality": Goethe as Measuring Stick

Young Germany contains many of the same tensions and ambivalences as the other volumes, but the manner in which they are managed is to a certain extent different from in the rest of the work. This is due first and foremost to the nature of the material, which as mentioned no longer emitted the same transfiguring glow it once had for the young Brandes, and neither was it commensurable with his later understanding of literary art. What had seemed to him to be a definitive conclusion to the work, as long as he still thought in terms of an abstract philosophy of history, was less so after he had moved on from the Hegelian world spirit in favor of an experiential and biographical aesthetics, according to which art was conceived as "the expression of mental perturbations" with "the aim of calling forth mental perturbations" (Brandes 1890a:50). Young Germany as a political movement was perhaps a necessary enough current within "the great rhythmic ebb and flow of history" (Brandes 1890a:571), yet parceled out into individual artistic biographies, the group was too marginal and uninteresting from a literary perspective to form the foundation of the final volume of *Main Currents*. Equally as importantly, it was too artistically insignificant to maintain the author's interest.

As indicated, Brandes attempted to resolve the problem by providing much more space for Heine, by lengthening the period under study, and by incorporating a series of figures whose alleged connection to Young Germany perhaps does not always seem convincing. Among these figures the most important is without a doubt Goethe, whose place in German literary history of the first half of the nineteenth century is incontestable. Yet he plays such a prominent role at the end of volume six that we can well understand the aforementioned correspondent's astonishment: how could Brandes assign to Goethe – the *Geheimrat* who not only found himself on the wrong side of the barricades in the "emancipatory struggle of humanity" but was furthermore not particularly interested in politics – such a place of honor in a narrative account of the movements and currents that came to a head in the 1848 revolutions? The answer is of course already provided by the critic's shifted interest from currents toward great individuals; none of the figures of Young Germany were greater than the universal spirit that was Goethe.

The most remarkable aspect of Goethe's role in the sixth volume of *Main Currents* is not, however, that he is placed center stage every time Brandes sees a chance to do so. On the contrary, it is that throughout the immense amount of material treated in *Young Germany*, he functions as a kind of measuring stick for Brandes' evaluation of the other authors and their placement within the volume; indeed, in some passages analyzing Goethe almost seems to be the main objective of the narrative. This is perhaps most apparent in the long chapters on the three female figures, Rahel Varnhagen, Bettina von Arnim, and Charlotte Stieglitz, who are evaluated according to their views of Goethe, and whose place in the narrative is justified by reference to his significance: "through studying the most remarkable female figures of the time, we discover that between 1810 and 1835, the most deeply penetrating event, the subtlest and deepest secret of the time, was that the worldview of Goethe, point by point, had displaced the Church and had conquered all the great instincts and authentic movements of the era" (Brandes 1890a:384). Moreover, of Varnhagen Brandes even notes that "her critical literary significance" is due to the fact "it was her who first in Berlin sensed and expressed the worth of Goethe" (Brandes 1890a: 396). In short, these three women earned a place in Brandes' narrative because they distinguished themselves by being especially sensitive seismographs, measuring the depths and the impact of Goetheism. Here it is almost as if Goethe has become the overriding concern, and that anything that can contribute to a clearer illustration of the status of this universal spirit within German intellectual life is automatically justified.

A less eccentric use of Goethe, on the other hand, is in the discussion of the relation between art and politics, which runs like an undercurrent through *Young Germany* and is among the clearest indications of how far Brandes has moved since he began *Main Currents*. First on the witness stand is Börne, and Brandes immediately confronts him by pointing to his uncompromising attitude toward Goethe: "perhaps nothing has more damaged Börne's present reputation than his vehement denunciation of Goethe" (Brandes 1890a:54). Brandes goes to great lengths to understand the origins of this uncompromising hatred. A considerable measure of explanation is found in their biographies: both Goethe and Börne were from Frankfurt, yet they might as well have come from different worlds. Goethe was born into the upper bourgeoisie, while Börne grew up in the city's Jewish quarter. Whereas Goethe came into the world with the proverbial silver spoon in his mouth, as a Jew Börne was a pariah without civil rights, subject to derision and confined to the inhumane ghetto of cramped, dark alleyways he dared not leave during the daytime. Brandes concludes that "it is clear that such conditions must have exerted an influence on an impressionable young mind" (Brandes 1890a:58). Wisely enough, Brandes is hesitant to draw overly broad conclusions from these conditions; his point is narrower – that Börne's political views were intimately bound up with these childhood experiences, which at once laid the ground for his sense of justice and for his contempt of Goethe, that servant of the princes. While Brandes does not agree with Börne's argument that Goethe's work as a minister of state should be understood as a political betrayal, he is faithful in reproducing this critique and must concede that Börne "has pointed out weak points in Goethe's greatness and the limits of his being," even if much of this solicitude immediately withers on the vine, when shortly thereafter he adds that "certain merits of Goethe could only be purchased in exchange for these lacks, and that in order not to splinter his many-sided genius he had been compelled to set firm limits for himself" (Brandes 1890a:105).

Whatever the degree of understanding and insight Brandes brings to his treatment of Börne, we are nowhere in doubt about the outcome of this initial boasting match. In comparison to the ocean that is Goethe, Börne is and remains a pond, and even when he is at his strongest, he is at once too uncompromising – indeed almost Manichean in his vision of right and wrong – and too hot-tempered and naïve. In this regard, Börne's political analyses of the French July Revolution in 1830 are telling, since they, according to Brandes, appear outrageously naïve and, due to the "contradiction between what is predicted and what happens, become so striking that the effect is comical" (Brandes 1890a:129). Börne's letters from Paris bear witness to his honor and passion – and especially to his political fantasies. But the problem is first and foremost of an aesthetic nature. Positively formulated: "it can hardly surprise us, that he in whose spiritual makeup a sense of justice had developed so sharply and so finely that it formally served as a substitute for an actual aesthetic sensibility, must see such as lacking in Goethe, whose desire for justice was relatively undeveloped" (Brandes 1890a:129). Negatively formulated: "Börne did not possess an artistic sensibility in the strong sense of the word (…) that domain of *Bildung*, which considers art as art, was closed to him" (Brandes 1890a:91–92). This can of course be understood as a kind of explanation of the relation between art and politics: in Börne's eyes, an artistic sensibility is uninteresting or even a (moral) impediment to true political engagement; literature and politics belong to two different spheres and never the twain shall meet. Yet this solution is hardly satisfying – especially for Brandes, who had outgrown such stereotypical binaries long before. Fortunately there is more to be said of Heine, the next witness to take the stand, and here Goethe truly comes into his own.

Aristocratic Radicalism: The Image of Heine
Heine's privileged position in *Young Germany* can be explained, as already mentioned, both biographically and literary-historically. That Brandes makes him the star witness in his discussion of the relationship between literature and politics is however first and foremost due to other circumstances. Like the majority of the authors of his generation, Heine had a strained relationship with Goethe, whose being and work consumed so

much that it could be difficult for younger poets to find a place at the table. Some reacted with an almost instinctive rejection, such as Börne, who did not conceal the fact that his political critique of the servant of the princes had deep roots: "As long as I have been able to feel, I have hated Goethe, as long as I have been able to think, I have known why" [Seit ich fühle, habe ich Goethe gehaßt, seit ich denke, weiß ich warum] (Börne 1964b:71). Heine's critique of Goethe is more ambivalent, but also much more principled. In contrast to Börne and others, Heine has much that is good to say about Goethe, both as a poet and as a critic of the reactionary and catholicizing tendencies of German Late Romanticism (Häntzschel 2001:63–67). Yet Goethe's virtues at the same time point to his problems. Rightly enough, Goethe drove the brothers Schlegel out of the temple, and for this he deserves gratitude, but in so doing he also established himself as the sole overlord of German literature, and for Heine that is a problem. Correspondingly, his immortal works "adorn our fatherland like pleasing statues adorn a garden, but they are statues. One can fall in love with them, but they are infertile" [zieren unser theures Vaterland, wie schöne Statuen einen Garten zieren, aber es sind Statuen. Man kann sich darin verlieben, aber sie sind unfruchtbar] (*Die Romantische Schule*, 1836; Heine 1979, 8:155). Finally Heine acknowledges that while Goethe's lack of interest in politics can possibly be justified by the nature of the age in which he lived, it is no longer appropriate to the era and thus morally irresponsible. Literature should – and on this point he is in agreement with Börne – seek to make a political impact, and the poet ought to be conscious of his social responsibility.

The reason Brandes makes Heine the test case for his discussion of the relationship of literature to politics is not just that he is the only poet of the age who in an artistic sense can measure up to Goethe, but also that in his ambivalence he is closer to Brandes' own position than the other Young Germany authors. And just as importantly, Heine's ambivalence is by no means limited to Goethe; it is in fact a part of his constitution. For Brandes this is clearly evident in Heine's political views, which at first glance appear less than thought out, or without principles. On the one hand he represents "an outburst of the most extreme radicalism" that emerges from "the most strident revolutionary attitude" (Brandes 1890a:160), while on the other Heine reassures us again and again that he is no Jacobin, indeed even that he does not see himself as a republican. How to explain this extraordinary duality? Previously, notes Brandes, it has either not been explained at all or has been seen as evidence of his characterlessness. But Heine, asserts Brandes, was far from characterless; on the contrary he was "from first to last a faithful soul to his principles" (ibid.). According to Brandes Heine was both "a profound lover of freedom and a marked aristocrat," at once a fiery opponent of every form of the denial of freedom and a great admirer of "human greatness." In other words, "there was not a drop of conservative blood in Heine's soul. His blood was revolutionary. Yet neither was there in his soul a drop of democratic blood. His blood was aristocratic, he would see genius acknowledged as leader and lord" (Brandes 1890a:165).

Brandes would hardly have formulated it as such in the 1870s, and certainly not with so much sympathy. It is conspicuous to say the least that Brandes repeatedly employs the word "aristocrat" as an ostensibly positive designation for a certain spiritual disposition, coupling it with the concepts of "radicalism" and "revolutionary." This tendency becomes still clearer in the following pages, in which Brandes' characterization of Heine's position threatens to detach itself from its object, becoming the point of departure for a more general critique of culture. Among other things Heine does not believe that "the philistine ideals of average *Bildung*" can lead to freedom, and he therefore rejects all forms of mediocrity, "including the liberal and republican forms, as the enemy of the great personality and of freedom" (Brandes 1890a:163–164). Heine feared nothing other than

> a life without beauty and especially a life without greatness, with equality of mediocrity as a religion, with hatred of genius and of the seekers and of those who openly reject the belief that Nazarene asceticism is the only actual form of morality. What he equally rejected was the society he knew, governed by a clergy devoid of spirit and an aristocracy devoid of refinement, and thus the society

he had foreseen, consisting of emancipated slave souls who had only revolted against the obsequiousness that was their nature, in order to give reign to the enviousness that remains at the core of all their decency. (Brandes 1890a:165)

As has been indicated, it is possible to see tendencies already pointing in this direction in *Emigrant Literature*, the Mill-inspired remark on the tension between the great personality and the tyranny of public opinion serving as an example. What clearly distinguishes the later formulation from similar sentiments expressed in the first volume is that the emancipatory program of enlightenment of 1871 has faded entirely into the background in favor of an unconcealed fascination with the great personality. Whereas freedom in *Emigrant Literature* was first and foremost tied to liberal ideas and civil rights, there is now more obscure talk of "the greater freedom" that is plainly threatened by the lesser liberal freedom. Taken as a more general determination of the relationship between political and "intellectual" freedom, Brandes openly seems to prefer the latter at the expense of the former, in so far as it can be measured in the degree of freedom for the individual: the authentic, true freedom is aristocratic freedom, which must necessarily be reserved for the few. In the course of the civilizing process the average person has however raised himself up over his natural instincts ("obsequiousness"), and through resentment and envy of the great personalities imposed a political-liberal understanding of freedom, which views the greater freedom as illegitimate and propagates the equality of all people.

Finally, passages such as this, right down to the level of the wording, bear the mark of the fact that the work on Heine occurred at the same time that Brandes was reading and beginning to correspond with Nietzsche (Brandes 1966:439–479). What particularly drew Brandes to Nietzsche was precisely the idea that the welfare of the majority – the utilitarian credo of "the greatest happiness for the greatest number" – could not be the purpose of history, which on the contrary could only consist of bringing forth "individual great men" (Brandes 1889:574). Not only had such ideas strengthened Brandes in the reflections he himself had worked out on this question, they also – as is evident in the introductory chapter on Heine in *Young Germany* – provided him with a conceptual unity and a speculative historical-philosophical framework that went far beyond the well-known Hegelian construct. "Slave morality," ressentiment as the driving force of history, Caesarism, the cultivated ruling caste, the "cultural philistine," and the last man – all this and more Brandes found in Nietzsche, and it was put to use in the characterization of Heine, who in the effective merging of radicalism and aristocracy is presented as the forerunner of Nietzsche's aristocratic radicalism.

This is not to say that there is no evidence in support of Brandes' reading of Heine, and even less that it is solely the views of Nietzsche or for that matter Brandes that function as the point of reference in this account of Heine's political views. Yet if we look at some of the passages in Heine that presumably form the basis for Brandes' paraphrase, it nevertheless becomes clear that Heine's undeniable distinction between "intellect" and politics is of a quite different nature than that presented by Brandes. This may be illustrated by the foreword to the French edition of *Lutetia* from 1855, a collection of articles and reportages Heine wrote for the *Augsburger Allgemeine Zeitung*. Here he explains among other things that when in these articles he "in the most anguished and concerned tone" foresaw a golden future for the socialists or – "to call the horror by its proper name" [pour nommer le monstre par son vrai nom] (Heine 1988, 8:166) – the communists, he was in no manner playing to the gallery. A longer citation is required to understand Heine's argumentation:

> in reality I look only with fear and horror at the time when these obscure iconoclasts will come to power: with their bare fists they will smash all the marble images of my beloved world of art, they destroy all the fantastical curiosities the poet admires so dearly; they fell my laurel groves and make them into potato fields (…) the roses, the useless nightingale couple they do no better; the nightingales, those useless singers, are driven away, and woe! my *Buch der Lieder* will be used by the merchant as a cornet to be filled with coffee

or snuff for the old ladies of the future. – Woe! All this I foresee, and I am seized with an unspeakable sorrow at the thought of the defeat with which communism threatens my poems and the entire old world order along with them – And still I frankly confess this thought (…) a supernatural power over my mind against which I cannot defend myself (…) a dreadful syllogism plagues me, and I cannot deny its premise: 'that all human beings have the right to eat,' such that I must also accept all its consequences (…) and in the end I am seized by a desperate magnanimity and cry out (…) blessed be the grocer who one day makes my poems into cornets and fills them with coffee and snuff for the poor old grandmas, who in the unjust world of today must do without such refreshments – *fiat justitia, pereat mundus!* [let justice be done, though the world perish]

[En effet, ce n'est qu'avec horreur et effroi que je pense à l'époque où ces sombres iconoclastes parviendront à la domination: de leurs mains calleuses ils briseront sans merci toutes les statues de marbre si chères á mon coeur; ils fracasseront toutes ces babioles et fanfreluches fantastiques de l'art, qu'aimait tant le poëte; ils détruiront mes bois de lauriers et y planteront des pommes de terre; (…) les roses, ces oisives fiancées des rossignols, auront le même sort; les rossignols, ces chanteurs inutiles, seront chassés, et hélas! mon Livre des Chants servira à l'épicier pour en faire des cornets où il versera du café ou du tabac à priser pour les vieilles femmes de l'avenir. Hélas! je prévois tout cela, et je suis saisi d'une indicible tristesse en pensant à la ruine dont menace mes vers, qui périront avec tout l'ancien. Et pourtant, je l'avoue avec franchise, ce même communisme, exerce sur mon âme un charme dont je ne puis me défendre; (…) Un terrible syllogisme me tient ensorcelé, et si je ne puis réfuter cette prémisse: "que les hommes ont tous le droit de manger", je suis forcé de me soumettre aussi à toutes ses conséquences (…) et à la fin un désespoir généreux s'empare de mon coeur et je m'écrie: (…) Et béni soit l'épicier qui un jour confectionnera avec mes poésies des cornets où il versera du café et du tabac pour les pauvres 18 bonnes vieilles qui, dans notre monde actuel de l'injustice, ont peut-être dû se passer d'un pareil agrément – *fiat justitia, pereat mundus*!] (Heine 1988:167)

As always with Heine, it is easy to lose balance in the subtle tripwires of the irony, yet the point of view is without doubt sincerely meant. Presented with the choice between art for the privileged few and welfare for the many, one must be incredibly hard-hearted to feel the smallest measure of moral compulsion to choose the former. The content of the discord expressed by Heine here thus may be likened to the contradiction Brandes poses between the liberal-political and aristocratic conceptions of freedom, yet the particular weight placed on each side is an entirely different matter. Heine's discussion of the problem transposes classical theodicy from theology to art: how can art be justified in a world in which hunger and need are the norm for the majority of people? His answer is precisely that it cannot, if a moral measuring stick is employed. Nietzsche's answer to the same question is that "only as an aesthetic phenomenon is existence and the world eternally justified" [dass nur als ein aesthetisches Phänomen das Dasein und die Welt gerechtfertigt erscheint] (Nietzsche 1972:148). Whereas Heine allows himself to be swayed by the "slave army of the starving," Nietzsche views its existence as perhaps tragic, although just as much an inescapable condition of existence, on which art alone can impart meaning.

Brandes' own leanings on this issue at this time are clear, for in his reckoning there are few traces of Heine's scruples. The social question is more or less written out of the authorship and replaced with a Nietzschean philosophy of art, contemptuous of the base, ressentiment-fueled slave morality that stands in the way of great art and its deliverers. The Danish philosopher Harald Høffding, interestingly enough, reached a similar conclusion, when in 1889 he registered a protest against Brandes' portrait of Nietzsche in the famous essay on *Aristocratic Radicalism*. Høffding argued that Brandes' presentation of the philosopher was rather too sympathetic, and that the critic's "purely aesthetic tendency" led to "an overestimation of the great men" at the expense of the democratic welfare principle, which "prohibits the forgetting of the suffering of the many in favor of the enjoyment of the few" (Høffding 1889:864).

Close examination of the central commentaries on Börne and Heine in *Young Germany* reveals that the tendency is thus a clear upgrading of the apolitical "spirit" and the great personalities at the expense of the political engagement that otherwise must be said to be characteristic of the movement. When Brandes weighs Börne and finds him wanting, the measuring stick is the "artistic sensibility," for which Börne had no greater respect than he did for Goethe as an authority. Heine, in contrast, manages to escape more gracefully from being measured against "the greatest style of the past," even though he too does not always measure up to the comparison with Goethe in all respects: "in the comparison we frequently see him come up short, though not all too rarely rising up to an almost equivalent status. It is honor enough for him that it is possible and occasionally necessary to compare him to Goethe" (Brandes 1890a:237). With respect to Heine in and of himself, however, it is conspicuous how little his political engagement figures in Brandes' evaluation of his authorship. Now and then it almost seems as if he is more concerned with defending the antidemocratic and intellectual aristocratic version of Heine than presenting him as a part of the Young Germany movement.

Yet what blinds him in one eye sharpens the other. While his contemporaries found it difficult to see in Heine anything other than his critique of Prussia and his ironic and frivolous poetry, Brandes exhibits a penetrating gaze for other aspects that not infrequently point to literary-historical connections that had previously been neglected. This is perhaps best expressed in the brilliant excursus on the image of Napoleon in German literature, in which Brandes, precisely because of his strong focus on "the great personality in general," is able to show that Heine's admiration for Napoleon is far from the "isolated event in the German literature of the century" his contemporaries had made it into, but on the contrary was part of a long tradition stretching from the Weimar Classicist author Christoph Martin Wieland through Goethe, Schiller, Hegel, and the Dane Jens Baggesen.

Chapters like this one, which both breaks with customary understandings of and clichés about Heine and places him in a novel literary-historical context, demonstrate what the unbiased comparatist could accomplish, when he was at his best.

Reception and Afterlife

Danish and Nordic Reception

"The Danish edition fell to the earth like a stain. Throughout the year hardly a paper mentioned it" (Brandes 1908:285). The disappointment is still palpable when Brandes mentions the paltry discussion provoked by *Young Germany* in his memoirs, and he was not alone in resenting the dearth of reviews. When Brandes' faithful squire Sophus Schandorph discussed the volume in June 1891 in the journal *Tilskueren*, he began by lamenting the newspapers' neglect of Brandes: "rarely do we see Dr. Brandes' great books reviewed. If his many enemies had been able to do him harm, they would hardly have denied themselves the joy in doing so, and if his friends had been able to say something of significance on the occasion of his masterwork, they would surely also have done so" (Schandorph 1891:420). The explanation for the fact that neither friend nor enemy had taken up a pen to write about him, according to Schandorph, must be that he is too much for them to handle. Friends remained silent out of a feeling of awe or wonder, enemies because they could not find anything to criticize. Brandes "towers so far above everyone here in this country" that only the "poor devils" who basely occupied themselves with fact-checking or pettily pointing out that "Brandes has not used quotation marks to a significant degree" dared to write about his masterwork (ibid.).

Schandorph's explanation must be taken with a grain of salt, for in his own words he is "an affectionate admirer and faithful friend of the author" (ibid.), as is attested to excess in the 25 pages of his uncritical and admiring summary of *Young Germany*. On the other hand, it illustrates quite clearly how polarized the reception of Brandes was, and why critics of a bourgeois persuasion in some instances would rather refrain from saying something about Brandes in general than reviewing his books either favorably or with nuance. In spite of everything it demanded courage to break with consensus in the ideological conflict between Brandes' allies and opponents. A prominent example of one who lacked such courage was Fr. Winkel Horn, a reviewer at *Berlingske Tidende*, who at the request of Schandorph wrote to Brandes, indicating that while he admired his greatness, circumstances prevented him from expressing it publicly (Knudsen 1994:388). This is doubtless also the reason why a part of the contemporary criticism appears polarized and stereotypical. One was either on Brandes' team and followed him through thick and thin like his friends Schandorph and Oscar Levertin, each of whom shared virtually all of Brandes' political views and aesthetic idiosyncrasies, or, on the opposing side, one categorically dismissed his work for political, religious, or other reasons. An example of the latter approach is seen in a review in the Swedish newspaper *Post- och Inrikes Tidningar*; *Young Germany* only seems to strengthen the deeply hostile reviewer's sense that Brandes agitates for a thoroughly negative "work of destruction directed at the family, religion and thus the entirety of the orderly life of the state" (Wirsén 1890).

More interesting are the reviews that at least attempt to take the critical task seriously. This is partially the case for the review published in the Norwegian paper *Morgenbladet*, whose anonymous author bravely tries to find a balance between criticism and praise, and who is alone among Scandinavian reviewers in recognizing that Nietzsche can play a role in the "characterization of Heine that is in many respects highly interesting (…) it is as if Brandes here tests out the correctness of the Nietzschean theory of the overman" (Anon. 1891). Marginally more critical is "H-n L" in his review in the Swedish *Aftonbladet*, which begins with an acute, yet not hostile characterization of Brandes, who is said to be just as all-encompassing in his presentation of the material as he is one-sided in his evaluation and judgment of it (H-n L. 1890). This is followed by a severe critique of Brandes' treatment of especially Heine and Börne, while other (and more peripheral) sections of the volume are deemed successful. This was undoubtedly painful for Brandes to read. Finally, there are discussions that first and foremost use the publication as an occasion to cast a glance back over the entirety of *Main Currents* and to incorporate the final volume into the whole composition. This is the case with Johannes Jørgensen's commentary on the front page of *Kjøbenhavns Børs-Tidende*, which prefaces its discussion of *Young Germany* with a lengthy chronological review of the first five volumes. The tone is strikingly respectful, yet the piece is not actually evaluative. It is moreover conspicuous that the political-ideological tendentiousness of *Main Currents* is not even mentioned, and that it is uncertain whether it is Brandes or Jørgensen himself who has been bewitched by "the wondrous fairytale night of German Romanticism" (Jørgensen 1891).

Though there was not much encouragement in the reviews of the daily papers, Brandes found some in the private letters he received. In December of 1890, Jonas Lie wrote from Paris: "for more than a month now, I have had for my refreshment your latest splendid work, *Young Germany*, – it has been my only reading material while I, finished with *my* book, exhausted, have waged my hopeless struggle to sweep away all the various projects I have promised to complete" (Brandes 1939:448). Lie remembers to emphasize Heine and Börne, thanking the author for "this superb crowning touch on a grandly and gloriously executed work of intellect." No less enthusiastic was the reaction from Alexander Kielland in Norway, who bemoans that he has only now (August 1891) read the book, and offers it the highest praise: "it is with sorrow that one closes such a book, that it did not last longer, – that one does not always have such a work before himself. I do not think you have ever written anything better" (Brandes 1939:365). He also emphasizes the portrait of Heine: "what you write about Heine in your book is manna for my soul (…) you manage to say about Heine what should be said by someone who has correctly understood and evaluated him" (Brandes 1939:366). As his response to Kielland divulges, these words were cold comfort to Brandes: "many thanks to you for your heartening words on my old book, which otherwise has not been blessed with a strong reception and has sold perhaps five hundred copies, about which I am hardly giddy" (Brandes 1939:367).

Reception in Germany
While the majority of the Scandinavian critics often directly acknowledged that they did not know much about the authors of Young Germany and thus concentrated on the sections of the volume that treated subjects about which they were already knowledgeable (Heine, Goethe), and otherwise had to trust Brandes' review of the material, the German criticism is unsurprisingly distinguished by a greater knowledge of both the period and the common literary-historical treatments of it. In the longer reviews of the volume critics often reference other narrative accounts, just as they comment on Brandes' weighing of the material and his grasp of it. Minority views and idiosyncrasies are not a rarity in the German criticism either, but rarely do they revolve around Brandes' person or political-ideological questions. A significant role, however, is played by Brandes' relation to contemporary positivistic literary-historical writing. The majority of the reviewers discuss the remarkable fact that Brandes seems to have a much wider appeal than contemporary German literary-historical writing, and most explain this by noting that he is a literary critic and aestheticist rather than a literary historian and philologist. Some see this as a problem, criticizing the looser form and "salon style" (S. Lublinski), the missing references and the careless citation practice, criticisms which in certain instances are accompanied by more or less well-founded accusations of plagiarism (A. Gerhard). Others see the fact that Brandes writes in a manner accessible to non-specialists as itself a great service: "it feels like a refreshing bath when one comes from the swamp of official literary history" [Sie wirkt wie ein erfrischendes Bad, wenn man aus den Sümpfen der offiziellen Literarhistorie herkommt], writes Franz Mehring in *Die neue Zeit*, while Moritz Necker asserts in *Neue Freie Presse* that Brandes is "the only literary critic who enjoys a measure of authority and popularity among the more educated German public" [der einzige literarische Kritiker ist, der sich bei dem größeren Publicum der Gebildeten Deutschlands einer gewissen Autorität und Beliebtheit erfreut] (Mehring 1893/94).

Interestingly enough, behind such evaluations are the contours of a conflict over values that marked German intellectual circles from the beginning of the 1890s all the way through to the interwar years. The conflict was fueled by the challenge of the *Lebensphilosophie* to the established scientific culture, which in the wake of Nietzsche's critique of historicism was charged with being unproductive and barren, lost in irrelevant questions about details, and against its intentions leading to the collapse of values instead of creating healthy human beings and contributing to a genuine form of education. Brandes was naturally familiar with this discussion from both Nietzsche and his vulgar epigone Julius Langbehn, whose immensely influential *Rembrandt als Erzieher* (1890), published anonymously under the name of "a German," had been reviewed by Brandes in the first volume of *Freie Bühne* (Brandes 1890b) – and astoundingly favorably at that, in light of its national chauvinistic tendencies and anti-academic radicalism ("the professor is the German national disease" [Der Professor ist die deutsche Nationalkrankheit], Langbehn 1890:94). Yet with respect to the critique of institutions and of science formulated by the *Lebensphilosophie*, Brandes did not make a stand. As in the Scandinavian reception of *Young Germany*, he functioned more as a catalyst in an already ongoing *Weltanschauung* debate, though the content of this debate in Germany was different, and less tied to his own person.

Despite these differences between the Scandinavian and German receptions of *Young Germany*, the interest primarily focused on Börne and Heine in Germany as well. For Ludwig Geiger, who reviewed the final volume of *Main Currents* over many pages in the weekly *Die Nation*, the portrait of Heine was especially successful. According to him, Brandes succeeds with great virtuosity in saying something new about an authorship believed to have been exhaustively described. He is less enthusiastic, however, about the rest of the book. Some of this can surely be explained or excused by the lack of homogeneity and the thrown-together nature of the material, yet Brandes clearly also had problems in illuminating and arranging it, writes Geiger. On the other hand he does not see it as a problem that the other Young Germany authors (Gutzkow, Laube, Mundt, Wienbarg) are treated relatively quickly: "the works of these men (…) are entirely passé for us, and even a master like Brandes cannot manage to bring these colorless figures to life" [Die Werke jener Männer … sind für uns völlig abgethan und selbst ein Meister wie Brandes vermag aus diesen Schemen kein Leben zu erwecken] (Geiger 1890–1891:633). For Geiger the problem is rather in the omissions (for example of Grillparzer), and moreover in the more or less peripheral material included (for example the chapter on neutral literature). That his review is overall so positive is therefore due wholly to the chapters on Heine and Börne, which – as Geiger points out – take up half the book. In line with Geiger, yet still more effusive, is Wilhelm Bölsche, who in his review, published in the same volume of *Freie Bühne* as Brandes' aforementioned review of *Rembrandt als Erzieher*, likewise asserts that "this is a *book about Heine*" [das ist ein *Buch über Heine*] (Bölsche 1890:1179), and for the same reason does not find it necessary to comment on the other sections. Bölsche begins with general observations on the status of Heine in Imperial Germany, declaring his agreement with Brandes' explanation of the contemporary marginalization of Heine and expressing only words of praise for his rehabilitation, which is described as a salutatory act of the politics of memory in an age incapable of erecting a monument to the poet in the city of his birth. Interestingly enough, Bölsche further identifies Brandes' analysis of Heine's aristocratic radicalism as particularly successful – "the real key" to unlocking the political Heine – and states that Nietzsche was presumably a determining factor in this interpretation (Bölsche 1890:1180).

In the German criticism Brandes could not entirely escape being reminded of his Scandinavian detractors and enemies. Among the reviewers of *Young Germany* we thus also encounter Laura Marholm, Brandes' earlier translator and confidant who had married Ola Hansson and now, from the artist colony of Friedrichshagen outside Berlin, took part in her husband's effort to contend with Brandes as the foremost mediator of Scandinavian literature in Germany. Marholm begins her text – more essay than review – with a long recollection of her childhood reading of Gutzkow's novels, which leads into an interesting diagnosis of the present era (the "age of nervousness"), before at last discussing two new books about Young Germany, one of which is Brandes'. As expected, she has little favorable to say about the author or the work, which is viciously characterized as a book for

Danes and other foreigners who have no knowledge of German literature and culture, written by "the demagogue among the literary historians" [der Demagog unter den Literaturhistorikern] (Marholm 1893:205), who perhaps once had firsthand knowledge of the material, but after moving back to Denmark no longer has his finger on the pulse. Thereafter is passed the merciless verdict: "Perhaps an acute and profound psychological divination like that known to us from Frenchmen such as Taine and Bourget could have remedied these necessary deficiencies, but Brandes proceeds all too anecdotally, all too superficially" [Ueber diese nothgedrungenen Mängel hätte eine sehr feine und tiefe psychologische Divination hinweghelfen können, wie die Franzosen, wie Taine und Bourget sie haben, aber auf diesem Gebiet arbeitet Brandes allzusehr anekdotisch und auf der Oberfläche] (Marholm 1893:207). As if to add insult to injury, there follows an especially laudatory discussion of Johannes Prölß's *Young Germany* from 1892, which according to Marholm distinguishes itself by being everything Brandes' book is not: "this is not a book that is a reflection of its author, but a book that wholly strives to make its contents comprehensible (...) It is a very German book in technique and presentation, and thereby it stands in the greatest imaginable contrast to Brandes' French schooling" [Es ist kein Buch, das seinen Verfasser spiegelt, sondern ein Buch, das ganz von dem Bestreben ausgeht, seinen Inhalt durchsichtig zu ansehen . . . Es ist ein sehr deutsches Buch in Technik und Darstellung, und dadurch steht es im starken Gegensatz zu Brandes' französicher Schulung] (Marholm 1893:207). Incidentally the laurel-wreathed Prölß was naturally aware of Brandes' narrative, which is quite briefly discussed in the introduction to his book, but does not seem to have played any role in his own presentation.

The Afterlife of *Young Germany*
Not much indicates that later literary historians should have been more influenced by Brandes' presentation of Young Germany than that of Prölß. Many explanations can be provided for this, but presumably most important is the already noted circumstance that literary criticism and, according to its own understanding, strictly scientific literary history did not have

much to do with each other in Germany at this time, and that Brandes was always placed within the former group. Even though Brandes and Wilhelm Scherer, a professor at the University of Berlin and possibly the most famous positivistic literary historian of the era, held each other in high esteem, shared a passionate interest in Goethe, and associated with one another while Brandes lived in Berlin, they were far apart in their activities as representatives of, respectively, philologically and positivistically-oriented literary history, and aesthetic literary criticism – even if the distance between them was understood to be much shorter in Danish as opposed to German eyes. On this point Prölß is aligned with Scherer, when despite complementing Brandes on his "brilliantly written character analyses" [geistvoll geschriebene Charakteranalysen] he makes short work of his book, dismissing it as insufficiently based in source material (lacking in "scrupulous knowledge of the sources and the records" [die genaue Kenntnis der Quellen und Akten]), and moreover as subordinated to a political-ideological tendentiousness ("the aggregate purpose of the whole" [Totalzweck des Ganzen] Prölß 1892:4–5). Thus Brandes was set aside, so to speak, and no further discussion was required.

Nonetheless it is also necessary here to distinguish between volume six first as a unified historiographic presentation of Young Germany, and second as the sum of its individual sections, especially the chapters on Heine. While Brandes' literary-historiographic scheme does not seem to have made an impact on literary history, his portrait of Heine has fared better in more recent scholarship on the German reception of the poet. This is due on the one hand to his nuanced presentation of the conflict between Börne and Heine, as well as his defense of Heine in that conflict, which is described as "unusual" and "diverging from German criticism" [ungewöhnlich . . . von der deutschen Kritik abweichend] (Hohendahl 2008:139–140), and on the other to his refusal to take part in the almost unanimous branding of Heine as a "traitor" after 1848, instead insisting that Heine was no less patriotic than his enemies. It is not surprising that Brandes, who himself was often attacked for being unpatriotic, had a sharp eye for such accusations.

Finally, the same author points out that Brandes' portrait of Heine by all accounts resonated immensely with Heinrich Mann, who in reference to *Young Germany* in 1892 noted that Heine's modernity first and foremost consisted of his "psychological complexity" [psychologische Komplexität] (Hohendahl 2008:203). As an admirer of the French Enlightenment tradition and republicanism, neither was it difficult for him to affirm Brandes' presentation of the world citizen Heine, his critique of German Romanticism, his anticlericalism, and his proud individualism – all of which were later incorporated into Heinrich Mann's own portrait of Heine in *Geist und Tat* (1910). Because he does not actually refer to Brandes in this work, it is unclear how much Heinrich Mann was in debt to Brandes' understanding of Heine. There is no doubt, however, that Heine came to play an important role in the determination of the aesthetic and political views of both Heinrich and Thomas Mann, just as he became a central historical and political point of contention in the famous fratricidal conflict between German culture and French civilization that manifested itself in the First World War, and which found concentrated expression in the question of the character of Heine's patriotism and modernity. But that is another story, in which Brandes is only indirectly involved.

BIBLIOGRAPHY

BRANDES BEFORE *MAIN CURRENTS*: THE MAKING OF A CRITIC

Ahlström, Gunnar (1937): *Georg Brandes' Hovedstrømninger*. Lund and Copenhagen.
Bourguignon, Anne, Harrer, Konrad, and Clausen, Jørgen Stender (Eds) (2010): *Grands courants d'échanges intellectuels: Georg Brandes et La France, L'Allemagne, L'Angleterre. Actes de la deuxième conférence internationale Georg Brandes, Nancy, 13–15 Novembre 2008*. Bern: Peter Lang.
Brandes, Georg (1866): *Dualismen i vor nyeste Philosophie*. Copenhagen: Gyldendalske Boghandel.
Brandes, Georg (1870a): *Kritiker og Portraiter*. Copenhagen.
Brandes, Georg (1870b): *Den franske Æsthetik i vore Dage. En Afhandling om H. Taine*. Copenhagen.
Brandes, Georg (1872a): *Hovedstrømninger i det 19de Aarhundredes Litteratur. Emigrantlitteraturen*. Copenhagen.
Brandes, Georg (1908): *Levned*, Vol. I. Copenhagen.
Brandes, Georg (1923): *Hovedstrømninger i det 19de Aarhundredes Litteratur. Emigrantlitteraturen*. Copenhagen.
Brandes, Georg (1978): *Breve til Forældrene 1859–71*, edited by Morten Borup, Vol. I. Copenhagen.
Brandes, Georg and Edvard (1939): *Brevveksling med nordiske Forfattere og Videnskabsmænd*, edited by Morten Borup et al., Vol. I. Copenhagen.
Braudel, Fernand (1997): *Écrits sur l'histoire*, Vol. II. Paris: Flammarion.
Dahl, Per (1998): *Georg Brandes-tidstavle 1842–1927* [*Working Papers* 18-1998. Department of Comparative Literature, Aarhus University]. Aarhus.
Fenger, Henning (1955): *Georg Brandes' læreår. Læsning. Ideer. Smag. Kritik*. Copenhagen.
Fenger, Henning (1957): *Den unge Brandes. Miljø, venner, rejser, kriser*. Copenhagen: Gyldendalske Boghandel – Nordisk Forlag.
Gibbons, Henry J. (1980): "Georg Brandes. The reluctant Jew," in: Hertel and Kristensen 1980:55–89.
Harsløf, Olav (Ed.) (2004): *Georg Brandes og Europa. Forelæsninger fra 1. internationale Georg Brandes Konference, Firenze, 7-9 november 2002*. Copenhagen: Museum Tusculanum.
Hertel, Hans and Kristensen, Sven Møller (Eds) (1973): *Den politiske Georg Brandes*. Copenhagen: Hans Reitzel.
Hertel, Hans and Kristensen, Sven Møller (Eds) (1980): *The Activist Critic. A symposium on the political ideas, literary methods and international reception of Georg Brandes* [*Orbis Litterarum*. Supplement 5]. Copenhagen: Munksgaard.
Hjortshøj, Søren Blak (2021): *Son of Spinoza. Georg Brandes and Modern Jewish Cosmopolitanism*. Aarhus: Aarhus University Press.
Hvidt, Kristian (2005): *Edvard Brandes, portræt af en radikal blæksprutte*. Copenhagen: Gyldendal.
Knudsen, Jørgen (1985): *Georg Brandes. Frigørelsens vej 1842-77*. Copenhagen: Gyldendal.
Kristensen, Sven Møller (1980): *Georg Brandes. Kritikeren, liberalisten, humanisten*. Copenhagen: Gyldendal.
Larsen, Pelle Oliver (2016): *Professoratet. Kampen om Det Filosofiske Fakultet 1870-1920*. Copenhagen: Museum Tusculanum.
Nolin, Bertil (1976): *Georg Brandes* [*Twayne's World Authors Series*, 390]. Boston: Twayne Publishers.
Nolin, Bertil (1980): "The critic and his paradigm. An analysis of Brandes' role as a critic 1870–1900 with special reference to the comparatistic aspect," in: Hertel and Kristensen 1980:21–36.
Rubow, Paul V. (1927): *Georg Brandes og hans Lærere* [*Studier fra Sprog- og Oldtidsforskning*, 144].
Rubow, Paul V. (1928): *Litterære Studier*. Copenhagen: Levin.
Rubow, Paul V. (1932): *Georg Brandes' Briller*. Copenhagen: Levin & Munksgaard.

Rubow, Paul V. (1976): *De Franske*. Copenhagen: Gyldendal.
Taine, Hippolyte (1866): *Histoire de la littérature anglaise*, Vol. I, 2nd revised edition. Paris: Libr. Hachette.
Taine, Hippolyte (1877): *Den engelske Literaturs Historie. Første Deel*. Copenhagen: Gyldendalske Boghandel.

THE TEXTUAL HISTORY OF *MAIN CURRENTS*

Ahlström, Gunnar (1937): *Georg Brandes' Hovedstrømninger*. Lund and Copenhagen.
Bjerring-Hansen, Jens (2008): "Brandes, Brentano og Bernkonventionen. Om Georg Brandes' revision af Den romantiske Skole i Tydskland," *Danske Studier* 2008, pp. 150–167.
Brandes, Georg (1870a): *Kritiker og Portraiter*. Copenhagen.
Brandes, Georg (1870b): *Den franske Æsthetik i vore Dage. En Afhandling om H. Taine*. Copenhagen.
Brandes, Georg (1872a): *Hovedstrømninger i det 19de Aarhundredes Litteratur. Emigrantlitteraturen*. Copenhagen.
Brandes, Georg (1872b): *Forklaring og Forsvar. En Antikritik*. Copenhagen.
Brandes, Georg (1873): *Hovedstrømninger i det 19de Aarhundredes Litteratur. Den romantiske Skole i Tydskland*. Copenhagen.
Brandes, Georg (1874): *Hovedstrømninger i det 19de Aarhundredes Litteratur. Reactionen i Frankrig*. Copenhagen.
Brandes, Georg (1875): *Hovedstrømninger i det 19de Aarhundredes Litteratur. Naturalismen i England*. Copenhagen.
Brandes, Georg (1876): [review of Holger Drachmann: En Overkomplet], in *Det nittende Aarhundrede*, July 1876, IV,3, p. 312.
Brandes, Georg (1877): *Søren Kierkegaard. En kritisk Fremstilling i Grundrids*. Copenhagen.
Brandes, Georg (1882): *Hovedstrømninger i det 19de Aarhundredes Litteratur. Den romantiske Skole i Frankrig*. Copenhagen.
Brandes, Georg (1883a): *Det moderne Gjennembruds Mænd*. Copenhagen.
Brandes, Georg (1883b): *Mennesker og Værker*. Copenhagen.
Brandes, Georg (1889): *Essays. Danske Personligheder*. Copenhagen.
Brandes, Georg (1890): *Hovedstrømninger i det 19de Aarhundredes Litteratur. Det unge Tyskland*. Copenhagen.
Brandes, Georg (1891): *Hovedstrømninger i det 19de Aarhundredes Litteratur. Den romantiske Skole i Tyskland*, second edition. Copenhagen.
Brandes, Georg (1892): *Hovedstrømninger i det 19de Aarhundreds Litteratur. Reactionen i Frankrig*, second edition. Copenhagen.
Brandes, Georg (1895–1896): *William Shakespeare*, Vols 1–3. Copenhagen.
Brandes, Georg (1906): [foreword to *Gesammelte Schriften*, 1902], in *Samlede Skrifter*, Vol. 17, pp. 285–289. Copenhagen.
Brandes, Georg (1907): *Levned*, Vol. 2. Copenhagen.
Brandes, Georg (1923): *Hovedstrømninger i det 19de Aarhundredes Litteratur. Emigrantlitteraturen*. Copenhagen.
Brandes, Georg (1952): *Correspondance de Georg Brandes*, edited by Paul Krüger, Vol. 1. Copenhagen.
Brandes, Georg (1978): *Breve til Forældrene 1859-71*, edited by Morten Borup, Vol. 1. Copenhagen.
Brandes, Georg and Edvard (1939): *Brevveksling med nordiske Forfattere og Videnskabsmænd*, edited by Morten Borup et al., Vol. 1. Copenhagen.

Brandes, Georg and Emil Petersen (1980): *En Brevveksling*, edited by Morten Borup. Copenhagen.
Conrad, Flemming (2006): *For læg og lærd. Studier i dansk litteraturhistorieskrivning 1862-ca. 1920.* Copenhagen.
Fehrman, Carl (1999): *Litteraturhistorien i Europaperspektiv. Från komparatism till kanon.* Lund.
Fenger, Henning (1955): *Georg Brandes' læreår. Læsning. Ideer. Smag. Kritik.* Copenhagen.
Fenger, Henning (1978): *Georg Brandes og det nyere franske drama. Teateranmeldelser og dramaturgiske forelæsninger 1865-1872.* Copenhagen.
Graff, Gerald (1987): *Professing Literature. An Institutional History.* Chicago.
Knudsen, Jørgen (1994): *Georg Brandes. Symbolet og manden. 1883-95.* Copenhagen.
Koch, Carl Henrik (2000): *Strejftog i den danske filosofis historie.* Copenhagen.
König, Christoph and Lämmert, Eberhard (1993): *Literaturwissenschaft und Geistesgeschichte 1910 bis 1925*, hrsg. von Christoph König und Eberhard Lämmert. Frankfurt/Main.
Stenström, Thure (1961): *Den ensamme. Et motivstudie i det moderna genombrottets litteratur.* Stockholm.
Weimar, Klaus (1989): *Geschichte der deutschen Literaturwissenschaft.* Munich.

BRANDES AFTER *MAIN CURRENTS*: POLITICAL JOURNALISM, OPPRESSED PEOPLES

Allen, Julie K. (2012): *Icons of Danish Modernity. Georg Brandes and Asta Nielsen.* Seattle: University of Washington.
Appiah, Kwame Anthony (2005): *The Ethics of Identity.* Princeton, NJ: Princeton University.
Berthelsen, Sune and Egebjerg, Ditte Marie (2004): "Europa i Danmark, Danmark i Europa. Georg Brandes som national kosmopolit," in Hans Hertel, Ed., *Det stadig moderne gennmbrud.* Copenhagen: Gyldendal, 99–122.
Brandes, Georg (1875): *Hovedstrømninger i det 19de Aarhundredes Litteratur. Naturalismen i England.* Copenhagen: Gyldendal.
Brandes, Georg (1883): *Det moderne Gjennembruds Mænd.* Copenhagen: Gyldendal.
Brandes, Georg (1887): "Et Brev fra Dr. G. Brandes." *Politiken,* July 4, 1887.
Brandes, Georg (1888): *Indtryk fra Polen.* Copenhagen: Gyldendal.
Brandes, Georg (1889): "Aristokratisk Radikalisme." *Tilskueren,* September 1889: 565–613.
Brandes, Georg (1890): "Det store Menneske. Kulturens Kilde." *Tilskueren,* January 1890: 1–25.
Brandes, Georg (1895–1896): *William Shakespeare,* 3 vols. Copenhagen: Gyldendal.
Brandes, Georg (1898): *Henrik Ibsen.* Copenhagen: Gyldendal.
Brandes, Georg (1902a): "Tanker ved Aarhundredeskiftet," in *Samlede Skrifter* XII. Copenhagen: Gyldendal, 142–162.
Brandes, Georg (1902b): "Om Nationalfølelse," in *Samlede Skrifter* XII. Copenhagen: Gyldendal, 187–204.
Brandes, Georg (1905): "Tale paa Møen," in *Samlede Skrifter* XV. Copenhagen: Gyldendal, 440–445.
Brandes, Georg (1906a): "Hunnertalen," in *Samlede Skrifter* XVII. Copenhagen: Gyldendal, 74–77.
Brandes, Georg (1906b): "Finland," in *Samlede Skrifter* XVII. Copenhagen: Gyldendal, 60–64.
Brandes, Georg (1906c): "Til Skoleungdommen i russisk Polen," in *Samlede Skrifter* XVII. Copenhagen: Gyldendal, 42–47.
Brandes, Georg (1910): "Zionism," in *Samlede Skrifter* XVIII. Copenhagen: Gyldendal, 407–412.
Brandes, Georg (1915): *Wolfgang Goethe,* 2 vols. Copenhagen: Gyldendal.
Brandes, Georg (1916): "En Appel," in *Verdenskrigen.* Copenhagen: Gyldendal, 254–261.

Brandes, Georg (1916–1917): *Françoise de Voltaire*, 2 vols. Copenhagen: Gyldendal.
Brandes, Georg (1917a): *Napoleon og Garibaldi*. Copenhagen: Gyldendal.
Brandes, Georg (1917b): *Verdenskrigen*, 4th edition. Copenhagen: Gyldendal.
Brandes, Georg (1918): *Cajus Julius Caesar*, 2 vols. Copenhagen: Gyldendal.
Brandes, Georg (1919): *Sønderjylland under prøjsisk Tryk*. Copenhagen: Gyldendal.
Brandes, Georg (1921): *Michelangelo Buonarotti*. Copenhagen: Gyldendal.
Brandes, Georg (1932): "Imperialisme," in *Kulturbilleder: Studien og strejftog*. Copenhagen: Hage & Clausen: 156–174.
Dahl, Per (2019): "The Textual History of Main Currents." georgbrandes.dk.
D'haen, Theo, Domínguez, César, and Thomsen, Mads Rosendahl (2013): *World Literature: A Reader*. London: Routledge.
Engberg-Pedersen, Anders (2019): "The Reaction i France." georgbrandes.dk.
Fjord Jensen, Johan (1966): *Homo Manipulatus: Essays omkring Radikalismen*. Copenhagen: Gyldendal.
Harsløf, Olav. "Fra kulturpolitik til politikal journalistik," in Hans Hertel and Sven Møller Kristensen, Eds, *Den politisk Georg Brandes*. Copenhagen: Hans Reitzel: 135–138.
Hertel, Hans (2004): "Det stadig moderne gennembrud?" in Hans Hertel, Ed., *Det stadig moderne gennmbrud*. Copenhagen: Gyldendal: 7–16.
Høffding, Harald (1889): "Demokratisk Radikalisme. En Indsigelse." *Tilskueren* November–December 1889: 849–872.
Knudsen, Jørgen (2004): *Georg Brandes: Uovervindelig taber, 1914-1927*. Copenhagen: Gyldendal.
Moretti, Franco (2010): "The Grey Area: Ibsen and the Spirit of Capitalism." *New Left Review* 61, January–February 2010: 117–131.
Nordby, Thomas (1973): "Georg Brandes og imperialismen," in Hans Hertel and Sven Møller Kristensen, Eds, *Den politisk Georg Brandes*. Copenhagen: Hans Reitzel: 139–156.
Paulsen, Adam (2019): "Young Germany." georgbrandes.dk.
Pjetursson, Leif (1984): *Drømmen om det absolute: den kulturradikale kulturstrømning*. Copenhagen: Hans Reitzel.
Shaw, Albert (1905): "Some Danish Fiction Writers of Today." *The American Monthly Review of Reviews* XXXI, January 1905: 107.

EMIGRANT LITERATURE (1872)

Ahlström, Gunnar (1937): *Georg Brandes' Hovedstrømninger*. Lund: C.W.K. Gleerup.
Allen, Julie K. (2010): "Brandes as a German Journalist: Shaping Cultural Identity through the Mass Media," in Anne Bourguignon et al. 2010: 227–242.
Bhabha, Homi K. (2004): *The Location of Culture*. New York: Routledge.
Bohnen, Klaus (2005): *Georg Brandes in seiner deutschen Korrespondenz*. Copenhagen/Munich: Wilhelm Fink Verlag.
Bourguignon, Anne, Harrer, Konrad, and Clausen, Jørgen Stender (Eds) (2010): *Grands courants d'échanges intellectuels: Georg Brandes et La France, L'Allemagne, L'Angleterre. Actes de la deuxième conference internationale Georg Brandes, Nancy, 13–15 Novembre 2008*. Bern: Peter Lang.
Brahm, Otto (1913): *Kritische Schriften über Drama und Theater*. Berlin: S. Fischer Verlag.
Brandes, Georg (1866): *Dualismen i vor nyeste Philosophie*. Copenhagen: Gyldendalske Boghandel.
Brandes, Georg (1870a): *Den franske Æsthetik i vore Dage. En Afhandling om H. Taine*. Copenhagen: Gyldendalske Boghandel.

Brandes, Georg (1870b): *Kritiker og Portraiter*. Copenhagen: Gyldendalske Boghandel.
Brandes, Georg (1872a): *Emigrantlitteraturen*. Copenhagen: Gyldendalske Boghandel.
Brandes, Georg (1872b): *Die Hauptströmungen der Literatur des neunzehnten Jahrhunderts*, in *Die Emigrantenliteratur*. Berlin: Duncker.
Brandes, Georg (1873): *Den romantiske Skole i Tydskland*. Copenhagen: Gyldendalske Boghandel.
Brandes, Georg (1882): *Die Literatur des neunzehnten Jahrhunderts in ihren Hauptströmungen dargestellt*, in *Die Emigrantenliteratur*, 2nd edition. Leipzig: Veit & Co.
Brandes, Georg (1886): *Die Hauptströmungen der Literatur des neunzehnten Jahrhunderts*, in *Die Emigrantenliteratur*, 3rd edition. Leipzig: Barsdorf.
Brandes, Georg (1894): *Die Hauptströmungen der Literatur des neunzehnten Jahrhunderts*, in *Die Emigrantenliteratur*, 4th enlarged edition. Leipzig: Barsdorf.
Brandes, Georg (1897): *Die Hauptströmungen der Literatur des neunzehnten Jahrhunderts*, in *Die Emigrantenliteratur*, 5th revised and enlarged edition. Leipzig: Barsdorf.
Brandes, Georg (1952): *Correspondance de Georg Brandes*, in *La France et l'Italie*. Copenhagen: Rosenkilde og Bagger.
Brandes, Georg (1956): *Correspondance de Georg Brandes*, II: *L'Angleterre et la Russie*. Copenhagen: Rosenkilde og Bagger.
Brandes, Georg (1966): *Correspondance de Georg Brandes*, III: *L'Allemagne*. Copenhagen: Rosenkilde og Bagger.
Brandes, Georg (1978): *Breve til forældrene 1859-71*, edited by Morten Borup, I–III. C.A. Reitzel.
Brandes, Georg and Brandes, Edvard (1939–1942): *Brevveksling med nordiske Forfattere og Videnskabsmænd*, I–VIII. Copenhagen: C.A. Reitzel.
Braudel, Fernand (1997): *Ecrits sur l'histoire* II. Paris: Flammarion.
Briens, Sylvian (2010): *Paris. Laboratoire de la littérature scandinave moderne (1880-1905)*. Paris: L'Harmattan.
Bruns, Alken (1977): "Strodtmanns Brandes-Rezeption," in Bruns: *Übersetzung als Rezeption. Deutsche Übersetzer skandinavischer Literatur von 1860 bis 1900* [Skandinavische Studien 8]. Neumünster 1977: 106–120.
Casanova, Pascale (1999): *La republique mondiale des lettres*. Paris: Éditions du Seuil.
Dahl, Per (1998): *Georg Brandes-tidstavle 1842–1927* [Working Papers 18-1998. Department of Comparative Literature, Aarhus University]. Aarhus.
Dahlerup, Pil (1983): *Det moderne gennembruds kvinder*. Copenhagen: Gyldendal.
Fenger, Henning (1955): *Georg Brandes' Læreår. Læsning, ideer, smag, kritik 1857-1872*. Copenhagen: Gyldendalske Boghandel – Nordisk Forlag.
Fenger, Henning (1957): *Den unge Brandes. Miljø, venner, rejser, kriser*. Copenhagen: Gyldendalske Boghandel – Nordisk Forlag.
Gibbons, Henry J. (1980): "Georg Brandes. The reluctant Jew," in Hertel and Kristensen 1980: 55–89.
Harsløf, Olav (Ed.) (2004): *Georg Brandes og Europa. Forelæsninger fra 1. internationale Georg Brandes Konference, Firenze, 7-9 november 2002*. Copenhagen: Museum Tusculanum.
Hertel, Hans and Kristensen, Sven Møller (Eds) (1973): *Den politiske Georg Brandes*. Copenhagen: Hans Reitzel.
Hertel, Hans and Kristensen, Sven Møller (Eds) (1980): *The Activist Critic. A symposium on the political ideas, literary methods and international reception of Georg Brandes* [Orbis Litterarum. Supplement 5]. Copenhagen: Munksgaard.
Hjortshøj, Søren Blak (2021): *Son of Spinoza. Georg Brandes and Modern Jewish Cosmopolitanism*. Aarhus: Aarhus University Press.
Juncker, Beth (1973): "Debatten omkring Emigrantlitteraturen," in Hertel and Kristensen 1973: 27–66.
Knudsen, Jørgen (1985): *Georg Brandes. Frigørelsens vej 1842-77*. Copenhagen: Gyldendal.

Kristensen, Sven Møller (1980): *Georg Brandes. Kritikeren, liberalisten, humanisten.* Copenhagen: Gyldendal.
Larsen, Pelle Oliver (2016): *Professoratet. Kampen om Det Filosofiske Fakultet 1870-1920.* Copenhagen: Museum Tusculanum.
Madsen, Peter (2004): "World Literature and World Thoughts," in Christopher Prendergast (Ed.): *Debating World Literature.* London: Verso, 54–75.
Nolin, Bertil (1965): *Den gode europén. Studier i Georg Brandes' idéutveckling 1871-1893 med speciell hänsyn till hans förhållande till tysk, engelsk, slavisk och fransk litteratur.* Uppsala: Svenska Bokförlaget/Nordtedts.
Nolin, Bertil (1976): *Georg Brandes* [*Twayne's World Authors Series* 390]. Boston: Twayne Publishers.
Nolin, Bertil (1980): "The critic and his paradigm. An analysis of Brandes' role as a critic 1870–1900 with special reference to the comparatistic aspect," in Hertel and Kristensen 1980: 21–36.
Rogations, Laurence (2016): "Images et imaginaire. La Scandinavie et les Scandinaves dans la presse française à l'aube du XXe siècle," in *Deshima. Revued'histoire globale des pays du nord* 2016: 10, 165–178.
Rubow, Paul V. (1927): *Georg Brandes og hans Lærere* [*Studier fra Sprog- og Oldtidsforskning*, 144].
Rubow, Paul V. (1928): *Litterære Studier.* Copenhagen: Levin.
Rubow, Paul V. (1932): *Georg Brandes' Briller.* Copenhagen: Levin & Munksgaard.
Rubow, Paul V. (1976): *De Franske.* Copenhagen: Gyldendal.
Rømhild, Lars Peter (1980): "Georg Brandes and Comparative Literature," in Hertel and Kristensen 1980: 284–302.
Said, Edward W. (1993): *Culture and Imperialism.* London: Chatto & Windus.
Said, Edward W. (2002): *Reflections on Exile and other Essays.* Cambridge, Mass.: Harvard University Press.
Segrestin, Marthe (2010): "Ibsen et Strindberg face au théâtre français. L'étranger en règle et l'étranger sans papier," in *Deshima. Revued'histoire globale des pays du nord* 2010: 4, 287–302.
Sørensen, Bengt Algot (1980): "Georg Brandes als 'deutscher' Schriftsteller. Skandinavische moderne und deutscher Naturalismus," in Hertel and Kristensen 1980: 127–145.
Taine, Hippolyte (1866): *Histoire de la littérature anglaise*, 1, 2nd revised edition. Paris: Libr. Hachette.
Taine, Hippolyte (1877): *Den engelske Literaturs Historie. Første Deel.* Copenhagen: Gyldendalske Boghandel.

Contemporary Reception of Emigrant Literature

Anon. (1873): "G. Brandes: Die Hauptströmungen der Literatur des 19. Jahrhunderts," in *Literarisches Centralblatt*, 28 June, No. 26, pp. 819–821.
Anon. (1876): "G. Brandes: Hovedstrømninger i det 19de Aarhundredes Literatur," *Morgenbladet*, 10 February.
Anon. (1877): "Georg Brandes Hovedstrømninger m.m.," in *Norsk Tidskrift for Literatur*, 29 July.
Anon. (1893): "Die Hauptströmungen der Literatur des 19. Jahrhunderts," *Nord und Süd*.
Anon. (1894): "Die Hauptströmungen der Litteratur des neunzehnten Jahrhunderts," *Westermanns Monatshefte*.
Barine, Arvède (1883): "Un critique danois – M. George Brandes," *La Revue Bleue*, June: 759–764.
Bury, Henri Blaze de (1873): "Les grands courants de la littérature française au dix-neuvième siècle," *La Revue des deux mondes*, Vol. 108, December: 5–36.
Jung, Alexander (1877): "Das Literaturwerk von G. Brandes," *Blätter für literarische Unterhaltung* 22, 23, 24.

Kreyssig, F. (1874): "Die Hauptströmungen der Literatur des neunzehnten Jahrhunderts," in *Deutsche Rundschau*, October: 139–141.
Kuh, Emil (1876): "Die Hauptströmungen der Literatur des neunzehnten Jahrhunderts," in *Beilage zur Wiener Abendpost*, 11, 12, 13, 14 April.
Lublinski, Samuel (1900): "Albert Geiger, Georg Brandes und ich," *Das Magazin für Litteratur*, September.
Mehring, Franz (1893–1894): "Georg Brandes. Die Hauptströmungen der Literatur des neunzehnten Jahrhunderts," *Die neue Zeit*: 309–311.
St., Th. [Theodor Storm] 1872: "Dänemark," *Das Magazin für die Literatur des Auslandes* 49: 640.
Thorel, Jean (1893): "La Critique internationale. M. George Brandes," *Revue des deux mondes*, 15 September 1893, Vol. 2: 337–358.
Weddigen, Otto (1882): "Das Literaturwerk von Brandes in neuer Bearbeitung," *Blätter für literarische Unterhaltung*: 748–750.

THE ROMANTIC SCHOOL IN GERMANY (1873)

Ansel, Michael (2003): *Prutz, Hettner und Haym. Hegelianische Literaturgeschichtsschreibung zwischen spekulativer Kunstdeutung und philologischer Quellenkritik*. Tübingen: Max Niemeyer Verlag.
Becker-Cantarino, Barbara (2000): *Schriftstellerinnen der Romantik. Epoche – Werk – Wirkung*. Munich: C.H. Beck.
Behler, Ernst (2011): "Kierkegaard's Concept of Irony with Constant Reference to Romanticism," in Cappelørn, N.J. and Stewart, J. (Eds): *Kierkegaard Revisited. Proceedings from the Conference "Kierkegaard and the Meaning of Meaning It"*, Copenhagen, May 5–9, 1996. Berlin, Boston: De Gruyter, pp. 13–33.
Bjerring-Hansen, Jens (2008): "Brandes, Brentano og Bern-konventionen. Om Georg Brandes' revision af Den romantiske Skole i Tydskland." *Danske Studier*, Vol. 103, pp. 150–168.
Bohnen, Klaus (1980): "'Persönlichkeit' bei Georg Brandes. Zu einer Kategorie der Kritik und ihrer Rezeption in Deutschland," in Hertel, Hans and Kristensen, Sven Møller (Eds): *The Activist Critic. A Symposium on the political ideas, literary methods and international reception of Georg Brandes. Orbis Litterarum*, Supplement No. 5. Copenhagen: Munksgaard, pp. 237–251.
Bohnen, Klaus (2001): "Der grenzüberschreitende Mentor. Georg Brandes' kritische Strategie in seiner deutschen Korrespondenz," in Detering, Heinrich et al. (Eds): *Dänisch-deutsche Doppelgänger. Transnationale und bikulturelle Literatur zwischen Barock und Moderne*. Göttingen: Wallstein Verlag.
Bohnen, Klaus (2004): "Georg Brandes og de intellektuelle miljøer i Tyskland og Østrig," in Harsløf, Olav (Ed.): *Georg Brandes og Europa. Forelæsninger fra 1. internationale Georg Brandes konference*, Firenze, 7–9 November 2002. Copenhagen: Det Kongelige Bibliotek and Museum Tusculanums Forlag, pp. 155–160.
Bohnen, Klaus (2013): "Nachwort. Zur Rezeption des 'Niels Lyhne' im deutschen Sprachraum," in Jacobsen: *Niels Lyhne. Roman*. Leipzig: Reclam, pp. 256–267.
Bohrer, Karl Heinz (1989): *Die Kritik der Romantik. Der Verdacht der Philosophie gegen die literarische Moderne*. Frankfurt: Suhrkamp.
Brandes, Georg (1873): *Den romantiske Skole i Tydskland*. Copenhagen: Gyldendalske Boghandel.
Brandes, Georg (1907): *Levned*, Vol. 2. Copenhagen-Kristiania: Gyldendalske Boghandel – Nordisk Forlag.

Busk-Jensen, Lise (2009): *Romantikkens forfatterinder*, Vols 1–3. Copenhagen: Gyldendal.
Cerf, Steven (1981): "Georg Brandes' view of Novalis: A current within Thomas Mann's 'Der Zauberberg'," in *Colloquia Germanica*, Vol. 14, No. 2, pp. 114–129.
Conrad, Flemming (1996): *Smagen og det nationale. Studier i dansk litteraturhistorieskrivning 1800-1861*. Copenhagen: Museum Tusculanums Forlag.
Dehrmann, Mark-Georg (2017): "Lucinde," in Endres, Johannes (Ed.): *Friedrich Schlegel-Handbuch: Leben – Werk – Wirkung*. Stuttgart: Metzler Verlag, pp. 171–178.
Dierkes, Hans (1983): "Friedrich Schlegel's Lucinde, Schleiermacher und Kierkegaard." *Deutsche Vierteljahresschrift für Literaturwissenschaft und Geistesgeschichte* 57: 3, pp. 431–449.
Fenger, Henning (1980): "Georg Brandes and Kierkegaard," in Hertel, Hans and Kristensen, Sven Møller (Eds): *The Activist Critic. A Symposium on the political ideas, literary methods and international reception of Georg Brandes*. Orbis Litterarum, Supplement No. 5. Copenhagen: Munksgaard, pp. 49–54.
Haym, Rudolf (1870/1961): *Die romantische Schule. Ein Beitrag zur Geschichte des deutschen Geistes*. Hildesheim: Georg Olms Verlagsbuchhandlung.
Heitmann, Annegret (2006): "Die Moderne im Durchbruch (1870-1910)," in Glauser, Jürg (Ed.): *Skandinavische Literaturgeschichte*. Stuttgart: Metzler Verlag, pp. 183–229.
Hohendahl, Peter Uwe (1985): *Literarische Kultur im Zeitalter des Liberalismus 1830-1870*. Munich: C.H. Beck.
Huggler, Jørgen (2006): "Rudolf Haym om tysk romantik og tysk idealisme. Die romantische Schule. Ein Beitrag zur Geschichte des deutschen Geistes (1870)," in *Litteraturkritik & Romantikstudier* 43. Copenhagen: Dansk Selskab for Romantikstudier.
Kierkegaard, Søren (1997): *Om Begrebet Ironi*, in *Søren Kierkegaards Skrifter*, Vol. 1, edited by Niels Jørgen Cappelørn. Copenhagen: Søren Kierkegaard Forskningscenteret and Gad.
Knudsen, Jørgen (1985): *Georg Brandes Frigørelsens vej 1842-77*. Copenhagen: Gyldendal.
Knudsen, Jørgen (1988): *Georg Brandes. I modsigelsernes tegn 1877-83*. Copenhagen: Gyldendal.
Knudsen, Jørgen (1994): *Georg Brandes. Symbolet og manden 1883-1895*. Copenhagen: Gyldendal.
Lundtofte, Anne Mette (2003): *The Case of Georg Brandes. Brandes between Taine, Hegel, Kierkegaard, and Goethe – and the Institutions of Literature in 19th Century Denmark*. Dissertation, New York University.
Mortensen, Finn Hauberg (1993): "Den radikale Kierkegaard-læsning." *Nordica. Tidsskrift for nordisk tekstshistorie og æstetik*, 10: 41–70.
Nolin, Bertil (1965): *Den gode europén. Studier i Brandes' idéutveckling 1871-1893 med speciell hänsyn til hans förhållande till tysk, engelsk, slavisk og fransk litteratur*. Uppsala: Svenska bokförlaget.
Oesterreich, Peter L. (1994): "Ironie," in Schanze, Helmut (Ed.): *Romantik-Handbuch*. Stuttgart: Kröner Verlag, pp. 351–365.
Piatti, Barbara (2008): *Die Geographie der Literatur. Schauplätze, Handlungsräume, Raumphantasien*. Göttingen: Wallstein Verlag.
Polheim, Karl Konrad (1999): "Kleine Bibliographie," in Schlegel, Friedrich: *Lucinde. Ein Roman. Studienausgabe*. Stuttgart: Reclam Verlag, pp. 213–215.
Rosiek, Jan (2008): *Romantiske veksler. Løfter og efterliv*. Hellerup: Forlaget Spring.
Rømhild, Lars Peter (1996): *Georg Brandes og Goethe*. Copenhagen: Museum Tusculanums Forlag.
Safranski, Rüdiger (2007): *Romantik. Eine deutsche Affäre*. Munich: Carl Hanser Verlag.
Schlegel, Friedrich (2000): *Athenäum-fragmenter og andre skrifter*. Copenhagen: Gyldendal.
Schulz, Gerhard (1983): *Die Deutsche Literatur zwischen Französischer Revolution und Restauration. Erster Teil 1789-1806*. Munich: C.H. Beck.
Schwering, Markus (1994): "Politische Romantik," in Schanze, Helmut (Ed.): *Romantik-Handbuch*. Stuttgart: Kröner, pp. 477–507.

Stewart, Jon (2015): "Kierkegaard and Romantic Subjectivism," in Stewart, Jon: *Søren Kierkegaard: Subjectivity, Irony, and the Crisis of Modernity*. Oxford: Oxford University Press. Oxford Scholarship Online: November 2015. DOI: 10.1093/acprof:oso/9780198747703.001.0001.

Sørensen, Bengt Algot (1980): "Georg Brandes als deutscher Schriftsteller. Skandinavische Moderne und deutscher Naturalismus," in Hertel, Hans and Kristensen, Sven Møller (Eds): *The Activist Critic. A Symposium on the political ideas, literary methods and international reception of Georg Brandes. Orbis Litterarum*, Supplement No. 5. København: Munksgaard, pp. 127–145.

Sørensen, Peer E. (2017): "Georg Brandes og modernismen," in Dam, Anders Ehlers and Stidsen, Marianne (Eds): *Distancens patos*. Copenhagen: U Press, pp. 75–85.

Thomsen, Niels (1998): *Hovedstrømninger 1870-1914. Idélandskabet under dansk kultur, politik og hverdagsliv*. Odense: Odense Universitetsforlag.

Zovko, Jure (2017): "Ironie, Witz," in Endres, Johannes (Ed.): *Friedrich Schlegel-Handbuch: Leben – Werk – Wirkung*. Stuttgart: Metzler Verlag, pp. 309–312.

Newspaper book reviews (in chronological order):

Pry, Paul: "Bref från Köpenhamn." *Göteborg-Posten* 25.6.1873.

Ahnfelt, Arvid (A.W.A): "Litteratur-Tidning. Sören Kierkegaard och Romantiken. G. Brandes: Hovedströmninger i det 19:de Aarhundredes litteratur.2." *Aftonbladet* 3.7.1873.

Anon.: "Hovedstrømninger i det 19de Aarhundredes Literatur. Den romantiske Skole i Tydskland." *Dagens Nyheder* 6.7.1873, No. 177.

G.r: "Hovedstrømninger i det 19de Aarhundredes Literatur." *Lolland-Falster Stifts-Tidende* 29.7.1873.

Warburg, Karl (K.Wg): "Dansk litteratur. Georg Brandes: Hovedströmninger i det 19:de Aarh.s Lit. II. Den romantiske Skole i Tydskland." *Göteborg Handels- og Sjöfarts Tidning*, 22.8.1873.

A.L.G.: "Literatur. G. Brandes. Hovedströmninger i det 19:de Aarhundredes Literatur. Den romantiske Skole i Tydskland." *Sydsvenska Dagbladet* 5.9.1873.

H.E.: "G. Brandes: Hovedstrømninger i det 19de Aarhundredes Literatur. Den romantiske Skole i Tydskland." *Jyllands-Posten* 3.10.1873, No. 230.

Anon.: "Brandes, G: die Hauptströmungen der Literatur des neunzehnten Jahrhunderts. 2. Bd. Die romantische Schule in Deutschland." *Literarisches Zentralblatt*, 18.10.1873, No. 42.

Anon.: "Den romantiske Skole i Tydskland." *Dags-Telegrafen* 17.11.1873, No. 311.

Gosse, Edmund W.: "A Dane on the German Romanticism." *The Athenæum*, 6.12.1873, No. 2406.

S: "G. Brandes: Hovedstrømninger i det 19de Aarhundredes Literatur. Den romantiske Skole i Tydskland." *Fyns Stiftstidende* 18.12.1873.

Jessen, E: "Denmark." *The Athenæum*, 27.12.1873, No. 2409.

C.R. Nyblom: "G. Brandes. Hovedströmninger i det 19:de Aarhundredes Literatur. Den romantiske Skole i Tydskland. Kjöbenhavn 1873." *Svensk Tidskrift för Literatur, Politik och Ekonomi*, Stockholm 1873, pp. 401–422.

H.H.: "Ein Däne über die Romantik." *Magazin für die Literatur des Auslands*, Vol. 33, 1873, pp. 487–489.

Anon. = Kristian Elster: "Fra Danmark." *Aftenbladet*, Kristiania, 3.1.1874.

Kreyssig, F: "Literarische Rundschau. Die Hauptströmungen der Literatur des neunzehnten Jahrhunderts. Vorlesungen, gehalten an der Kopenhagener Universität von G. Brandes. Uebersetzt und eingeleitet von Adolf Strodtmann. Band 1, 2 und 3. Berlin, Franz Duncker." *Deutsche Rundschau*, Bd. 1, Heft 1, Oktober 1874, pp. 139–141.

Anon.: "G. Brandes: Hovedstrømninger i det 19de Aarhundredes Literatur." *Morgenbladet* 12.2.1876.

Kuh, Emil: "Die Hauptströmungen der Literatur des neunzehnten Jahrhunderts. Zweiter Band: die romantische Schule in Deutschland." *Beilage zur Wiener Abendpost*, 13.4.1876.

Jung, Alexander: "Das Literaturwerk von G. Brandes." *Blätter für literarische Unterhaltung*, Leipzig, 31.5.1877, No. 22, pp. 337–342.

Anon.: "Om G. Brandes: Hovedstrømninger i det 19:de Aarhundredes Literatur I-IV." *Norsk Tidsskrift for Literatur*, 29.7.1877.

Anon.: "Die Literatur des neunzehnten Jahrhunderts in ihren Hauptströmungen, dargestellt von Georg Brandes. II. Band: Die romantische Schule in Deutschland (Leipzig, Veit & Co)." *Magazin für die Literatur des In- und Auslands*, 1887, Vol. 4, p. 55.

Anon.: "Brandes, Georg: Die Literatur des neunzehnten Jahrhunderts in ihren Hauptströmungen, 2. Bd: Die romantische Schule in Deutschland, Leipzig, 1887. Veit & Co." *Literarisches Centralblatt*, 23.4.1887, No. 17.

Dr. Puls: "Wie Georg Brandes deutsche Literaturgeschichte schreibt." *Archiv für das Studium der neueren Sprachen und Literaturen*, Vol. XLII., No. 80., 1888.

Vetterlund, Frederik: "Georg Brandes, Hovedstrømninger i det 19:de Aarhundredes Litteratur. Den romantiske Skole i Tyskland. Anden omarbejdede udgave, København 1891." *Nordisk Tidskrift för Vetenskap, Konst och Industri*, Vol. 4, Stockholm 1891.

Jørgensen, Johannes (J.J.): "Den nye Udgave af Georg Brandes: Romantiken i Tyskland." *Kjøbenhavns Børs-Tidende* 14.8.1891.

Anon.: "The Romantic School in Germany." *The Independent*, New York, Vol. 54, No. 2800, 31.7.1902.

Anon.: "Essays and Criticism. Main Currents I, The Emigrant Literature, Main Currents II, The Rom. School in Germany." *The Forum*, New York, July 1902.

THE REACTION IN FRANCE (1874)

Ahlström, Gunnar (1937): *Georg Brandes' Hovedstrømninger. En ideologisk undersökning*. Lund: C.W.K. Gleerup.

Auerbach, Erich (1946): *Mimesis: Dargestellte Wirklichkeit in der abendländischen Literatur*. Bern: A. Francke Verlag.

Baldensperger, Fernand (1927): "Georg Brandes (1842–1927)." *Revue de littérature comparée* 7, pp. 368–371.

Brandes, Edvard and Georg (1972): *Edvard og Georg Brandes' brevveksling 1866-1877, et udvalg*. Copenhagen: Gyldendals Uglebøger.

Brandes, Georg (1872): *Emigrantlitteraturen*. Copenhagen: Gyldendalske Boghandel.

Brandes, Georg (1873): *Den romantiske Skole i Tydskland*. Copenhagen: Gyldendalske Boghandel.

Brandes, Georg (1874): *Reactionen i Frankrig*. Copenhagen: Gyldendalske Boghandel.

Brandes, Georg (1875): *Naturalismen i England*. Copenhagen: Gyldendalske Boghandel.

Brandes, Georg (1882): *Den romantiske Skole i Frankrig*. Copenhagen: Gyldendalske Boghandel.

Brandes, Georg (1887): "Et Brev fra Dr. G. Brandes." *Politiken*, 4 July.

Brandes, Georg (1890): *Det unge Tyskland*. Copenhagen: Gyldendalske Boghandel.

Brandes, Georg (1903): *Den franske Æstetik i vore Dage*, in *Samlede Skrifter*, Vol. 13. Copenhagen: Gyldendalske Boghandels Forlag.

Brandes, Georg (1907): *Levned*, Vol. 2. Copenhagen: Gyldendalske Boghandel.

Brandes, Georg (1966): *Correspondance de Georg Brandes. Lettres chosies et annotées par Paul Krüger*, Vol. 3, *L'Allemagne*. Copenhagen: Rosenkilde og Bagger.

Brandes, Georg (1999): Diary 21 July 1861 – 22 July 1863. Unpublished. Royal Danish Library, Copenhagen. Available in digital form: www.kb.dk.

Fenger, Henning (1957): *Den unge Brandes. Miljø. Venner. Rejser. Kriser.* Copenhagen: Gyldendalske Boghandel.
Gervinus, Georg Gottfried (1853): *Einleitung in die Geschichte des neunzehnten Jahrhunderts.* Leipzig: Verlag von Wilhelm Engelmann.
Gervinus, Georg Gottfried (1855–1866): *Geschichte des neunzehnten Jahrhunderts seit den Wiener Verträgen,* 1–8. Leipzig: Verlag von Wilhelm Engelmann.
Hegel, Georg Wilhelm Friedrich (1986): *Vorlesungen über die Philosophie der Geschichte.* Frankfurt am Main: Suhrkamp Verlag.
Houe, Poul (2013): "Georg Brandes (1842–1927)," in M.A.R. Habib (Ed.), *The Cambridge History of Literary Criticism,* Vol. 6. *The Nineteenth Century, c. 1830–1914.* Cambridge: Cambridge University Press, pp. 464–477.
Kant, Immanuel (2001): *Kritik der Urteilskraft.* Hamburg: Felix Meiner Verlag.
Knudsen, Jørgen (1985): Georg Brandes. *Frigørelsens Vej, 1842-77.* Copenhagen: Gyldendal.
Larsen, Pelle Oliver (2016): *Professoratet. Kampen om Det Filosofiske Fakultet 1870-1920.* Copenhagen: Museum Tusculanums Forlag.
Larsen, Svend Erik (2012): "Georg Brandes. The telescope of comparative literature," in Theo D'haen, David Damrosch, Djelal Kadir (Eds), *The Routledge Companion to World Literature.* London: Routledge, pp. 21–31.
Lublinski, Samuel (1900): "Albert Geiger, Georg Brandes und ich." *Das Magazin für Litteratur,* 35, Sept.–Oct. Berlin: Verlag Siegfried Cronbach.
Lundtofte, Anne Mette (2003): *The Case of Georg Brandes: Brandes between Taine, Hegel, Kierkegaard, and Goethe – and the Institutions of Literature in 19th Century Denmark.* Unpublished PhD-dissertation.
Madsen, Peter (2004): "World Literature and World Thoughts," in Christopher Prendergast (Ed.), *Debating World Literature.* London: Verso, pp. 54–75.
Nolin, Bertil (1965): *Den gode européen. Studier i Brandes' idéutveckling 1871-1893 med speciell hänsyn till hans förhållande till tysk, engelsk, slavisk och fransk litteratur.* Uppsala: Svenska bokförlaget.
Taine, Hippolyte (1866): *Histoire de la littérature anglaise,* Vol. 1. Paris: Libr. Hachette.
Wellek, René (1955): "The lonely Dane: Georg Brandes," in *A History of Modern Criticism: 1750–1950,* Vol. 4, *The Later Nineteenth Century.* New Haven: Yale University Press.

Book reviews

Anon. (1874): "Brandes. G. Die Hauptströmungen der Literatur des 19. Jahrhunderts." *Literarisches Centralblatt,* 19 December.
Anon. (1874): "G. Brandes. Hovedstrømninger i det 19:de århundredes litteratur. Reactionen i Frankrig." *Aftonbladet,* 28 March.
Anon. (1874): "Notitser. Literatur. [G.B. Hovedstrømninger. Reaktionen i Frankrig]." *Ny illustrerad Tidning,* 18 April.
Anon. (1874): "Reactionen i Frankrig." *Berlingske Tidende,* 9 April.
Anon. (1874): "Reactionen i Frankrig." *Fyens Stiftstidende,* 20 October.
Anon. (1876): "G. Brandes: Hovedstrømninger i det 19de Aarhundredes Literatur." *Morgenbladet,* 10 February.
Anon. (1877): "Georg Brandes Hovedstrømninger m.m." *Norsk Tidsskrift for Literatur,* 29 July.
Anon. (1893): "Die Hauptströmungen der Literatur des 19. Jahrhunderts." *Nord und Süd.*
Anon. (1894): "Die Hauptströmungen der Litteratur des neunzehnten Jahrhunderts." *Westermanns Monatshefte.*

Anon. (1903): "The Reaction in France." *The Independent*, 26 February.
Jung, Alexander (1877): "Das Literaturwerk von G. Brandes." *Blätter für literarische Unterhaltung*, Vols 22, 23, 24.
Kreyssig, F. (1874): "Die Hauptströmungen der Literatur des neunzehnten Jahrhunderts." *Deutsche Rundschau*, October.
Kuh, Emil (1876): "Die Hauptströmungen der Literatur des neunzehnten Jahrhunderts." *Beilage zur Wiener Abendpost*, 11, 12, 13, 14 April.
Lublinski, Samuel (1900). "Albert Geiger, Georg Brandes und ich." *Das Magazin für Litteratur*, September.
Mehring, Franz (1893–1894): "Georg Brandes. Die Hauptströmungen der Literatur des neunzehnten Jahrhunderts." *Die neue Zeit*.
Morgenstern, Gustav (1894): "Georg Brandes: Die Hauptströmungen der Litteratur des 19. Jahrhunderts." *Die Gesellschaft*.
Sauer, August (1898): "Brandes G. Die Hauptströmungen der Litteratur des 19. Jahrhunderts." *Euphorion*.
Schandorph, Sophus (1893): "G. Brandes: Reaktionen i Frankrig." *Tilskueren*, June–July.

NATURALISM IN ENGLAND (1875)

Abrams, M.H. (1971): *Natural Supernaturalism: Tradition and Revolution in Romantic Literature*. New York: W.W. Norton & Co.; London: Oxford University Press.
Ahlström, Gunnar (1937): *Georg Brandes' Hovedstrømninger*. Lund: C.W.K. Gleerup; Copenhagen: Levin & Munksgaard.
"B" (1878): Review of Thomas Moores Lalla-Rookh, *Fædrelandet* 28 December, pp. 2–3.
Birrell, Augustine (1916): "A Foreign Critic of Byron and Wordsworth" (1905), in Birrell, *Self-Selected Essays*. London and Edinburgh: Thomas Nelson and Sons, pp. 209–216.
Bleibtreu, Carl (1887): *Geschichte der englischen Litteratur im neunzehnten Jahrhundert*. Leipzig: W. Friedrich.
Boyesen, Hjalmar Hjorth (1895): *Essays on Scandinavian Literature*. London: David Nutt.
Brandes, Georg (1872): *Emigrantlitteraturen*. Copenhagen: Gyldendalske Boghandel.
Brandes, Georg (1873): *Den romantiske Skole i Tydskland*. Copenhagen: Gyldendalske Boghandel.
Brandes, Georg (1874): *Reactionen i Frankrig*. Copenhagen: Gyldendalske Boghandel.
Brandes, Georg (1875a): *Naturalismen i England*. Copenhagen: Gyldendalske Boghandel.
Brandes, Georg (1875b): "Percy Bysshe Shelley." *Det nittende Aarhundrede: Maanedskrift for Literatur og Kritik* (April–September), pp. 139–161, 221–240.
Brandes, Georg (1876): "Svar fra Georg Brandes til Frederik Paludan-Müller." *Det nittende Aarhundrede: Maanedsskrift for Literatur og Kritik* (February–March), pp. 473–475.
Brandes, Georg (1878a): "Forord," in P.B. Shelley, *Beatrice Cenci. Tragedie af Percy Bysshe Shelley*. Translated into Danish by Johannes Magnussen. Copenhagen: Brødrene Salmonsen.
Brandes, Georg (1878b): *Benjamin Disraeli, Jarl af Beaconsfield. En litterær Charakteristik*. Copenhagen: Gyldendalske Boghandels Forlag.
Brandes, Georg (1883): *Det moderne Gjennembruds Mænd*. Copenhagen: Gyldendalske Boghandels Forlag.
Brandes, Georg (1888): *Indtryk fra Polen*. Copenhagen: Gyldendalske Boghandels Forlag.
Brandes, Georg (1896): "Indtryk fra London," in *Samlede Skrifter*, Vol. 11. Copenhagen: Gyldendalske Boghandel, 1902, pp. 304–336.

Brandes, Georg (1905): "Tale i The Authors Club i London" (1895), in *Samlede Skrifter*, Vol. 15. Copenhagen: Gyldendalske Boghandel / Nordisk Forlag, pp. 428–429.
Brandes, Georg (1907): *Levned*, Vol. 2. Copenhagen: Gyldendalske Boghandel / Nordisk Forlag.
Brandes, Georg (1908): *Levned*, Vol. 3. Copenhagen: Gyldendalske Boghandel / Nordisk Forlag.
Brandes, Georg (1923): "Forord til sjette gennemsete Udgave," in *Emigrantlitteraturen*. Copenhagen: Gyldendal.
Byron, George Gordon (1833): *The Works of Lord Byron: With his Letters and Journals*, Vol. 8. London: John Murray.
Downs, Brian W. (1948): "Anglo-Danish Literary Relations 1867–1900. The Fortunes of English Literature in Denmark." *The Modern Language Review*, pp. 145–173.
Elze, Karl (1876): *Lord Byron*, translated by K. Kroman. Copenhagen: J.H. Schubothes Boghandel.
Engelberg, Karsten (2008): "Shelley in the Nordic Countries: Would They be Seeking Him if He Had Not Been Found?", in Susanne Schmid and Michael Rossington (Eds), *The Reception of Shelley in Europe*. London and New York, pp. 156–168.
Fenger, Henning (1955): *Georg Brandes' læreår: Læsning, ideer, smag, kritik 1857-1872*. Copenhagen: Gyldendal.
Friis, Finn (1965): "Gottfried Keller og hans danske oversættere." *Danske Studier* 1965, pp. 55–74.
Gamsa, Mark (2010): *The Reading of Russian Literature in China: A Moral Example and Manual of Practice*. New York: Palgrave Macmillan.
Gosse, Edmund (1911): *Two Visits to Denmark 1872, 1874*. London: John Murray.
Hansen, Adolf (1876): *G. Brandes: Naturalismen i England. En Anmeldelse*. Copenhagen: Den Gyldendalske Boghandel.
Hansen, Adolf (1902): *Den engelske og den nordamerikanske Litteraturs Historie i Omrids*. Copenhagen: Gyldendalske Boghandels Forlag.
Heiberg, Johan Ludvig (1833): *Om Philosophiens Betydning for den nuværende Tid. Et Indbydelses-Skrift til en Række af philosophiske Forelæsninger*. Copenhagen: C.A. Reitzel.
Heuch, Johan Christian (1877): *Dr. G. Brandes' Polemik mod Kristendommen*. Copenhagen: Gyldendalske Boghandel.
Ipsen, Alfred (1902): *Georg Brandes, en Bog om Ret og Uret, Bidrag til dansk Aandslivs Historie i de sidste Decennier af det 19de Aarhundrede*. Copenhagen: Olaf O. Barfod.
Jensen, Christian Hermann (1980): "Georg Brandes and the Literary Debate in China during the Transitional Years," in Hans Hertel and Sven Møller Kristensen (Eds), *The Activist Critic: A Symposium on the Political Ideas, Literary Methods and International Reception of Georg Brandes*, *Orbis Litterarum*, Supplement No. 5. Copenhagen: Munksgaard, pp. 228–235.
Jespersen, Otto (1912): "Brandes og engelsk litteratur," in *Tilskuerens Festskrift til Georg Brandes*. Copenhagen: Gyldendalske Boghandel, pp. 84–96 (= *Tilskueren* 1912, pp. 194–206).
Kabell, Aage (1944): "Shelley og Georg Brandes: Et Bidrag til 'Hovedstrømninger's Historie." *Orbis litterarum* 1944. Copenhagen: Munksgaard, pp. 188–215.
Knudsen, Jørgen (1985): *Frigørelsens vej, 1842-1877*. Copenhagen: Gyldendal.
Knudsen, Jørgen (2008): *GB. En Georg Brandes-biografi*. Copenhagen: Gyldendal.
Krejöi, Karel (1963): "Klasszicizmus és szentimentalizmus a keleti és nyugati szlávok irodalmában." *Filológiai közlöny* 9(1), pp. 28–51.
Kristensen, Sven Møller (1980): *Georg Brandes: Kritikeren, liberalisten, humanisten*. Copenhagen: Gyldendal.
Levin, Harry (1963): *The Gates of Horn: A Study of Five French Realists*. New York: Oxford University Press.
Masson, David (1874): *Wordsworth, Shelley, Keats, and Other Essays*. London: Macmillan and Company.

Mazzini, Giuseppe (1970): "Mazzini on Byron and Liberty", reprint from *The Life and Writings of Joseph Mazzini* (London, 1864–1870), Vol. 6, 61–94, in Andrew Rutherford (Ed.), *Lord Byron: The Critical Heritage*. London: Routledge, pp. 330–341.
Morgenbladet (1876): "Review of *Naturalismen i England*, 13 February."
Morton, Timothy (2006): "Receptions," in T. Morton (Ed.), *The Cambridge Companion to Shelley*. Cambridge: Cambridge University Press.
Nielsen, Harald (1922): "Brandes og Southey," in *Usurpatoren*. Copenhagen: Aschehoug, pp. 56–84.
Nielsen, Jørgen Erik (1976): *Den samtidige engelske litteratur og Danmark 1800-1840*, Vol. 1. Copenhagen: Nova.
Nielsen, Jørgen Erik (1983): "Myth and Reality in Early Danish Byron Criticism," in Karsten Engelberg (Ed.), *The Romantic Heritage: A Collection of Critical Essays*. Copenhagen: Department of English and the Faculty of Humanities: University of Copenhagen, pp. 173–184.
Nielsen, Jørgen Erik (2003): "English Literature in Denmark in the First Half of the Nineteenth Century," in Jørgen Sevaldsen (Ed.), *Britain and Denmark: Political, Economic and Cultural Relations in the 19th and 20th Centuries*. Copenhagen: Museum Tusculanum Press, pp. 357–372.
Nielsen, Jørgen Erik (2004): "'Look to the Baltic': Byron between Romanticism and Radicalism in Denmark," in Richard A. Cardwell (Ed.), *The Reception of Byron in Europe*, Volume II: *Northern, Central and Eastern Europe*. London and New York: Thoemmes Continuum, pp. 365–374.
Nolin, Bertil (1965): *Den gode européen. Studier i Georg Brandes' idéutveckling 1871-1893 med speciell hänsyn till tysk, engelsk, slavisk og fransk litteratur*. Uppsala: Svenske Bökforlaget.
Oehlenschläger, Adam (1833): "Æsthetik. Om det Musikalske, det Philosophiske, det Maleriske og det Historiske i Poesien." *Prometheus: Maanedskrift for Poesie, Æsthetik og Kritik*, pp. 97–127.
Paludan-Müller (1876): "Et Brev fra Prof. Fr. Paludan-Müller." *Det Nittende Aarhundrede: Maanedsskrift for Literatur og Kritik* (February–March), pp. 471–473.
Peattie, Elia W. (1905): "Brandes' Naturalism in England." *Chicago Daily Tribune*, 1 July, p. 9, kol. 4–5.
Rasmussen, Jens Rahbek (2003): *Modernitet eller åndsdannelse?: Engelsk i skole og samfund 1800-1935*. Copenhagen: Museum Tusculanums Forlag.
Rix, Robert W. (2018): "The Reception of Blake in Denmark and Norway," in Morton D. Paley and Sibylle Erle (Eds), *The Reception of William Blake in Europe*. London: Bloomsbury.
Rubow, Paul V. (1932): *Georg Brandes' Briller* (revised edition). Copenhagen: Levin og Munksgaards Forlag.
Rubow, Paul V. (1934): "Georg Brandes," in Povl Engelstoft and Svend Dahl (Eds), *Dansk Biografisk Leksikon* (second edition), Vol. 3. Copenhagen: Gyldendal, pp. 629–643.
Rutherford, Andrew (Ed.) (1995): *Byron: The Critical Heritage* [1970]. London and New York: Routledge.
"S" (1876): "Review of Elzes Byron-bibliography." *Fædrelandet* 31 March, p. 3.
Saintsbury, George (1924): *A Last Scrapbook*. London: Macmillan.
Sjöholm, Stig (1940): *Övermänniskotanken i Gustaf Frödings diktning*. Göteborg: Elanders Boktryckeri Aktiebolag.
Shoutung, Zhu (2004): "Uden for Europa: Brandes og Kina," in Olav Harsløf (Ed.), *Georg Brandes og Europa: Forelæsninger fra 1. internationale Georg Brandes Konference, Firenze, 7.-9. november 2002*. Copenhagen: Museum Tusculanum.
The Spectator (1876): "A Foreign Critic on English Poetry", 29 January, pp. 17–19.
Stabler, Jane (2013): *Byron*. Oxford and New York: Routledge.
Stephen, Leslie (1902): *Studies of a Biographer*, Vol. 4. New York: G.P. Putnam's Sons; London: Duckworth & Co.
Stenström, Thure (1961): *Den ensamme: En motivstudie i det moderna genombrottets litteratur*. Stockholm: Natur och Kultur.

Taine, Hippolyte (1864): *Histoire de la littérature anglaise*, Vol. 4. Paris: Libraire de L. Hachette.
Thomése, Ika A. (1923): *Romantik und Neuromantik: mit besonderer Berücksichtigung Hugo von Hofmannsthals*. Haag: Martinus Nijhoff.
Thomsen, Grimur Thorgrimson (1845): *Om Lord Byron*. Copenhagen: A.F. Høst.
Tyler, Graeme (1982): *Physiognomy in the European Novel: Faces and Fortunes*. Princeton, NJ: Princeton University Press.
Waller, Phillip J. (2008): *Writers, Readers, and Reputations: Literary Life in Britain, 1870–1918*. Oxford; New York: Oxford University Press.
Wellek, René (1968): *A History of Modern Criticism: 1750–1950*, Vol. 4. The Later Eighteenth Century (7th printing). New Haven: Yale University Press.

THE ROMANTIC SCHOOL IN FRANCE (1882)

Anon. (1883): "Nyheter från den nya Skolan. Literaturbref från Köpenhamn." *Sydsvenska Dagbladet* 5.1.1883.
Aristoteles (1991): *Retorik*, translated by Thure Hastrup. Copenhagen: Museum Tusculanum.
Aristoteles (1999): *Poetik*, translated by Poul Helms. Copenhagen: Hans Reitzels forlag.
Barry, William (1904): "From Hugo to Balzac. The School of Romanticism in France. Main Currents of Nineteenth Century Literature by Dr. George Brandes." *The Bookman*, London, Vol. XXVI, No. 153, June 1904, pp. 97–98.
Basch, Victor, (1902): "Introduction," in Georg Brandes, *L'Ecole romantique en France*. Berlin/Paris: Barsdorf.
Brandes, Georg (1872): *Hovedstrømninger i det 19de Aarhundredes Litteratur. Emigrantlitteraturen*. Copenhagen: Gyldendal.
Brandes, Georg (1882): *Hovedstrømninger i det 19de Aarhundredes Litteratur. Den romantiske Skole i Frankrig*. Copenhagen: Gyldendal.
Brandes, Georg (1883): *Det moderne Gjennembruds Mænd. En Række Portræter*. Copenhagen: Gyldendal.
Brandes, Georg and Edvard (1940): *Brevveksling med nordiske Forfattere og Videnskabsmænd*, edited by Morten Borup, Vol. 3. Copenhagen: Gyldendal.
Brandes, Georg (1952): *Correspondance de Georg Brandes*, Vol. 1. Copenhagen: Rosenkilde og Bagger.
Brandes, Georg (1994): *Breve til Forældrene 1872-1904*, edited by Torben Nielsen, Vols 1–3. Copenhagen: C.A. Reitzel.
Brandes, Georg: *Dagbog*, 24.11.1882. The Royal Library, www.kb.dk.
Combe, Dominique (1991): *La Pensée et le style*. Paris: editions universitaires.
Knudsen, Jørgen (1988): *Georg Brandes. I modsigelsernes tegn. Berlin 1877-83*. Copenhagen: Gyldendal.
Rubow, Paul V. (1932): *Georg Brandes' Briller, Ny forøget Udgave*. Copenhagen: Levin & Munksgaards Forlag.
Schandorph, Sophus (1883): "Den romantiske Skole i Frankrig." *Ude og Hjemme* 14.1.1883.
Thorel, Jean (1893): "La Critique Internationale. M. Georg Brandes. Die Litteratur des neunzehnten Jahrhunderts in ihren Hauptströmungen dargestellt." *Revue des deux mondes*, Vol. 119, pp. 337–358.
Vodskov, Hans Sophus (1883): "Den romantiske Skole i Frankrig. II." *Illustreret Tidende* 25.2.1883.

YOUNG GERMANY (1890)

Anon. (1926): "The Last of the Great Humanists – The Sage of Copenhagen. Georg Brandes at Eighty-four", *New York Herald Tribune* 18 April.
Anon. (1896): "[Review of] *Die Literatur des 19. Jahrhunderts in ihren Hauptströmungen dargestellt von Georg Brandes. Sechster Band: Das junge Deutschland*", *Illustrierte Zeitung Leipzig* 13 June.
Anon. (1894): "[Review of] *Die Literatur des 19. Jahrhunderts in ihren Hauptströmungen dargestellt von Georg Brandes. Sechster Band: Das junge Deutschland*", *Westermanns Monatshefte*, pp. 379–380.
Anon. (1893): "Uskjønsomhed", *Berlingske Tidende* 22 September.
Anon. (1891): "Den sande Prokrustes [review of *Det unge Tyskland*]", *Morgenbladet* 16 June.
Anon. (1891): "[Review of] *Die Literatur des 19. Jahrhunderts in ihren Hauptströmungen dargestellt von Georg Brandes. Sechster Band: Das junge Deutschland*", *Preussische Jahrbücher*, Vol. 67, pp. 712–714.
Anon. (1891): "[Review of] *Die Literatur des 19. Jahrhunderts in ihren Hauptströmungen dargestellt von Georg Brandes. Sechster Band: Das junge Deutschland*", *Blätter für literarische Unterhaltung, Jahrgang 1891, Erster Band (Januar bis Juni)*, pp. 54–55.
Anon. (1890): "[Review of *Det unge Tyskland*]", *Göteborgs-Posten* 6 December.
Anon. (1890): "[Review of] *Hovedstrømninger i det 19:de Aarhundredes Litteratur. Bind 6: Det unge Tyskland*", *Nyaste Öresunds-Posten* 12 November.
Anon. (1883): "Ved Dr. Brandes' anden Forelæsning paa Universitetet i Aftes…", *Dags-Avisen* 2 March.
Anon. (1883): "Dr. Brandes holdt i Aftes sit første offentlige Foredrag om 'Det unge Tyskland'…", *Dags-Avisen* 27 February.
Allen, Julie K. (2013): *Icons of Danish Modernity: Georg Brandes and Asta Nielsen*. Seattle: University of Washington Press.
Arens, Franz (1927): "Georg Brandes' literarhistorisches Hauptwerk", *Archiv für Politik und Geschichte* 6, pp. 663–668.
[C.B.] (1890): "Georg Brandes i Tyskland", *København* 27 December.
Bjerring-Hansen, Jens (2016): "Romantik, Modernität und Copyright. Georg Brandes auf dem deutschen Buchmarkt", in Bjerring-Hansen, Jens et al. (Eds): *Die skandinavische Moderne und Europa. Transmission – Exil – Soziologie*. Vienna: Praesens Verlag, pp. 121–142.
Bohnen, Klaus (2001): "Der grenzüberschreitende Mentor: Georg Brandes' kritische Strategie in seiner deutschen Korrespondenz", in Detering, Heinrich et al. (Eds): *Dänisch-deutsche Doppelgänger. Transnationale und bikulturelle Literatur zwischen Barock und Moderne*. Göttingen: Wallstein Verlag, pp. 196–211.
Bohnen, Klaus (1999): "Ein Kulturvermittler der Jahrhundertwende. Georg Brandes in seiner deutschen Korrespondenz", in *Zagreber Germanistische Beiträge, Festschrift für Viktor Žmegač* Beiheft 5, pp. 205–219.
Borgards, Roland et al. (Eds) (2009): *Büchner-Handbuch. Leben – Werk – Wirkung*. Stuttgart: Verlag J.B. Metzler.
Bölsche, Wilhelm (1890): "Heinrich Heine bei Georg Brandes", in *Freie Bühne* 1 (Drittes und viertes Quartal), pp. 1177–1181.
Börne, Ludwig (1964a) [1826]: "Einige Worte über die angekündigten Jahrbücher der wissenschaftlichen Kritik," in Börne, Ludwig: *Sämtliche Schriften*, Vol. 1, edited by Inge and Peter Rippmann. Düsseldorf: Joseph Melzer Verlag, pp. 622–632.
Börne, Ludwig (1964b) [1830]: "Vierzehnter Brief," in Börne, Ludwig: *Sämtliche Schriften*, Vol. 3 (= Briefe aus Paris), edited by Inge og Peter Rippmann. Düsseldorf: Joseph Melzer Verlag, pp. 64–72.

Brandes, Georg (1978): *Breve til Forældrene 1859–71*, Vol. II (= Italy 1871), edited by Morten Borup. Copenhagen: Det Danske Sprog- og Litteraturselskab/C.A. Reitzels Boghandel.

Brandes, Georg (1908): *Levned*, Vol. 3: *Snevringer og Horizonter*. Copenhagen: Gyldendalske Boghandel.

Brandes, Georg (1900): *Samlede Skrifter*. Sjette Bind (= *Den romantiske Skole i Frankrig, Det unge Tyskland*). Copenhagen: Gyldendalske Boghandel.

Brandes, Georg (1890a): *Hovedstrømninger i det 19de Aarhundredes Litteratur. Forelæsninger holdte ved Kjøbenhavns Universitet i Aarene 1883 og 1887. Det unge Tyskland*. Copenhagen: Gyldendalske Boghandels Forlag.

Brandes, Georg (1890b): "[Review of] Rembrandt als Erzieher" in *Freie Bühne* 1 (Erstes und zweites Quartal), pp. 390–392.

Brandes, Georg (1889): "Aristokratisk Radikalisme. En Afhandling om Friedrich Nietzsche" in *Tilskueren* VI (= August), pp. 565–613.

Brandes, Georg (1887): "Et Brev fra Dr. G. Brandes." *Politiken*, 4 July.

Brandes, Georg (1885): *Berlin som tysk Rigshovedstad. Erindringer fra et femaarigt Ophold*. Copenhagen: P.G. Philipsen.

Brandes, Georg (1872): *Hovedstrømninger i det 19de Aarhundredes Litteratur. Forelæsninger holdte ved Kjøbenhavns Universitet i Efteraarshalvaaret 1871. Emigrantlitteraturen*. Copenhagen: Gyldendalske Forlag.

Brandes, Georg and Edvard (1939): *Brevveksling med nordiske Forfattere og Videnskabsmænd*, Vol. IV (Første Halvbind), edited by Morten Borup. Copenhagen: Gyldendalske Boghandel/Nordisk Forlag.

Brandes, Georg (1966): *Correspondance de Georg Brandes. Lettres choisies et annotées par Paul Krüger*, Vol. 3, *L'Allemagne*. Copenhagen: Rosenkilde og Bagger.

Christensen, Erik M. (2001): "Ein Europäer in Berlin," in Christensen, Erik M.: *Zurückbleiben. Tryk 1943-2001*. Berlin: Nordeuropa-Institut, pp. 239–255.

Dahl, Per (2016): "Georg Brandes: Hovedstrømninger" (= Uddrag af Brandes-bibliografi). Upublished manuscript.

Dahl, Per (1998): *Georg Brandes-tidstavle 1842-1927* [*Working Papers* 18-1998. Department of Comparative Literature, Aarhus University]. Aarhus.

Dahl, Per (1985): "Georg Brandes und Heinrich Heine," in Bohnen, Klaus et al. (Eds): *Heinrich Heine. Werk und Wirkung in Dänemark* (= *Text & Kontext Sonderreihe*, Band 19). Copenhagen/Munich: Wilhelm Fink Verlag, pp. 91–113.

[e.] (1891): "[Review of] *Die Literatur des 19. Jahrhunderts in ihren Hauptströmungen dargestellt von Georg Brandes. Sechster Band: Das junge Deutschland*." *Nord und Süd*, p. 309.

Geiger, Ludwig (1890/91): "Georg Brandes: Das junge Deutschland." *Die Nation* 8(41), pp. 631–634.

Gerhard, A. (1894): "[Om Georg Brandes' omtale af Rahel i Das junge Deutschland]." *Das Magazin für Literatur* 12, pp. 378–380.

Hansson, Ola (1890): "Georg Brandes und die skandinavische Bewegung." *Freie Bühne* 1 (Erstes und zweites Quartal), pp. 233–236.

[K.V.H.] (1890): "[Review of] *Hovedstrømninger i det 19. Aarhundredes Litteratur. Bind 6: Det Unge Tyskland*." *Verdens Gang*, 6 November.

Häntzschel, Günter (2001): "Das Ende der Kunstperiode? Heinrich Heine und Goethe," in Eibl, Karl et al. (Eds): *Goethes Kritiker*. Paderborn: Mentis, pp. 57–70.

Heine, Heinrich (1988) [1855]: "Lutezia. Berichte über Politik, Kunst und Volksleben", fr.udg. "Lutèce, Préface", dat. Paris, 30.3.1855, in *Heine. Düsseldorfer Ausgabe. Historisch-kritische Gesamtausgabe der Werke*, v. Manfred Winfuhr, Vol. 13, pp. 163–169.

Hermand, Jost (Ed.) (1974): *Das Junge Deutschland. Texte und Dokumente*. Stuttgart: Reclam.

Hohendahl, Peter Uwe (2008): *Heinrich Heine: Europäischer Schriftsteller und Intellektueller*. Berlin: Erich Schmidt Verlag.

Hohendahl, Peter Uwe (2004): "Emancipation and Critique," in Wellbery, David E. (Ed.): *A New History of German Literature*. Cambridge: Harvard University Press, pp. 564–572.

Høffding, Harald (1889): "Demokratisk Radikalisme. En Indsigelse." *Tilskueren* VI (= November-December), pp. 849–872.

Jørgensen, Johannes (1891): "[Review of] Georg Brandes: Det unge Tyskland (Gyldendal)." *Kjøbenhavns Børs-Tidende*, 30 January.

Knudsen, Jørgen (1994): *Georg Brandes. Symbolet og manden 1883-1895*. Copenhagen: Gyldendal.

[H-n L.] (1890): "Brandes Hovedströmninger." *Aftonbladet*, 31 December.

[Langbehn, Julius] (1890): *Rembrandt als Erzieher. Von einem Deutschen*. Leipzig: Hirschfeld 1890.

Levertin, Oscar (1890): "[Review of] Georg Brandes: Sidste Bind af Hovedstrømninger: Det unge Tyskland." *Politiken*, 12 December.

Levertin, Oscar (1890): "Ett afslutadt verk." *Dagens Nyheter*, 8 December.

Lublinski, S. (1900): "Albert Geiger, Georg Brandes und ich." *Das Magazin für Literatur* 35, pp. 867–877.

Marholm, Laura (1893): "Vom alten 'Jungen Deutschland'." *Nord und Süd* 65, pp. 200–210.

Mehring, Franz (1893/94): "[Review of Vol. 6 of] Die Hauptströmungen der Literatur des neunzehnten Jahrhunderts." *Die Neue Zeit*, pp. 309–311.

Mill, John Stuart (2003) [1859]: *On Liberty*, edited by David Bromwich et al. New Haven: Yale University Press.

Morgenstern, Gustav (1894): "[Review of] Die Literatur des 19. Jahrhunderts in ihren Hauptströmungen. Vierte, vermehrte Auflage, 5 Bände." *Die Gesellschaft. Monatsschrift für Literatur, Kunst und Sozialpolitik* 8, p. 964.

Moritzen, Julius (1924): *A Guide to Georg Brandes's "Main Currents in 19th Century Literature"*. U.st.: Haldeman-Julius Company.

Møller, Niels (1896): "Hovedstrømningerne." *Studenterbladet* 124–125, pp. 67–69.

[M.N.] (1892): "Was sollen wir lesen? Georg Brandes über Börne und Heine (Die Literatur des neunzehnten Jahrhunderts in ihren Hauptströmungen. Sechster Band: Das junge Deutschland)." *Wiener Literatur-Zeitung*, Vol. 5, pp. 16–17.

Necker, Moritz (1894): "Georg Brandes." *Neue Freie Presse*, 20 January.

Nietzsche, Friedrich (1988) [1872]: "Die Geburt der Tragödie aus dem Geiste der Musik" i Nietzsche, Friedrich: *Kritische Studienausgabe*, Vol. 1, edited by Giorgio Colli et al. Berlin/New York: de Gruyter, pp. 9–156.

Nolin, Bertil (1965): *Den gode europén. Studier i Georg Brandes' idéutveckling 1871-1893 med speciell hänsyn till hans förhållande till tysk, engelsk, slavisk och fransk litteratur*. Uppsala: Svenska Bokförlaget/Norstedts.

Peters, George F. (2000): *The poet as provocateur: Heinrich Heine and his critics*. Rochester, NY: Camden House.

Prölß, Johannes (1892): *Das junge Deutschland. Ein Buch deutscher Geistesgeschichte*. Stuttgart: J.G. Cotta'sche Buchhandlung.

Rømhild, Lars Peter (1996): *Georg Brandes og Goethe*. Copenhagen: Museum Tusculanums Forlag.

Sauer, August (1898): "[Review of] Die Literatur des 19. Jahrhunderts in ihren Hauptströmungen. 5., gänzlich umgearbeitete, vermehrte und mit einem Generalregister versehene Auflage. Jubiläumsausgabe. 6 Bände," in *Euphorion* 5, pp. 373–374.

Schandorph, Sophus (1891): "[Review of Vol. 6 of] Hovedstrømninger i det 19de Aarhundredes Literatur." *Tilskueren* VIII (= June), pp. 420–443.

Skriver, Svend (2017): "Den radikale europæer. Internationaliseringsstrategier i Emigrantlitteraturen af Georg Brandes – en historiografisk analyse." *Spring* 40, pp. 208–231.

[O. St.] (1896): "[Review of] Die Literatur des 19. Jahrhunderts in ihren Hauptströmungen dargestellt von Georg Brandes. Sechster Band: Das junge Deutschland." *Die Zeit*, 30 May.

Söderhjelm, W. (1894): "Det 'unga Tyskland', skildradt af Georg Brandes." *Finsk Tidskrift för vitterhet, vetenskap, konst och politik* XXXVI, pp. 252–272.

Sørensen, Bengt Algot (1980): "Georg Brandes als 'deutscher' Schriftsteller. Skandinavische Moderne und deutscher Naturalismus," in Hertel, Hans et al. (Eds): *The Activist Critic. A symposium on the political ideas, literary methods and international reception of Georg Brandes* (= *Orbis Litterarum*, Supplement 5). Copenhagen: Munksgaard, pp. 127–145.

Verbot der Schriften des "Jungen Deutschland" vom 10. Dezember 1835 (31. Sitzung der Bundesversammlung), http://www.heinrich-heine-denkmal.de/dokumente/beschluss.shtml (accessed 01.06.2018).

Wirsén, Carl David af (1890): "[Review of] Hovedströmninger i det 19:de Aarhundredes Litteratur. Det unge Tyskland. Kjbh. 1890]." *Post- och Inrikes Tidningar*, 22 November.

[O.W.] (1893): "[Review of] Die Literatur des 19. Jahrhunderts in ihren Hauptströmungen dargestellt von Georg Brandes. Sechster Band: Das junge Deutschland." *Nord und Süd*, pp. 134–135.

CONTRIBUTORS

William Banks is a writer, editor, and translator. He has edited *Georg Brandes: Human Rights and Oppressed Peoples. Collected Essays and Speeches* (University of Wisconsin Press, 2020). His latest book is *The Great Debate. Nietzsche, Culture and the Welfare Society. Georg Brandes and Harald Høffding* (University of Wisconsin Press, 2023).

Jens Bjerring-Hansen is Associate Professor of Scandinavian Literature at the University of Copenhagen, specializing in eighteenth- and nineteenth-century literature. Recent publications include the volumes *Scandinavian Exceptionalisms. Culture, Society, Discourse* (Nordeuropa-Institut der Humboldt Universität, 2021, co-edited with Torben Jelsbak and Anna Estera Mrozewicz) and *Georg Brandes: Pioneer of Comparative Literature and Global Public Intellectual* (Brill, 2023, co-edited with Anders Engberg-Pedersen and Lasse Horne Kjældgaard).

Per Dahl is Associate Professor (emeritus) of Comparative Literature at the University of Aarhus, specializing in The Modern Breakthrough/ Georg Brandes, Johannes V. Jensen, and editing. Recent publications include *Georg Brandes: Vorlesungen über Friedrich Nietzsche (1888) – Aristokratischer Radicalismus (1889/1890). Dänisch-deutsche Parallelausgabe* (Schwabe, 2021, with Gert Posselt), *Dansk Editionshistorie*, Vol. 3 (Museum Tusculanum Press, 2021, edited by Johnny Kondrup), and *Johannes V. Jensen: Himmerlandshistorier 1-2* (The Society for Danish Language and Literature / Gyldendal, 2018, with Aage Jørgensen).

Anders Engberg-Pedersen is Professor of Comparative Literature at the University of Southern Denmark and Chair of Humanities at the Danish Institute for Advanced Study. His research focuses on German, French, and Scandinavian literature, warfare, and media. Recent publications include *Martial Aesthetics: How War Became an Art Form* (Stanford University Press, 2023), *War and Literary Studies* (Cambridge University Press, 2023, co-edited with Neil Ramsey), and *Georg Brandes: Pioneer of Comparative Literature and Global Public Intellectual* (Brill, 2023, co-edited with Jens Bjerring-Hansen and Lasse Horne Kjældgaard).

Torben Jelsbak is Associate Professor of Scandinavian Literature at the University of Copenhagen. He researches in Danish and Scandinavian literatures in the interdisciplinary field between media and cultural history. Recent publications include *Dansk-tyske krige. Kulturliv og kulturkampe* (U Press, 2020, co-edited with Anna Sandberg) and *Scandinavian Exceptionalisms. Culture, Society, Discourse* (Nordeuropa-Institut der Humboldt Universität, 2021, co-edited with Jens Bjerring-Hansen and Anna Estera Mrozewicz).

Lasse Horne Kjældgaard is CEO of the Carlsberg Foundation and Professor of Danish Literature at the University of Southern Denmark. He has authored and edited several monographs and anthologies on Danish literary and cultural history, most recently *The Original Age of Anxiety: Essays on Kierkegaard and His Contemporaries* (Brill, 2021) and *Georg Brandes: Pioneer of Comparative Literature and Global Public Intellectual* (Brill, 2023, co-edited with Jens Bjerring-Hansen and Anders Engberg-Pedersen).

Carsten Meiner is Professor of French literature at the University of Copenhagen, specializing in French literary history from the seventeenth to the early twentieth century. Recent publications include "The double Topology. Reflections on the Function and History of Literary Topoi", in *Poetics Today* (43:1, 2022), *Literature and Contingency* (Routledge, 2020, co-edited with Tina Lupton), and *Mutating Idylls. Uses and Misuses of the Locus Amoenus in European Literature 1850–1930* (Peter Lang, 2019).

Adam Paulsen is Associate Professor of Comparative Literature at the University of Southern Denmark, specialising in German-language literature and culture. Recent publications include the volumes *Soldat, arbejder, anark. Ernst Jüngers forfatterskab* (Eksistensen, 2017, co-edited with Anders Ehlers Dam) and *Identitetspolitik, litteratur og kunstens autonomi* (U Press, 2022, co-edited with Leander Møller Gøttcke).

Robert W. Rix (PhD, Dr Phil.) is Associate Professor of Literature at the University of Copenhagen. He has published widely in several areas relating to the eighteenth and nineteenth centuries: politics, religion, language, nationalism, Nordic antiquarianism, and book history. Rix's most recent publications include the edited volume *Nordic Romanticism: Translation, Transmission, Transformation* (Palgrave, 2022, co-edited with Cian Duffy) and the monograph *The Vanished Settlers of Greenland: In Search of a Legend and Its Legacy* (Cambridge University Press, 2023).

Anna Sandberg is Associate Professor of German Studies at the University of Copenhagen, specializing in Danish-German cultural relations from 1750 onwards. Other fields of research are Romanticism, eco and green studies, and migration literature. Recent publications include the volumes *Dansk-tyske krige. Kulturliv og kulturkampe* (U Press, 2020, co-edited with Torben Jelsbak) and a special issue on The German Circle in Copenhagen 1750–1770 in *European Journal of Scandinavian Studies* 2022 (co-edited with Andreas Hjort-Møller).